THE PERSON IN PSYCHOLOGY

THE PERSON
IN PSYCHOLOGY

Selected Essays by

GORDON W. ALLPORT

BEACON PRESS   BOSTON

I wish to acknowledge with thanks permission to reprint certain materials from the following sources:

Acta Psychologica for "The Fruits of Eclecticism: Bitter or Sweet?", 1964.

The Press of Case Western Reserve University for "Six Decades of Social Psychology," Chap. 1 in S. Lundstedt (ed.), *The Preparation of Social Psychologists*, 1968, © 1968 by the Press of Case Western Reserve University.

American Psychological Association for "Traits Revisited" from *American Psychologist*, 1966; for "Personal Religious Orientation and Prejudice" from *Journal of Personality and Social Psychology*, 1967; and for "Productive Paradoxes of William James" from *Psychological Review*, 1943.

Harvard Educational Review for "Psychological Models for Guidance," 1962.

Duke University Press for "The Unique and the General in Psychological Science" from *Journal of Personality*, 1962.

University of Toronto Press for "Imagination in Psychology" in *Imagination and the University*, 1963.

Journal of Religion and Health for "Mental Health: A Generic Attitude," 1964, and "Behavioral Science, Religion, and Mental Health," 1963.

Teachers College Record for "Values and Our Youth," 1961, and "Crises in Normal Personality Development," 1964.

Journal of Social Issues for "Prejudice: Is It Societal or Personal?", 1961.

Prentice-Hall, Inc., for "Prejudice and the Individual," Chap. 17 in *American Negro Reference Book*, 1966.

Journal for the Scientific Study of Religion for "The Religious Context of Prejudice," 1966.

Harper and Row, Inc., for "The Personalistic Psychology of William Stern," in B. Wolman (ed.), *Historical Roots of Contemporary Psychology*, 1968. Copyright © 1968 by Benjamin B. Wolman.

Open Court Publishing Company for "Dewey's Individual and Social Psychology," Chap. 9. in A. Schlipp (ed.), *The Philosophy of John Dewey*, 1939.

The Journal Press for "Karl Bühler" in the *Journal of General Psychology*, 1966.

Journal of Personality for "The Genius of Kurt Lewin," 1947.

Journal of Pastoral Care for "The Spirit of Richard Clarke Cabot," 1966.

Appleton-Century-Crofts for "Autobiography" in E. G. Boring and G. Lindzey (eds.), *A History of Psychology in Autobiography*, Vol. V, Meredith Publishing Company, 1967. Copyright © 1967 by Meredith Publishing Company. Reprinted by permission of Appleton-Century-Crofts.

CONTENTS

PREFACE

To ME the title of this book seems presumptuous, but justifiable. Let me explain.

The essays here reprinted do not pretend to cover all aspects of the concept of *person* as it crops up in all varieties of *psychology*. At the same time each of the essays—indeed all of my published work in the past forty years—bears upon the place of the person in the diversified science of psychology.

Sometimes I have dealt with purely social aspects of personal behavior (rumor, morale, communication), sometimes with expression (handwriting, expressive movement), often with structural dynamic components (traits, the religious sentiment, prejudice, motivation, values), and occasionally with practical problems of guidance, mental health, control of prejudice, and pedagogy. This is but a partial list of the aspects of personhood in psychology that I have tried to deal with.

While systematic expositions of my position are available (e.g., in *Pattern and Growth in Personality*, published in 1961), some readers say that they need to consult my occasional essays to round out their view of my theoretical position. They refer, for example, to a previous volume of "selected essays" entitled *Personality and Social Encounter* (Beacon, 1960, 1964).

Here I offer a second such volume composed chiefly of recent essays dealing with additional aspects of personhood in psychology. It has seemed appropriate to include also a few biographical pieces (including one of myself), although the studies of James, Dewey, and Stern are not of recent vintage.

Let me give one word of comment concerning the *Bibliography*. With the aid of Eleanor D. Sprague and Karen L. Lindsley it has been kept up to date and is, I trust, accurate (through 1967). At the same time it is marred by one irregularity. After 1963 it has proved to be impossible to keep up with the many reprintings of articles, chapters, excerpts. I am leaving the records of such reprintings prior to 1963 as they were, but ask the reader to understand my surrender to the pressures from anthologies, books of readings, collections, and other printed concoctions whipped together chiefly with scissors and paste.

The dedication of this volume to Peter A. Bertocci, Borden Parker Bowne Professor of Philosophy in Boston University, is an attempt to recognize not only his specific help in bringing this and other publications to the light of day, but also his invigorating instruction in the philosophical dimensions of personhood; and, above all, it is an attempt to thank him for many years of close intellectual and personal friendship.

G. W. A.

PART I

WHICH MODEL FOR THE PERSON?

I

The Fruits of Eclecticism: Bitter or Sweet?

ECLECTICISM is often a word of ill-repute. An artist or composer, even a psychologist who is "eclectic" seems to lack a mind and a style of his own.

Yet in a wide sense there is surely some portion of truth in every thoughtful theory or observation. How shall the broad-minded theorist take this fact into account unless he holds an eclectic perspective?

This article attempts to state the condition under which one may pursue a permissible eclecticism—an eclecticism which could lead psychology, now badly dismembered in contradictory theories, to a fruitful and ultimately *systematic* eclecticism.

This address was an invited lecture at the Seventeenth International Congress of psychologists held at Washington in August 1963. The original publication occurred in The Congress Proceedings, in *Acta Psychologia*, 1964, *23*, 27–44.

† † †

One of the sharpest critics of eclecticism is the Honorary President of this Congress, my colleague and good friend, Professor Boring. In writing of the content *versus* act controversy at the turn of the century he remarks that any effort to compromise the issue is "sheer eclectic laziness" (1950, p. 453). Again in praising the productiveness of controversy in psychology he expresses admiration for the great men who fight for a disputed prize, and he scorns the thieving eclectic who meanwhile runs off with it, "sticking it into a textbook for sophomores written from no point of view and in defense of nothing whatsoever." This low creature he calls an "eclectically-minded, middle-of-the-road nonentity" (1929, p. 99).

Long ago Goethe likewise decried namby-pamby eclecticism. He likened directionless eclectics to jackdaws who aimlessly carry anything and everything to their nests (Schmidt, 1934, pp. 144f.).

I shall assume that we all share these dark opinions of spiritless eclecticism. It reminds us of the agreeable martyr who when offered his choice between death on the rack or by flame replied, "Please, I'll take a little of each." And of King James II of whom it was said that when confronted by two bad alternatives he always chose both.

Yet the time has come to look more closely at the issue, especially today when we are faced with considerable anarchy in psychological theorizing, and when the forces acting on us are so strongly anti-eclectic that the anarchy is increasing. Specialization is in the saddle. Bad enough is the parochialism resulting from traditional national cleavages (an anachronism in a shrunken world). Much worse is the fact that theorizing, especially in the grand manner, is frowned out of court in psychology—though not in other sciences. Conant (1951) tells us that the course of science is toward larger and larger abstractions. Psychology seems headed in the opposite direction. Minuscule theories we have, but scarcely any that are comprehensively human in their reference. (Of necessity I am speaking primarily of American developments, although what I say, I believe, has relevance to other lands.)

The trend toward conceptual specialization, I fear, is earning for us a reputation among other sciences for triviality. Psychology, we are told, is not proving itself relevant to human needs as are physics, chemistry, or medicine.

Recently, I attended a conference on public understanding of the role of science. Since science shapes our lives today, the public should know more about it—such was the theme.

During a week's conferring there was scarcely any mention of behavioral science, and none at all of psychology explicitly. In response to my complaint, a natural scientist said, "You psychologists lay hold of some fragment of human nature, snatch it out of context, and exaggerate its importance." In a similar vein, C. P. Snow writes, "We think that when we have said something about the egotisms, the weaknesses, the vanities, the power-seeking of men, that we have said everything." Quietly he adds that men "are sometimes capable of more" (1959, p. 52). In all this criticism we sense an echo of William James's judgment of sixty years ago: "Psychology," he impetuously declared, "is a nasty little subject—all one cares to know lies outside" (H. James, 1920, p. 2).

Such criticism is constructive if it leads us to admit in humility that psychology today does in fact lack a comprehensive and generally accepted conception of the nature of man, capable of compelling the respectful attention of other sciences, of the arts, the healing professions, of religion, and philosophy, and I would add with special urgency, of our statesmen in all lands. At present the sad fact is that our contributions seem to many a bagatelle irrelevant to human needs.

I have exaggerated my point a bit. Certain special contributions are recognized and used. (See Likert and Hayes, 1957; also Berelson and Steiner, 1964.) We think of intelligence and personality tests, of industrial studies, of research on prejudice, and recently of the efforts of colleagues in various lands to find firmer psychological ground on which to advance world peace. But for the most part even our successful work is *ad hoc*. We are still a science without firm postulates, without a commonly accepted comprehensive theory of man (Cf. Bertocci and Millard, 1963).

WHAT IS ECLECTICISM?

By eclecticism in psychology I shall mean a system that seeks the solution of fundamental problems by selecting and uniting what it regards as true in the several specialized approaches to psychological science.

As of today it is clearly not possible to synthesize all plausible theories. The task is beyond the limits of present intelligence. Yet eclecticism in this ambitious sense is still an ideal and a challenge. As such it merits serious thought.

In the field of philosophy the French scholar Victor Cousin (1792–1867) was convinced that each of the great systems of philosophy—namely: naturalism, idealism, skepticism, and mysticism—contain part of Truth. It was his aim to select and unite their respective elements of Truth under what he called "the guidance of common sense" (Janet, 1885, Chap. 17).[1]

The weakness of eclecticism, of course, is the difficulty of finding guiding principles for uniting fragments. To follow Cousin's guidance of common sense would place us at the mercy of subjective temperament, for my common sense is not necessarily your common sense. Nor can the guiding principles be drawn from any one fragment. It would be a complete contradiction of eclecticism, for example, to permit either Behaviorism or Gestalt to take the other into camp. If error and truth are present in every system then we need superordinate criteria for discriminating truth from error in any given system.

Let us look at Professor Boring's proposed solution. In spite of the shafts he has hurled against eclecticism, he once wrote a seductive essay, entitled "Psychology for Eclectics" (1930), and for the duration of this essay at least, considered himself

---

[1] The spirit of Cousin is reflected in the following passage:

"Ce que je professe avant tout, ce n'est pas telle ou telle philosophie, mais la philosophie elle-même; ce n'est pas l'attachement à tel système, mais l'esprit philosophique supérieur à tous les systèmes. La vraie muse de l'historien de la philosophie n'est pas la haine, mais l'amour; et la mission de la critique n'est pas seulement de signaler les extravagances de la raison humaine, mais de démêler et de dégager du milieu de ses erreurs les vérités qui peuvent et doivent y être mêlées, et par là de relever la raison humaine à ses propres yeux, d'absoudre la philosophie dans le passé, de l'enhardir et de l'éclairer dans l'avenir" (Janet, 1885, pp. 442f.).

an eclectic. He makes the important point that an eclectic must above all else be historically oriented—keenly aware of, and charmed by, the work of his predecessors. (Eclecticism is not, of course, a regurgitation of history, but rather a perspective on history.) Boring makes the further point that eclectics are "very numerous and probably constitute the majority of psychologists. Their presence, however, often goes unrecognized because they have no class name and no group consciousness, no intolerance, and therefore, no urge to controversy" (p. 115). He also points out correctly that American psychologists, in contrast to Germans, seem to be eclectically minded.

But when it comes to defining his own guiding principles, Boring draws the boundaries narrowly. The eclectic, he says,

> . . . goes to all the psychologies and examines them genetically as historical developments. He accepts whatever has shown vitality and fertility over a long period of time, and rejects the rest. Thus he accepts determinism and rejects freedom, he embraces experimentalism and avoids other empiricism. His choice is not based upon decisions as to truth and falsity, but upon the pragmatic test of fertility (1930, p. 126).

Thus for Boring an eclectic is one who admits only determinism, a narrow empirical method, and is neutral as regards truth. I fear this is too limited a guiding principle. What is required of an eclectic is that he theorize in such a way that his chosen superordinate principles never exclude valid evidence concerning human nature drawn from whatever source.

A TYPICAL PROBLEM

We may illustrate the issue from the field of learning. Every so often a thoughtful investigator, driven to distraction, tells us that there are many forms and types of learning. Tolman (1949) and Gibson (1950) have done so. Taken by itself such a statement is merely an example of piecemeal eclecticism. Some textbooks, including my own, list separate theories and leave the matter there. Such jackdaw behavior may be better than one-sided partisanship, but no one is happy with a mere list.

But how, with our present lack of a comprehensive model, can we synthesize such monstrously diverse forms of learning as contiguity and insight, latent learning and biographical learning, to say nothing of the opposing facts that we often learn from our successes, but sometimes learn much more from our failures and sufferings—and what we learn is by no means mere "avoidance behavior"? If you believe, as I do, that all these antimonies are valid, where is the comprehensive theory that allows each its proper place? Since it does not yet exist we either become jackdaws, or else invoke the strategy of denial which enables us to repress evidence that does not fit our preferred partial model of learning.

There are, in fact, only three possibilities before us: (a) we can resort to this strategy of denial which includes, of course, the verbal sleight-of-hand by which we take into camp evidence that does not fit. (b) We can be piecemeal eclectics and take all theories of learning into our jackdaw nest. (c) Or finally, we can struggle on for a comprehensive view that will find a place for all valid data: subjective and objective, machine-like and social, peripheral and propriate. And these same three possibilities confront us not only in respect to the problems of learning, but in all our fields of inquiry; perception, emotion, conflict, cognition, conscience, and all the rest.

DATA AND THEORY

In striving to unite what is true in various approaches both data and theory are clearly involved. Most of us are eclectic in data-gathering. When we put together findings from various experiments and from other reliable sources we achieve an "empirical generalization." An example would be the broad generalization that praise is a strong incentive. Although we can think of exceptions, we are content on a probabilistic basis to accept this uniformity as stated.

John Stuart Mill pointed out (1857, Book VI, Chap. 5) that such an empirical generalization tells us that a uniformity "is true," but it cannot tell us just "what is true," nor why. To know precisely what is true demands an understanding of underlying conditions, in other words, a theory. Is it true that some synaptic flow is facilitated by the benign affect aroused by praise? To give this explanation is to subsume the empirical generalization under a theory. Or is it true that the subject's need for affiliation is gratified by praise, and that it is the affiliative need that engenders future productivity? Or again, is praise a verbal secondary reinforcer? Or does the individual strive to keep the level of the "phenomenal ego" high? All these, and a dozen other, current theories can absorb the empirical generalization. What is true thus depends not on empirical fact but on the theory we adopt.

Already we have thousands of probabilistic empirical generalizations derived from painstaking research. But for each we may have a dozen or more alternative conceptualizations under which different investigators are likely to subsume a given generalization.

I am saying that we are all eclectic in the sense that we accept whatever empirical generalizations are discovered and verified by competent investigators. But we are not constrained to accept any one theory concerning what is really going on. We tend rather to fit the generalization to our pre-existing conceptual framework. We are eclectic in our store of facts but not in our categories and concepts.

The first requirement for eclecticism of theory is to recognize that human behavior may derive from many causes acting separately or conjointly. Thus it may be that praise is a strong incentive (insofar as it is) because man *is* a conditionable organism, *does* require an enhancement of his phenomenal ego, and *does* have a need for affiliation, and for still other reasons. Only when we face this pluralistic possibility can we move beyond an eclecticism of data and toward an eclecticism of theory.

The prospect is bewildering. It requires that any adequately comprehensive pluralism face the fact that valid explanations (as well as descriptions) can be made in terms of many models: neural and mental; conscious and unconscious; active and reactive; at low levels and high; based on local energies and on total synergies. But it is not enough to say, therefore, that all these models are equally valid. As they stand they are often contradictory. The theories we need will have to absorb antinomies while avoiding flat self-contradiction.

The situation at present is that each theorist typically occupies himself with one parameter of human nature, and builds himself a limited model to fit his special data and personal style. Those who concern themselves with either the brain or with phenomenology may be said to focus on one important parameter (body-mind); depth psychologists on the conscious-unconscious parameter; trait theories on the stability-variability parameter; others on self and non-self. Trouble arises when an investigator maintains that his preferred parameter, or his chosen model, overspreads the whole of human personality.

(It is fortunate that psychologists do not suffer the consequences of their partiality in theorizing. A surgeon cannot afford the luxury of partial, impulsive, one-sided theories. Life or death is the price. By comparison, psychologists can be childishly eager, aggressively one-sided, and even light-hearted about their theorizing. But, as I have already said, such lack of seriousness brings discredit upon a presumably mature profession. We are in fact being punished for our particularism though we do not yet realize it.)

Speaking of models I would point out that though currently fashionable they are by nature reductionist, nontheoretical, and anti-eclectic. A model is an analogue, either substantive or formal in type (Nagel, 1961). To say that human behavior is "like the input and output of a computer" is a substantive model; to say that behavior fits a mathematical theorem is a formal model. Having pointed to a substantive or formal analogy the modelist stops dead in his tracks. He has no further theory to offer. He is not telling us what behavior *is:* he is simply saying that man behaves *as if* were he something else (Cf. Boring, 1957). This is not theorizing; it is analogizing.

Its danger was pointed out long ago in the Indian proverb of the blind men and the elephant. One finds its tail very like a rope; another his hoof like a pillar; to a third the ear is like a saddle. But none is able to characterize the elephant. Similarly, modelists who say man is very like a machine, a pigeon, a mathematical theorem, mistake the part for the whole, and sometimes even mistake the *simulata* for the thing simulated. Systematic eclecticism works less with models than with theories. And its eventual aim is a comprehensive metatheory of the nature of man.

PARTICULARISM—BITTER AND SWEET

Model building is a product of particularistic thinking, and particularism has an important place. Its adherents are usually skilled workmen, close reasoners, and are acclaimed for the elegance of their investigations. Their temperament contrasts sharply with that of the aspiring eclectic for whom they have an epithet of exquisite opprobrium. "You are an intuitionist," they say. "Our propositions are testable, yours metaphysical."

Stung by the rebuke the intuitionist retorts, "At least we have hybrid vigor. Pure strains have proved to be sterile. See what happened to simon-pure Titchenerism, simon-pure Watsonianism, simon-pure Freudianism. They have run out. Only when infused with Gestalt, with purposivism, with ego-psychology, have they again become fertile." To the S-R colleague the intuitionist says, "You consider the reflex (e.g., the patellar) as a basic model. Fine, but where would you locate in it the laughter of the self-transcending subject who feels silly as he watches his patella respond to the hammer?" To the psychoanalyst he says, "Depth psychology is fine, but even in geometry depth is a senseless dimension unless there is also height."

Contrasting temperaments aside, let us be orderly about the issues at stake. There is much to be said in favor of particularism, of the use of miniature models, of wringing all possible juice from one conceptual system, and for what is loosely called reductionism.

History itself is the best argument. Think of the mighty impetus we have derived from Herbart, Fechner, Charcot, Freud, Pavlov, Watson, McDougall, Titchener, Bridgman, Thurstone, Hull, Skinner, and others who have pressed hard in one channel. If their contributions seem one-sided, what of it? Each has hurled a challenge to the other, and has energized the profession as a whole. Some have been tentative and tolerant, others dogmatic and acidulous. Each in his way is an historical argument for particularism. Some, we may think, have wielded only a frail conceptual wand, but all have cast a profound spell upon us.

Further, particularism clarifies and expedites communication among all who will learn its language. Operationism, for example, has proved to be a good general guide to describing experiments. Only when overextended does it break down. Pressed as a universal principle it succeeds merely in bleaching out the facts of human experience. Or take psychoanalysis which brilliantly discloses certain aspects of our being—notably our impulses and self-deceptions. But it too stammers badly when applied to other aspects—to our self-respect, sense of duty, cultural dependence, and self-identity as persons.

To sum up: particularism, especially for certain temperaments, has great incentive value. It is doubtful whether psychology in the past, present, or future, could show progress without it. It makes for clarity in discourse, a high morale within a select intellectual commonwealth. It stimulates productive opposition. It saves one from the painful paradoxes of eclecticism. And finally even when overextended it leaves a rich residue. No one believes today that Fechner solved the mind-body problem, but psychophysics is still our cherished legacy. No one believes with Titchener that trained introspection is the only legitimate method, but it still has its uses. No one believes with McDougall (1933) that human propensities are 18 in number, but his hormic insistence still challenges every worker in the field of motivation.

Such are the undoubted merits of particularism. Its faults are really only two in number. Both are related to the peril of overextension to which I have alluded. In the first place, the particularist may ignore everything that refuses to come into line with his scheme. By this strategy his powers of explanation seem to him unlimited. Take S-R models, for example. They are splendid, provided one overlooks the insistent consciousness of selfhood. Environmentalism is excellent provided one remains ignorant of genetics. The unconscious works neatly, provided one forgets that most of our conflicts are well-configured in consciousness. Whitehead has said that the intolerant use of abstractions is the "major vice of the intellect" (1925, p. 24). L. L. Whyte (1962, p. 5) goes further, warning us that the danger of our age is "total obsession with partial ideas." In the political world we have seen how disastrous total obsession with partial ideas can be.

The second pitfall of particularism lies in a curious inversion of logic. All analogies and models are derived in the first instance from a perceiving and cognizing mind. It is from our own experience with our regulatory processes that we derive the idea of regulatory systems in both animate and inanimate nature. The analogy we create does not include the creator. Rather the analogy is dependent upon (is an aspect of) the creator. Thus it is only *aspects* of our total life that are like computers, like biochemical compounds, rats in a maze, or like the social behavior of insects. It is only the tail aspect of the elephant that is like a rope.

A recent example of this fallacy is found in the stimulating book by Miller, Galanter, and Pribram (1960). This work argues that the concept of purpose is at last scientifically respectable since machines are now constructed that behave "purposively." In this formulation, machines, which are only partially analogous to human processes and are wholly dependent on them for their existence, are suddenly exalted to displace (or account for) the prior human processes. Such a curious inversion of reasoning can be explained only in terms of today's euphoric subservience to the idols of technology.

Leeper (1963) has rightly pointed out that the success of our miniature models is much greater for limited, short-run, here-and-now behavior than for long-sustained representational processes. Where, for example, is the model, technological or otherwise, that covers the steady purpose (with vastly varied conduct) of careers like those of Wundt, Gandhi, or of Einstein? As their energy decreased with the years their synergy of purpose grew firmer.

ORDINARY ECLECTICISM

Turning now from particularism to eclecticism, one brand is beneficial and causes no logical difficulties. I refer to the absorption of great ideas into the stream of intellectual history. During the Enlightenment man became reflective and self-aware. This impetus still carries us along today. Darwin, Galton, Pavlov, Freud came on the crest of the movement. Their work is in our bloodstream.

Furthermore, one can validly say, with Boring, that American psychology itself is a sort of eclectic edifice. Virtually all our leading concepts are borrowed from Europe. With light fingers we have lifted attitudes from Würzburg, conditioning from Leningrad, inkblots from Zurich, Gestalten from Berlin, the unconscious (as well as neopositivism) from

Vienna, the I.Q. from both Breslau and Paris, statistics from England, pathology from France. To these we have added the starch of stiffer method, a draft of our own pragmatism, and a dash of optimism. We have even engaged in conceptual cohabitation, by joining psychoanalysis with stimulus-response as well as with the culture concept; also by joining Pavlov with psychotherapy; not to mention existentialism with Elvis Presley.

How is it with our journals? The early American psychological periodicals were eclectic jackdaws, gathering all sorts of contributions ranging from brass instruments to philosophy. The reader of these early journals was invited to integrate the diversity if he could. If he couldn't, he was at least reminded of the range and breadth of psychology's subject matter. This desirable juxtaposition is still, I think, characteristic of most journals in Latin America, Europe, and the Orient. American periodicals on the other hand have grown more and more specialized, each having developed a party line. By reading the entire output of all of our journals a kind of vertiginous eclecticism will result, but so too will death by suffocation.

As an ex-editor, I am saddened by the restrictive folklore that inhibits most of our journals. Too often an editor says, "We want no theoretical articles unless they lead to testable propositions." Now the fact is that only very narrow theory, framed so as to exclude most of the contingencies of life, can be put to experimental testing. What about broader theories (or, if you prefer, metatheories) which allow for the ordering of a large number of phenomena, pointing to comprehensive relationships and uniting experimental fact with observations of behavior in many situations? Have they no place in modern psychological literature? Apparently not in the U.S.A.

Ideally eclecticism should, of course, disregard national boundaries. Noting the contrasting emphasis on rationality and irrationality of man in Russian and American psychology respectively, the Millers (1962, p. 29) remark, "The chasm between Pavlov and Freud is deep and it follows a main line of cleavage between our two cultures." One asks, is human nature so different east and west as to justify the chasm? One doubts it.

ATTEMPTS AT SYSTEMATIC ECLECTICISM

What can we say about efforts to establish a systematic, or quasisystematic, eclecticism? Is there progress to report?

Many years ago G. Stanley Hall advocated what he called "synthetic psychology" (Boring, 1950, p. 522). It led him into many pioneering ventures: in child psychology, adolescence, senescence, space perception, physiology, religion, the founding of journals, the presidency of Clark University. But of synthesis there was none. His versatility ended in jackdaw eclecticism.

William James, like any particularist of today, desired with all his heart to be a strict scientist. But his conflict was acute, for he refused to accept presuppositions that ran counter to the totality of human experience. He knew that in any particular system "the juices of metaphysical assumption leak in at every joint." In various contexts he himself accepted contradictory assumptions, so that he piled paradox upon paradox (G. W. Allport, 1943) but with the saving grace of insight. His *Principles*, he knew, was "unsystematic and loose." Yet he preferred looseness to the "terrible flavor of humbug" that marks the work of those who claim perfect consistency, exactitude, and adequacy for their slender formulations. Further he saw that by their own theories of human nature psychologists have the power of elevating or degrading this same nature. Debasing assumptions debase human beings; generous assumptions exalt them. And he adds, "There never can be a state of facts to which new meaning may not truthfully be added, provided the mind ascend to a more enveloping point of view . . ." (1902, p. 428).

More than any other psychologist James agonized over the problems of systematic eclecticism. We all know the tentative solutions he reached in *Pragmatism, The Pluralistic Universe,* and *Essays in Radical Empiricism.* His final position is still skeptical. A truly eclectic system to him would seem "too buttoned-up and white-chokered and clean-shaven a thing to speak for the vast slow breathing unconscious Kosmos" (1912, pp. 277f.).

Without going into detail, let me mention a few other approaches to eclecticism. There was, for example, Robert Woodworth with his "middle-of-the-road" position (perhaps a bit tipped toward Würzburg experimentalism). There was the structural concept of Felix Krueger (leaning toward the Leipzig tradition). One thinks of Edward Tolman's "purposive behaviorism" (still partial to the animal laboratory). Karl Bühler's *Krise der Psychologie* and William Stern's *Allgemeine Psychologie* point eclectic paths. If none of these figures reaches a full synthesis their aspirations nonetheless lie in that direction.

In recent years we have *Schichtentheorie* which has the artful ability to accommodate unintegrated behavior at lower levels, and fully integrative functions at higher levels. Its thoroughgoing assumption of hierarchical structure provides a ready-made framework for a certain type of eclecticism (Gilbert, 1957).

A promising movement in America is "general systems theory." Its chief danger, I feel, is that in the hands of positivists it loses altogether the concepts of personality and self. Yet properly employed the basic principle of *open system* is, I believe, the most fruitful approach to systematic eclecticism. (See G. W. Allport, 1961; also Collier, 1962.)

Yet another potential host for eclectic theorizing is modern existentialism. Van Kaam (1963) insists that the existential outlook is above all things comprehensive. It rejects nothing that is true about human nature. Man's relation to outer objects, to other persons, and to himself (*Umwelt, Mitwelt, Eigenwelt*) are all included. Particular psychologies, he insists, deal only with "isolated profiles of human behavior." Typically they relate these profiles to something nonhuman, sometimes to lower animals, sometimes to mathematics, sometimes to machine models. The consequence is that the resulting constructs cannot include findings drawn from other, equally valid, particular approaches. For a full integration of data, neither the mathematical, statistical, physical, physiological, neurological, or biochemical constructs is sufficient. Far better to relate these partial images to the totality of human existence.

True, existentialism at present has no complete and definite theory of man capable of articulating all the facts assembled from all these sources (and according to Jaspers never can have such a theory). Still it is at least an attitude of mind that may help bring to focus a more articulated eclecticism in the future.

In addition to these promising developments I am impressed by the wide range of authors of the present day who are demanding a fuller image of man and his behavior. Murray (1959) offers what he calls "a scaffold of a comprehensive system." F. H. Allport (1955) presents an ambitious "event-structure" metatheory. An open-ended eclecticism frames the versatile contributions of Gardner Murphy (see, e.g., 1947). Recent vigorous voices have been raised by Wellek (1963), Loevinger (1963), Chein (1962). Koch contends sharply that ". . . psychology has been far more concerned with being a science than with courageous and self-determining confrontation of its historical subject matter" (1961, p. 624). To confront such rich subject matter requires an eclectic outlook.

From our survey we conclude that eclecticism, whatever else it may be, is a counsel of historically oriented moderation, and that a would-be systematic eclecticism aims to achieve moderation through the principle of inclusiveness.

IS SYSTEMATIC ECLECTICISM POSSIBLE?

Can inclusiveness ever be achieved in view of the diversity of our subject matter, diversity of metaphysical assumptions, and diversity of personal preference among theorists?

Almost every psychological theory carries with it some presupposition regarding the body-mind relation, the function of consciousness, the issue of freedom, the nature of the self—to name a few of our riddles of the Sphinx. The more you try to solve these riddles the worse they seem to grow. Many current theories point their solutions in terms of strict determinism, epiphenomenalism, and a Humean denial of the self, although authors are often unaware of the assumptions they make. I once asked a doctoral candidate a question. His thesis dealt with physiological and psychological indicators of stress. "How does your thesis bear on the body-mind problem," I asked. "What's that?" he asked, "I never heard of it."

The truth is that we can never have a fully systematic eclecticism until we can resolve the two central antinomies—the issue of dualism and the problem of purpose. An analytically sharp particularism, as I have indicated, tends to meet these issues by the strategy of denial; or by the strategy of synecdoche that substitutes a miniature model for the whole.

As for dualism, we hear that it is dated: that it is dreadful; that it is dead. Yet the solution via epiphenomenalism is surely trivial. And I would add that physicalistic and deterministic theories tend so to restrict our science as to render it incapable of having fruitful bearing upon practical life. And theories that don't work in practical life cannot be entirely sound. Among particularistic theories that follow the fashion of physical monism and determinism, are behaviorism, stimulus-response, empty organism, reinforcement, conditioning, stimulus-generalization, exclusive environmentalism, orthodox psychoanalysis, cybernetics, information theory, homeostasis, computer analogies, and others.

Theories written *exclusively* in such terms cannot be reconciled easily with theories of a second group which hold that in some way man participates in his own destiny. Here one may list modern ego-psychology, personalism, existentialism, most versions of phenomenology, conceptions of motives anchored to the self image (such as aspiration level, competence, life-style, self-consistency, self-actualization, autonomy, identity, propriate striving).

You may ask, Do not all theories in this second group involve an ascription of "freedom" that is denied by theories of the first group? My answer is that all theories of the second group do deal with the person's orientation to his future, and allow for planning, striving, and hope. If you define freedom as planning-striving-hope, then yes, there is in these theories an ascription of freedom. Yet freedom in this sense does not necessarily mean a suspension of lawful regularity. Here, as so often, our impasse in the problem of freedom hinges on the matter of definitions.

Many attempts are made by theorists of the first class to account for the events that interest theorists of the second class. Thus, it has long been known to S-R psychologists who abound in both the U.S.A. and U.S.S.R., that a subject who administers the conditioned stimulus to himself will form a conditioned reflex more rapidly than one who does not. In this fact they find a paradigm for self-control and for will. Or to take a different example, some S-R psychologists give a grudging role to expectancy or to mental set, but usually only in connection with a specific response elicited under experimental conditions. The question of who has the expectancy and why, and what its place may be in the long-range projects of the life is seldom raised. And as for the self-administered conditioned stimulus, the question of who is the self who administers the stimulus is not faced. I think it fair to say that all reinterpretations by reactive theories of active theories never get beyond the immediate response, and so do not cover the long-range phenomena that are of special interest to the second class of theories.

I am not saying that there is no validity in the reactive models or that they have no place in modern eclecticism. We know too much about the mechanical character of much behavior to rule out theories of the first class. What we are saying is that exclusive devotion to theories of the first class makes it impossible to proceed far in understanding the planful, inventive, aspiring, hopeful behavior of man. For all the subtlety of "reinforcement schedules" the characters in Professor Skinner's *Walden Two* remain as reactive as an array of patellar knee-jerks. In real life a *challenge* is something more than a *stimulus*. Thinking creatively with symbols is something beyond responding to signals.

How is it with theories of the second class? A writer who is too much obsessed with the proactive aspect of human nature cannot come to terms with theories of the first group. Thus if he holds that the *only* motive of man is self-actualization or "keeping the phenomenal ego level high" he is debarred from absorbing into his theory the valid facts concerning the reactive aspects of man's behavior accumulated under the inspiration of mechanical and infrahuman models.

But unless I am mistaken the majority of writers from the proactive point of view are not exclusionists. They are saying in effect to their "reactive" colleagues, "You have done a good job on the mechanical aspects of behavior. We do not question them. But we think you have stopped short of the full-bodied person. There is something more to his nature than you are able to explore, even when you overstrain your preferred model."

On this issue of purpose (freedom) it helps to look backward for a moment. Condillac derived everything from sensation; Fichte derived everything from the activity of the self. Condillac neglected the autonomous and Fichte neglected the automatic. Each was blind; yet each was right. The same imbalance on precisely the same issue obtains today. What Condillac and Fichte affirmed was correct. What they by implication denied was their blunder. The same is true today: denial by implication is the major source of weakness in psychological theorizing.

Considering these two basic collisions (dualism and purpose) should we not despair of a systematic eclecticism, to say nothing of an eventual "scientific monism"? On the whole I think not. I have already mentioned some energetic attempts at synthesis—including those of James, Woodworth, Tolman, Bühler, *Schichtentheorie,* existentialism, systems theory. While all of these endeavors hold promise, I am most hopeful that systems theory, properly developed, may yield the comprehensive solution we seek.

Elsewhere I have presented the concept of personality as an open system (1960). Needless to say, the type of system suited to eclecticism must be of the broad organismic variety, since as von Bertalanffy shows (1952) organization in the organic realm is fundamentally different from organization in the mechanical. Further, the open organismic system can admit the criteria of a closed (mechanical) system whereas no closed or quasiclosed system can admit the criteria of an open system. Personality is the most eclectic concept in psychology, and an open system view the most eclectic interpretation of this concept.

Various organic systems differ in their degree of openness. Unless the human personality is ascribed the maximum degree of openness the model will account for neither purpose nor for pattern. As Polanyi says, "by looking at the atomic topography of a frog, no human intelligence could apprehend that it *is* a frog" (1962, p. 615). I would add that no one looking exclusively at behavior could tell that it is a person who is behaving. Patterns tend to vanish if we scan them through the lens of a particularistic model, however magnified (or overmagnified) it may be.

But an open system eclecticism places alarming demands upon us. It shall allow for pattern but also for atomic topography; for the recognition of what is neural and what is not; for what is past (as covered by learning theories) but also for the forward thrust in a life that has organizing power over habit; for the importance of ego-defenses but also for conflict-free ego structure; for computer-like behavior as well as for spontaneity; for infantile remnants in the superego but also the adult sense of moral obligation; for the importance of stimulus and also for the importance of challenge. It shall utilize the procedures of dimensional analysis but at the same time invent needed morphogenic (idiographic) procedures in order to account for what is unique as well as for what is general (see G. W. Allport, 1962).

The task is vast. Yet as an item of faith I submit that a metatheory of man as an open system may lead us to the resolution of each separate antinomy, and toward a systematic eclecticism reflecting a viable image of man.

A CATEGORICAL IMPERATIVE FOR THEORISTS

Although the vision is distant it might be reached if investigators, whatever their preferred level of work, agree to a new categorical imperative to guide their research and theory. The imperative contains two admonitions.

1. Do not forget what you have decided to neglect. If you have a neat S-R formula for a certain type of learning—fine; just don't forget that you have decided to neglect other forms of learning. If you are working with animal drives—fine; but don't forget that you have bracketed human aspirations.

2. Theorize in such a way that what is true in any region of mental life can be verified to be so. (See Bronowski, 1959, p. 74.) This admonition holds that truth is the motive at the center of psychological science. Dogmatic theories often inhibit the discovery of uncongenial truth. Whatever else truth may be it is the process of confronting the valid work of one man with that of another, of grafting each onto each. What is unforgivable, but not uncommon, is to close one's approach to truth so that grafting becomes impossible. The imperative says that no psychologist has the right to interpret his results in such a way as to block the solution of related problems.

Until a systematic eclecticism is achieved, if ever it can be, a pluralism is in order. And pluralism means that neither human nature, nor the universe itself, is yet complete. Hence the imposition of any form of final closure is not allowable.

————, "Psychology for eclectics," in Murchison, C. C. (ed.), *Psychologies of 1930*, Worcester: Clark Univ. Press, 1930, 115–127.

————, *History of experimental psychology*, 2d ed., New York: Appleton-Century-Crofts, 1950.

————, "When is human behavior predetermined?" *Sci. Monthly*, 1957, *84*, 189–196.

Bronowski, J., *Science and human values*, New York: Harper, Torchbook, 1959.

Chein, I., "The image of man," *J. soc. issues*, 1962, *18*, 1–35.

Collier, R. M., "Independence: an overlooked implication of the open system concept," *J. indiv. psychol.*, 1962, *18*, 103–113.

Conant, J. B., *Science and common sense*, New Haven: Yale Univ. Press, 1951.

Gibson, J. J., "The implications of learning theory for social psychology," in Miller, J. G. (ed.), *Experiments in social process*, New York: McGraw-Hill, 1950, pp. 149–167.

Gilbert, A. R., "On the stratification of personality," in David, H. P., and von Bracken, H. (eds.), *Perspectives in personality theory*, New York: Basic Books, 1957, 218–241.

James, H. (ed.), The letters of William James, Vol. 2, Boston: Atlantic Monthly, 1920.

James, W., *Varieties of religious experience*, New York: Longmans, Green, 1902.

————, *Essays in radical empiricism*, New York: Longmans, Green, 1912.

Janet, P., *Victor Cousin et son oeuvre*, Paris: Clamann Levy Edit., 1885.

van Kaam, A., "Existential psychology as a comprehensive theory of personality," *Exist. Psychol. & Psychiat.*, 1963, *3*, 11–26.

Koch, S., "Psychological science versus the science-humanism antinomy," *Amer. Psychologist*, 1961, *16*, 629–639.

Leeper, R. W., "Learning and the fields of perception, motivation, and personality," in Koch, S. (ed.), *Psychology: a study of science*, Vol. 5, New York: McGraw-Hill, 1963.

Likert, R., and Hayes, S. P., Jr., *Some applications of behavioural research*, Paris: Unesco, 1957.

Loevinger, Jane, "Conflict of commitment in clinical research," *Amer. Psychologist*, 1963, *18*, 241-251.

McDougall, W., *The energies of men*, New York: Scribner, 1933.

Mill, J. S., *A system of logic*, New York: Harper, 1867.

Miller, G. A.; Galanter, E.; and Pribram, K. H., *Plans and the structure of behavior*, New York: Holt, Rinehart & Winston, 1960.

Miller, Jessie L., and Miller, J. G., "Behavioral scientists visit the Soviet Union," *Behavioral Sci.*, 1962, 7, 3–36.

Murphy, G., *Personality: a biosocial approach to origins and structure*, New York: Harper, 1947.

Murray, H. A., "Preparations for the scaffold of a comprehensive system," in Koch, S. (ed.), *Psychology: a study of science*, Vol. 3, New York: McGraw-Hill, 1959, 7–54.

Nagel, E., *The structure of science*, New York: Harcourt, Brace & World, 1961.

Polanyi, M., "Tacit knowing: its bearing on some problems of philosophy," *Reviews of mod. Physics*, 1962, *34*, 601–616.

Schmidt, H., *Philosophisches Wörterbuch*, Leipzig: Kröner Verlag, 1934 (9th ed.).

Skinner, B. F., *Walden Two*, New York: Macmillan, 1948.

Snow, C. P., *The two cultures and the scientific revolution*, New York: Cambridge Univ. Press, 1959.

Tolman, E. C., "There is more than one kind of learning," *Psychol. Rev.*, 1949, *56*, 144–155.

Wellek, A., Die Wissenschafts-problematik der Psychologie als einer anthropologischen Disziplin, *Psychol. Rundschau*, 1963, *15*, 75–92.

Whitehead, A. N., *Science and the modern world*, New York: Macmillan, 1925.

Whyte, L. L., *The unconscious before Freud*, New York: Doubleday-Anchor, 1962.

2

Six Decades of Social Psychology

SINCE IT IS ALWAYS PLEASANT to indulge in personal reminiscence I enjoyed writing this article. Its contents tell the story. The reader need only to be told that it was prepared for, and delivered at, the Conference on the Teaching of Social Psychology held in New York City in December 1966. The Chairman for the occasion was Dr. Sven Lundstedt, who also edited the proceedings in which this paper appears as Chapter 1: *The Preparation of Social Psychologists*, Cleveland: Western Reserve University Press, 1967.

† † †

THE FIRST DECADE

Social psychology was christened in 1908 when its first two textbooks were published.[1] This was a remarkable event in that the infant was christened some years before it was born. Indeed one may ask whether this particular embryo science is not still lingering long in gestation.

The two textbooks were not only progenitive but also prophetic. E. A. Ross's approach is sociological, William McDougall's psychobiological. The former deals with the "psychic planes and currents" that run through social congregates and societal aggregates; the latter focuses upon the instincts and sentiments of the individual person that prepare him for his social memberships.

The numerous progeny of these progenitive authors have a tendency, as all offspring have, to favor either one parent or the other. Approximately half the offspring favor the group (or macro) approach, half the individual (or micro) approach. Needless to say the situation engenders some sharp sibling rivalries. The macros scorn the micros for their narrowness of vision; and the micros abuse the macros for their conceptual looseness. But on the whole the two genetic strains manage a peaceful coexistence.

For all their historic importance both texts were in a sense abortive. Ross's production was *fin de siècle*, a final restatement of dissociation theory, snatched from Charcot's séances with hysterics, and applied to mass phenomena in the manner of Tarde, Sighele, and Le Bon. Although this movement holding over from the 1890's was certainly ancestral to modern social psychology, its influence from Ross's time onward declined.

McDougall's book too, in spite of innumerable reprintings down to the present day, was abortive. Instincts as explanatory concepts went rapidly out of fashion in America although somewhat more slowly in Britain. In America it was chiefly the rising behaviorists who administered the *coups de grâce* to instincts: Watson, Kuo, Dunlap, Holt, and others. I can clearly recall that we younger social psychologists would not be caught dead with an instinct in our possession, not even with Freud's *thanatos*, although if instinctual energies (as opposed to simple drives) were to be admitted at all we preferred Freud's steam-boiler conception to McDougall's careful architectonic. But in fairness to McDougall it should be noted that his thoughtful treatment of the self-regarding sentiment had at least 30-years' head start over neo-Freudian ego psychology. Much that Hartmann, Horney, Erikson had later to say about the integrative ego functions was resident in McDougall's self-regarding sentiment.

Summing up the first decade we may say that the twin channels of social psychology—the functions of the individual on the one hand and the processes of group organization on the other—were both clearly demarcated. This bifurcation exists down to the present day. But in all fairness it should be said that both schools of thought even in the earlier years made overtures to the other. McDougall recognized from the start that his approach was one-sided, and so he promised a complementary treatment of social psychology, a promise he endeavored to fulfill in *The Group Mind*[2] which is clearly a "macro" book on social structure and dynamics. At the same time the Chicago School felt the need for a doctrine of individual motives to underpin social process, and this they found in Thomas's doctrine of the four wishes.[3] And other sociologically oriented social scientists began to draw on Freud for such motivational concepts as they felt the need of. One should recall in this connection the writings of James Harvey Robinson, Everett Dean Martin, Harold Laswell, and others.

THE SECOND DECADE

Let me approach the second decade somewhat autobiographically, for this is where I came in. My story here concerns chiefly social psychology at Harvard. I justify my parochialism by the conviction that for all its oddities Harvard does reflect the *Zeit*, the *Geist*, and the *Schicksal* of American social psychology during the past 50 years.

The first course at Harvard titled *Social Psychology* was offered in the spring of 1917 by Edwin Bissell Holt. About 20 students enrolled. Upon the outbreak of the war in April most of us took a hasty final examination and departed for basic military training. Yet for the space of two months we were exposed to what is surely the queerest hodgepodge of all the hodgepodges ever offered under the rubric of social psychology. Our assigned reading consisted of Tarde's book on *Imitation* and Schopenhauer's essay on the *Primacy of the Will in Self-consciousness*. The texts by McDougall and Ross were ignored. McDougall's purposivism irritated Holt's behavioristic soul; and since Ross was Tarde at second hand why not read the original?

In class Holt discussed only his own current interests. The

Dutch physiologist, Bok, excited him with his concept of the circular reflex. Added to Pavlov this concept gave Holt his "echo principle" which he felt to be the keystone of all psychology, although I personally could never see that it explained anything save the first stages of the child's learning of the language along with pat-a-cake and bye-bye.

His other enthusiasm was for the new book by Félix Le Dantec, *L'Egoisme*. He would translate pages in class and smack his lips over the iconoclastic treatment of social institutions. All of them, including the Ten Commandments, were reduced to arrant hypocrisies invented to insure the survival of the individual in a society of wolves. I still think that no author—be it Hobbes, Stirner, Freud, or Bertrand Russell—has ever given so devastating a commentary on the self-seeking aspects of human nature. And since there is plenty of self-seeking around even in the modern welfare state, Le Dantec's book remains a classic, unknown to most modern social psychologists.

Holt's course was erratic, but it started me on my way. For me it held a two-pronged goad. One was the impetus that comes from studying the efforts of good minds in the past to solve the puzzles of man's social nature. The other prong comes from the on-the-spot inquiry. In those days we did not have laboratory or field projects, but Holt's wrestling with the construction of an original theory (the echo principle) served the same purpose. For balance in social psychology the sagacity of the past and the forward thrust of the frontier, two forces are needed. The first without the second is regressive; the second without the first is illiterate.

Instruction in social psychology at Chicago no doubt antedated instruction at Harvard. Under Cooley, Mead, Park, Burgess, Faris, and others the emphasis at Chicago was clearly sociological; whereas at Harvard for at least three decades social psychology was tied to the general academic tradition of individual psychology. Such, I am told, is my own continuing bias. Indeed I am variously accused of being anti-cultural, anti-institutional, and anti-social. My sins in these respects, I feel, are exaggerated.

During the early 1920's I was exposed to two remaining influences in social psychology at Harvard. One was the incubation of my brother's text *Social Psychology*[4]—a combination of behavioristic and Freudian thought. The other was McDougall's seminar in social psychology from which I gained some historical insights and an exposure to purposivism. I mention these crosscurrents for they help explain my leaning toward eclecticism, a leaning accentuated by a period of study of the structural, Gestalt, and personalistic trends in Germany, and of cultural factors with Bartlett in England. All these contrary forces made me long for an appropriate eclecticism in psychological theory.[5]

The theoretical ferment in the second decade concerned chiefly the controversy over meanings of the "group mind," the place of Freudian concepts, and the applicability of strict behavioral principles to the study of social conduct. It was also a decade of important methodological inventions. Attitude measurement came into being, stimulated chiefly by Thurstone. Controlled group experiments were initiated by Moede in Germany, imported by Muensterberg to Harvard, and developed by F. H. Allport, Dashiell, Goodwin Watson, and others.[6] Lewin's clever experimental methods were incubating in Germany, but they did not affect American social psychology until the end of the third decade.

THE THIRD DECADE

Commencing around 1930, the third decade was marked by a push to bring the basic social sciences into confrontation. The slogan was "culture and personality," and the sponsor was the Social Science Research Council, which, in a series of conferences and volumes, juxtaposed the research and thinking of anthropologists, sociologists, and psychologists. It was a stimulating movement, lasting well into the fourth decade, and no doubt having a diffuse influence in the present day.

The culture-personality movement to my mind illustrates two persistent characteristics of our science. One is the honest search for means to unite the individual and the group approaches, what Parsons calls the personality system and the social system. The other characteristic is our easy boredom and slippery change of venue. We do not solve our problems; we only grow tired of them. New labels, we think, bring new problems. We grow weary of suggestibility and so investigate persuasibility; personality and culture give way to systems theory; the group mind drifts into organizational theory; rationalization becomes cognitive dissonance; friendship masquerades as interpersonal attractiveness; problem-solving dissolves into programming; pleasure and pain become positive and negative reinforcement; maladjustment becomes alienation; volition gives way to decision-making; no longer does one possess character, one has ego-strength. The average life of popular concepts is, I estimate, about two decades. After that they begin to taste as flat as yesterday's beer.

It is possible, of course, that new formulations represent true progress, but to me such shifting often seems merely weary and evasive—a device for overlooking previously relevant studies.

During the third decade *attitude* became a pivotal concept. Here we should pause and take stock, for, contrary to what I have just said, "attitude" seems to be a truly indestructible core concept in our science. As long ago as 1918, Thomas and Znaniecki defined social psychology as the scientific study of attitudes. I myself examined the concept in detail in Murchison's *Handbook of Social Psychology* in 1936, and it will no doubt feature largely in the forthcoming revision of the Lindzey *Handbook*. And yet one cannot overlook the dissatisfaction of many writers who have avoided or recast the concept. Lewin found attitude too isolated from the total field of force and for the same reason others avoid it. The finding of great inconsistency among attitudes and in their expression has led to minimizing their explanatory value. There have been many attempts to externalize attitudes, as it were, from a neurodynamic role in personality into the stimulus situation conceived as acting on an empty organism. Situationism, objectivism, positivism, and operationism do not care for the intervening character of the attitude concept. Donald Campbell has tried to steer a middle and conciliatory course.[7] And yet all in all it seems to me that if we have any common focus in social psychology it is in the concept of attitude.

A further feature of the third decade was its tender-mindedness. The great depression, the rise of Hitler, the influx of German refugees—including many psychologists—the approach of World War II profoundly accepted psychologists touched with social concern (and most of them, hard-nosed as they may be, are soft as marshmallows inside). The Society for the Psychological Study of Social Issues was formed in 1936. My impression is that most of the active social psychologists at that time became members, and many of them pursued serviceable lines of research in industry, among the unemployed, and in the field of national morale.

In preparation for the fourth decade we should cite here the memorable paper of Kurt Lewin on "Some social psychological differences between Germany and America."[8] I well recall his telling me of the background of this simple but pungent observational study. He said that in pre-Hitler Germany he considered himself a true social-democrat; but that when he savored the free political and social atmosphere in America he felt that he had never known what, psychologically speaking, democracy meant. With what I would consider the simplicity of true genius, he tried to put down the grounds for this elusive experience of what democracy means. He noted that German barriers to social intercourse lay closer to the surface than in America, where professors keep their office doors open, and where newspapers pub-

lish all but the innermost secrets of personal lives. His arrival
in this country and this initial paper are the harbingers of a
highly important development in the fourth decade, to which
we now turn.

THE FOURTH DECADE

History, no doubt, will record three theoretical advances in
the 40's. One of these is the Lewinian theory of group dynamics. For about two decades the experimental study of
groups had remained at the level of social influence, that is
to say, the effects that the presence of coacting partners have
upon the psychological performance of the individual. Lewin
expanded the problem to study any and all forces that affect
any and all members of a face-to-face group. He introduced
concepts such as cohesiveness, group decision, styles of leadership, experimental social change. Under his influence the
social psychology of groups took a stride forward.

A second advance was in the formulation of principles that
might apply to urgent social problems. A prime example is
the preparation and publication of *The Authoritarian Personality*.[9] Here, of course, the source lay partly in attitude
measurement and partly in Freudian theory; but its focus,
as in Lewin's work, was on the functioning of democracy in
a time of crisis. In wartime the demands were not primarily
for tight theoretical elegance, but even so it would be wrong
to think that the many studies in rumor, propaganda, morale,
race conflict, and public opinion did not lead to marked advances in method and in theory. Besides *The Authoritarian
Personality* one should recall the theoretical contributions that
lay in the extensive research reports by Stouffer and his associates in *The American Soldier*,[10] of Alexander Leighton in *The
Governing of Men*,[11] and in various studies of a demoralized
Germany made by social psychologists in connection with the
so-called "bombing survey."

A third advance came partly as a sleeper effect of the Ge-

stalt revolution of previous decades. Social perception became
the watchword. And here again we have in part Lewin to
thank. Perception, cognition, phenomenology wormed their
way into social psychology, assisted by the deliberate efforts
of MacLeod,[12] Heider,[13] and the "new look" perceptionists.
Gardner Murphy and many others aided the movement
which showed that man's awareness of his social environment
varies with his inner needs, cultural situation, and economic
status. A text establishing the validity and value of the phenomenological approach to social psychology appeared at this
time—the text by Krech and Crutchfield.[14]

THE FIFTH DECADE

Moving into the fifth decade the phenomenological movement becomes somewhat more consolidated. Asch's text (like
Krech and Crutchfield's) is a strong statement of a theoretical
position.[15] But Asch goes beyond phenomenology in stressing
the essential reasonableness of man's efforts to cope with his
environment. Much that we have called illusion, rationalization, projection, suggestion, and imitation, he insists, is a
rational form of coping with life's problems. Not since the
days of the Enlightenment (Condorcet, Locke, Godwin)
have we had so sweet and reasonable an interpretation of
man's social behavior.

The fifth decade brought, also, a frenzy of methodological
sophistication. Factor analysis, mathematical models, computers, minute empiricism, multivariate analysis of variance,
and elaborate mendacious experimentation, began to flourish.
Our addiction to the pompous and erroneous term "methodology" betrays our preoccupation. We inflate our methods
into "methodologies" because we are so conscious of them
and so childishly proud.

Now no one can object to clear methods, to an accurate
handling of data, or to severe self-scrutiny in research. But the
obsessiveness we encounter in our journal articles during the
fifth and sixth decades seems to betoken a drift whose signifi-

cance is not yet fully clear. Let me suggest two interpretations; neither may be correct, or perhaps both may be valid.

(1) All science seems to be tending toward metatheory. One indication is the search for mathematical models; another is computer theory which assumes an embracing uniformity to cover mental, behavioral, mechanical events in the same deterministic way. Another symptom is the popularity of information theory, and of linguistic analysis. If one only knew his syntactical rules one could compass all of man's cognitive, ethical, and spiritual experience at one fell swoop. We note that all these examples of metatheory call for clarification and precision of method. All metatheories in the last analysis are methodological; none is substantive. It may therefore be that the recent preoccupation with method is a preparation for the abandonment of a substantive social psychology in favor of more abstract conceptualization in which social psychology would join other sciences in a common search for a unifying metatheory.

(2) An alternative interpretation is in terms of cultural disintegration. We cannot hope (says the modern man to himself) to find intelligible generalizations. Who knows what imitation, suggestion, crowd contagion, communication networks, group decision, cooperation, competition, or leadership may be? Or who any longer cares? Such rubrics are too coarse and too representational. Modern art is no longer representational. The time is past when we can set our problem in terms of face appearance. Modern painting, music, poetry have given up attempts at consecutiveness and synthesis.

Can it be that social psychology is following suit, and seeking only momentary fragments of experience? If with elaborate methods I can confirm my hypothesis that a child will talk to its mother more often than to a stranger, or that adults are often inconsistent in their behavior, the obviousness of my findings does not perturb me so long as they are confirmed and reconfirmed beyond the .001 level of probability. May it also be that the goad to "publish or perish" encourages swift, piecemeal, unread, and unreadable publications,

crammed with method but scant on meaning? The prevalence
of fragmentation seems illustrated by the present cloudburst
of books of disjointed and astigmatic *Readings*. The student
is fed fragments, not theory.

Support for the argument that social psychology follows
the general trend of culture comes from a recent content
study made by Earl Carlson.[16] He finds that over the past several decades psychologists have given less and less attention to
the pleasant emotions—to elation, joy, sympathy; and greatly
increased attention to fear, anxiety, and anger. The trend is
very marked, and seems to mirror our era of existential
anxiety and of angry young men. Social psychology, like
general psychology, deals more with frustration than with
fondness, and more with hostility than with compassion.

If we take the forthcoming revision of Hollander and Hunt's
Current Perspectives in Social Psychology as representative
of contemporary interests we note that of the 65 topical en-
tries none seems to deal with sympathy, with humor, with
conscience, or with religion.[17] Clearly the flight from tender-
ness is still under way.

THE SIXTH DECADE

Yes, to some extent the latter part of the fifth and early part
of the sixth decade have been jerky, nervous, and largely
atheoretical in nature. But it would be a mistake, I think, to
characterize the present only in these terms.

There is still a strong trend toward substantive studies.
Some excellent investigators have taken a wholesome bath in
method but have not drowned in it. They are proud of the
fact that of all the social sciences ours has always been the
most aware, and the most inventive, of sharp instruments of
research, and has gone further in attempting to apply them
to difficult areas of inquiry. At the same time they remain
primarily problem-centered in orientation. Sound books on
leadership, industrial relations, social movements, prejudice,

communication, the socialization of children, and the psychological conditions of international understanding and peace continue to appear. They employ improved modern methods but are not (like many of our journal articles) tied, gagged, and suffocated by their pretentious "methodologies."

Let us consider for a moment two areas in which vast progress has been made in the past 20 years: the field of group conflict and prejudice and the field of peace research. There can be no doubt that social psychologists have contributed heavily to the increase in understanding of these (and other) major social problems. And yet, to be entirely frank, we have not contributed enough to help remedy our social distress. We have a long way yet to go.

Toward the end of his career E. B. Holt was mightily fed up with the pretensions of academic social psychology. He warned the student against it, saying that the student will find any textbook "a farrago of vague, pedantic, and utterly useless abstractions." He goes on to say, "The mental blindness of nearly every academic social psychologist for any observable fact of human nature is so unfailing and complete as almost to compel admiration." All this Holt wrote in 1935 in a paper entitled "The whimsical condition of social psychology and of mankind."[18]

Holt's dyspepsia was chronic. But if we are honest with ourselves do we not all have our moments of depression when we doubt our justification as scientists? Unlike the engineer we cannot demonstrate the validity of our theories or the utility of our methods—not even when we inflate them into "methodologies." It is not hard to understand our occasional retreat into gamesmanship.

I recall a conversation I had with a high official in the State Department. Bluntly he asked me, "Honestly, do you social psychologists have anything that would help me in my day-to-day work on the India desk?" I replied, "Honestly, I do not know, but I am furious with you for not using it." We left the matter at this impasse.

CONCLUSION

What then shall we conclude? For one thing we do well to face frankly our failure thus far to demonstrate our claim to be a powerful theoretical and applied social science. We should face this fact even though we may not agree with Holt that we are poor observers and whimsical in our dabbling.

But to return to my earlier point: our science is young—indeed it is still aborning. As Swanson and Faris show in the present symposium it is a peculiarly American product—and six decades is not such a long time when we look at the longer history of the physical, biological, and medical sciences. Furthermore the tempo of our progress both in method and in problem orientation is increasing—in spite of our occasional excursions into trivial bypaths.

All in all my own outlook is optimistic. I think we may yet become the central science for the understanding and amelioration of mankind. But the way is long and difficult and our wisdom is thin.

When I say that social psychology is only six decades old I do not mean, of course, that the previous history of human thought is not rich in insight. We have much, much to learn from political science past and present, from philosophy, and from all theories of the social nature of man.

But we have much also to learn from the past six decades, and it is here that I should like to hurl my parting shaft.

I have tried to discover in a superficial way how much contemporary social psychologists know about the past six decades. So far as my tidbit of evidence goes the answer is "Not very much." Take a look at the references given at the end of articles in the *Journal of Social Psychology and Personality* in the July and August editions of 1966. Among articles properly classified as social psychology, 94 per cent of the references are to publications during the previous decade and a half, that is, since the year 1950. There may be good reasons for this topsidedness. Recent work may be better than older work; to some extent recent work may be cumulative of the earlier work (but considering our tendency to re-label our problems I doubt this explanation). Perhaps the most plausible explanation is that in our hectic tempo of production investigators build only on their immediate predecessors. Whatever the reason, the fact remains that 94 per cent of the threads deliberately woven into our current research fabric reach back only 15 years.

While the modern social psychologist does indeed need experimental, statistical, and computer skills he also needs historical perspective. He needs immersion in theories (both macro and micro). Above all he needs an ability to relate his problem to the context in which it properly belongs. Sometimes the context lies in the traditions of academic psychology, often in sociology or anthropology, sometimes in philosophy or theology, occasionally in history or in economics, frequently in the political life of our day. Sometimes the science of genetics or clinical experience provides the context.

In short, although social psychology has its own body of history, theory, problems, and methods it is not a self-sufficient science. It thrives best when cross-cultivated in a rich and diversified intellectual garden.

NOTES

1. E. A. Ross, *Social psychology*, New York: Macmillan, 1908; Methuen, 1908.
2. W. McDougall, *The group mind*, New York: G. P. Putnam, 1920.
3. W. I. Thomas, *The unadjusted girl*, Boston: Little, Brown, 1923.
4. F. H. Allport, *Social psychology*, Boston: Houghton Mifflin, 1924.
5. Cf. G. W. Allport, "The fruits of eclecticism: bitter or sweet?" *Acta Psychologia*, 1964, *23*, 27–44.
6. For a history of early experimental methods, see G. W. All-

port, "The historical background of modern social psychology," Chapter 1 in G. Lindzey (ed.), *Handbook of social psychology*, Reading, Mass.: Addison-Wesley, 1954. This same source contains references to other historical events mentioned, but not documented, in the present paper.

7. D. T. Campbell, "Social attitudes and other acquired behavioral dispositions," in S. Koch (ed.), *Investigations of man as socius: their place in psychology and the social sciences*, New York: McGraw-Hill, 1963.

8. K. Lewin, "Social-psychological differences between the United States and Germany," Chapter 1 in *Resolving social conflict*, New York: Harper, 1948.

9. T. W. Adorno, Else Frenkel-Brunswik, D. J. Levinson, and R. N. Sanford, *The authoritarian personality*, New York: Harper, 1950.

10. See, for example, discussions of relative deprivation in S. A. Stouffer, E. A. Suchman, L. C. DeVinney, Shirley A. Star, R. M. Williams, Jr., *The American soldier*, Volume 1, Princeton: Princeton University Press, 1949.

11. A. H. Leighton, *The governing of men*, Princeton, N.J.: Princeton University Press, 1945.

12. R. B. MacLeod, "The phenomenological approach to social psychology," *Psychological Review*, 1947, *54*, 193–210.

13. F. Heider, "Social perception and phenomenal causality," *Psychological Review*, 1944, *51*, 358–374.

14. D. Krech and R. S. Crutchfield, *Theory and problems of social psychology*, New York: McGraw-Hill, 1948.

15. S. E. Asch, *Social psychology*, New York: Prentice-Hall, 1952.

16. E. R. Carlson, "The affective tone of psychology," *Journal of General Psychology*, 1966, *75*, 65–78.

17. E. P. Hollander and R. G. Hunt, *Current perspectives in social psychology*, New York: Oxford University Press, rev. ed., 1967.

18. E. B. Holt, "The whimsical condition of social psychology and of mankind," in H. M. Kallen and S. Hook (eds.), *American philosophy: today and tomorrow*, New York: Lee Furman, 1935.

3

Traits Revisited

IMPORTANT—indeed central—to my theoretical position is my own particular conception of "trait" (or its variant, "personal disposition"). I take it for granted that we all have in our neuropsychic equipment, in addition to habits and other smaller structures, integrated systems of action tendencies that comprise the molar units of the total structure of personality. These units are often dynamic in their motive power, being "functionally autonomous" of their historical forms.

When the American Psychological Association granted me its Award for "distinguished scientific contribution" in 1964 it became my obligation to offer this paper one year later at the 1965 meeting in Chicago.

It so happened that my maiden speech at the Ninth International Congress of Psychology at Yale in 1929 was titled "What Is a Trait?" It seemed to me a fitting idea to pursue the original theme and even to parody the original title 35 years later. The *American Psychologist* printed the article in January 1966.

†   †   †

Years ago I ventured to present a paper before the Ninth International Congress at New Haven (G. W. Allport, 1931). It was entitled "What Is a Trait of Personality?" For me to return to the same topic on this honorific occasion is partly a sentimental indulgence, but partly too it is a self imposed task to discover whether during the past 36 years I have learned anything new about this central problem in personality theory.

In my earlier paper I made eight bold assertions. A trait, I said,

1. Has more than nominal existence.
2. Is more generalized than a habit.
3. Is dynamic, or at least determinative, in behavior.
4. May be established empirically.
5. Is only relatively independent of other traits.
6. Is not synonymous with moral or social judgment.
7. May be viewed either in the light of the personality which contains it, or in the light of its distribution in the population at large.

To these criteria I added one more:

8. Acts, and even habits, that are inconsistent with a trait are not proof of the nonexistence of the trait.

While these propositions still seem to me defensible they were originally framed in an age of psychological innocence. They now need reexamination in the light of subsequent criticism and research.

CRITICISM OF THE CONCEPT OF TRAIT

Some critics have challenged the whole concept of trait. Carr and Kingsbury (1938) point out the danger of reification. Our initial observation of behavior is only in terms of adverbs of action: John behaves aggressively. Then an adjective creeps in: John has an aggressive disposition. Soon a heavy substantive arrives, like William James's cow on the doormat: John has a trait of aggression. The result is the fallacy of misplaced concreteness.

The general positivist cleanup starting in the 1930s went even further. It swept out (or tried to sweep out) all entities, regarding them as question-begging redundancies. Thus Skinner (1953) writes:

When we say that a man eats *because* he is hungry, smokes a great deal *because* he has the tobacco habit, fights *because* of the instinct of pugnacity, behaves brilliantly *because* of his intelligence, or plays the piano well *because* of his musical ability, we seem to be referring to causes. But on analysis these phrases prove to be merely redundant descriptions [p. 31].

It is clear that this line of attack is an assault not only upon the concept of trait, but upon all intervening variables whether they be conceived in terms of expectancies, attitudes, motives, capacities, sentiments, or traits. The resulting postulate of the "empty organism" is by now familiar to us all, and is the scientific credo of some. Carried to its logical extreme this reasoning would scrap the concept of personality itself—an eventuality that seems merely absurd to me.

More serious, to my mind, is the argument against what Block and Bennett (1955) called "traitology" arising from many studies of the variability of a person's behavior as it changes from situation to situation. Every parent knows that an offspring may be a hellion at home and an angel when he goes visiting. A businessman may be hardheaded in the office and a mere marshmallow in the hands of his pretty daughter.

Years ago the famous experiment by La Piere (1934) demonstrated that an innkeeper's prejudice seems to come and go according to the situation confronting him.

In recent months Hunt (1965) has listed various theories of personality that to his mind require revision in the light of recent evidence. Among them he questions the belief that personality traits are the major sources of behavior variance. He, like Miller (1963), advocates that we shift attention from traits to interactions among people, and look for consistency in behavior chiefly in situationally defined roles. Helson (1964) regards trait as the residual effect of previous stimulation, and thus subordinates it to the organism's present adaptation level.

Skepticism is likewise reflected in many investigations of "person perception." To try to discover the traits residing within a personality is regarded as either naïve or impossible. Studies, therefore, concentrate only on the *process* of perceiving or judging, and reject the problem of validating the perception and judgment. (Cf. Tagiuri & Petrullo, 1958.)

Studies too numerous to list have ascribed chief variance in behavior to situational factors, leaving only a mild residue to be accounted for in terms of idiosyncratic attitudes and traits. A prime example is Stouffer's study of *The American Soldier* (Stouffer et al., 1949). Differing opinions and preferences are ascribed so far as possible to the GI's age, marital status, educational level, location of residence, length of service, and the like. What remains is ascribed to "attitude." By this procedure personality becomes an appendage to demography (see G. W. Allport, 1950). It is not the integrated structure within the skin that determines behavior, but membership in a group, the person's assigned roles—in short, the prevailing situation. It is especially the sociologists and anthropologists who have this preference for explanations in terms of the "outside structure" rather than the "inside structure" (cf. F. H. Allport, 1955, Ch. 21).

I have mentioned only a few of the many varieties of situationism that flourish today. While not denying any of the evidence adduced I would point to their common error of interpretation. If a child is a hellion at home, an angel outside, he obviously has two contradictory tendencies in his nature, or perhaps a deeper genotype that would explain the opposing phenotypes. If in studies of person perception the process turns out to be complex and subtle, still there would be no perception at all unless there were something out there to perceive and to judge. If, as in Stouffer's studies, soldiers' opinions vary with their marital status or length of service, these opinions are still their own. The fact that my age, sex, social status help form my outlook on life does not change the fact that the outlook is a functioning part of me. Demography deals with distal forces—personality study with proximal forces. The fact that the innkeeper's behavior varies according to whether he is, or is not, physically confronted with Chinese applicants for hospitality tells nothing about his attitude structure, except that it is complex, and that several attitudes may converge into a given act of behavior.

Nor does it solve the problem to explain the variance in terms of statistical interaction effects. Whatever tendencies exist reside in a person, for a person is the sole possessor of the energy that leads to action. Admittedly different situations elicit differing tendencies from my repertoire. I do not perspire except in the heat, nor shiver except in the cold; but the outside temperature is not the mechanism of perspiring or shivering. My capacities and my tendencies lie within.

To the situationist I concede that our theory of traits cannot be so simpleminded as it once was. We are now challenged to untangle the complex web of tendencies that constitute a person, however contradictory they may seem to be when activated differentially in various situations.

ON THE OTHER HAND

In spite of gunfire from positivism and situationism, traits are still very much alive. Gibson (1941) has pointed out that the "concept of set or attitude is nearly universal in psychological thinking." And in an important but neglected paper—perhaps the last he ever wrote—McDougall (1937) argued that *tendencies* are the "indispensable postulates of all psychology." The concept of *trait* falls into this genre. As Walker (1964) says, trait, however else defined, always connotes an enduring tendency of some sort. It is the structural counterpart of such functional concepts as "expectancy," and "goal-directedness."

After facing all the difficulties of situational and mood variations, also many of the methodological hazards such as response set, halo, and social desirability, Vernon (1964) concludes, "We could go a long way towards predicting behavior if we could assess these stable features in which people differ from one another [p. 181]." The powerful contributions of Thurstone, Guilford, Cattell, and Eysenck, based on factor analysis, agree that the search for traits should provide eventually a satisfactory taxonomy of personality and of its hierarchical structure. The witness of these and other thoughtful writers helps us withstand the pessimistic attacks of positivism and situationism.

It is clear that I am using "trait" as a generic term, to cover all the "permanent possibilities for action" of a generalized order. Traits are cortical, subcortical, or postural dispositions having the capacity to gate or guide specific phasic reactions. It is only the phasic aspect that is visible; the tonic is carried somehow in the still mysterious realm of neurodynamic structure. Traits, as I am here using the term, include long-range sets and attitudes, as well as such variables as "perceptual response dispositions," "personal constructs," and "cognitive styles."

Unlike McClelland (1951) I myself would regard traits (i.e., some traits) as motivational (others being merely stylistic). I would also insist that traits may be studied at two levels: (*a*) dimensionally, that is, as an aspect of the psychology of individual differences, and (*b*) individually, in terms of *personal dispositions*. (Cf. G. W. Allport, 1961, Ch. 15.) It is the latter approach that brings us closest to the person we are studying.

As for factors, I regard them as a mixed blessing. In the investigations I shall soon report, factorial analysis, I find, has proved both helpful and unhelpful. My principal question is whether the factorial unit is idiomatic enough to reflect the structure of personality as the clinician, the counselor, or the man in the street apprehends it. Or are factorial dimensions screened so extensively and so widely attenuated—through

item selection, correlation, axis manipulation, homogeniza-
tion, and alphabetical labeling—that they impose an artifact of
method upon the personal neural network as it exists in nature?

This question leads me to propose an epistemological position
for research in personality. Most of us, I suspect, hold this
position although we seldom formulate it even to ourselves.
It can be called a *heuristic realism*.

Heuristic realism, as applied to our problem, holds that the
person who confronts us possesses inside his skin generalized
action tendencies (or traits) and that it is our job scientifically
to discover what they are. Any form of realism assumes the
existence of an external structure ("out there") regardless of
our shortcomings in comprehending it. Since traits, like all
intervening variables, are never directly observed but only
inferred, we must expect difficulties and errors in the process
of discovering their nature.

The incredible complexity of the structure we seek to understand is enough to discourage the realist, and to tempt him
to play some form of positivistic gamesmanship. He is
tempted to settle for such elusive formulations as: "If we
knew enough about the situation we wouldn't need the concept of personality"; or "One's personality is merely the way
other people see one"; or "There is no structure in personality
but only varying degrees of consistency in the environment."

Yet the truly persistent realist prefers not to abandon his
commitment to find out what the other fellow is really like.
He knows that his attempt will not wholly succeed, owing
partly to the complexity of the object studied, and partly to
the inadequacy of present methods. But unlike Kant who
held that the *Ding an Sich* is doomed to remain unknowable,
he prefers to believe that it is at least partly or approximately
knowable.

I have chosen to speak of *heuristic* realism, because to me special emphasis should be placed on empirical methods of discovery. In this respect heuristic realism goes beyond naïve realism.

Taking this epistemological point of view, the psychologist first focuses his attention on some limited slice of personality that he wishes to study. He then selects or creates methods appropriate to the empirical testing of his hypothesis that the cleavage he has in mind is a trait (either a dimensional trait or a personal disposition). He knows that his present purposes and the methods chosen will set limitations upon his discovery. If, however, the investigation achieves acceptable standards of validation he will have progressed far toward his identification of traits. Please note, as with any heuristic procedure the process of discovery may lead to important corrections of the hypothesis as originally stated.

Empirical testing is thus an important aspect of heuristic realism, but it is an empiricism restrained throughout by rational considerations. Galloping empiricism, which is our present occupational disease, dashes forth like a headless horseman. It has no rational objective; uses no rational method other than mathematical; reaches no rational conclusion. It lets the discordant data sing for themselves. By contrast heuristic realism says, "While we are willing to rest our case for traits on empirical evidence, the area we carve out for study should be rationally conceived, tested by rational methods; and the findings should be rationally interpreted."

THREE ILLUSTRATIVE STUDIES

It is now time for me to illustrate my argument with sample studies. I have chosen three in which I myself have been involved. They differ in the areas of personality carved out for study, in the methods employed, and in the type of traits established. They are alike, however, in proceeding from the standpoint of heuristic realism. The presentation of each study must of necessity be woefully brief. The first illustrates what might be called *meaningful dimensionalism;* the second *meaningful covariation;* the third *meaningful morphogenesis.*

Dimensions of Values

The first illustration is drawn from a familiar instrument, dating almost from the stone age, *The Study of Values* (Allport & Vernon, 1931). While some of you have approved it over the years, and some disapproved, I use it to illustrate two important points of my argument.

First, the instrument rests on an a priori analysis of one large region of human personality, namely, the region of generic evaluative tendencies. It seemed to me 40 years ago, and seems to me now, that Eduard Spranger (1922) made a persuasive case for the existence of six fundamental types of subjective evaluation or *Lebensformen.* Adopting this rational starting point we ourselves took the second step, to put the hypothesis to empirical test. We asked: Are the six dimensions proposed—the *theoretic,* the *economic,* the *esthetic, social, political,* and *religious*—measurable on a multidimensional scale? Are they reliable and valid? Spranger defined the six ways of looking at life in terms of separate and distinct ideal types, although he did not imply that a given person belongs exclusively to one and only one type.

It did not take long to discover that when confronted with a forced-choice technique people do in fact subscribe to all six values, but in widely varying degrees. Within any pair of values, or any quartet of values, their forced choices indicate a reliable pattern. Viewed then as empirical continua, rather than as types, the six value directions prove to be measurable, reproducible, and consistent. But are they valid? Can we obtain external validation for this particular a priori conception of traits? The test's *Manual* (Allport & Vernon, 1931) contains much such evidence. Here I would add a bit more, drawn from occupational studies with women subjects. (The evidence for men is equally good.) The data in Table 1 are derived partly from the *Manual*, partly from Guthrie and McKendry (1963) and partly from an unpublished study by Elizabeth Moses.

TABLE I

MEAN SCORES FOR OCCUPATIONAL GROUPS OF WOMEN:
STUDY OF VALUES

	Female collegiate norms $N = 2,475$	Graduate nurses training for teaching $N = 328$	Graduate students of business administration $N = 77$	Peace Corps teachers $N = 131$
Theoretical	36.5	40.2	37.3	40.6
Economic	36.8	32.9	40.4	29.9
Esthetic	43.7	43.1	46.8	49.3
Social	41.6	40.9	35.0	41.2
Political	38.0	37.2	41.8	39.7
Religious	43.1	45.7	38.7	39.2

For present purposes it is sufficient to glance at the last three columns. For the *theoretic* value we note that the two groups of teachers or teachers in preparation select this value significantly more often than do graduate students of business administration. Conversely the young ladies of business are relatively more *economic* in their choices. The results for the *esthetic* value probably reflect the higher level of liberal arts background for the last two groups. The *social* (philanthropic) value is relatively low for the business group, whereas the *political* (power) value is relatively high. Just why nurses should more often endorse the *religious* value is not immediately clear.

Another study of external validation, showing the long-range predictive power of the test, is an unpublished investigation by Betty Mawardi. It is based on a follow-up of Wellesley graduates 15 years after taking the Study of Values.

Table 2 reports the significant deviations (at the 5% level

TABLE 2

SIGNIFICANT DEVIATIONS OF SCORES ON THE STUDY OF VALUES FOR OCCUPATIONAL GROUPS OF WELLESLEY ALUMNI FROM WELLESLEY MEAN SCORES

Occupational groups	N	Theoretical	Economic	Esthetic	Social	Political	Religious
Business workers	64	Lower	Higher				
Medical workers	42	Higher	Lower			Lower	
Literary workers	40	Higher	Lower	Higher			
Artistic workers	37			Higher	Lower		
Scientific workers	28	Higher		Lower			
Government workers	24	Higher			Lower		Lower
Social workers	26				Higher		
Religious workers	11					Lower	Higher

or better) of various occupational groups from the mean
scores of Wellesley students. In virtually every case we find
the deviation meaningful (even necessary) for the occupation
in question. Thus women in business are significantly high in
economic interests; medical, government, and scientific workers in *theoretical;* literary and artistic workers in *esthetic;*
social workers in *social;* and religious workers in *religious*
values.

One must remember that to achieve a relatively high score
on one value, one must deliberately slight others. For this
reason it is interesting to note in the table the values that are
systematically slighted in order to achieve a higher score on
the occupationally relevant value. (In the case of social workers it appears that they "take away" more or less uniformly
from other values in order to achieve a high social value.)

Thus, even at the college age it is possible to forecast in a
general way modal vocational activity 15 years hence. As
Newcomb, Turner, and Converse (1965) say, this test clearly
deals with "inclusive values" or with "basic value postures"
whose generality is strikingly broad. An evaluative posture
toward life saturates, or guides, or gates (choose your own
metaphor) specific daily choices over a long expanse of years.

One reason I have used this illustration of trait research is
to raise an important methodological issue. The six values
are not wholly independent. There is a slight tendency for
theoretic and esthetic values to covary; likewise for economic
and political values; and so too with social and religious. Immediately the thought arises, "Let's factor the whole matrix
and see what orthogonal dimensions emerge." This step has
been taken several times (see *Manual*); but always with confusing results. Some investigators discover that fewer than six
factors are needed—some that we need more. And in all cases
the clusters that emerge seem strange and unnamable. Here is a
case, I believe, where our empiricism should submit to rational
restraint. The traits as defined are meaningful, reliably measured, and validated. Why sacrifice them to galloping gamesmanship?

Covariation: Religion and Prejudice

Speaking of covariation I do not mean to imply that in restraining our empirical excesses we should fail to explore the patterns that underlie covariation when it seems reasonable to do so.

Take, for example, the following problem. Many investigations show conclusively that on the broad average church attenders harbor more ethnic prejudice than nonattenders. (Some of the relevant studies are listed by Argyle, 1959, and by Wilson, 1960.) At the same time many ardent workers for civil rights are religiously motivated. From Christ to Gandhi and to Martin Luther King we note that equimindedness has been associated with religious devoutness. Here then is a paradox: Religion makes prejudice; it also unmakes prejudice.

First we tackle the problem rationally and form a hypothesis to account for what seems to be a curvilinear relation. A hint for the needed hypothesis comes from *The Authoritarian Personality* (Adorno, Frenkel-Brunswik, Levinson, & Sanford, 1950) which suggests that acceptance of institutional religion is not as important as the *way* in which it is accepted. Argyle (1959) sharpens the hypothesis. He says, "It is not the genuinely devout who are prejudiced but the conventionally religious [p. 84]."

In our own studies we have tentatively assumed that two contrasting but measurable forms of religious orientation exist. The first form we call the *extrinsic* orientation, meaning that for the churchgoer religious devotion is not a value in its own right, but it is an instrumental value serving the motives of personal comfort, security, or social status. (One man said he went to church because it was the best place to sell insurance.) Elsewhere I have defined this utilitarian orientation toward religion more fully (G. W. Allport, 1960, 1963). Here I shall simply mention two items from our scale, agreement with which we assume indicates the extrinsic attitude:

What religion offers me most is comfort when sorrows and misfortune strike.

One reason for my being a church member is that such membership helps to establish a person in the community.

By contrast the *intrinsic* orientation regards faith as a supreme value in its own right. Such faith strives to transcend self-centered needs, takes seriously the commandment of brotherhood that is found in all religions, and seeks a unification of being. Agreement with the following items indicates an intrinsic orientation:

My religious beliefs are what really lie behind my whole approach to life.

If not prevented by unavoidable circumstances, I attend church, on the average (more than once a week) (once a week) (two or three times a month) (less than once a month).

This second item is of considerable interest, for many studies have found that it is the irregular attenders who are by far the most prejudiced (e.g., Holtzmann, 1956; Williams, 1964). They take their religion in convenient doses and do not let it regulate their lives.

Now for a few illustrative results in Table 3. If we correlate the extrinsicness of orientation with various prejudice scales we find the hypothesis confirmed. Likewise, as predicted, intrinsicness of orientation is negatively correlated with prejudice.

In view of the difficulty of tapping the two complex traits in question, it is clear from these studies that our rationally derived hypothesis gains strong support. We note that the trend is the same when different denominations are studied in relation to differing targets for prejudice.

Previously I have said that empirical testing has the ability to correct or extend our rational analysis of patterns. In this particular research the following unexpected fact emerges. While those who approach the intrinsic pole of our con-

TABLE 3
CORRELATIONS BETWEEN MEASURES OF RELIGIOUS
ORIENTATION AMONG CHURCHGOERS AND VARIOUS
PREJUDICE SCALES

Denominational sample	N	r
Unitarian	50	
Extrinsic—anti-Catholicism		.56
Intrinsic—anti-Catholicism		−.36
Extrinsic—anti-Mexican		.54
Intrinsic—anti-Mexican		−.42
Catholic	66	
Extrinsic—anti-Negro		.36
Intrinsic—anti-Negro		−.49
Nazarene	39	
Extrinsic—anti-Negro		.41
Intrinsic—anti-Negro		−.44
Mixed[a]	207	
Extrinsic—anti-Semitic		.65

[a] From Wilson (1960).

tinuum are on the average less prejudiced than those who approach the extrinsic pole, a number of subjects show themselves to be disconcertingly illogical. They accept both intrinsically worded items and extrinsically worded items, even when these are contradictory, such as:

> My religious beliefs are what really lie behind my whole approach to life.

> Though I believe in my religion, I feel there are many more important things in my life.

It is necessary, therefore, to inspect this sizable group of muddleheads who refuse to conform to our neat religious logic. We call them "inconsistently proreligious." They simply like religion; for them it has "social desirability" (cf. Edwards, 1957).

The importance of recognizing this third mode of religious

orientation is seen by comparing the prejudice scores for the groups presented in Table 4. In the instruments employed the lowest possible prejudice score is 12, the highest possible, 48. We note that the mean prejudice score rises steadily and significantly from the intrinsically consistent to the inconsistently proreligious. Thus subjects with an undiscriminated proreligious response set are on the average most prejudiced of all.

TABLE 4

TYPES OF RELIGIOUS ORIENTATION AND
MEAN PREJUDICE SCORES

	Mean prejudice scores			
	Consistently intrinsic	Consistently extrinsic	Moderately inconsistent (proreligion)	Extremely inconsistent (proreligion)
Anti-Negro	28.7	33.0	35.4	37.9
Anti-Semitic	22.6	24.6	28.0	30.1

Note.—$N = 309$, mixed denominations. All differences significant at .01 level.

Having discovered the covariation of prejudice with both the extrinsic orientation and the "pro" response set, we are faced with the task of rational explanation. One may, I think, properly argue that these particular religious attitudes are instrumental in nature; they provide safety, security, and status—all within a self-serving frame. Prejudice, we know, performs much the same function within some personalities. The needs for status, security, comfort, and a feeling of self-rightness are served by both ethnic hostility and by tailoring one's religious orientation to one's convenience. The economy of other lives is precisely the reverse: It is their religion that centers their existence, and the only ethnic attitude compatible with this intrinsic orientation is one of brotherhood, not of bigotry.

This work, along with the related investigations of Lenski (1963), Williams (1964), and others, signifies that we gain important insights when we refine our conception of the nature of the religious sentiment and its functions. Its patterning properties in the economy of a life are diverse. It can fuse with bigotry or with brotherhood according to its nature.

As unfinished business I must leave the problem of nonattenders. From data available it seems that the unchurched are less prejudiced on the average than either the extrinsic or the inconsistent churchgoers, although apparently more prejudiced on the average than those whose religious orientation is intrinsic. Why this should be so must form the topic of future research.

Personal Dispositions: An Idiomorphic Approach

The final illustration of heuristic realism has to do with the search for the natural cleavages that mark an individual life. In this procedure there is no reference to common dimensions, no comparison with other people, except as is implied by the use of the English language. If, as Allport and Odbert (1936) have found, there are over 17,000 available trait names, and if these may be used in combinations, there is no real point in arguing that the use of the available lexicon of a language necessarily makes all trait studies purely nomothetic (dimensional).

A series of 172 published *Letters from Jenny* (G. W. Allport, 1965) contains enough material for a rather close clinical characterization of Jenny's personality, as well as for careful quantitative and computational analysis. While there is no possibility in this case of obtaining external validation for the diagnosis reached by either method, still by employing both procedures an internal agreement is found which constitutes a type of empirical validation for the traits that emerge.

The *clinical* method in this case is close to common sense. Thirty-nine judges listed the essential characteristics of Jenny as they saw them. The result was a series of descriptive adjectives, 198 in number. Many of the selected trait names were obviously synonymous; and nearly all fell readily into eight clusters.

The *quantitative* analysis consisted of coding the letters in terms of 99 tag words provided by the lexicon of the General Inquirer (Stone, Bales, Namenwirth, & Ogilvie, 1962). The frequency with which these basic tag words are associated with one another in each letter forms the basis for a factor analysis (see G. W. Allport, 1965, p. 200).

Table 5 lists in parallel fashion the clusters obtained by clinical judgment based on a careful reading of the series, along with the factors obtained by Jeffrey Paige in his unpublished factorial study.

TABLE 5
CENTRAL TRAITS IN JENNY'S PERSONALITY AS
DETERMINED BY TWO METHODS

Common-sense traits	Factorial traits
Quarrelsome-suspicious ⎫	
Aggressive ⎬	Aggression
Self-centered (possessive)	Possessiveness
Sentimental	⎰Need for affiliation
	⎱Need for family acceptance
Independent-autonomous	Need for autonomy
Esthetic-artistic	Sentience
Self-centered (self-pitying)	Martyrdom
(No parallel)	Sexuality
Cynical-morbid	(No parallel)
Dramatic-intense	("Overstate")

In spite of the differences in terminology the general paralleling of the two lists establishes some degree of empirical check on both of them. We can say that the direct common-sense perception of Jenny's nature is validated by quantification, coding, and factoring. (Please note that in this case factor analysis does not stand alone, but is tied to a parallel rational analysis.)

While this meaningful validation is clearly present, we gain (as almost always) additional insights from our attempts at empirical validation of the traits we initially hypothesize. I shall point to one instance of such serendipity. The tag words (i.e., the particular coding system employed) are chiefly substantives. For this reason, I suspect, *sexuality* can be identified by coding as a minor factor; but it is not perceived as an independent quality by the clinical judges. On the other hand, the judges, it seems, gain much from the running style of the letters. Since the style is constant it would not appear in a factorial analysis which deals only with variance within the whole. Thus the common-sense traits *cynical-morbid* and *dramatic-intense* are judgments of a pervading expressive style in Jenny's personality and seem to be missed by factoring procedure.

Here, however, the computer partially redeems itself. Its program assigns the tag "overstate" to strong words such as *always, never, impossible,* etc., while words tagged by "understate" indicate reserve, caution, qualification. Jenny's letters score exceedingly high on overstate and exceedingly low on understate, and so in a skeletonized way the method does in part detect the trait of dramatic intensity.

One final observation concerning this essentially idiomorphic trait study. Elsewhere I have reported a small investigation (G. W. Allport, 1958) showing that when asked to list the "essential characteristics" of some friend, 90% of the judges employ between 3 and 10 trait names, the average number being 7.2. An "essential characteristic" is defined as "any trait, quality, tendency, interest, that you regard as of major importance to a description of the person you select." There is, I submit, food for thought in the fact that in these two separate studies of Jenny, the common-sense and the factorial, only 8 or 9 central traits appear. May it not be that the essential traits of a person are few in number if only we can identify them?

The case of Jenny has another important bearing on theory. In general our besetting sin in personality study is irrelevance, by which I mean that we frequently impose dimensions upon persons when the dimensions fail to apply. (I am reminded of the student who was told to interview women patients concerning their mothers. One patient said that her mother had no part in her problem and no influence on her life; but that her aunt was very important. The student answered, "I'm sorry, but our method requires that you tell about your mother." The *method* required it, but the *life* did not.)

In ascribing a list of traits to Jenny we may seem to have used a dimensional method, but such is not the case. Jenny's traits emerge from her own personal structure. They are not imposed by predetermined but largely irrelevant schedules.

CONCLUSION

What then have I learned about traits in the last four decades? Well, I have learned that the problem cannot be avoided— neither by escape through positivism or situationism, nor through statistical interaction effects. Tendencies, as McDougall (1937) insisted, remain the "indispensable postulates of all psychology."

Further, I have learned that much of our research on traits is overweighted with methodological preoccupation; and that we have too few restraints holding us to the structure of a life as it is lived. We find ourselves confused by our intemperate empiricism which often yields unnamable factors, arbitrary codes, unintelligible interaction effects, and sheer flatulence from our computers.

As a safeguard I propose the restraints of "heuristic realism" which accepts the common-sense assumption that persons are real beings, that each has a real neuropsychic organization, and that our job is to comprehend this organization as well as we can. At the same time our profession uniquely demands that we go beyond common-sense data and either establish their validity or else—more frequently—correct their errors. To do so requires that we be guided by theory in selecting our trait slices for study, that we employ rationally relevant methods, and be strictly bound by empirical verification. In the end we return to fit our findings to an improved view of the person. Along the way we regard him as an objectively real being whose tendencies we can succeed in knowing—at least in part—beyond the level of unaided common sense. In some respects this recommended procedure resembles what Cronbach and Meehl (1955) call "construct validation," with perhaps a dash more stress on external validation.

I have also learned that while the major foci of organization in a life may be few in number, the network of organization, which includes both minor and contradictory tendencies, is still elusively complex.

One reason for the complexity, of course, is the need for the "inside" system to mesh with the "outside" system—in other words, with the situation. While I do not believe that traits can be defined in terms of interaction effects (since all tendencies draw their energy from within the person), still the vast variability of behavior cannot be overlooked. In this respect I have learned that my earlier views seemed to neglect the variability induced by ecological, social, and situational factors. This oversight needs to be repaired through an adequate theory that will relate the inside and outside systems more accurately.

The fact that my three illustrative studies are so diverse in type leads me to a second concession: that trait studies depend in part upon the investigator's own purposes. He himself constitutes a situation for his respondents, and what he obtains from them will be limited by his purpose and his method. But this fact need not destroy our belief that, so far as our method and purpose allow, we can elicit real tendencies.

Finally, there are several problems connected with traits that I have not here attempted to revisit. There are, for example, refinements of difference between trait, attitude, habit, sentiment, need, etc. Since these are all inside tendencies of some sort, they are for the present occasion all "traits" to me. Nor am I here exploring the question to what extent traits are motivational, cognitive, affective, or expressive. Last of all, and with special restraint, I avoid hammering on the distinction between common (dimensional, nomothetic) traits such as we find in any standard profile, and individual traits (personal dispositions) such as we find in single lives, e.g., Jenny's. (Cf. G. W. Allport, 1961, Ch. 15, also 1962.) Nevitt Sanford (1963) has written that by and large psychologists are "unimpressed" by my insisting on this distinction. Well, if this is so in spite of four decades of labor on my part, and in spite of my efforts in the present paper—I suppose I should in all decency cry "uncle" and retire to my corner.

REFERENCES

Adorno, T. W.; Frenkel-Brunswik, Else; Levinson, D. J.; & Sanford, R. N., *The authoritarian personality*, New York: Harpers, 1950.

Allport, F. H., *Theories of perception and the concept of structure*, New York: Wiley, 1955.

Allport, G. W., "What is a trait of personality?" *Journal of Abnormal and Social Psychology*, 1931, *25*, 368–372.

————, Review of S. A. Stouffer et al., *The American soldier*, in *Journal of Abnormal and Social Psychology*, 1950, *45*, 168–172.

————, "What units shall we employ?" in G. Lindzey (ed.), *Assessment of human motives*, New York: Rinehart, 1958.

————, "Religion and prejudice," in *Personality and social encounter*, Boston: Beacon Press, 1960. Chapter 16.

————, *Pattern and growth in personality*, New York: Holt, Rinehart & Winston, 1961.

————, "The general and the unique in psychological science, *Journal of Personality*, 1962, *30*, 405–422.

————, "Behavioral science, religion and mental health," *Journal of Religion and Health*, 1963, *2*, 187–197.

———— (ed.), *Letters from Jenny*, New York: Harcourt, Brace & World, 1965.

————, & Odbert, H. S., "Trait-names: A psycholexical study," *Psychological Monographs*, 1936, 47 (1, Whole No. 211).

————, & Vernon, P. E., *A study of values*, Boston: Houghton Mifflin, 1931. (Reprinted: With G. Lindzey, 3rd ed., 1960.)

Argyle, M., *Religious behaviour*, Glencoe, Ill.: Free Press, 1959.

Block, J., & Bennett, Lillian, "The assessment of communication," *Human Relations*, 1955, *8*, 317–325.

Carr, H. A., & Kingsbury, F. A., "The concept of trait," *Psychological Review*, 1938, *45*, 497–524.

Cronbach, L. J., & Meehl, P. E., "Construct validity in psychological tests," *Psychological Bulletin*, 1955, *52*, 281–302.

Edwards, A. L., *The social desirability variable in personality assessment and research*, New York: Dryden Press, 1957.

Gibson, J. J., "A critical review of the concept of set in contemporary experimental psychology," *Psychological Bulletin*, 1941, *38*, 781–817.

Guthrie, G. M., & McKendry, Margaret S., "Interest patterns of Peace Corps volunteers in a teaching project," *Journal of Educational Psychology*, 1963, *54*, 261–267.

Helson, H., *Adaptation-level theory*, New York: Harper & Row, 1964.

Holtzman, W. H., "Attitudes of college men toward non-segregation in Texas schools," *Public Opinion Quarterly*, 1956, *20*, 559–569.

Hunt, J. McV., "Traditional personality theory in the light of recent evidence," *American Scientist*, 1965, *53*, 80–96.

La Piere, R., "Attitudes *vs.* actions," *Social Forces*, 1934, 230–237.

Lenski, G., *The religious factor*, Garden City, N.Y.: Doubleday, 1961.

McClelland, D. C., *Personality*, New York: Dryden Press, 1951.

McDougall, W., "Tendencies as indispensable postulates of all psychology," in *Proceedings of the XI International Congress on Psychology: 1937*, Paris: Alcan, 1938, 157–170.

Miller, D. R., "The study of social relationships: Situation, identity, and social interaction," in S. Koch (ed.), *Psychology: A study of a science* (Vol. 5, *The process areas, the person, and some applied fields: Their place in psychology and the social sciences*), New York: McGraw-Hill, 1963, 639–737.

Newcomb, T. M.; Turner, H. H.; & Converse, P. E., *Social psychology: The study of human interaction*, New York: Holt, Rinehart & Winston, 1965.

Sanford, N., "Personality: Its place in psychology," in S. Koch (ed.), *Psychology: A study of a science* (Vol. 5, *The process areas, the person, and some applied fields: Their place in psychology and in science*), New York: McGraw-Hill, 1963, 488–592.

Skinner, B. F., *Science and human behavior*, New York: Macmillan, 1953.

Spranger, E., *Lebensformen* (3d ed.), Halle: Niemeyer, 1922. (Translated: P. Pigors, *Types of men*, Halle: Niemeyer, 1928.)

Stone, P. J.; Bales, R. F.; Namenwirth, J. Z.; & Ogilvie, D. M., "The general inquirer: A computer system for content analysis and retrieval based on the sentence as a unit of information," *Behavioral Science*, 1962, 7(4), 484–498.

Stouffer, S. A., et al., *The American soldier*, Princeton: Princeton Univer. Press, 1949. 2 vols.

Tagiuri, R., & Petrullo, L., *Person perception and interpersonal behavior*, Stanford: Stanford Univer. Press, 1958.

Vernon, P. E., *Personality assessment: A critical survey*, London: Methuen, 1964.

Walker, E. L., "Psychological complexity as a basis for a theory of motivation and choice," in D. Levine (ed.), *Nebraska symposium on motivation: 1964*, Lincoln: Univer. Nebraska Press, 1964.

Williams, R. M., Jr., *Strangers next door*, Englewood Cliffs, N.J.: Prentice-Hall, 1964.

Wilson, W. C., "Extrinsic religious values and prejudice," *Journal of Abnormal and Social Psychology*, 1960, 60, 286–288.

4

Psychological Models for Guidance

THE READER may recognize that the three models I describe reflect not only the principal procedures in the field of guidance but likewise the main trends in present-day psychology. One sometimes hears of three "forces" in psychology: the first of these being behavioristic; the second, depth psychology; and the third, an effort to find a more adequate humanistic conception of human nature that will incorporate the many enterprises of psychological science. My discussion of guidance follows closely these models.

The paper, like most papers in this volume, was commissioned by an interest group. The *Harvard Educational Review* asked me to contribute to a special issue devoted to problems of guidance published in 1962. Three years later the issue was revised and expanded in a book entitled *Guidance: an examination* (Harcourt, Brace, & World, 1965).

† † †

However excellent his natural eyesight may be, a counselor always looks at his client through professional spectacles. It could not be otherwise. After all, he has invested time and money in his psychological training. Of what use is it unless it adds special prisms to his own unaided eyesight?

The lenses we wear are ground to the prescription of our textbooks and teachers. Even while we are undergraduates a certain image of the nature of man is fitted to our eyes. We grow accustomed to the image and when we become practitioners or teachers we may still take it for granted.

But every so often comes a time for optical reexamination. Perhaps the image we have is still the best fit we can get; perhaps it is not. We can tell only by examining alternative lenses. In particular I believe that three are worthy of special scrutiny:

   1) *Man seen as a reactive being.* Under this rubric I would include outlooks known as naturalism, positivism, behaviorism, operationism, physicalism; these are also sometimes called—mistakenly, I think—"scientific psychology."
   2) *Man seen as a reactive being in depth.* Here I include what is variously called psychoanalysis, psychodynamics, depth psychology.
   3) *Man seen as a being-in-process-of-becoming.* This label covers recent trends known as holism, orthopsychology, personalistics, existential psychology.

These three images provide a focus not only for guidance practices, but for all other professional psychological activity whether it be teaching, research, counseling, or therapy.

MAN: A REACTIVE BEING

One hundred years ago in his *Beiträge* Wilhelm Wundt mapped a program for the newly conceived science of psychology. His own view of the proper development of this science was broad and permissive, especially in the field of social psychology. But what has taken hold in the Anglo-American tradition is the experimental outlook of his *Physiologische Psychologie.* Fusing with Darwinism, Machian positivism, the quantitative outlook of Galton and his successors, as well as with techniques invented by Binet, Pavlov, Hull, and others—this experimental outlook prevailed and has ground the lens that is fitted to the eyes of almost all undergraduate students of psychology. Many of us who continue in the profession feel no need for further correction in this image of man.

Seen through this lens man is no different in kind from any other living reactor; and therefore, like the paramecium or pigeon, may be studied biologically, behaviorally, mathematically. To be sure a few special concepts need to be devised to take care of the vast complexity of human behavior, but all these concepts—among them habit hierarchy, secondary reinforcement, input and output of information, and the like—are consistent with the postulates of physicalism and naturalism.

If we ask, "What does it mean to be a human being?" this school of thought replies, "Man is one more creature of nature; his behavior though complex is predictable in principle. His present state is determined by his past state. A man's consciousness is unreliable and must be distrusted, preferably disregarded altogether. We seek the general laws of nature, not personal uniqueness. We study man, not men; objective reality, not subjective."

In principle this broad positive tradition, which we all know so well, puts a desirable end to psychological naïveté. It cautions us not to believe every verbal report that comes to our ears; it warns us to be skeptical of our own naked eyesight; and from it we learn to check ourselves for observer reliability. It teaches us to use precise and repeatable methods. Because of its stress on reliable methods this favored tradition in psychology has become known as "scientific psychology." Its methods are indeed scientific; but its primary postulate— that man is simply a reactive organism—is no more scientific than any other postulate.

It is here that the counselor encounters his first difficulty. Trained in tests, statistics, and experimental design, he may think, quite mistakenly, that to employ these useful aids he must also view his client as a reactive being—an exclusive product of stimulus impact, homeostasis, drive-reduction, and reinforcement learning. The term "scientific" has spread like a grease spot from method to theory. Just because most of our methods evolved through the positivistic tradition does not mean that the postulates of this tradition concerning the nature of man are the only acceptable postulates for scientific psychology.

A counselor whose theoretical spectacles disclose a merely reactive being, is likely to think of his client in terms of past conditioning and potential reconditioning; in terms of reinforcements, in terms of environmental determinism. He will assume that his client's basic motives are drive-reduction or second-order conditionings which in some shadowy way are supposed to account for all his adult interests and vocational ambitions.

The vocabulary emanating from this type of postulate is replete with terms like *reaction, response, reinforcement, reflex, respondent, reintegration*—all sorts of *re*-compounds. The reference is backward. What *has* been is more important than what *will* be. Terms such as *proaction, progress, program, production, problem-solving*, or *propriate* are characteristically lacking. One would think that the client seated opposite would *pro*test, for the language of response negates the subject's immediate certainty that his life lies in the future.

The positivistic view of man as a reactor has performed a good service, shaking us out of common sense naïveté, endowing us with useful methods, and correctly informing us that man is, in *some* aspects of his being, a simple respondent to simple pressures. Its postulates are, however, questionable. It sees reality as ordered but not as personal; it sees consciousness as a nuisance; it looks at man as reactive, not proactive.

It is probably true that no counselor fully follows this creed in his daily practice. Indeed he could not do so. It is too impoverished a view of real life. When a convinced positivist attempts to fit his image of man to concrete human situations, as B. F. Skinner has done in *Walden Two*, the result strikes many of us as threadbare, even pitiable.

Probably for this reason many behaviorists (starting even as far back as E. B. Holt in *The Freudian Wish and Its Place in Ethics*) attempt to combine stimulus-response with psychoanalysis. Neal Miller and John Dollard in their *Personality and Psychotherapy* offer a good example. Man as a reactive being is combined with man as a reactive being in depth.

MAN: A REACTIVE BEING IN DEPTH

So influential is this image of man that we find it everywhere: dominant in literature, in social work, in guidance, in therapeutic practice, and in the market place. There is no need today to describe this image to any educated, or even semi-educated, American adult. Freudianism, like positivism, is our daily dish.

What I should like to do is to make clear that Freudianism (in spite of its less reliable methods) is a close kin of traditional positivism. The only change in the image of man lies in adding the depth dimension. To the long psychological vocabulary of re-compounds, depth psychology adds *repression, regression, resistance, abreaction, reaction formation,* and many others.

Like other simple naturalistic views of man, psychoanalysis puts its chief weight upon the press of pleasure and pain. This pressure produces in the organism a tendency to seek an equilibrium between the force of his drives and the circumstances of reality. The fact that Freud maximizes the role of sex and locates the whole constellation of reactive forces chiefly in the unconscious does not alter the essential similarity.

For Freud causation lies in the past history of the individual just as it does for the conditioned-response theorist. Both have a dismaying disregard for the person's phenomenology of the future, for his sense of personhood and sense of freedom. The ego is a reactive agent, having no energy of its own, but borrowing from the unsocialized Id.

Central to depth psychology, and important for guidance, is the doctrine of *recall* and *recovery* (two more *re*-compounds). Therapy, and presumably guidance, proceeds by disclosing to the client some buried motive, or a troublesome and repressed psychic trauma. The client's salvation, if indeed he has any, lies in this vital recall. A troublesome memory is brought to cognizable form. Presumably the result is helpful to the individual in solving his conflicts. The theory, however, does not allow for any interaction between the person and the recovered memory. Simple reinstatement is itself, as Freud says, the "pure gold" of psychoanalysis. What values a client should live by when once the reinstatement has taken place is not the "pure gold" of psychoanalysis. That all adult values are simply sublimated aim-inhibited wishes, is the central doctrine. Freud never allows for the individual's capacity to disregard his past or to reshape it freely. Indeed, since the structure of the Id never changes, the future can at best be a redirection, never a transformation, of one's purposes. What one becomes is essentially what one is, and what one was.

Among the valid portions of psychoanalysis of special use to all counselors, is the brilliant account given us by Freud and by his daughter Anna, of the defensive mechanisms of the ego. In dealing with our client we do well to follow the advice of psychoanalysis and watch for rationalizations, denials of reality through repression, and displacements of aggression. All these, and other, ego-defenses belong to the nature of man, and therefore must find a place in any theory of human personality.

But what perplexes me is why so many of the ego-processes described by psychoanalysis should be merely protective strategies. Are there no ego-processes that lead to a transformation of what is recovered? To a creative cognition? To a revised sense of personhood and a new phenomenology of the future? To Freud the person seems never to be truly proactive, seldom even active. Almost always he is seen as reactive to early fixations—perhaps to some castration threat that occurred years ago, or to some other unsocialized infant complex, especially to Oedipal fantasies. My difficulty with this image of man is summed up most tersely by the late satirist, Max Beerbohm, who said, "They were a tense and peculiar family—those Oedipuses."

There is, I am well aware, a large group of theories that derive from the psychodynamic tradition but at the same time deviate considerably from the orthodox view of reactivity-in-depth. All these theories, in my judgment, move in a desirable direction. Here I shall mention only some of the relevant authors: Adler, Jung, Hartmann, Horney, Erikson, Fromm. Still more deviant from Freud are Goldstein, Maslow, Rogers, and Robert White. These and other writers offer a type of theory that views man as a being in the process of becoming. Many of them ask the pivotal question differently from the reactivist schools of thought. And it makes a good deal of difference just how a question is asked.

> A story is told about two priests. They were arguing whether it was proper to smoke and to pray at the same time. One said "Yes," the other "No." To settle the matter they decided that both should write to the Holy Father for his opinion. Sometime later they met and compared notes. Each claimed that the Holy Father had supported his view. They were perplexed. Finally one asked, "How did you phrase your question?" The other replied: "I asked whether it was proper to smoke while one is praying; and the Pope answered, 'Certainly not, praying is serious business and permits no distractions.' And how did you phrase your question?" "Well," said the other, "I asked if it were proper to pray while smoking, and the Pope answered, 'Certainly, prayer is always in order.'"

Instead of asking Aristotle's question, "What is the place of man in Nature?" many authors today are asking St. Augustine's question, "Who am I?" This question, rephrased in the Twentieth Century, has opened the floodgates to a new theorizing of the broad type often labeled *existentialist*.

MAN: BEING IN THE PROCESS OF BECOMING

Seelye Bixler, former president of Colby College, tells of a student who recently remarked, "I can't tell you how much satisfaction I take in my existential despair." In some student circles despair has always been popular. To label it "existentialist" makes it doubly attractive, in fact irresistible.

But overlooking the fashionable flavor of existentialism it is surely necessary for the modern counselor to take seriously the present-day anxieties of the younger generation. No longer can youth contemplate its future under the protection of the great social stabilizers of the past. No longer can one counsel within the framework of Victorian decorum, theological certainties, or the Pax Britannica. It is obvious to us all that some sort of shattering transformation is under way. The comfortable stabilities of culture, caste, the gold standard, and military supremacy are no longer ours.

Nor are the comfortable stabilities of traditional psychology adequate. Of what use is it to invoke an impersonal theory of learning, a biological theory of motivation, and a late Victorian formula for the unconscious, when youth's problems today are acutely conscious, intensely personal, and propelling him like an unguided astronaut into an unknown future? A counselor is not equipped for his job unless he can share in some degree the apprehensions of modern youth, and sense the swampy underpinning on which youth treads. Over his desk the counselor might well tack the wisdom of the Spanish writer Unamuno, "Suffering is the life blood that runs through us all and binds us together." While not every youth who comes to the counselor is at that moment a sufferer, it is a safe assumption that he comes for guidance that will fortify him for the inevitable suffering that he will encounter in his course of life.

TENTATIVENESS AND COMMITMENT

From the existential point of view the ideal counselor will strive to develop two attitudes in his client. Taken separately they seem antithetical; but fused into a world view they provide strength for the future. One attitude is *tentativeness* of outlook. Since certainties are no longer certain, let all dogmas be fearlessly examined, especially those cultural idols that engender a false sense of security: dogmas of race supremacy, of naïve scientism, of unilinear evolutionary progress. Let one face the worst in oneself and in the world around him, so that one may correctly estimate the hazards.

Taken by itself such tentativeness, such insightfulness, might well lead to ontological despair. Yet acceptance of the worst does not prevent us from making the best of the worst. Up to now psychologists have not dealt with the remarkable ability of human beings to blend a tentative outlook with firm commitment to chosen values. The poet Tennyson perceived the point.

> There lives more faith in honest doubt,
> Believe me, than in half the creeds.

A commitment is, as Pascal has said, a wager. One may lose it, but one may also win. Cardinal Newman warned us that our religion can never be a matter of certainty. It is at best a subjective condition of certitude which he defined as "probability supported by faith and love." Yet a mature religion, thus defined, can be infinitely sustaining and heroically motivating. Existentialism, whether theistic or atheistic, makes the same point. We have the freedom to commit ourselves to great causes with courage, even though we lack certainty. We can be at one and the same time half-sure and wholehearted.

William James, probably America's greatest thinker, tried to teach us this lesson, but fifty years ago we were not ready for it. It is surely noteworthy that, writing as he did in a period of social stability, James saw clearly how ultimately uncertain are our foundations of value. Wealth, he saw was a false god, leading us into a national disease that has recently been called "galloping consumption." The more we build up our material resources, the more we fear poverty. In religion, James knew, there was no certainty; yet, like Cardinal Newman, he recognized the constructive power of a mature religious commitment. Whatever ideal leads to long-range constructive consequences is psychologically sound. It is also pragmatically true. And who is to say that we have a test for truth more absolute than our own commitment insofar as it is validated by fruitful consequences?

Neither positivistic nor psychodynamic schools of thought allow for the fact that our psychological constitution permits both total tentativeness and total commitment. Such a paradox reminds us of the electron that is able to go in two opposite directions at the same time. Taken by itself tentativeness is disintegrative; commitment is integrative. Yet the blend seems to occur in personalities that we admire for their soundness and perspective. Presumably through teaching and guidance we may develop both attitudes in our youth.

Whenever the two attitudes coexist in a life we find important desirable by-products from the fusion. One is a deep sense of compassion for the lot of the human race in general and in each separate social encounter that marks our daily life. The other by-product is likewise graceful; it is the sense of humor. Humor requires the perspective of tentativeness, but also an underlying system of values that prevents laughter from souring into cynicism. As Meredith said, humor is a capacity to laugh at the things you love and still to love them.

RATIONALISM VS. IRRATIONALISM

The chief criticism made of existentialism is that it leads away from reason and exalts irrationalism. While this charge may apply to certain literary and theological trends in the existential movement I doubt that it jeopardizes the future of scientific psychology. The attitudes of tentativeness and commitment of which I speak are perfectly sound concepts—call them "intervening variables" if you wish. Indeed insofar as they reflect important states in human personality, and thus lead to improvement in understanding, prediction, and direction of human behavior, they are sounder scientific concepts than many of those we have been using.

And just what is rationalism? We venerate the ancient Greeks for their exaltation of human reason; and as psychologists we venerate Aristotle for asking the question, "What is man's place in nature." But Greek rationalism was broader than the limited, method-centered, scientism into which it has degenerated. The Greeks themselves saw a place for tentativeness and commitment within the scope of reason. The case is beautifully stated in an ancient inscription found somewhere on the coast of Greece:

> A shipwrecked sailor buried on this coast
> Bids you set sail.
> Full many a bark, when we were lost,
> Weathered the gale.

The dead sailor urges us to make the wager, take the risk, although we cannot be sure of coming through to our destination.

IMPLICATIONS FOR THEORY

What does all this mean in terms of psychological theory, and in terms of guidance? First of all it means that in order to achieve a more realistic image of man and his potentialities, we need to revise our current theories of learning and growth, of motivation and personality structure. Elsewhere (in *Pattern and Growth in Personality*, 1961) I have discussed some of the needed changes in detail, and so shall say only a few words about each.

The trouble with our current theories of learning is not so much that they are wrong, but that they are partial. They fit best the learning of animals and young children. The concepts of conditioning, reinforcement, identification, seem a bit hollow when the counselor tries to apply them to his work. They are not very helpful, for example, in explaining how a youth may learn both tentativeness of outlook and firmness of commitment. Supplementary theories in terms of organizational, biographical, and propriate learning are needed.

Except in the sense of physical maturation the concept of *growth* scarcely exists in psychology at all. Nor will it have its proper place until we have agreed upon normative standards for the maturity of personality. Up to now normative problems, except in the sense of statistical norms, are much neglected.

As for motivation and personality structure psychologists are in a state of turmoil and disagreement. That the past stages of a life do not fully explain the motivational "go" of the present, I for one am firmly convinced. Therefore we need a concept (*functional autonomy*, I think will do) to represent that portion of a life that is oriented toward the future and not toward the past. Also we need a theory of personal structure (of *personal dispositions*) to represent the important cleavages and foci of a given, concrete personality. Such a theory will, I am convinced, carry us much further than a conception of uniform variables to which every client is forcibly ordered, whether we call these variables factors, needs, dimensions, or common traits.

Most of all we need to surrender the models that would compress human personality into the routine homeostatic situation that we find in quasi-closed systems. Human personality is a wide-open system, responsive to tangible and intangible culture, on the lookout for new ideas, and capable of asking an altogether new type of question—asked by no other creature in nature, viz., "Who am I?"

There are, I am glad to say, many psychologists who feel as strongly as I that these various types of improvement need to be made before the counselor will have a fully fashioned science of psychology to undergird his practice.

IMPLICATIONS FOR GUIDANCE

Guidance is not a matter of gimmicks, nor of rules of thumb. A guide, like a philosopher and friend, is a person who loves wisdom and loves his fellow men. True, he has skills to mark him off from the professional philosopher or the untrained friend. To some extent the counselor's present-day skills are useful. Standard tests and measurements are helpful; so too achievement records and focused interviews. Most of our devices come from researches conducted under the positivistic outlook, or (in the case of projective techniques) under the psychodynamic. While many of them are serviceable I look forward to the invention of new instruments still better suited to the study of the central or propriate aspects of single personalities.

Most important, of course, are the spectacles the counselor wears. The image should no longer be borrowed from the tradition of simple naïve reactivism. Just as centimeters, grams, seconds are outmoded in modern physics so too are simple stimulus-response connections in modern psychology. In psychology, even more than in physics, we need theory capable of dealing with fluid becoming.

The plain fact is that man is more than a reactive being, more even than a reactive being in depth. If he were comfortably fixed at these levels we could with confidence apply a uniform stencil in studying his nature. But the life process is no less paradoxical than the processes of modern physics. How can one deal with space that is both finite and unbounded, with light that is both wave and particle, with electrons that pass from orbit to orbit without traversing the space between? Similarly, a human person is both structure and process, a being both biological and noetic, a being who changes his identity even while he retains it. Small wonder that at the end of his life, the famous physicist, P. W. Bridgman, said, "The structure of nature may eventually be such that our processes of thought do not correspond to it sufficiently to permit us to think about it at all."

We need not, I think, be quite so pessimistic. Our first duty is to affirm a new and wider rationalism; that is to say, to redouble our efforts to find a more adequate image of man to guide us in fashioning a more suitable science of personality.

And what about our personal attitudes as guidance specialists or teachers? Should we not cultivate the same twin virtues that we recommend to client and student: tentativeness and commitment? We can hold our own present image of man on trial, reviewing our own past psychological training in critical perspective. At the same time we can embrace courageously our task of interpreting the wisdom of the past in such a way as to make it most available to the youthful personality who is facing an uncertain, but not uninviting, future. Tentativeness and commitment are twin ideals for both counselor and client. To my mind they lie at the heart and center of guidance, of teaching, and of living.

5

The General and the Unique in Psychological Science

IN 1961 the Berufsverband deutscher Psychologen invited me to speak at its annual meeting held in Hamburg. Almost forty years previously I had spent a fruitful semester of study there, chiefly with Professor William Stern. (See Chapter 15 of the present volume.) This circumstance speeded my acceptance. I wished to honor my teacher in the University he himself had helped to found and from which two decades later Hitler had ousted him.

The topic I deal with had perplexed me ever since Stern had led me to see its importance. The German title of the address was "Das Allgemeine und das Eigenartige in der psychologischen Praxis," published in *Psychologische Beiträge;* 1962. The English version appeared in the *Journal of Personality* in 1962.

† † †

Let me take my text from the opening sentence of *Ethical Standards of Psychologists,* the official code set forth by the American Psychological Association (1959). This sentence defines a psychologist as a person "committed to increasing man's understanding of man." The code itself makes it abundantly clear that both *man in general* and *man in particular* are the objects of our concern. Thus the psychologist, as psychologist, can properly make two sorts of statement; he can say:

1) the problem of human personality concerns me deeply;
2) the problem of Bill's personality concerns me deeply.

Although superficially similar the two statements are poles apart. In the second we are speaking of one and only one person; in the first we are abstracting elusive properties from all of the three billion inhabitants of the earth. Both statements are true; both appropriate; and both fall squarely within the domain of psychological science.

Some people, to be sure, object to this broad coverage. Artists, literati, some psychiatrists, perhaps a few clinical psychologists would say that to generalize about personality is to lose it. Bill, as an integral datum, we are told, cannot belong to scientific psychology. He can be represented only by the methods of biography, drama, or other artistic portraiture. Bill himself might say to the psychologist, "If you think those pockmarks on your silly IBM card represent *me*, you have another guess coming."

Among scientific psychologists the objection takes a somewhat different form. Usually we repress one half of the APA definition, and say that our job is to reach only generalized formulae—propositions that hold across the board for all mankind, or at least for some identifiable section of the population. We recognize the single case as a useful source of hunches—and that is about all. We pursue our acquaintance with Bill long enough to derive some hypothesis, and then spring like a gazelle into the realm of abstraction, drawing from Bill a "testable proposition" but carrying with us no coordinated knowledge of him as a structural unit. We tolerate the single case only as a takeoff point. We forgive Ebbinghaus for performing 163 experiments on himself, since almost immediately his findings were confirmed on other subjects. Luckily these subjects, like him, displayed a logarithmic relationship between the percentage of material forgotten and the time elapsing after the original act of learning. We forgive Köhler and Wallach for intensive work on their own figural aftereffects, for it was soon confirmed that others also show a displacement of the percept, after long stimulation, away from the retinal area stimulated.

But imagine the consternation if some deviant psychologist (perhaps I myself) were to say, "Can't we linger longer with Ebbinghaus and discover in his life what relationships might exist between his memory functions and *his* motives and *his* cognitive style and *his* aspirations?" The objection would be: "Of what use is that? Even if we find the relationship we'd have to generalize to other people or else we'd have nothing of any scientific value."

Such is the prevailing "response set" of our specialty. The intricacy of internal structure in concrete lives seldom challenges or detains us. Our concern is with commonalities and comparabilities across individuals.

This response set is undoubtedly derived from our submissiveness to the goals and procedures of natural science. And this submissiveness is not in itself a bad thing. Up to now it has taught us much. The question is whether we have become so enslaved that we overlook an important half of our particular professional assignment which is "increasing man's understanding of man."

It does no good to argue that every individual system in nature is unique; every rat, every porpoise, every worm; and that it is only the general laws of their functioning that lead to comprehension. No, we can't take this easy way out of the dilemma. The human system, unlike all others, possesses a degree of openness to the world, a degree of foresight and self-awareness, a flexibility and binding of functions and goals that present a unique structural challenge far more insistent than that presented by any other living system. It is because of their essential stereotypy and lack of variation that psychologists like to draw their generalizations from lower animals. But for my part I venture the opinion that all of the infrahuman vertebrates in the world differ less from one another in psychological functioning and in complexity of organization, than one human being does from any other.

And so I wonder whether the time has not come for students of personality to shake themselves loose from a too-rigid response set, and perhaps even to reverse it. Instead of growing impatient with the single case and hastening on to generalization, why should we not grow impatient with our generalizations and hasten to the internal pattern? For one thing we should ask, are our generalizations really relevant to the case we are studying? If so, do they need modification? And in what ways is this individual the asymptote of all our general laws?

Or to state the procedure more simply: Why should we not start with individual behavior as a source of hunches (as we have in the past), and then seek our generalizations (also as we have in the past), but finally come back to the individual—not for the mechanical application of laws (as we do now), but for a fuller, supplementary, and more accurate assessment than we are now able to give? I suspect that the reason our present assessments are now so often feeble and sometimes even ridiculous, is because we do not take this final step. We stop with our wobbly laws of personality and seldom confront them with the concrete person.

THE DIMENSIONAL AND THE MORPHOGENIC

The issue before us is not new. More than a hundred years ago John Stuart Mill proposed that we distinguish sharply between psychology, the science of mind-in-general, and *ethology*, a science of character (having no relation to what is called ethology today). To his mind ethology should trace the operation of psychological laws in specifically individual combinations—such as the pattern of the single person or of a single culture or nation. Somewhat similar was Dilthey's proposal to distinguish between "explanatory" and "understanding" psychology. Said Dilthey, "We explain nature, but we understand human beings." Widelband too would recognize two classes of science: the nomothetic (seeking general laws) and the idiographic (dealing with structured pattern).

In confronting this same problem William James almost threw up his hands in despair. It is well known that after writing his textbook, he concluded that general psychological laws are poor stuff. He declared that psychology has not produced "a single law in the sense in which physics shows us laws. . . . This is no science, it is only the hope of a science" (1961 edit., p. 335). Perhaps the ensuing half-century of intensive research would have strengthened his faith in general laws; but I doubt it. At any rate he not only questioned the validity of general laws but, champion of the individual though he was, he seemed to feel that the concrete person must also inevitably elude psychology. In his *Memories and Studies* (1912) he wrote,

> . . . in every concrete individual, there is a uniqueness that defies all formulation. We can feel the touch of it and recognize its taste, so to speak, relishing or disliking, as the case may be, but we can give no ultimate account of it, and have in the end simply to admire the Creator (pp. 109f.).

And so at the end of his career James seems to despair of psychology as a science of either the general or the concrete.

The problem has not yet been solved, but I for one detect signs of progress. For one thing it increasingly haunts us, in our dual roles as experimenter and clinician, as theorist and practitioner. Nearly a decade ago Meehl (1954) wrote a distinguished treatise on the subject entitled *Clinical vs. Statistical Prediction*. His own position he declared to be "ambivalent." Some called it middle-of-the-road (but only those, I think, whose own adaptation level was somewhere to the right of Sarbin and Lundberg).

Meehl's book draws an important distinction. It points out that in comparing so-called clinical with so-called statistical procedures we may be talking (a) about the methods we employ and the type of data we use, or (b) about the way we piece together these data and reach a final assessment. Thus the data, on the one hand, may be percentile scores or other quantifiable dimensional data; or they may be looser types of information, case records, free associations, and the like. Further, in reaching a conclusion from these data we may use statistical procedures with mechanical regularity, or we may— as Dilthey advises—simply try to "understand" the pattern. Meehl's chief concern is with the latter issue. Does one handle the data (whatever they be) more successfully through using the statistical cookbook, or through global comprehension? While this issue is surely central, it is not the focus of my interest in the present paper. Here I am concerned rather more with Meehl's first problem: the type of data that should go into our assessments.

More recently a German author (Graumann, 1960) put the problem this way: shall our units of analysis in the study of personality be derived from general psychological concepts, or from lives as actually lived? Another statement of the issue is found in the presidential address of L. S. Hearnshaw (1956) to the British Psychological Society. He first calls attention to the strain that exists between the demands of conventional scientific method and "the appreciation of the richness of human individuality." He pleads for "a constant search for concepts which, while capable of scientific definition and employment, nevertheless possess humanistic implications" and reflect patterned structure accurately.

It would serve no good purpose here to review the long-standing debate between partisans of the nomothetic and idiographic methods, between champions of explanation and understanding. Indeed to insure more rapid progress I think it best to avoid traditional terms altogether. For the purposes of our present discussion I shall speak of "dimensional" and "morphogenic" procedures. Let me explain the latter term.

The science of molecular biology shows us that life-substances are identical across species. The building blocks of life—vegetable and animal—turn out to be strikingly uniform in terms of nucleic acids, protein molecules, and enzymatic reactions. Yet an antelope differs from an ash tree, a man from

an antelope, and one man is very unlike another. The challenge of morphogenesis (accounting for pattern) grows more
rather than less acute as we discover the commonalities of life.
Yet biologists admit that morphogenic biology lags far behind
molecular (or dimensional) biology. So too does morphogenic
psychology lag far behind dimensional psychology.

The commonalities in personality are the horizontal dimensions that run through all individuals. We focus our attention
chiefly upon these commonalities: for example, upon the common traits of achievement, anxiety, extraversion, dominance,
creativity; or upon the common processes of learning, repression, identification, aging. We spend scarcely one per cent of
our research time discovering whether these common dimensions are in reality relevant to Bill's personality, and if so how
they are patterned together to compose the Billian quality of
Bill. Ideally research should explore both horizontal and vertical dimensions.

I have already rejected the easy solution that assigns the
general to science and the unique to art. I should like also to
dispose of another proposed solution. Some psychologists
would say that Bill, our individual, is known primarily by his
conformity to, or deviation from, universal norms or group
norms. His private and unique qualities are only the residual
peculiarities left over when we have accounted for most of
his behavior in terms of general norms. My colleagues, Professors Kluckhohn and Murray (1953, p. 53) have expressed the
thought by saying

> . . . every man is in certain respects:
>   a. like all other men (universal norms)
>   b. like some other men (group norms)
>   c. like no other men (idiosyncratic norms).

Now it is certainly true that we often *wish* to use universal
and group norms. We want to know whether Bill, relative to
others, is high or low in intelligence, in dominance, in affilia-
tiveness. But although Bill can be compared profitably on

many dimensions with the average human being or with his cultural group, still he himself weaves all these attributes into a unique idiomatic system. His personality does not contain three systems, but only one. Whatever individuality is, it is not the residual ragbag left over after general dimensions have been exhausted. The *organization* of Bill's life is first, last, and all the time, the primary fact of his human nature.

Since we cannot brush our problem aside we do well to ask how a truly morphogenic psychology (sadly neglected up to now) can become a scientific asset. To become such it will have to learn certain lessons from dimensional empiricism, and from positivism—most of all the lesson of observer reliability. It is not sufficient to "intuit" the pattern of Bill or Betty. All of their friends do this much, with greater or less success. A science, even a morphogenic science, should be made of sterner stuff. The morphogenic interpretations we make should be testable, communicable, and have a high measure of predictive power.

My purpose is to suggest certain procedures that seem to me to be morphogenic in nature, or at least semimorphogenic, and yet to be at the same time controlled, repeatable, reliable. Before I do so, let us look more closely at the question of successful prediction, which, we are told, is the acid test of a valid science.

PREDICTION: DIMENSIONAL AND MORPHOGENIC

Prediction based on general or dimensional information is called actuarial. For many purposes it is surprisingly accurate. One marvels, for example, at the correctness with which insurance companies predict the number of deaths that will occur by highway accidents, from cancer, or from suicide. The chances of a hypothetical average man for survival or death are all the insurance business wants to know. Whether Bill himself will be one of the fatal cases it cannot tell—and that is what Bill wants to know.

The situation is exactly the same in psychology. Actuarial prediction enables us, with fair success, to predict what proportion of boys, having a certain type of physique and family history, will become delinquent; what percentage of engaged couples, having various types of background, will enjoy successful marriage. Actuarial prediction can tell approximately what the average student's university record will be on the basis of his elementary school record or I.Q. It can advise industry concerning crucial cutting points on psychological tests by designating the score below which most applicants would probably fail on the job.

Note please that these actuarial predictions are far more useful to insurance companies, school authorities, police, and industrial management than to Bill himself. As a person he is frozen out, for although statistical generalizations hold with small error for large populations they do not hold for any given individual. And as practitioners we have fully as much responsibility to Bill as to his employers or to the public. Nay, if we follow our own professional code of ethics, we have more.

Suppose we take John, a lad of 12 years, and suppose his family background is poor; his father was a criminal; his mother rejected him; his neighborhood is marginal. Suppose that 70 per cent of the boys having a similar background become criminals. Does this mean that John himself has a 70 per cent chance of delinquency? Not at all. John is a unique being, with a genetic inheritance all his own; his life-experience is his own. His unique world contains influences unknown to the statistician: perhaps an affectionate relation with a certain teacher, or a wise word once spoken by a neighbor. Such factors may be decisive and may offset all average probabilities. There is no 70 per cent chance about John. He either will or will not become delinquent. Only a complete understanding of his personality, of his present and future circumstances, will give us a basis for sure prediction.

It was this line of argument, I believe, that led Meehl

(1954) to say, "Let us see what the research evidence is regarding the relative success of dimensional and morphogenic prediction." Surveying such relevant studies as were available, Meehl concludes that morphogenic (what he calls "clinical") prediction seems to be actually inferior. More successful are predictions made mechanically with the aid of a standard formula. Best to keep strictly to our Rorschach diagnostic signs, to our I.Q. measures, to our profiles on the Minnesota Multiphasic Personality Inventory, and to other standard predictive indexes. We can, of course, weight the signs, but we must do so according to rule. We may give one sign twice as much weight as another, just as a cook uses two cups of flour but only one of sugar. Meehl appropriately calls the procedure he advocates the "cookbook" method.

The point is that whenever we deal with well-defined variables, possessing a known relation to a pathological type, or to success in occupation or in school, we are usually safer in following the cookbook method of combining scores according to a formula known to have a good average validity. If strictly followed the logical outcome of this procedure would be the early elimination of the clinician or practitioner as assessor or diagnostician. A computing machine could handle the data more accurately than a fallible psychologist. In coming years we shall, no doubt, increasingly encounter IBM diagnoses and IBM predictions in psychological practice. It does no good to shudder at such a lèse majesté to human dignity. It will surely come to pass. But already we can sense its limitations.

LIMITATIONS OF THE COOKBOOK

In the first place, as Meehl (1957) himself has pointed out, the cookbook is usable only under restricted circumstances. The dimensions studies must be objectively defined, reliably measured, validly related to the target of prediction (e.g., to vocational success), clearly normed for a population to which the subject belongs. Most of the dimensions we employ have not attained this level of objective perfection.

The question of weighting signs gives us special difficulty. Suppose John has a good engineering profile, but also scores high in aesthetic interests; suppose he is introverted, but has high ego-strength; and with all this suffers some physical disability—what then does the final pattern signify? Cookbook enthusiasts might say a computer could tell us. But could it? In all the world there are not enough cases of this, or of any other, personal pattern to warrant assured actuarial prediction.

Again, by keeping within a previously established dimensional frame the cookbook procedure rules out insights peculiarly relevant to the individual. True, the computer can tell whether Sam should be diagnosed as schizophrenic. But whether Sam's love for his sister and her way of dealing with him are such as to effect his recovery, the computer cannot tell. A dimensional frame is a rigid thing. It is like giving to the cook ingredients that will produce only dumplings while imagining that she has the freedom to produce a cake.

Further, the dimensions imposed on the individual are dimensions of interest to the investigator, or to the hospital, school, or firm. For this reason they may not be relevant in guiding John. The most salient features of his life—his aspirations, his sense of duty, his existential pattern, may be left untouched. In every dimensional analysis there are inevitably many "empty cells."

Finally, as for the discovery that clinical or morphogenic predictions are in fact poorer than cookbook predictions, I can only say, "What a pitiful reflection on the inventiveness and sensitivity of psychologists!" The findings—which, by the way, are not necessarily the last word on the matter—prove only that we do not yet know how to maximize clinical skill through training. I suspect that our present emphasis on tests and cookbooks may actually be damaging the potential skill of young clinicians and advisers. There are studies that indicate that clinicians grow confused when they have too many data concerning an individual life, and that for this reason their predictions are better when they fall back on a mere formula (Sarbin, Taft, Bailey, pp. 262–264). But this finding, too, points chiefly to our neglect in inventing and training in sensitive morphogenic methods.

Recently Meehl (1959) has shown that under certain circumstances a combined actuarial and clinical—a kind of "configural"—procedure is superior in predictive power to either method used alone. This is progress indeed. But I would raise two objections: (1) the level of success achieved is still too low; (2) the diagnostic instruments employed in the first instance are too one-sided. The original instruments on which the predictions are based are nearly always of a dimensional or horizontal order (extending across people) and seldom of an intensive vertical order (within the person).

My point is that while dimensional diagnostic methods are an indispensable half of the psychologist's tools of trade, the other half of the tool box is, up to now, virtually empty. I recall that a few years before his death I was discussing this matter with the beloved psychologist, Edward Tolman. He said to me with his characteristic twinkle, employing the then-current terminology, "I know I should be more idiographic in my research, but I just don't know how to be." My reply now, as then, is, "Let's learn!"

MORPHOGENIC METHODS

To start simply: it is worth asking whether we ought to seek only objective validation for our measuring instruments. Why not demand likewise, where possible, subjective validation by asking our subject what he himself thinks of the dimensional diagnosis we have made? (If the subject is a child, a psychotic, or manifestly defensive, this step, of course, has no point.) Too often we fail to consult the richest of all sources of data, namely, the subject's own self-knowledge. During the war, psychiatrists were assigned the task of screening candidates for the armed services. While they employed various dimensional tests, it is said that the best predictive question turned out to be, "Do you feel that you are emotionally ready to enter military service?" The men themselves were often the best judges—although, of course, not infallible.

One might think that the existential outlook in psychology (now spreading at considerable speed) could logically be expected to bring a revolution in methods of psychological assessment. Its basic emphasis is upon the individual as a unique being-in-the-world whose system of meanings and value-orientations are not precisely like anyone else's. Hence an existential psychologist, be he conducting research, assessment, or therapy, would seem to need procedures tailored to each separate case. But up to now followers of this school of thought have not been as inventive as their own basic postulate requires. There is a methodological lag.

It is true that psychiatrists and clinical psychologists have long known that they should take the patient's own story as a starting point. But almost immediately they redact this story into general categories, dismembering the complex pattern of the life into standard dimensions (abilities, needs, interest inventories, and the like), and hasten to assign scores on their favorite variables. One notes too that therapists who claim to be existential in their orientation also tend to employ standard procedures in treatment. Their techniques and even their interpretations are sometimes indistinguishable from orthodox psychoanalysis (G. W. Allport, 1961a).

Our conceptual flexibility is greater than our methodological flexibility. Let me illustrate the point by reference to the valuable and extensive bibliography of nearly 500 items prepared by Ruth Wylie (1961). Most of these items deal with empirical studies of the self-concept. (The very fact that the self in recent years has been readmitted to good standing in psychology is proof of our conceptual flexibility.) A close inspection, however, shows that virtually all the studies approach the self-concept only via general dimensions. We encounter such descriptions as the following: "this test infers self-esteem from scores on an anxiety questionnaire"; or "nine bipolar semantic differential scales are employed"; or "self-ratings on

18 trait words on a five-point scale from which self-acceptance is inferred." I am not objecting to these studies but point out that they are methodologically stereotyped.

But let us turn now to what at present lies available in the morphogenic half of our tool box. My inventory will be illustrative rather than exhaustive. I shall be brief in describing each method, hoping that the array as a whole will help to make clear what I mean by morphogenic method, and, best of all, may stimulate further invention.

1. Familiar is the method of matching, used with profit by both German and American investigators (see G. W. Allport, 1961b, pp. 387f. and 446f.). This method invites us to fit together any record of personal expression, however complex, with any other record. We test our skill in seeing that this case record must fit such-and-such a test profile; or that this handwriting goes with that voice. It is a good way to discover how much of a perceptible form-quality saturates separate performances. Although the method gives us no insight into causal relationships, it is, so far as it goes, a good example of a 100 per cent morphogenic procedure.

2. Another wholly morphogenic technique was devised by Baldwin (1942), who made use of a long series of personal letters written by one woman, Jenny by name. Her unique thought-structure, i.e., associative complexes, was the object of interest. If she talked about women, money, or nature, with what feeling tone did she mention them? If she mentioned her son, what else did she mention in the same context? This technique, called by Baldwin "personal structure analysis," is highly revealing, and is carried through without reference to any general or dimensional norms.

3. Somewhat similar, and wholly morphogenic, is the procedure recommended by Shapiro (1961) for psychiatrists. On the basis of a five-hour intensive interview with a patient he constructs a questionnaire which from that time on is standard for this patient but not directly relevant to any other patient. Administered over intervals of months or years, the instru-

ment will show the course of development, including improvement or deterioration in health.

4. A somewhat more ambitious attempt, still wholly morphogenic, would be to attempt to discover the number and range of all the major structural foci a given life possesses. Many years ago in his *Experiment in Autobiography*, H. G. Wells asserted that there were only two major themes in his life: interest in world-government and in sex. Elsewhere I have explored the possibility that a life may be understood almost completely by tracing only a few major themes or intentions. Probably two is too few for most lives (perhaps especially for H. G. Wells), although it is said that Tolstoy after his conversion had only one major theme: viz., the simplification of life. More typical, I believe, would be the case of William James, who, according to his biographer, R. B. Perry (1936, Chaps. 90–91), had eight dominant trends. In some preliminary explorations with my students (G. W. Allport, 1958), I find that they regard it possible to characterize a friend adequately on the average with 7.2 essential characteristics, the range falling for the most part between 3 and 10.

What to call these central motifs I do not exactly know. They are "essential characteristics," for the most part motivational in type although some seem to be stylistic. F. H. Allport (1937), in proposing the term "teleonomic trends," suggests that we proceed to regard them as life-hypotheses held by the individual, and count carefully how many of his daily acts can accurately be ordered to one or more of these trends. The idea has merit, but it has not yet been systematically tried out. One question is whether we can obtain sufficiently high observer-reliability (i.e., reliable judgments of the fit of specific acts to the hypothesized trend). At present it is only one of the avenues of research needing exploration.

5. Suppose we are interested in an individual's value system. Direct questioning is, of course, useful. "What would you rather have than anything else in the world?" "What experiences give you a feeling of completeness, of fully func-

tioning, or of personal identity?" "What," in Maslow's terms, "are your peak experiences of life?" Elsewhere I have argued strongly for the use of such direct questions as these, for in important matters we should grant our client the right to be believed. Projective methods should never be used without direct methods, for we cannot interpret the results of projective testing unless we know whether they confirm or contradict the subject's own self-image (see G. W. Allport, 1960, Chap. 6).

But how can we grow more precise in this type of work, benefiting from lessons learned from objective dimensional procedures? One such technique is the "self-anchoring scale," devised by Kilpatrick and Cantril (1960). It consists of a simple diagram of a ladder, having 10 rungs. The subject is asked first to describe in his own terms the "very best or ideal way of life" that he can imagine. Then he is told that rung 10 at the top of the ladder represents this ideal. Similarly he is asked to describe the "worst possible way of life" for himself. This he is told is the bottom of the ladder. Now he is asked to point to the rung on the ladder where he thinks he stands today—somewhere between the bottom and top rungs. He can also be asked, "Where on this scale were you two years ago? Five years ago? Where do you think you will be five years hence?"

This device has considerable value in personal counseling. It is also used by the authors to study rising or falling morale in different countries, e.g., in those having undergone recent revolution as compared with those living in a static condition. In this case, a curious thing happens; a completely morphogenic instrument is adapted for use as a tool for nomothetic research. Ordinarily, of course, the situation is reversed: it is a nomothetic mold that is forced upon the individual.

All these various examples suffice to show that it is possible to examine the internal and unique pattern of personal structure without any dependence whatsoever on universal or group norms. All the methods I have mentioned up to now are completely morphogenic, although they are seldom explicitly recognized as such.

Let us turn our attention to certain procedures that are highly useful for exploring individuality even though they are in part also dimensional.

6. First, there is the common dimensional instrument, the rating scale. Many years ago Conrad (1932) asked teachers to rate pupils on 231 common traits. The teachers were thus forced to make the assumption that all children did in fact possess all 231 traits in some degree. Proceeding on this assumption the teachers agreed poorly, as reflected in a median reliability coefficient of .48. After this nomothetic orgy, the same teachers were asked to star *only* those traits that they considered to be of "central or dominating importance in the child's personality." On this part of their task the teachers agreed almost perfectly, their judgments correlating .95. This result shows that low reliability may be due to the essential irrelevance of many of the dimensions we forcibly apply to an individual. On well-configurated prominent dispositions there is likely to be good agreement.

A related method is the simple adjective checklist. Here the rater is confronted with perhaps hundreds of common trait-names (which are, of course, common linguistic dimensions). But he is required to use only those that seem to him appropriate to the primary trends in the individual life.

Both the method of starring and the use of the checklist have the advantage of permitting us to discard irrelevant dimensions—a feature lacking in most other dimensional procedures.

7. Another halfway method is the *Role Construct Repertory Test*, devised by Kelly (1955). The method asks the subject to tell in what way two concepts are alike and how they differ from a third. The concepts might, for example, be *mother, sister, wife*. The subject could, for instance, reply that mother and sister are alike because both are comforting; and the wife different because she is demanding. Not only is

the particular response revealing of his family attitudes, but over a long series of comparisons it may turn out that the subject has a characteristic cognitive style in which the polarity of comfortableness versus demandingness may recur time and time again. This method is not wholly morphogenic since it prescribes for the subject what "significant others" he shall characterize, and in other ways limits his spontaneous choices, but it allows nonetheless for a certain amount of morphogenic discovery.

8. Certain other devices for approaching cognitive style likewise move in a desirable direction. I have in mind Broverman (1960), who employs standard tests with his subjects, but makes his interpretations entirely in terms of the subject's tendency to do well or poorly on a given type of test relative to his own mean for all tests. By the use of such ipsative scores he is able to determine which responses are strong or weak with respect to other responses within the same individual.

If this line of thought were extended we would be moving toward a psychophysics of one person—a desirable advance indeed. We would at last know, so to speak, the relation between Bill's sensory acuity and his interests, between his cognitive style and his tempo, between his respiration and extraversion. To what extent it is necessary to start, as Broverman does, with standard dimensional measures, is a question for the future. I doubt that we can answer it a priori.

9. Another mixed method is the Allport-Vernon-Lindzey *Study of Values* (1960), devised to measure the relative prominence of each of the six Spranger *Lebensformen* within a particular person. The resulting profile does not tell how high or low a given person stands on the economic, theoretic, or religious value in the population at large, but only which value is relatively most, or next most, or least prominent in his own life. This type of profile is semidimensional, semimorphogenic.

10. Sometimes the Q-sort (Stephenson, 1953) is said to be an idiographic technique. Yet it, like other devices we are

now considering, goes only part way. It has the merit of making use of self-report, and can be used for measuring changes in the self-concept. As ordinarily used, however, only a standard set of propositions is employed, thus creating for the subject little more than a standard rating scale. And if the subject is forced, as he often is, to produce a quasi-normal distribution among his sorts, he is further restricted. In short, the method can be rigidly dimensional. Yet it is a flexible method, and some variants are highly promising, perhaps especially when combined with inverse factor analysis.

11. For example, Nunnally (1955) studied one therapy case over a two-year period, using sixty statements selected for their unique relevance to this person (and this, I think, is a great improvement over the use of uniform lists). The patient made her sorts under many different sets of instructions on many occasions. Using an inverse factor analysis it was possible to find three fairly independent factors that comprised her total self-concept. During therapy these factors showed only a moderate change.

It strikes me as curious that out of the thousands and thousands of factor-analytic studies that smother us today, scarcely any are carried through in such a manner as to discover the internal, unique, organizational units that characterize a single life. Even inverse factor analysis does not fully achieve this goal unless the initial information employed is selected for its morphogenic relevance. A good deal of creative work still lies ahead for factor-analysis. It has potentiality, I think, for discovering the main foci of organization in a given life, but has not yet moved far enough in this direction.

FINAL WORD

This survey of possible relevant methods is not complete but may indicate that by a deliberate shift of procedures we can bring the laggard end of our science up to a more flourishing level. To effect the shift we shall have to restrain to some extent our present dimensional debauch.

71784

In this paper I have introduced the term "morphogenic psychology," borrowed from, but not identical with the usage in, biology. It is, I think, a good term, better than "idiographic," which so many students of personality misuse and misspell. I hope the concept "morphogenic" catches on, but even more do I hope that the types of research to which I have ventured to apply the label will flourish and spread. Already we know that personality (in general) is an interesting topic for study. But only when morphogenic methods are more highly developed shall we be able to do justice to the fascinating individuality that marks the personalities of Bill, John, and Betty.

I feel deeply that such progress is needed to bring our young science to the age of maturity. It is our one-sided preoccupation with the general that renders our encounters with concrete personalities often inept and sometimes even clownish. Perhaps we should take more seriously than we do the scorn that is sometimes directed against our profession. A recent peppery critic, G. Sykes in *The Hidden Remnant,* has accused psychologists of being "half-educated, presuming to speak above their intellectual and moral stations."

This is a demoralizing jibe. Insofar as it contains truth, I believe that the fault lies less with our sins of commission than with our sins of omission. I look forward to raising our level of virtue through a more equitable distribution of our ingenuity in both research and theory, and to a more even spread of our interest over the whole broad field of personality.

REFERENCES

Allport, F. H., "Teleonomic description in the study of personality," *Charact. & Pers.,* 1937, *6,* 202–214.

Allport, G. W., "What units shall we employ?" Chap. 9 in G. Lindzey (ed.), *Assessment of human motives,* New York: Rinehart, 1958. Also, Chap. 7 in G. W. Allport, *Personality and social encounter,* Boston: Beacon, 1960.

————, "The trend in motivational theory," Chap. 6 in *Personality and social encounter*, Boston: Beacon, 1960.

————, Vernon, P. E., Lindzey, G., *A Study of Values*, third ed., Boston: Houghton Mifflin, 1960.

————, Comment. In R. May (ed.), *Existential psychology*, New York: Random, 1961, pp. 94–99. (a)

————, *Pattern and growth in personality*, New York: Holt, Rinehart & Winston, 1961. (b)

————, "Das allgemeine und das eigenartige in der psychologischen praxis," *Psycholog. Beitr.*, 1962, *6*, 630–650. English translation: "The unique and the general in psychological science," in J. A. Ross and R. Thompson (eds.), *Proceedings of the Summer Conference*, Western Washington State College, 1961, pp. 25–37.

American Psychological Association, "Ethical standards of psychologists," *Amer. Psychologist*, 1959, *14*, 279–282.

Baldwin, A. L., "Personal structure analysis: a statistical method for investigation of the single personality," *J. Abnorm. Soc. Psychol.*, 1942, *37*, 163–183.

Broverman, D. M., "Cognitive style and intra-individual variation in abilities," *J. Pers.*, 1960, *28*, 240–256.

Conrad, H. S., "The validity of personality ratings of preschool children," *J. Educ. Psychol.*, 1932, *23*, 671–680.

Graumann, C. F., "Eigenschaften als Problem der Persönlichkeits-Forschung. Chap. 4 in P. Lersch and H. Thomae (eds.), *Persönlichkeitsforschung und Persönlichkeitstheorie*, Gottingen: Hogrefe, 1960.

Hearnshaw, L. S., *Bull. xxx Brit. Psychol. Soc.*, No. 36, *1*, 1956. See also, Leytham, G. W. H., "Psychology and the individual," *Nature*, vol. 189, no. 4763, 1961, pp. 435–438.

James, W., *Memories and studies*, New York: Longmans, Green, 1912.

————, *Psychology: the briefer course* (G. W. Allport, ed.), New York: Harper, Torchbooks, 1961.

Kelly, G. A., *The psychology of personal constructs*, New York: Norton, 1955, vol. 1.

Kilpatrick, F. P., and Cantril, H., "Self-anchoring scale: a measure of the individual's unique reality world," *J. Indiv. Psychol.*, 1960, *16*, 158–170.

Kluckhohn, C. M., Murray, H. A., and Schneider, D. M. (eds.), *Personality in nature, society, and culture*, New York: Knopf, 1953.

Meehl, P. E., *Clinical vs. statistical prediction*, Minneapolis: Univ. Minnesota Press, 1954.

———, "When shall we use our heads instead of a formula?" *J. Counsel. Psychol.*, 1957, *4*, 268–273.

———, "A comparison of clinicians with five statistical methods of identifying psychotic MMPI profiles," *J. Counsel. Psychol.*, 1959, *6*, 102–109.

Nunnally, J. C., "An investigation of some propositions of self-conception: the case of Miss Sun," *J. Abnorm. Soc. Psychol.*, 1955, *50*, 87–92.

Sarbin, T. R., Taft, R., and Bailey, D. E., *Clinical inference and cognitive theory*, New York: Holt, Rinehart & Winston, 1960.

Shapiro, M. B., "The single case in fundamental clinical psychological research," *Brit. J. Med. Psychol.*, 1961, *34*, 255–262.

Stephenson, W., *The study of behavior*, Chicago: Univ. Chicago Press, 1953.

Sykes, G., *The hidden remnant*, New York: Harper, 1962.

Wylie, R. C., *The self-concept: a critical survey of pertinent research literature*, Lincoln: Univ. Nebraska Press, 1961.

6

Imagination in Psychology: Some Needed Steps

IN THIS PAPER I examine the "disorganized complexity" of much modern culture, and show how psychological science partakes of the same general dismemberment. I try to point out how psychology's threads may be reknit so that larger and more significant units of mental organization may be imaginatively studied. In a way this paper may be regarded as restating the position I develop in Chapter 1, "The Fruits of Eclecticism."

The address was one in a series of the Frank Gerstein Lectures and was published in the York University Invitation Lecture Series, *Imagination in the University*, University of Toronto Press, 1964.

† † †

Some people will shudder at the very thought that psychology may develop more imagination than it has. They will say, "Look at what you psychologists have already done. You have addled us with teaching machines, computers, and simulators; and have measured all of our quotients (IQ's, EQ's, AQ's, and even PQ's—personality quotients). You have submitted us to truth drugs and lie detectors, to opinion polls and questionnaires, to mazes and other crazes; and worst of all you have mistaken us for that strange and upsetting Viennese family of Oedipuses. . . . We want no more of your imagination. What we need is a strategy by which we can resist your impertinence. Our admiration is for the poor fellow who applied for a job with the British Intelligence service. He had the reputation of hitting the bottle. So a psychologist was asked to discover whether this was his weakness. Whereupon the psychologist gave him a word association test.

"Tell me what first comes to your mind when I say: *Haig!*" "Oh," replied the applicant, "Haig—you know—a famous general—First World War—North Africa, and all that."

"*Gordon!*" "Oh yes, another general: Chinese Gordon; Boxer rebellion."

"*Booth!*" "Oh yes, another general. This time, the Salvation Army."

"*Vat 69!*" "Well . . . , could that be the Pope's telephone number?"

With this sort of resistance I too am in sympathy. But the present impertinence of psychology will best be cured not by depriving it of its imagination, but by endowing it with more.

AN ERA IN TRANSITION

At the present moment psychology resembles a youth, awkward and arrogant perhaps, but plainly flourishing and full of promise. Its situation can best be understood in the perspective of the intellectual history of the present century.

Early monumental figures in psychology—shall we name Wilhelm Wundt, William James, William McDougall, and John Dewey?—moved us away from purely speculative philosophy toward a broadly empirical view of human nature. While they favored empirical evidence from laboratory or clinic they did not have much of it available; nor did they wish to lose their synoptic view of the subject matter of psychology, namely, the total constitution of human nature.

Their revolt against philosophy did not go far enough to please certain enthusiasts who said, in effect: We can give you a simple formula for human nature. Freud, for example, offered us a comfortable conceptual tripod: the id, ego, and superego. Watson and the behaviorist school said it was all a matter of reactions to stimuli. There developed a number of easily understood reductionist concepts, including the unconscious, conditioning, reinforcement, habit hierarchy. Reductionism is the doctrine that says that all the intricacies of human nature can be explained in principle with the aid of one mechanism or group of mechanisms favored by a particular theorist.

But the *Zeitgeist* of this century moved even further. Psychology was caught in the same web as were other sciences along with philosophy, art, and literary criticism. An era of extreme positivistic reductionism set in. All theories became suspect because of their verbal seductiveness and slender empirical support. Wundt and James, McDougall and even Freud were offering us essentially one man's view, a personal interpretation. This is not science, we were told, for it is based on personal meanings, and all meanings are subjective.

Better, it was said, become objective; avoid introspection; eschew personal meanings. Make a clean sweep; define terms operationally. Whenever practicable fit all data to mathematical or computer models; employ statistics; determine probabilities. Minimize intervening variables; better still, think in terms of an "empty organism," so that all measurements and concepts may be publicly verifiable.

It is important to note that this trend toward extreme positivism was not limited to psychology. It had a precise parallel in philosophy which widely repudiated metaphysics and value theory in favor of language analysis and methodology. It had a parallel in literary neocriticism wherein a poem is shorn of its context, separated from the personality of the author, and analyzed as a string of words in isolation, employing nothing more than the textual evidence itself. In art, realism and representation, dependent as they are on meaning and on tradition, went into the discard. Abstractions, reflecting only the momentary experience of the artist, were the vogue.

All fields of human endeavor were saying in effect: let's forget our traditional baggage of words, words, words. Nothing is trustworthy unless you can reduce it to physical and measurable operations. Nothing is true unless language analysts can define the concept of truth. In the case of literary and artistic creation let us stick to present definable fragments of experience and to textual evidence.

This period of the recent past, which we might call the era of the "clean sweep," is by no means ended. In psychology we note the effects of reductionism all along the line. Current theorizing, in contrast to earlier synoptic theorizing, is greatly simplified. Sometimes there is a reduction to biologism—a trend we already perceive in Freud; sometimes to physicalism, as in stimulus-response psychology; sometimes to operationism, to cybernetic analogies, to computer analogies, to mathematical formulae, including of course factor-analysis and other forms of bitter-end empiricism. The products of such reductions have been, and to a considerable extent still are, regarded as the psychologist's final word.

This era, as I say, has not yet ended, and we hope it will not completely vanish since the lessons it teaches are too valuable to be lost. No one, excepting perhaps a few philosophic sages, would want to return to the a priori systems of psychological theory which had little or no empirical monitoring.

At the same time a conspicuous reaction is already taking place. One marks the resurgence of the concept of self during the past two decades. One thinks of the existential movement which is peculiarly adroit in accepting the fragmentation of life and the dissipation of values while at the same time seeking through its concepts of "transcendence," "commitment," and the "will to meaning" to counteract the atomization of thought and the disintegration of purpose. One thinks of the upsurge of interest in the goals of therapy, and also in the goals of the nation. The revival of phenomenology as a psychological method is a prominent development. Related to this broad general movement is the turning of psychoanalysis toward so-called "ego psychology." One notes that new journals are springing up devoted to individual psychology, to existential psychology, to humanistic psychology. The trend is so marked that it has been called the "third force" in modern psychology.

And so we come to the era that lies ahead. Can it maintain the critical gains of recent decades and yet escape the trivialization of outlook that accompanies extreme reduction? Is it possible to reach a new level of synoptic theory with its respect for the totality of the human mind without sacrificing the gains in critical method so recently achieved? My answer is a cautious Yes. To do so requires first of all identifying those features of human nature that have been lost to sight in the reductionist stampede. The second requirement, of course, is to keep clearly in view the methodological lessons that we so recently learned.

MORPHOGENESIS AND PERSONALITY

We can illustrate the dual need by considering a problem from the field of human personality.

Everyone knows that each human neuropsychic system is unique. With unique genotypes of inheritance and never-repeated personal environments, it could not be otherwise. And everyone knows that while there is no final unity in a given personality system, each system nonetheless is highly organized and patterned in a self-consistent way. Has the science of psychology up to now adequately dealt with this situation? I think not. The picture that psychology offers is principally a picture of dimensions not of persons.

Individual differences (or dimensions) are freely allowed for, but personality is something more than an intersection of dimensions. That is to say, your personality is not simply your array of scores on achievement, ascendance, introversion, intelligence, neuroticism, or on Factors A, B, and C. In point of fact these general or nomothetic dimensions, which are the psychologist's present stock in trade, may not even be relevant to your personal structure. If some are relevant (in an approximate way) the question is not how do your scores on these variables differ from the scores of other people, but rather how do these qualities modify one another in your own functioning system.

Imagination is needed to provide us with methods appropriate to the pattern and growth of the single person. We have considerable distance to go before we improve our assessment and understanding of the individual and our prediction and control of his behavior. To me it is not acceptable to argue that this challenge of uniqueness lies outside the domain of science, since science, it is said, deals only with general laws and never with unique occurrences. Whatever the dogma may be in the natural sciences, I insist that psychology is assigned the problem of human personality and that to handle it adequately it must focus on the morphogenesis of the single pattern as it exists. A psychologist is defined in the official ethical code of the American Psychological Association (1959) as a person "committed to increasing man's understanding of man." And man, I submit, exists only in concrete, specifiable, and unique forms. If you reply that every object in nature is unique —every stone, every tree, every bird—I remain unmoved. The fact is that the individual human system is so enormously complex and so amazingly varied in its transactions with the world, and so intricate in its self-regulation, that one cannot shrug off the challenge of uniqueness by taking refuge in analogies with inanimate nature or lower forms of life.

The issue before us is not new. It has been discussed many times, for example by Meehl (1954), Sarbin, Taft, and Bentley (1960), and most recently by Holt (1962). If I am not mistaken most of the discussions conclude with an elaborate defense of dimensional analysis. We are told in a variety of ways that it is not possible for science to deal with patterned uniqueness, or are assured that in the last analysis there is no difference between molecular (i.e., dimensional) study and morphogenic study. Every biologist knows the difference between molecular and morphogenic biology, but psychologists are slow to recognize the parallel distinction in their own science.

As Meehl pointed out, there are two separate issues in this dispute. One concerns the *process* of understanding. How does the psychologist assemble into a unitary image all the fragments of information he obtains regarding a person? This question raises the troublesome matter of the roles of inferential or associational knowledge as against intuitive or configural knowledge. Unsolved epistemological issues are here raised. For psychology the question has been framed in terms of the relative predictability that results from following the method of statistical (or actuarial) forecasting based on the behavior of the average human being of a given class, as compared with success in predicting on the basis of clinical (individual) insights. Since we are far from reaching an acceptable solution in this dispute I call for imagination in devising more appropriate methods of submitting the matter to empirical testing.

A second issue in the dimensional-morphogenic dispute concerns the type of *data* needed for assessing individual behavior. Are scores derived from dimensional scales, from projective tests, or from questionnaires the only data we need? In general this is the type of evidence with which we are now working.

The theoretical limitation of this prevalent approach is clear. When we assess an individual in terms of questionnaires or Rorschach scores, or anything similar, we are assuming that the basic constitution of his personality is qualitatively like that of all other people. The self-same dimensions are imposed on all subjects. They are allowed to vary quantitatively but only in respect to the dimensions imposed by the experimenter. But what if the cleavages in our own lives, our "personal dispositions," do not correspond to the slicing in terms of "common traits"? (Allport, 1961, chaps. 14, 15.) Would we not then need a new base line, a new device for finding out the nature of these unique personal dispositions?

To take an example. Suppose we wish to discover a person's primary interests or values. We now have several precoded scales that we can administer (Kuder, Strong, Allport-Vernon-Lindzey). What we discover, of course, is precisely what we expected: quantitative variations on the dimensions prescribed by the experimenter, and not necessarily prescribed by the life we are studying.

More directly morphogenic is the old-fashioned device of asking the subject point blank what he wants in life. And there is still much to be said for this simple procedure. The trouble with it is that Freud has made us aware of the self-deceptions that may creep in, and it is also true that some people may not be able to articulate their own values, some may not even know what they are.

Recently Cantril and Free (1962) have approached this problem with the sort of imagination I think we need. Subjects in many different lands (including India, Nigeria, Brazil, and Poland in addition to the United States) are asked to define as well as they can the "best possible" way of life for themselves. As the next step, the subject is shown a picture of a ladder and told that the top rung (of 10) represents this way of life. He is then asked on which of the 10 rungs he would locate himself today in the process of climbing toward his aspirations. Where did he stand five years ago? Where does he expect to stand five years hence? In this way interesting reflections of morale and outlook are obtained on a scale that is self-anchoring. The subject is also asked to describe the worst possible way of life that he can imagine for himself. This dreaded contingency is located at the bottom of the ladder. Interestingly enough the most dreaded way of life is seldom a logical opposite of the best possible way, even though the ladder forms some sort of psychological continuum in the subject's mind. Here is a clear instance where the logical dimensions of an experimenter may fail to represent the phenomenological dimensions of the person he is studying.

You may ask, well, granted that this method establishes a

unique base line for the individual, by which we can locate his intentions and measure his progress, what can be done with such a mass of solipsistic data? Doesn't it merely prove that every individual is hopelessly solitary?

No, in analyzing thousands of cases, Cantril finds that an elaborate code may be constructed, consisting of about 145 items, which will include in different proportions most of the ways of life that were mentioned in all the countries studied. Ah, you may say, thus we return to a dimensional scheme. Yes, for purposes of comparisons we do, but with two marked differences from our usual dimensionalism. In the first place no individual is forced into the common code if in fact his aspirations are *sui generis;* and secondly, the dimensions used are derived *inductively* from aspirations as actually experienced and not invented in the laboratory by the experimenter.

I mention this one example of an imaginative step that has been taken to draw scientific psychology closer to the study of morphogenic patterning. The example happens to deal with the field of personal values. But one can mark off other areas of patterning for study. Shapiro (1961), working with psychiatric patients, has likewise shown imagination. On the basis of a five-hour intensive interview with an incoming patient he constructs a questionnaire which from that time on is standard for this particular patient, although not directly relevant to any other patient. Used over intervals of months or years, the instrument shows the course of improvement or deterioration in health, as well as changes in attitudes and outlook.

Elsewhere (Allport, 1962) I have gathered together a number of other recently devised methods which to my mind exemplify the neglected morphogenic approach to personality study. I shall not repeat the listing here, but shall say that while such methods are by no means common they show that in principle imagination is possible. Some techniques seem to blend dimensional and morphogenic procedures, such as the Q-sort and the "Rep" test, and these too are partial gains. But we still have far to go in the direction I describe. Let me say clearly: our customary dimensional methods have their merit. My point is simply that they are one-sided and need imaginative supplementation.

OTHER NEEDED STEPS

In what other areas besides personality assessment does psychology need to stretch its imagination? I cannot, of course, write a scientific agenda for the future, but I shall venture to call attention briefly to a few particularly needy fields.

Reductionism has left us with a peculiarly threadbare account of human learning. I say this in spite of the fact that learning is probably the most worked-on topic in our science. Conditioning and reinforcement take us only a short distance in understanding the mysteries of acquiring knowledge, skills, and motives. Yet conditioning and reinforcement are enormously popular concepts. With true reductionist zeal they are often offered as a universal formula. Today, I suspect, more and more psychologists realize that to predict adult learning in terms of past reinforcements is an unwarranted extrapolation of isolated and inappropriate experiments. In fact the very concept of "learning" seems inadequate. What a human being does, at least after the stage of infancy, is to absorb, master, engulf whatever is relevant to his conception of himself. And he does not do so, I submit, in order to reduce tensions, as prevalent learning theory would hold, but in order to maintain the tensions that are appropriate to his sense of self-identity. Clearly this is a highly complex issue and will require imaginative reformulation in the future.

Take the more specific topic of conscience. It was Freud's important insight that in children the parental mandate is interiorized in the form of a superego. The question arises whether this "must" conscience of childhood has normally any functional tie at all with the mature adult's sense of moral obligation. May it not be that the "ought" conscience of adults in normal lives is functionally autonomous of the "must" conscience of childhood? For a discussion of these two forms of conscience, see Allport, 1955, pages 72–73.

Freud, we gratefully admit, gave us the gift of self-scrutiny, including the art of the backward glance toward childhood. But now that we are able to stand on his shoulders we can see farther than he could see—before as well as behind. Conscience we discover has a wider horizon than he knew. Religion also. According to Freud the religious sentiment is an elaboration of our childhood view of the earthly father. And so it may be to a limited degree. But a more full-bodied study of the role of the religious sentiment in normal adults will surely show how slender is Freud's reductionist formula. One could speak also of Freud's liberating treatment of sex. But whether sex is the whole of the complex sentiment of love is doubtful. It is to the credit of Fromm and others that this question is now being raised in a new psychological context.

It is an odd fact that psychologists by preference conduct scores of investigations on aggression for every one on affiliation or love. They study stress but not relaxation; pain but not joy; deprivation but not fulfillment; prejudice but not friendship. Just why the seamier aspects of life have chiefly attracted psychologists up to now, I do not know. Perhaps it is for the same reason that young people like horror in their comic books.

It would be choppy indeed to list in this brief way additional areas that would benefit from wider imagination. Instead of such staccato listing let us return finally to the problem of theory-building.

THEORY-BUILDING

We have spoken of *reductionist* theories. The opposite type may properly be called pluralistic. A pluralist in psychology is a thinker who will not exclude any attribute of human nature that seems important in its own right. Like the pluralist in philosophy, he favors multiplicity and diversity of interpretation. The result, of course, is a curious medley of theories.

There is an analogy to the concept of "cultural pluralism." Whenever we defend cultural pluralism we are in effect advocating a nation in which each ethnic strain maintains its identity. To be sure we hope at the same time for some form of overall national unity, but the only unity possible turns out to be rather loose and incomplete, and in some respects discordant. Those who think it better for a nation to aim at complete assimilation are analogous to reductionists. It is better, they say, to work for organic unity rather than risk the looseness and disjointedness of pluralism.

So far as psychological theory-building is concerned the same dilemma exists. Everything conceivable about human nature is conceived in specific human minds, and specific human minds are limited. No one type of mind is able to discern the totality of truth. On this simple fact William James constructed his own brand of pluralism. No single formula, he held, could possibly cover all that is conceivably true. The diversity of valid knowledge is such that no one theory-builder can embrace the totality.

At the same time our rational ability insists on making conceptual systems—and the more closed and tight the system is, the more rational it seems to be, and the more satisfying. We are, therefore, caught in the dilemma: we want coherent systems but we are not able to include in our limited coherence all the diversity of mental functioning that we encounter. The reductionist is the person who solves the dilemma by favoring coherence over adequacy. He is willing to blind himself, permanently or temporarily, to the complexities of his subject in order to reap the rewards of rationalism. The pluralist, on the other hand, is willing to sacrifice rational coherence in order to keep alive his recognition of diversity and subtlety.

The most obvious way to be a pluralist is to be an eclectic. An eclectic chooses doctrines and principles from various systems of thought, and somehow blends them to suit his own temperament. If his temperament can tolerate contradictions he will find himself holding one theory at one moment and an

opposite theory the next. If accused of illogicality he can retort, with Emerson, that "consistency is the hobgoblin of little
minds." Nothing that seems true in any context can be denied,
not even if these special truths fail to cohere.

In the psychology of William James we encounter many
paradoxes of this order (Allport, 1943). His hospitable mind
was able in different contexts to give assent to determination
and also freedom; to mentalism and to physicalism; to parallelism and to interactionism. He both affirmed and denied the
unconscious; he expressed both hope and despair concerning
the future of psychology as a science.

James, of course, claimed justification for his paradoxes
within the embracing doctrine of pragmatism. Pragmatism
tells us that the whole purpose of thinking is to develop concepts that will guide us in practical action. If the consequences
of this action are fruitful then we know that we have laid hold
successfully of some aspect of truth.

James knew that his position was "unsystematic and loose."
But he preferred it to what he called the "terrible flavor of
humbug" that marks the work of any psychologist who
claims perfect consistency and adequacy for his theory. He
would, therefore, not approve of modern reductionism with
its claims of sufficiency for psychoanalytic, stimulus-response,
operational, or some other rationally satisfying but partial
position. Pluralism has the merit of inviting imagination. Nothing need be ruled out simply because it rests on an heretical
hypothesis (as does telepathy) or upon an unfashionable
method (as do case studies). New frontiers are allowed and
exploration encouraged.

Let me repeat: pluralism would not deny the insights
yielded by reductionism. It would admit the evidence for
reinforcement along with the evidence for cognitive and ego-
relevant theories of learning. It would preserve the merits of
dimensional analysis while seeking out morphogenic procedures to round out the patterns of individuality. It would admit the truth that lies in theories of ego defense while giving

scope to the conflict-free propriate structure of the self. It would allow for infantile remnants in the superego but also for the adult sense of moral obligation. It would admit the role of stimulus, but also the role of challenge which is considerably more than stimulus.

We have not yet answered the question whether such pluralism is doomed to the illogic of temperamental eclecticism; or whether pragmatism is the only available conceptual cement. My own answer would be that, given imagination, the psychology of the future can evolve a stronger theoretical position—one that might be called *systematic pluralism*.

SYSTEMATIC PLURALISM

The goal of systematic pluralism is to fashion a conception of the human person that will exclude nothing that is valid, and yet at the same time preserve our ideal of rational consistency. It will allow for what is neural and what is mental; for what is conscious and what is unconscious; for what is determined and what is free; for what is stable and what is variable; for what is normal and what is abnormal; for what is general and what is unique. All these, and many other, paradoxes are actually resident in the human frame. All represent verifiable capacities and none can be ruled out of consideration in our theory-building.

It is not possible at this time, of course, to formulate an embracing theory of the human person in terms of systematic pluralism. Such a formulation requires imagination and is, therefore, assigned to our agenda of the future. Elsewhere (1960) I have suggested a possible line of approach.

The starting point, I believe, should be the admission that the human person is himself the primary system (unique, yes, but still a system); and he is a system of amazingly diverse potentialities. We are already familiar with many kinds of natural systems, ranging in type from the atom to the solar system, from an amoeba to a man, from an idiot to an Aristotle. But systems, we know, vary in their degree of openness. An inanimate system (a stone or a bridge) obeys chiefly the second law of thermodynamics. An animate system (a plant or a bird) is self-maintaining according to the principle of homeostasis. A human system is still more open. While it, like lower forms of life, maintains itself through homeostasis it has the capacity for vastly greater differentiation, and tries restlessly to become something more than it is through its foresight, imagination, and ideals. And it has infinitely more complex encounters with the environment and with other human systems.

The ingredients of the personal system comprise automatisms, reflexes and habits, operations of the unconscious, and of biological impulse, as well as the deposits of culture and social class. Exclusive stress on these particular aspects of human nature has led to the reductionist image of man as a simple reactive mechanism. While his system surely contains all these reactive features it also contains proactive, productive, propriate features that elude most of the current reductionist views.

In defining each man as a system, therefore, we should include all (and not simply a few) of the features intrinsic to this system. In doing so we shall neither rest content with reductionist theory nor deny the truth that lies therein. We shall not have to settle for arbitrary eclecticism, or for pragmatic pluralism, for *we shall have defined our subject matter in such a way that any and all valid data and all verified processes can be woven into our central conception of man as an open system.* Even though no single psychologist will be able to discern the totality he will fit his own specialty into a larger and more hospitable theoretical edifice. In this way we shall, I hope, reconstruct psychology so that it will be a more open-minded and also a more coherent science than it is at present.

IMPLICATIONS FOR SOCIETY

I have proposed these various imaginative steps not simply in the interests of fashioning a more adequate science of psychology, but likewise in order to improve its usefulness.

It is commonly said that the Free World needs above all

else to clarify its goals. We are up against dictators who know what they want, and since what they want enslaves the free spirit of man, we rightly resist their desires. But do citizens of our open society know what *they* want? Do our colleges and universities know? It appears that they concern themselves more with the scientific know-how than with the philosophic know-why of our existence. They talk about *what* more than about *what for*.

As I see it, an open system conception of the human person within the science of psychology could lead to a clearer definition of the root motives of mankind. It could do so through improved cross-cultural and cross-national research. Up to now such research has not focused on the central problem of the universal root desires and goals of mankind. Rather it has compared selected cultures in respect to their practices in child training, in their images of other peoples, in their responses to modern technology. All these studies are good so far as they go. But they originate in limited views of human nature, or sometimes in no view at all.

I can imagine a study that will aim to discover the root motives and also the universal modes of thought that may enable international policy-makers to improve upon their present opportunistic statecraft, and perhaps discover new formulas for peaceful living. Essential to such a study would be the drawing of a distinction between people's *demands* (which are nothing more than preconceived solutions to problems) and root *desires* which lie behind the demands. The needs of mankind are probably universal; the solutions proposed up to now are all parochial. As yet we lack sufficient knowledge of mankind to offset local particularistic political demands. Such knowledge is needed as a basis for novel solutions to present conflict. Admittedly it will be difficult to change the habits of politicians, but if psychology offers an imaginative lead perhaps it can be done.

You may object that we already know of mankind's desire for peace, and that even so we have made little progress toward implementing this desire. The hitch, I suspect, lies in the inability of policy-makers up to now to consider the whole pattern of concurrent desires, including the need for self-respect, for freedom from fear, for raising standards of living even while disarming, and for some cause to devote onself to above national aggrandizement. It is the whole system of the person that must be taken into account, not a single segment. And knowledge of the person-system must of course be supplemented by knowledge of the social system.

Apart from its importance for social policy, a systematic pluralism would give to students of the future a broader basis for exploring and testing their own individual values. As a teacher I have noticed that students tend to see their own lives in terms of whatever fashionable reductionist frame they are currently taught. It has been said of Freud, that compared with most psychologists he delves deeper into the unconscious, stays down longer, and comes up dirtier. I hope that the psychology of the future will delve still deeper, stay still longer, explore more widely, and emerge with a truer image of the totality of human nature.

This nature has marked limitations, but also rich potentiality. If it harbors evil it also harbors good. My vision is of a psychology that will know the best along with the worst; that will enable us to make the good better, and when necessary make the best of the worst.

It is understandable that up to now our youthful science has taken delight in iconoclasm, and has tested its rationality by inventing all sorts of engaging reductionist models, and has admired its own aseptic methods. But it has paid a price. It has grown remote from its assigned subject matter, and is often compulsive about its own rituals. But a youth outgrows his adolescence, and intellectual manhood comes at last.

REFERENCES

Allport, G. W., 1943. "The Productive Paradoxes of William James," *Psychological Review*, 50, 95–120. See also Chapter 16 of the present volume.

————, 1955. *Becoming: Basic Considerations for a Theory of Personality* (Yale University Press).

————, 1960. "The Open System in Personality Theory," Chapter 3 in *Personality and Social Encounter* (Beacon).

————, 1961. *Pattern and Growth in Personality* (Holt, Rinehart & Winston).

————, 1962. "The Unique and the General in Psychological Science," *Journal of Personality, 30*, 405–422.

American Psychological Association, 1959. "Ethical Standards of Psychologists," *American Psychologists, 14*, 279–282.

Cantril, H., and Free, L. A., 1962. "Hopes and Fears for Self and Country," *American Behavioral Scientist, 6*, Supplement.

Holt, R. R., 1962. "Individuality and Generalization in the Psychology of Personality," *Journal of Personality, 30*, 377–404.

Meehl, P. E., 1954. *Clinical versus Statistical Prediction* (University of Minnesota Press).

Sarbin, T. R., Taft, R., and Bailey, D. E., 1960. *Clinical Inference and Cognitive Theory* (Holt, Rinehart & Winston).

Shapiro, M. B., 1961. "The Single Case in Fundamental Clinical Psychological Research," *British Journal of Medical Psychology, 34*, 255–262.

PART II

PERSONAL CONDITIONS FOR GROWTH

7

Mental Health: A Generic Attitude

PSYCHOLOGICAL DISCOURSE often spills over into ethical assumption and value theory. It is scarcely possible to discuss growth, development, maturity, health, therapy without assuming standards for progress and for regress. Thus it often happens that psychologists write about value theory without being aware of their own assumptions and goals.

The four chapters in Part II are cases in point. While I deal more explicitly with psychological process than with normative assumptions, the latter are clearly present.

The present paper was prepared for a conference dealing with the potentially wider use of the clergy in rehabilitation work in cases of mental illness. Originally printed in the *Journal of Religion and Health*, 1964, Vol. 4, it has received wide distribution by the Johnson Foundation, Racine, Wisconsin.

† † †

The whole of my argument can be summed up in three stories —all of them true.

In a provincial Austrian hospital, a man lay gravely ill—in fact, at death's door. The medical staff had told him frankly that they could not diagnose his disease, but that if they knew the diagnosis they could probably cure him. They told him further that a famous diagnostician was soon to visit the hospital and that perhaps he could spot the trouble.

Within a few days the diagnostician arrived and proceeded to make the rounds. Coming to this man's bed, he merely glanced at the patient, murmured "Moribundus," and went on.

Some years later, the patient called on the diagnostician and said, "I've been wanting to thank you for your diagnosis. They told me that if you could diagnose me I'd get well, and so the minute you said 'moribundus' I knew I'd recover."

According to this story, even life itself may hang upon an attitude and an expectation.

My second story: a psychiatrist friend of mine—a believer in conditioned reflex therapy—tells of an alcoholic woman patient. To remove her appetite by the conditioning method, he placed a glass of whiskey in front of her while he administered a powerful emetic. Before long she learned to vomit whenever she smelled liquor. Needless to say, her consumption of alcohol completely ceased. Up to this point in the story we would say that a specific conditioning technique was ingeniously successful. Unfortunately, this therapy was her undoing. For whenever a salesman came to the door, or even her bosom friends, smelling (as many of them did) of alcohol, she straightway threw up on her visitors.

Curing the habit mechanically all by itself did not rehabilitate her. The cure was not set in the context of her total life.

The third story, with a rather brighter outcome, concerns a very small boy, an obsessive thumb-sucker. Every known method of reward and punishment—and reward and punishment are the be-all, end-all, and cure-all of therapy based on currently fashionable learning theory—such as tying the thumb, soaking it in bitter aloes, slapping, candy-giving and candy-withholding—all were tried, but to no effect. The habit grew firmer, and by the age of six the lad was a public spectacle.

One bright day he stopped his thumb-sucking completely. When the astonished parents dared to inquire why the ingrained habit had been so abruptly broken, the child replied simply, "Big boys don't suck their thumbs."

Somehow, somewhere, this generic idea had got through to him, and the specific compulsion vanished. The lad was cured.

THERAPIES: PARTICULARISTIC AND GENERIC

In different ways, these three stories all bear upon our problem. What is the problem? Simply this: How in the helping professions—and here I include psychiatry, the ministry, social work, applied psychology, and education—can we recover some of the common sense that we seem to have lost along the way? What has happened historically, I believe, is this: During the nineteenth century, the social and psychological and medical sciences found themselves unable to handle the whole vast complex of mental and social life. Therefore, in imitation of natural sciences, they set out to solve one small problem at a time. Events have causes, and so the logical thing is to focus upon a specific pathological event, find its cause, and remove it. The successes of Jenner, Lister, and Pasteur were vastly impressive. Their example seemed well worth following in the field of mental illness.

The conviction that man's psyche is secondary to his soma became set. The brain, of course, is a physiological organ. If you change this organ through drugs, conditioning, or even hypnosis, you change a man's attitudes and actions. The image of materia medica and surgery were dominant. John Whitehorn has called it the "pseudo-surgical formulation in psychotherapy."[1]

At the present time in the treatment of mental disorder and mental retardation, it is still fashionable, indeed more fashionable than ever, to administer all sorts of miracle drugs. Pharmacotherapy is an instance of specific therapy, based on a biochemical view of mental disorder. That such treatment often has favorable effects cannot be denied. Yet an observant nurse in a nearby clinic said to me, "Giving drugs without giving love is of no lasting benefit at all. The patient still has his problems; he still is frightened and insecure; he still feels isolated, rejected, forsaken by God and man."

And speaking of drugs, the baffling problem of addiction illustrates the point. In spite of his suffering, an addict gener-

ally returns to drugs after release from prison or from hospital.
Even psychotherapy, it is said, helps only from three to seven-
teen per cent of the cases. "The addict 'solves' all his problems
with the pill, the potion, the smoke or the needle."[2] To do so
is a way of life, a way common to between 25,000 and 40,000
persons, mostly youth, in New York City alone. These un-
happy persons are victims of a generic attitude that might be
called "magical thinking." E. M. Brown characterizes this
generic attitude as one that considers the concrete moment to
be the only reality, subjective reality to be more important
than external reality, and the person's point of view to be absolute and unconditional. The addict must feel himself to be
omnipotent. Frustration, loneliness, alienation send him to
dope. His addiction is a way of life. Only a total change of
outlook can be therapeutic, and admittedly a total change of
outlook is very hard to achieve.

In spite of its frequent failures, the particularistic pseudo-
surgical approach is in favor. The nineteenth-century scientific outlook still prompts us to seek specific causes for specific
effects. The result is an array of theories, concepts, and techniques that arouse scientific fervor—while they last. I have in
mind such fashionable concepts as *biochemical imbalance,
conditioning, reinforcement, milieu therapy, hypnoanalysis,
tension reduction, homeostasis, somatotype, cybernetics, neurological block, cognitive dissonance, stimulus-response,* and
certain popular principles of psychoanalysis, such as *transfer-
ence, Oedipal conflict, oral regression, identity diffusion,* and
a vast array of similar conceptual enthusiasms. None of these
approaches can be declared wholly erroneous; but they are all
partial, some to the point of triviality. Each calls attention to
some limited way in which some organisms may react some of
the time; but their proponents often imply that their favored
theory explains far more than it does.

Note the popularity of the term "organism." This label reflects the impersonal, biological, deterministic outlook of the
particularistic investigator. Theorists addicted to partial doc-

trines seldom speak of the human subject as a man, a woman, an individual, a person—certainly not as a soul.

The theoretical issue, however, is not the truth or falsity of any particular formulation for some particular occasion. The question is rather, *where do the primary dynamics of a human life lie?* Shall we say that our patient suffers from biochemical imbalance, or from an intolerable loss of self-respect? Both statements may be true; but to science, it seems more objective, less animistic and mystical, to attack the problem at the biochemical level where cause and effect are easier to perceive.

Dr. John Whitehorn tells of his own experience in this regard. Trained in his laboratory courses to seek specific natural causes for specific effects, he engaged in biochemical researches on schizophrenia. While making his experimental injections, he discovered that his conversations with the patients seemed to do them much more good than did his glucose and sodium acid phosphate. He also discovered that a ubiquitous theme ran through the minds of the patients: a fear of being submitted to coercive influence. They were struggling for integrity in their own way, and were frightened by outside influence.

Yet, as Whitehorn observes, a psychiatrist does inevitably influence his patient; his role demands that he be a leader. And so gradually Whitehorn tested various styles of leadership among psychiatrists and discovered that what he called an "evocative" leadership (a responding, encouraging, sympathetic manner) was more effective than either a directive or passively consultative leadership in bringing about improvement in schizophrenia.[3]

When scientific dogma alone rules the roost, a curious caste system develops, with the patient on the bottom. He alone is not informed, not responsible, not free, and not wise. Just how a patient is to regain these attributes of health when his therapist and even the attendants are supposed to be superior in scientific wisdom is not clear. This sort of condescension is, I suspect, the chief obstacle to cure.

Not all therapists, to be sure, entrench themselves behind their particularistic wisdom. Many of them employ evocative leadership, and in so doing are rediscovering an important chapter in the history of psychiatry. A hundred and fifty years ago, Philippe Pinel evolved a revolutionary approach to mental illness, which has been called "moral treatment" (although it would be more accurate to retain Pinel's term "morale"). It was a program of planned rehabilitation in a positive, sympathetic, social milieu marked by friendly association, discussion of difficulties, a busy day of occupational work in a family-like environment, during all of which activity the patient was to be treated as a normal person so that he might retain or regain his self-respect. Recently Dr. J. Sanbourne Bockoven has written up this forgotten period of the history of psychiatry. In America, model hospitals employing moral treatment were the Worcester State Hospital in Massachusetts and the Hartford Retreat in Connecticut. In these and other hospitals, compassion had replaced restraint and custody, and the recovery rates, according to Bockoven's analysis, were surprisingly high.[4]

Around 1860, the viewpoint of physical medicine became dominant. Treatment was considered best if it rested on a physical theory. Psychological sensitivity and insight that marked moral treatment were dismissed as mystical, sentimental, and unscientific. Neurological societies ruled out papers dealing with psychological factors in mental illness. And the recovery rate began to go down, reaching its lowest point between 1923 and 1950. Chronic and incurable cases piled up. Although outpatient clinics were being added and the method of keeping statistics was changing, on the whole it seems probable that the success of the earlier moral treatment (what I would like to call "attitudinal therapy") was greater than the success of our more recent scientific and particularistic methods.[5]

Now the cycle is changing again. Pinel and moral treatment are slowly returning to favor. The concept of science is gradually broadening, and within the framework of a broadened science, evidence is accumulating concerning the reasons for the success of the earlier moral treatment. Let me cite one study.

A few years ago, a student of Carl Rogers chose to study factors that would predict the successful reform of juvenile delinquents. The question was, which factors among many studied in a group of 75 boys would spot the lads who would pull out and be rehabilitated? Possible factors included, of course, the quality of the boy's neighborhood, his parents' attitudes, his friendships, his physique, his past record, his social class, his school adjustments, and a variety of environmental stresses—now fashionably lumped together under the label "psychosocial epidemiology." It turned out that while some of these factors had some predictive power, by far the most important was the degree of self-understanding that the lad displayed concerning his situation. Later, Rogers replicated this finding.[6] And still more recently, Dr. B. R. Hutcheson discovered a similar fact: that if a boy regards his antisocial acts as normal, ordinary, natural, the outlook for reform is bad indeed. If on the other hand his attitude toward his misconduct shows that to him it is unnatural and repugnant, he is likely to reform.[7] The generic attitude is of major importance.

GENERIC ATTITUDES

What do we mean by "generic attitude"? Let me offer a few examples.

President Lowell of Harvard was once asked how he managed to make so many important decisions during a single day of his busy life. He replied in effect, "Oh, it is not too difficult. There are only a few—perhaps half a dozen—principal standards of value by which I make my judgments. Almost every decision fits one of these broad categories."

In trying to classify her patients, Karen Horney found it helpful to distinguish three generic social attitudes: (a) approaching people; (b) avoiding people; (c) being antagonistic or hostile toward people. Each patient, she felt, could be known by the characteristic way in which his social conduct fitted one of these attitudes. Perhaps her typology is too coarse, but the point is there: each of us has a general schema or attitude of our own that selects or "gates" our responses to people.

Even laboratory researches show the pervasive influence of social schemata. Some people are so broadly affiliative that they use many adjectives in describing people, and when rearranging figurines of people they place them closer together than they were in the original arrangement.[8] Thus it is that general schemata guide specific conduct in specific situations. Some years ago, Cantril demonstrated the same primacy that marks generic attitudes in directing activities and in shaping detailed beliefs.[9]

Up to now, I regret to say, neither psychology nor psychiatry, nor for that matter neural physiology, has reached an adequate level of knowledge concerning the nature and operation of generalized mental sets. Some slight progress, however, is being made. Neurophysiologists are recognizing the selective or gating force that complex mental attitudes exert upon specific behavioral functions. Hebb, for example, traces this steering influence to what he calls "autonomous central processes" and "central motive states."[10]

Let us take the topic of ethnic prejudice. In most people, ethnic prejudice—or its opposite, tolerance—we now know, is a generalized attitude. That is to say, if John has antipathy toward Negroes, he is almost certain to have antipathy toward Jews, Mexicans, Orientals, Catholics (or Protestants)—almost any group of which he is not himself a member. Correspondingly, if he is tolerant toward one he is almost certainly tolerant toward all.[11]

Let me relate this finding (confirmed by many researches) to the problem of a generalized religious orientation—a topic I have recently been investigating. It is a disturbing finding (but again confirmed by many researches) that, on the average, churchgoers are more bigoted toward minority groups than nonchurchgoers. Our first reaction to this finding is to say, "But that can't be true. Look at the leaders of the civil rights movement; most of them seem to be religiously motivated. One thinks of Gandhi, Father John La Farge, the Rev. Martin Luther King, and many others." We are forced to conclude: if most churchgoers are more bigoted, but if some churchgoers are more tolerant, then there must be a vast difference in the type of religious orientation that people may hold. And such turns out to be the case.

Our research (not yet fully published) shows that churchgoers high in ethnic prejudice tend, on the whole, to have what I have called an extrinsic religious orientation.

Extrinsic religion. For many people, religion is a dull habit, or a tribal investment to be used for ceremony, for family convenience, or for personal comfort. It is something to *use* but not to *live*. It may be used to improve one's status, to bolster one's self-confidence. It may be used as a defense against reality, and as a divine sanction for one's own formula for living. Such a sentiment assures me that God sees things my way. In theological terms, the extrinsically religious person turns to God, but does not turn away from self. This type of religion is a shield for self-centeredness.[12]

Individuals of this type, it turns out, ordinarily are only occasional attenders at church. They are not truly devout. Their religion is a matter of convenience. Some of them, as the saying goes, attend church only thrice: when they are hatched, when matched, and when dispatched. Not surprisingly, it is this type of religion that correlates with high ethnic prejudice.

By contrast, *intrinsic* religion is not instrumental. It is not a means of handling fear, a mode of sociability and conformity, a sublimation of sex, or a wish-fulfillment. All these motives are somehow subordinated to an overarching motive. One's ethnic relations, one's domestic life, one's quandaries, guilt, and ultimate ontological anxiety are all handled under a comprehensive commitment, partly intellectual but more fundamentally motivational. It is integral, covering everything in experience, making room for scientific fact and emotional fact. It is a unifying orientation. Such religion does not exist to serve the person; rather the person is committed to serve it.

It is not surprising that people with this type of generic attitude are tolerant and compassionate toward fellow mortals.

While I have spoken of these types of religious orientation in relation to prejudice, I feel equally sure that mental health is facilitated by an intrinsic, but not by an extrinsic, religious orientation.

Please note that intrinsic religion, according to this hypothesis, cannot exist in order to be therapeutic or preventive. It is not something to use. The sufferer can aim only at religion; he cannot aim at treatment. If he has deeply interiorized his religion, he will find sanity and soundness as a by-product. Such is my hypothesis.

An additional example of generic attitudes is from a recent book by Father John Clifford that sets forth his own strategy for withstanding Chinese communist brainwashers.[13] His points are equally relevant to the strategy by which we ourselves withstand pressures that endanger our mental health: (a) a resolve to be unremittingly and yet passively uncooperative with evil influences; (b) a continual restatement of the positive values and beliefs of one's own life; (c) active planning of counterstrategy; (d) retaining a sense of humor, particularly about the antics and stratagems of the captors; (e) remembering that specific indignities are only part of a broader program; and what one does in a given case cannot always affect the final outcome.

Father Clifford's rule that one should continually restate one's positive values and beliefs approaches the heart of the matter. Martin Buber makes the point in a broader way. He writes, "As a condition of the individual soul evil is the convulsive shirking of direction. . . ."[14]

It is not easy for a counselor to know what a given person's own proper "direction" is, or should be; nor is it easy to help him control his characteristic "convulsive shirking." Yet the psychology of the matter is clear: evil is best controlled by affirming and strengthening the generic direction of the life. It is less a matter of specific bad habits or the violation of specific rules, and more a matter of maintaining total orientation. Christ, we recall, worried less about specific legalisms than about pride, self-centeredness, and hypocrisy. His generic formula for mental health and for righteousness was drawn from the Old Testament—to love the Lord God with all one's heart and soul and mind; and to love one's neighbor as oneself.

At the concrete level, we can learn something, I think, from the devices that healthy people use to maintain their "orientation of the soul." Father Clifford's maxims are an example. Some people resort to simple mottoes that distill for them an area of generic wisdom. A hardworking public servant of my acquaintance tells me that his whole life is guided by his generic belief that "if everyone works as hard as he can, and takes only what he and his family need, then there will be just enough to go around." A lovely lady said that her life was pretty much guided by her conviction that she had no right to poison the air that other people have to breathe. She never whined, complained, or gossiped. Many find mottoes in the scriptures: perhaps, "Be still and know that I am God," or Job's total orientation, "Though He slay me, yet will I trust Him." Needless to say, what is effective in one life is not necessarily effective in another; but the principle of discovering and holding fast to one direction is the first law of mental health.

THE ROLE OF THE RELIGIOUS COUNSELOR

When we emphasize the importance of man's total orientation, we approach at long last the role of the religious counselor, for this is his specialty.

The aim of attitudinal therapy is to free the individual so

that he may know himself—his values, his chosen direction, and his total orientation toward life. Within this context, he has to find a place for his current suffering.

No other person has the same context, and no one else has the same problems. It is within this frame of uniqueness that the minister begins his difficult task. Since I am not a pastoral counselor, I cannot speak from experience. Yet a few aspects of the minister's job strike me as especially noteworthy.

For one thing, I believe the advancement of mental health involves a paradox: the tie that binds serious attitudinal orientation with humor. So many tangles in life are ultimately hopeless that we have no appropriate sword other than laughter. I venture to say that no person is in good health unless he can laugh at himself quietly and privately, noticing where he has overreached, where his pretensions have been overblown or pedantic. He needs to note where he has been hoodwinked, too sure of himself, too shortsighted, and above all too conceited. The specific remedy for vanity, says Bergson, is laughter, and the one essentially laughable failing is vanity.

Yet there is an end to laughter. A mature person needs also a guiding philosophy of life. I do not mean that he must be highly articulate about his world view. He need not be a Heidegger, about whom it was said that he wrote his German philosophy in two volumes, the second volume of which contained the verbs.

We hear much nowadays about the tragedy of meaninglessness. Frankl has identified the corresponding neurosis, which he calls "noögenic."[15] I myself believe that this state of vacancy—the "existential vacuum"—is primarily an affliction of the sophisticated and educated (or miseducated) man. In fact, I suspect that existentialism, for all its insights, is pretty much a philosophy written by and for eggheads. Yet, in many patients, the condition of "existential vacuum" does exist, and the clergy and other therapists have to deal with it. In his pride, the sufferer claims that everything is illusion. He is neither a pilgrim nor even a tourist in life, but only a wanderer.

Here fall the clergy's duty and opportunity. Young people may have to go through a period of vacancy, of rebellion, and of disintoxication with life. I am thinking of the coed who said, beamingly, "I cannot tell you how much I enjoy my existential despair." But what is appropriate for a brief time in late adolescence is no guide for maturity.

Whether we speak of existential vacuum or of total orientation, of generic attitude or of central motive state, the clergyman is a specialist where the scientist is still a fumbler. (*Please note:* In saying that the scientist is still a fumbler, I have in mind psychological research and theory, not necessarily the daily practice of psychiatrists or of clinical psychologists. Many of the latter know from experience the patient's need for a constructive world view; many are respectful toward the religious orientation that constitutes a potential curative direction for a given patient's life. My complaint is rather that the intellectual foundations of the therapeutic professions have not yet been made consistent with the best in therapeutic practice.)

It is probable that the sufferer who comes to the clergyman has some religious ideas to start with. Hence the task is to help him deepen and enlarge them, so that they more adequately embrace his present distress and groping. To employ my earlier terms, the task is to help him move from his relatively extrinsic religion to a mature, all-embracing, intrinsic religion. This, I submit, is the primary assignment of every religious counselor.

Along the way, of course, the counselor may have to bring the sufferer in contact with psychiatric facilities. He may have to interpret such facilities as potential agents of help, and not a seal of doom. But to send the patient to a clinic, a hospital, or a school for retarded children does not automatically solve the problem; in fact, it may increase the strain. No patient or parent can comfortably give up his integrity to a hospital ward or school, where he encounters an array of impersonal treatments—electroconvulsive, hypnotic, pharmacological, or psychotherapeutic—without wanting to put them into perspective. To hand over responsibility to doctors, nurses, psychologists—however skillful they may be—is to surrender one's vital liberty. What the sufferer craves is to be comforted in his extremity, to feel that the spirit of the universe understands his predicament and accepts him. "Is there a place for me, a helpless failure?" This is what he wants to know.

Boisen reports among sufferers in mental hospitals religion is seldom an escape from reality. It is much more closely related to the texture of life, and insofar as it brings meaning to the suffering it is a potential asset. But to confront the totality of the patient's distress, his religion must be adequately comprehensive and integrative. For example, as Boisen insists, it is relatively worthless unless it can embrace in some meaningful way the patient's conflicts in the sexual sphere—not in terms of conventional prudery, but in a widely meaningful and integrative way.[16]

One psychiatrist has said that the sense of sin is the chief lesion found in mental illness. If this be true, the clergyman has a clear duty, for the poor psychiatrist and psychologist are ordinarily baffled by sin. More often than not, they view it as they might view an outgrown vermiform appendix—something that ought to be removed by a psychoanalytic scalpel. Here is one place where the minister has a more balanced wisdom. While there is a neurotic type of guilt, there is also in most people a deep sense of their own persistent, sinful, convulsive shirking. William James complained that modern Protestantism does not avail itself of sacramental confession often enough. I think he was right. Except in the Catholic tradition, we seem unready even for private sacramental penance under the seal of secrecy, let alone the open type of social confession advocated by Hobart Mowrer.[17]

The average clergyman has an additional advantage over the psychiatrist in that he is unlikely to close his ears to the religious ideas of a disturbed person. Provided that he does not grow argumentative or angered, he can listen with respect to what may be bizarre religious conceptions. Many patients complain that their therapists never inquire concerning the religious aspects of their turmoil, even though they themselves regard religious issues as central to their distress. Insofar as this is true, the therapist's neglect may sometimes come from his own lack of personal religion; but more often it is the result of his habituation to the grammar of science. He is accustomed to applying the stencils of particularistic theory and the stencils of particularistic treatment. In so doing, he may fail to recognize the power of healing that lies in generic faith.

I have been saying that the average clergyman in an average community has several advantages in the relief of distress that comes with mental ill health or into families where mental retardation has struck. He is inclined to view each individual as unique and important, not as an "organism" to which stenciled theories of therapy are applied. He knows that at heart most people (at least most sufferers) have deep religious concerns, and he is by training a specialist in the area of their concern. He can be attentive and intelligent in listening to the mixed-up religious ideas of sufferers and in urging them toward more constructive thinking. He has, or can have, an authoritative method of dealing with the sense of sin. In his heart he believes that an integrative and intrinsic religious outlook is health-giving, and with this basic faith he can go even further in attitudinal therapy than did "moral treatment" a century ago. He can perhaps increase its rate of success.

Of course, there are pitfalls along the way. One is the danger that a minister may exacerbate a disturbed condition by stressing aspects of religion that are pathogenic for a given individual. He may arouse pathological feelings of guilt, an abnormal degree of anxiety, or encourage some futile compulsive ritual. Or conversely, he may offer nothing but spiritual lozenges that are momentarily pleasant but in the long run ineffective.

Another obvious pitfall often pointed out is the danger that a little knowledge of psychiatry or psychoanalysis may tempt the clergyman to abandon his special function and become a second-string psychiatrist.

A more subtle pitfall—one that teachers fall into as well as clergymen—is to throw some solution at the sufferer in one verbal chunk. Any skillful teacher knows that he cannot present his student with a neat, well-formulated conclusion, no matter how many years of experience and labor lie behind it, and expect the student to assimilate it. The student hears what you say, but is unable to digest it.

I recall a case where a counselor prematurely offered advice. He said to his client, "Well, you know that's life. That's the way it is; you have to accept things like that." This bit of summary wisdom at the time fell on deaf ears. The therapy continued for some months, eventually making good progress. Just before its termination, the patient summed up his hard-won wisdom in the same words: "Well, you know that's life. That's the way things are. You have to accept them." The same words—but with a world of difference.

Change in attitudes comes about only through experience, not through prefabricated and secondhand solutions presented by clergy, teachers, or therapists.[18]

Now these and other pitfalls can greatly reduce a minister's effectiveness and may even damage the sufferer who comes to him for help. (In honesty I must add that other therapists have been known to bring damage rather than help.)

What is needed is training and more training. While many seminaries, of course, are laying good foundations, the need is a continuing one. Especially at this time, the average clergyman in the average community needs to have the whole problem laid before him step by step. The community's health resources should be explained; even more, the relation between the two logics of science and of religion. Training in the techniques of human relations (including the art of listening), theories of personality (including the common forms of mental distress), the place of religion in attitudinal therapy—all are part of the needed curriculum of continuous training. It is encouraging to know that a movement in this direction is now under way.

The main purpose of religion, I repeat, is not to make people healthy, but to help them fit themselves into the Creator's context for them. An adequate religion of this dimension serves incidentally to guard, maintain, and restore mental health. It casts out demons. The clergyman knows that a personality, to be sound and fully human, requires a guiding philosophy of life. I have called such a philosophy of life a "generic attitude." By the very nature of his calling, the minister himself is, or could become, a specialist in those generic attitudes that confer and maintain health of mind.

If I have stressed the role of the minister, it is not in order to disparage other helping professions. Many psychiatrists accomplish in practice a true cure of souls. I do, however, wish to establish two points. The clergy as such have a valid and valuable part to play in therapy and guidance—a part that few of them (and few psychiatrists) fully understand. As a theorist, I feel that the intellectual foundations of psychiatry are not yet adequately developed. Too much is said of psycho-surgical and particularistic factors and too little of the dynamics of the generic attitudes and assumptive worlds of the sufferer.

References

1. Whitehorn, John C., "Types of Leadership Involved in Psychotherapy," *American Journal of Psychotherapy*, 1962, *16*, 366–378.
2. Brown, E. M., "The Juvenile Narcotic Addict: a Profile," *The Pastoral Counselor*, 1963, *1*, 26–30.
3. Whitehorn, *op. cit.*
4. Bockoven, J. S., *Moral Treatment in American Psychiatry*. New York: Springer Publishing Co., 1963.
5. Cf. Adams, H. B., " 'Mental Illness' or Interpersonal Behavior?" *American Psychologist*, 1964, *19*, 191–197.

6. Rogers, C. R., "Toward a Science of the Person," in T. W. Wann (ed.), *Behaviorism and Phenomenology*. Chicago: University of Chicago Press, 1964, p. 125.
7. Hutcheson, B. R., *A Prognostic Classification for Juvenile Court First Offenders, Based on a Follow-up Study*. Quincy, Mass.: South Shore Mental Health Center, 1963.
8. Kuethe, J. L., "Pervasive Influence of Social Schemata," *Journal of Abnormal and Social Psychology*, 1964, *68*, 248–254.
9. Cantril, Hadley, "General and Specific Attitudes," *Psychological Monographs*, No. 192, 1932.
10. Hebb, D. O., *The Organization of Behavior*. New York: John Wiley & Sons, 1949.
11. Allport, G. W., *The Nature of Prejudice*. Reading, Mass.: Addison-Wesley, 1954, Chapter 5.
12. ———, "Behavioral Science, Religion and Mental Health," *Journal of Religion and Health*, 1963, *2*, 193ff.
13. Clifford, John W., S.J., *In the Presence of My Enemies*. New York: W. W. Norton & Co., 1963.
14. Buber, Martin, *Between Man and Man*. Boston: Beacon Press, 1959, p. 78.
15. Frankl, V. E., *Man's Search for Meaning*. Boston: Beacon Press, 1963.
16. Boisen, A. T., *The Exploration of the Inner World*. New York: Harper & Bros., 1936.
17. Mowrer, O. H., *The Crisis in Psychiatry and Religion*. New York: D. Van Nostrand & Co., 1961.
18. Cf. Gendlin, E. T., in P. Worchel and D. Byrne (eds.), *Personality Change*. New York: John Wiley & Sons, 1964.

8

Behavioral Science, Religion, and Mental Health

ALTHOUGH THIS PAPER DEALS with varied oppositions and affinities between modern behavioral science and religion, its chief interest lies in its use of the concepts "extrinsic" vs. "intrinsic" religion. The former refers to the familiar utilitarian exploitation of religion to provide comfort, status, or needed crutches in one's encounters with life. The latter concept applies to the life that is wholly oriented, integrated, and directed by the master value of "intrinsic" religion. These concepts are here brought to bear on the relationship between religious orientation and mental health.

In Chapters 13 and 14 the same distinction becomes pivotal for illuminating the relationship between religion and ethnic prejudice in individual lives.

Originally this paper was given for the Academy of Religion and Mental Health at Boston College, and published in the *Journal of Religion and Health* in 1963, Vol. 2.

† † †

Any genuinely human life is psychologically marginal. It is at best a short span of years compressed between two oblivions, spent chiefly in wonderment, and terminated in mystery. To be human implies moments of delight and glimpses of happiness; but also it implies ordeals of suffering, discord of purposes, frequent defeat of self, and painful reconquest of self. A mentally ill person is one who, at least temporarily, has lost the battle. He regrets his past, abhors his present, and dreads his future. If we ourselves have not gone over this brink, we have been close enough to it to sympathize with those who have.

And such sympathy today is widespread. The many current researches in universities and clinics, frequently supported by the federal government through the National Institute of Mental Health, and the founding and rapid growth of the Academy of Religion and Mental Health with its various activities, including the publication of this *Journal*, are signs of a new understanding and tokens of hope. Our common aim is to fortify the human spirit so that it can withdraw from the brink and to help those who have fallen to regain their footing.

In a general way, we know what mental health requires. It requires that we learn to grow muscles where our injuries were. In the words of the Eighty-fourth Psalm, that man is blessed "who, going through the vale of misery, uses it for a well." One thing we have learned is that a full discussion of mental health requires a rich bilingualism. It requires both the poetic and prophetic metaphors of religion and the precise, hard grammar of science.

This bilingual approach to mental health is something new under the sun. A long-standing gap in communication is closing at last. Richard McCann reports on interviews with a sample of psychiatrists practicing in a large city. Although more than half of them say that they personally are not religious, yet "none is opposed to religion; none expresses the idea that the religious view of reality as such may create problems for his patients; and all welcome the assistance and support that religious affiliations provide for their patients."[1]

On the side of religion, there have sprung up in recent years nearly 400 programs for clinical pastoral training for the younger clergy. Centers for pastoral counseling are mushrooming. Chaplaincies in mental hospitals constantly increase in number. Protestant, Catholic, and Jewish faiths all share in these developments.[2] To be sure, the bickering between psychiatry and religion has not yet ended, but a growing sense of teamwork is evident. Each specialty has wisdom to bring; each now knows that it is handicapped without the aid of the other.

RELIGION: ITS MERITS AND LIMITATIONS

For many centuries, religion has held priority in the field. By tradition, the church and the synagogue are "therapeutic communities." Throughout the ages, they, more than other institutions, have concerned themselves with the major crises of life. By comparison, psychiatry and its correlative behavioral sciences are recent upstarts. True, the language of the Scriptures seems dated in spots. (But already the language of Kraepelin and Charcot also seems old fashioned to our ears.) Fashions in terminology should not deceive us. To say that a sufferer is "afflicted with unclean spirits" is not far from scientific truth.

With its eyes on eternal verities, religion has little difficulty accommodating modern conceptions of psychopathology. When we say that the mentally sick person is one who regrets his past, abhors his present, and dreads his future, religion deepens the issue by adding, "Yes, and I can provide forgiveness for the past, acceptable meaning for the present, and hope for the future." And when we say that mental health requires that we grow muscles where our injuries were, religion echoes, "Yes, our mental health is proportional to the weight of the burden that we can carry." In recent years, psychiatry has been discovering what religion has always maintained: that there is no cure apart from love. Thus do the concepts of therapy and of redemption fuse. Healing follows the path of redemptive love, whether human or divine.

But however modern in principle, religion in practice has many shortcomings. For one thing, churches and synagogues, as they grow in numbers and in grandeur, lose much of their character as therapeutic communities. While 97 per cent of the people profess some form of religious devotion in their lives and 95 per cent say they believe in God, only about 6 per cent of the believers, according to one study, ever take their problems to a clergyman. And hardly any who do so regard their problems as basically spiritual. Even from the clergy they seek chiefly secular help. And among patients in mental hospitals having chaplains, only a few (perhaps two and a half per cent) say that they have received major help from this ministry.[3] From such data we conclude that, as of today, church and synagogue fall short in dealing with lives in acute emotional crisis and in helping the sufferer define his problem in spiritual terms.

Another charge that can fairly be laid against some religion is its use of pathogenic appeals. In some of its forms, religion instills an abnormal degree of terror, injurious especially to sensitive children; it may arouse pathological feelings of guilt; it may inculcate superstition. Or at the other extreme, it may bring superficial happiness, offering only those things that serve as cheap ego-defenses, talismans against reality, medicated lozenges momentarily pleasant but ineffective against the deeper virus of evil. Such religious practices do not make for muscle building.

One final criticism: as of today, we have no firm evidence that religious people on the average are more mentally healthy than nonreligious people. What demographic differences there are indicate that income and education are far more important variables in mental health and illness than is personal religion— at least as personal religion is measured today (chiefly in terms of denominational affiliation).[4] But to this problem I shall soon return.

It is sometimes argued, of course, that religion should not be assessed as if it were merely a servant of hygiene. Its purpose is not to make people healthy, but to save their souls. Even if we grant the theological point involved, our criticism still holds. All religions teach compassion for sufferers here and now, whatever their conception of ultimate salvation may be.

Christ himself healed the sick and cast out demons. Religion does have a duty to foster wholeness of personality. When it does not do so, it can be justly criticized.

PSYCHIATRY: ITS MERITS AND LIMITATIONS

The great achievement of psychiatry and correlative branches of modern behavioral sciences lies in giving us an objective view of the human mind and its workings. Though they are still far from solving mental mysteries, a significant revolution has occurred in comparatively recent times. It was only a little more than a century ago that radical reformers (Pinel and Dorothea Dix among them) started to break down ancient superstitions concerning the nature of insanity.

It took countless ages for man to develop the detachment required to discover and utilize any of the truths of science. At first, man perceived the world in the light of personal advantage. All truth had to be immediately relevant to the exigencies of survival. Only gradually did a third-person (or objective) point of view become possible. Fire, weather, gravity, man came slowly to realize, obeyed laws not related to personal advantage. Eventually he learned the laws of levers, pumps, steam engines, atomic energy, and of health and disease. Only now at long last are the laws of mental illness and health being discovered. And even today, relatively few people know that such laws exist. Like the cave man of old, most of us still let personal advantage rule our perceptions in our social relationships. Others, we insist, are to blame; we are blameless. The other fellow is always wrong; I am always right. As Emerson said, "What is sin in others is experiment for us." Our strategies of rationalization, of denial, of psychic blindness, of projection, of self-exculpation still show that for us (as for the cave man) what is to our personal advantage is true. We have a long way to go before we are able to apply the same scientific detachment to matters of the mind (our own or our neighbor's) that we apply to the impersonal phenomena of nature. It is to the credit of psychiatry and behavioral science that they lead us forward and focus our attention concretely on wholesome practices in child training, attitude change, environmental reform, and psychotherapy.

But if psychiatry and behavioral science are headed in the right direction, they still for the most part stumble at thresholds. We are still ignorant concerning the etiology of most forms of mental distress. Therapy for the most part is still experimental. Although we are able to give relief, we know we are not yet at the root of the matter. We are still far from being able to fashion balanced and productive lives, even though we take an objective view of our troubles. We rightly ask, "After tranquilizers, what? After energizers, what? After electroconvulsive therapy, what? After psychoanalysis, what?"

Here religion enters its claim. When the psychiatrist says, "We must integrate this life," religion replies, "I am the potential integration you need. As a master sentiment, I am able to dominate the nerve network, gating all impulses to accord with my generic motivation; I can dwell deep in the solar plexus; I can knit fragments together; I reach to the roots. When Freud says that anxiety is the alpha and omega of neurosis, I say, 'No: the alpha and omega of neurosis is vanity. And vanity is sin.' "

Here we encounter the characteristic difficulty of bilingualism. Whenever psychiatry and social science employ the hard, precise grammar of science, religion is likely to enter a counterclaim. There is in all religion, says Gabriel Marcel, a "mysterious primacy." It is never a matter of objective propositions amenable to verification. By its very nature, religion demands our participation rather than proof or verification. Religion, being total, contains both us as observers and the objects and events we single out for critical inspection. Working within a religious frame, we cannot expect to objectify entirely the frame that contains us. For example, if we sense that all being is engulfed in divine love, we cannot step completely outside this frame and objectify or measure the operations of this love.

To make the point more concrete: mental patients sometimes complain that their psychiatrists seldom or never inquire concerning their religious faith. And yet the same patients often insist that their religious faith somehow envelops their lives. The psychiatrists' customary neglect of this factor is, in part no doubt, due to their own lack of personal religion. In part it is due to their habituation to the grammar of science. In either case, they fail to recognize the power of healing that lies in generic faith.

OTHER BEHAVIORAL SCIENCES

Thus it is difficult for many psychiatrists to deal adequately with the "mysterious primacy" of religion. It is equally difficult for many exponents of faith to accept the psychiatrist's grammar of science. The situation is further complicated by the existence of a third voice. Behavioral science agrees with psychiatry in speaking the grammar of science; but it agrees with religion in its desire to broaden the horizon of the therapeutic relationship as it exists in hospitals or consulting rooms.

One of the behavioral sciences is psychology as distinct from psychopathology. Can one study or aid a broken personality without a deep knowledge of normal personality? A patient who recovers from a breakdown does not progress to a new personality. He returns essentially to the personality he had prior to his illness. For this reason, the doctor should know the norm for his patient. And he should also know how normal people manage to deal with the evils that befall them. How is it that most of us succeed in growing muscles where our injuries were? (I venture to protest the fact that the great majority of psychiatrists in their course of training are exposed to nothing but psychoanalytic theory. However applicable it may be to some disordered syndromes, psychoanalysis is often a poor, or very partial, fit to lives of normal constitution.)

Sociological disciplines, too, have much to contribute. Ethnic tradition, culture, family pattern, social class all affect the incidence and course of mental illness and are potentially important factors in prevention. We are learning much about the context of treatment in mental hospitals, about the structure of hospitals as small societies, about the therapeutic and pathogenic behavior of hospital personnel, about halfway houses, about ward improvement meetings and group therapy.[5]

Instead of two major disciplines demanding teamwork in the interests of mental health, there are clearly three: religion, psychiatry, and social science. Their interrelations are only now being understood.

TWO FORMS OF THE RELIGIOUS SENTIMENT

Let us now return to an earlier point. I remarked that we are still ignorant concerning the relation, if any, between mental soundness and the religious sentiment in a given life. To my mind, this is one of two most pressing problems demanding research. The other problem concerns the evaluation of psychotherapy itself—all types of therapy. No one yet knows surely that psychiatric intervention has permanent beneficial effects beyond the course of nature left to itself. But neither have we proved that religion in a life is curative or preventive.

I should like to present a hypothesis worth testing. It is my contention that the concept "religion" is too broad for discriminating use. In reality, the religious sentiment varies enormously from person to person. In some it is fragmentary, superficial, even trivial; in others it is deep and pervasive, lockstitched into the whole fabric of being. The religious sentiment varies not only in depth and breadth, but also in its content and its mode of functioning. Indeed, since every personality is unique, I have argued elsewhere that the religious sentiment in every life must take a unique form.[6]

Still, for research purposes it is allowable to select one important dimension of variability. The dimension I have in mind is a continuum ranging from the type of religious sentiment that has only instrumental or extrinsic significance in a life to the type of sentiment that is itself a major motive in life, and thus has intrinsic value. The latter type serves itself alone; it is subordinate to no other motives. If we can locate people approximately on this continuum, and if we are able to establish suitable criteria for mental healthiness, we should then be able to find an answer to our question: Are some forms of the religious sentiment more therapeutic and preventive than others?

For brevity's sake, let us speak then of *extrinsic* and *intrinsic* religion. My hypothesis is that extrinsic religion is less therapeutic or preventive than is intrinsic religion.

Extrinsic religion. For many people, religion is a dull habit, or a tribal investment to be used for occasional ceremony, for family convenience, or for personal comfort. It is something to *use*, but not to *live*. And it may be used in a variety of ways: to improve one's status, to bolster one's self-confidence, to enhance one's income, to win friends, power, or influence. It may be used as a defense against reality and, most importantly, to provide a super-sanction for one's own formula for living. Such a sentiment assures me that God sees things my way, that my righteousness is identical with His. I see the nature of being as conforming to the facts of my particular being. Two pious aged sisters were quarreling. One said with asperity to the other, "The trouble with you, Jane, is that you lack the grace of God in your heart." The grace of God, it seems, is hers, not Jane's.

One hypothesis already successfully tested is that this utilitarian or extrinsic form of religiosity correlates positively with racial and ethnic bigotry that is unfortunately widespread among churchgoers.[7] There is no reason why the same measures used in this research on religion and prejudice should not be applied to research on religion and mental health.

In theological terms, the extrinsically religious person turns to God, but does not turn away from self. For this reason, his religion is primarily a shield for self-centeredness. Had Freud been more perceptive, he would have seen that it is only this kind of religion that resembles a neurosis. It defends against anxiety. As with the cave man, religious perceptions serve personal advantage.

In motivational terms, the extrinsic religious sentiment is not a driving or integral motive. It serves other motives: the need for security, the need for status, the need for self-esteem. In terms of developmental psychology, the formation is immature. Like Piaget's children, the possessor holds an egocentric view of the universe. Habit, custom, family tradition are not critically reevaluated and recentered into an adult outlook.

If you ask, "But isn't religion legitimately a source of comfort?" I reply, "Of course it is. But the comfort it supplies can never be on our own terms—only on *its* terms. The burden cannot be evaded, nor can it be trimmed down. It must be borne. The comfort comes with courageous acceptance of the burden."

Like all other defenses, and like all instrumental habits, extrinsic religion is in danger of breaking down when the cross-purposes of life grow too discordant. It is for this reason that my hypothesis does not expect extrinsic religion to be either preventive or therapeutic in the long run, for life has a way of shooting its poisoned darts through defensive armor.

Intrinsic religion. Our hypothesis holds that, though religion of the extrinsic variety may hinder mental health, religion of the intrinsic variety may help. Each of us has known lives that remain serene in spite of inner turmoil, courageous in spite of the shattering shafts of fate. We have also known religious people who, in spite of neurotic fragments in their own lives, manage somehow to maintain control of their sanity—apparently because of a generic and embracing and guiding religious motive.

Intrinsic religion is not an instrumental formation. That is to say, it is not primarily a means of handling fear, or a mode of conformity, or an attempted sublimation of sex, or a wish-fulfillment. Earlier in life it may have been all these things. But now these specific needs are not so much served by, as they are subordinated to, an overarching motive. Quandaries, predicaments, cross-purposes, guilt, and ultimate mysteries are handled under the comprehensive commitment. This commitment is partly intellectual, but more fundamentally motivational. It is integral, covering everything in experience and everything beyond experience; it makes room for scientific fact and emotional fact. It is a hunger for, and a commitment to, an ideal unification of one's life, but always under a unifying conception of the nature of all existence.

It is important to note that this conception of intrinsic religion has nothing to do with formal religious structure. There are intrinsic Catholics and extrinsic Catholics, intrinsic Protestants and extrinsic Protestants, intrinsic and extrinsic Jews, Moslems, and Hindus. It is for this reason that I would not expect to find denominational or sectarian differences in the incidence of mental illness. My prediction rather is that mental health will vary according to the degree to which adherents of any faith are intrinsic in their interpretation and living of their faith.

It should be noted that intrinsic religion, according to our hypothesis, cannot exist in order to be therapeutic or preventive. Intrinsic religion is not a mustard plaster. The sufferer can aim only at religion; he cannot aim at treatment. If he has deeply interiorized his religion, he will find sanity and soundness as a by-product. Such is our hypothesis.

I have already conceded that there are pathogenic strains in some religions, such as excessive terror, superstition, a built-in hostility to science, or a palliative defensiveness. But these pathogenic strains are not found in the great creeds of the world religions; rather they are extrinsic accretions that lead some worshipers away from the intrinsic possibilities of their faith. If I am not mistaken, most of the damage that religion does and most of the criticisms directed against it are related to these accretions. They aim to make religion easy and palatable, but they fall short of the total outlook of the creed in question.

SANITY IN WORLD SOCIETY

Our approach, being psychological, has been person-cen-
tered and needs, therefore, a certain enlargement. To seek
one's own mental health smacks of hypochondriasis. Hence
we ask a final question: "Can one be truly sound in mind unless one takes upon himself some of the redemptive duties in
the world today?"

Physical science has already made it possible for all men to
die together. Is it not the task of psychological and social
science to discover ways by which we can live together? If
we do not soon do so, the last human survivor may write the
epitaph: "Over the whole earth lie the irradiated ashes of
homo sapiens, the only species to have committed self-extinc-
tion. Man learned too late that his sapience, his pursuit of
private mental health, was fatally one-sided."

Not long ago an editorial in a Southern newspaper caught
my eye. Titled "Science Isn't God," the editorial opens with
the question:

> Is it possible, as has been proposed, that a new science
> could be created to keep society from committing suicide
> with nuclear weapons? Can a science of human survival be
> developed, or is one necessary?

The writer says "No."

> We do not need a new science of human survival. What
> we need is to use the solution for human conflicts and fail-
> ure handed down to us by Christ and the Christian churches.
> . . . Human nature, upon which human survival depends,
> can be changed for the better and controlled only from
> within by the promptings of conscience and faith in God.
> We do not need a science for survival; we need faith.

At first, I dismissed the piece as just one more item of religious obscurantism. Then there came to my mind what
Bertrand Russell said, although he himself is a salty foe of
religion: "An indispensable condition of survival," he wrote,

is "the kindly feeling toward others which religion has advocated."

The editorial writer and Bertrand Russell are right in saying that religion has given us the guideline for international amity just as it has for personal mental health. No one can doubt this fact.

But religion by itself, in this complex world, simply cannot specify the means. Indeed, throughout the ages religious authority has often combated every increment of technical knowledge gained through the study of astronomy, of evolution, of vaccination. Some religion has held to belief in witchcraft, to the demonic theory of mental disease, to bigotry. Always available to man were the miracles of antibiotics, heart surgery, atomic energy, electronics, and the objective techniques of psychotherapy and social science. But these latent miracles were not available until scientists diverged from theology and commenced in their own way "to think God's thoughts after Him."

The editorial writer denies that scientific miracles may lie ahead in the realm of human relations. It is inconceivable, he says, that the new science may some day help man to control his aggressive impulses, improve relations in industry, in neighborhoods, between nations and races, and eventually to weave a firmer texture into all human character.

Fortunately, such obscurantism is on the wane. Religion is beginning to realize that it needs to team firmly with psychiatry and all the behavioral sciences in order that its vision may find implementation. How to love one's neighbor (or one's enemy) effectively is a question not of goodwill alone, but of knowledge derived from psychological and social science. Furthermore, scientific exploration, critically employed and applied to oneself, can help to clarify, sift, and test the purity of the religious motive, so that it will become more and more an intrinsic possession of aspiring man.

May it not be that the health (or wholeness) of any system —whether it be personal, national, or international—can be the product only of concerted wisdom, wherein the insights of religion and behavioral science blend? May we not hope that the present bilingualism of religion and behavioral science—good so far as it goes—may eventually lose its duality and emerge as a universal language suited to a final theory and implementation of both individual health and planetary peace?

REFERENCES

1. McCann, R. V., *The Churches and Mental Health*. Report of the Joint Commission on Mental Illness and Health, No. 8. New York: Basic Books, 1962, p. 206.
2. *Ibid.*, Chapters 4 and 7.
3. *Ibid.*, pp. 79, 153, 211.
4. *Ibid.*, Chapter 12.
5. Among recent significant contributions are: Greenblatt, M., Levinson, D. J., Williams, R. H. (eds.), *The Patient and the Mental Hospital*, Glencoe: The Free Press, 1957; Caudill, W., *The Psychiatric Hospital as a Small Society*, Cambridge: Harvard University Press, 1958; Kramer, B., *Day Hospital*, New York: Grune & Stratton, 1962; King, S. H., *Perceptions of Illness and Medical Practice*, New York: Russell Sage Foundation, 1962.
6. Allport, G. W., *The Individual and His Religion*. New York: The Macmillan Co., 1950.
7. ———, *The Nature of Prejudice*. New York: Doubleday Anchor, 1958, Chapter 28. See also Allport, G. W., "Religion and Prejudice," Chapter 16 in *Personality and Social Encounter*. Boston: Beacon Press, 1960.

9

Values and Our Youth

OCCASIONALLY I have asked myself what bearing my theories may have on practical classroom teaching. This paper comes as close as any of my work, I think, to telling how I envisage the process of *becoming* in relation to what the teacher says or does (or can say and do) in the classroom.

After presenting the paper to various groups of teachers I arranged for its publication in *Teachers College Record* in 1961.

† † †

One aim of education is to make available the wisdom of the past and present so that youth may be equipped to solve the problems of the future. If this is so, then we have good grounds for a feeling of consternation concerning the adequacy of our present educational procedures. The reason is that in the immediate future, the youth of today will have to live in a world very unlike the world of the past from which our store of wisdom has been drawn.

SOME PROSPECTS

Think of the vastly changed nature of life in the future, for which we have little relevant wisdom from the past to call upon:

1. The new generation of students will have to face an ever increasing domination of life by science, by technology, and by automation. (One thinks of the story of two

cows grazing along the roadside. An immense milk truck passes with the painted legend: Pasteurized, Homogenized, Vitamin B Added. One cow turns to the other and says, "Makes you feel inadequate, doesn't it?")

2. The new generation will have to recognize the impossibility of living any longer in a state of condescension toward the colored peoples of the world (about three-quarters of the world's population). Centuries of comfortable caste discrimination and segregation are from here on impossible to maintain.

3. The coming generation will have to deal with a population explosion whose predicted magnitude staggers our imagination.

4. It will need a completer understanding of world societies and their marked differences in values. In the past, we could be politely ignorant of such places as Africa, Latin America, and Asia in a way that is no longer possible.

5. It will have to create a world government or, at least, an effective confederation to forestall the threat of thermonuclear war.

6. As if a planetary world view were not difficult enough to achieve, the coming generation may have to develop an interplanetary point of view. (I find this prospect especially alarming because we seem to be solving the problems of outer space before those of the inner space of mind, character, and values.)

It is no wonder that this preview of problems confronting our youth throws us educators into a state of self-scrutiny bordering sometimes on panic. Where can youth find the needed equipment? Are they sound enough in mind and morale?

Sometimes our dismay finds an outlet in gallows humor. They tell of the benevolent lady who saw a depressing specimen of the very young generation sprawled on the curb of a city street, swilling down cans of beer. Greatly shocked, she asked, "Little boy, why aren't you in school?" "Cripes, lady," he replied, "I'm only four years old."

And they tell the story of the London bobby. London police, we know, are well trained for social work, even for psychotherapy. This bobby's beat was Waterloo Bridge. He spotted a man about to jump over and intercepted him. "Come now," he said. "Tell me what is the matter. Is it money?" The man shook his head. "Your wife perhaps?" Another shake of the head. "Well, what is it then?" The would-be suicide replied, "I'm worried about the state of the world." "Oh, come now," said the bobby. "It can't be so bad. Let's walk up and down the bridge here and talk it over." Whereupon they strolled for about an hour discussing the state of the world, and then they *both* jumped over.

Humor helps us put our dilemma into sane perspective, but it does not solve the problem. The vague apprehension we feel has led to certain empirical studies of the values of today's youth, with results, alas, that are not reassuring.

ASSESSING VALUES

Not long ago, Professor Phillip Jacob undertook to survey[5] all available studies concerning the values held by college students. He found a marked uniformity among them. Fully three-quarters of the students were "gloriously contented, both in regard to their present day-to-day activity and their outlook for the future." Their aspirations were primarily for material gratifications for themselves and their families. They "fully accepted the conventions of the contemporary business society as the context within which they will realize their personal desires." While they will not crusade against segregation and racial injustice, they will accept nondiscrimination when it comes as a "necessary convention in a homogenized culture." They subscribe to the traditional virtues of sincerity, honesty, and loyalty, but are indulgent concerning laxity in moral standards. They normally express a need for religion, but there is a hollow quality in their beliefs. They do not desire to have an influential voice in public policy or government. Their sense of civic duty stops at the elementary obligation of voting. They predict another major war within a dozen years, but they say that international problems give them little concern and that they spend no time on them. Only a minority value their college education primarily in terms of its intellectual gains. They regard it as good because it gives them vocational preparation, social status, and a good time. Such is the flabby value-fiber that Jacob discovers among college students of today.

The picture becomes more vivid when viewed in cross-national perspective. James Gillespie and I, in a comparative study[3] of the values of college youth in ten nations, asked students to write their autobiographies of the future ("My life from now until the year 2000") and also gave them an extensive questionnaire. The instrument was translated into nine different languages.

In comparison with youth of other nations, young Americans are delightfully frank and open, unsuspicious and co-operative. Their documents had no literary affectation (and, I may add, little literary quality). But the most important finding was that within these ten nations, American students were the most self-centered, the most "privatistic" in values. They desired above all else a rich, full life for themselves, and showed little concern for national welfare or for the fate of mankind at large. The context of their outlook was private rather than public, passive rather than pioneer. The essential point is made clear by two excerpts, the first drawn from the autobiography of a Mexican girl, 18 years of age, and the second from a Radcliffe student of the same age:

> Since I like psychology very much, I wish, on leaving this school, to study it, specializing in it and exercising it as a profession. I shouldn't like to get married right away, although like any woman I am desirous of getting married before realizing all my aspirations. In addition, I should like to do something for my country—as a teacher, as a psychologist, or as a mother. As a teacher, to guide my pupils in the best path, for at the present time they need solid bases in

childhood in order in their future lives not to have so many frustrations as the youth of the present. As a psychologist, to make studies which in some way will serve humanity and my beloved country. As a mother, to make my children creatures who are useful to both their country and all humanity.

Now follows the Radcliffe document. Its flavor of privatism is unmistakable:

> Our summers will be spent lobster fishing on the Cape. Later we'll take a look at the rest of the country—California, the Southwest, and the Chicago Stockyards. I want the children, when they get past the age of ten, to spend part of the summer away from home, either at camp or as apprentices to whatever profession they may show an interest in. Finally, I hope we will all be able to take a trip to Europe, especially to Russia, to see what can be done about Communism.

Many critics have called attention to the same American value predicament. Our current social pattern, they say, is almost completely geared to one objective alone, namely a profitable, expanding production. To insure expanding production, there must be more and more consumption. Hence comes the expensive glamour of our advertising and its control of our mass media. The sole objective seems to be to stimulate the accretion of goods. Self-respect and status, as well as comfort, are acquired in this way. Someone has called our national disease "galloping consumption." Half a century ago, William James saw the peril and was much worried by what he called "the American terror of poverty." He saw there was truth in the jibes that other countries direct at our "materialism."

HOPE IN UNEASINESS

Now a high standard of living is not in itself an evil thing. All the world wants what we already have. But the single-minded pursuit of production and consumption has brought a dulling of other values. One consequence is symbolized by the scandal of rigged quiz programs. These were in the service of advertising, which in turn was in the service of a profitable expanding economy. Another consequence is the accumulated froth of our TV, radio, and movies. Another is the widely discussed conformity of the organization man, as well as the futile rebellion of the beats. An especially peppery critic, Paul Goodman,[4] has shown that the starved lives of juvenile delinquents and of young people caught in the organizational grind are at bottom much alike. Both are attracted to the cult of easiness and aspire to nothing more than amiable mediocrity. Both styles of living fail to prepare youth for the problems that lie ahead for themselves and for the nation.

A somewhat vulgar story seems to me to summarize all this mordant criticism. Moses, a stalwart leader of the old school, said to the Israelites in Egypt, "Load up your camels, bring along your asses, and I'll lead you to the promised land." By contrast, the modern American prophet seems to urge, "Light up your Camels, sit on your asses, and I'll bring you the promised land."

All this familiar criticism is irritating; yet the fact that it flourishes is a hopeful sign. We suspect it may be too harsh. I am inclined to think so. It is rash indeed to indict a whole generation. At worst, Jacob's gloomy picture held for three-quarters of the college students studied, but not at all for a vital and far from negligible minority. And even though the gloomy generalizations have some truth in them, are the assets given fair attention? I myself have some favorable impressions, although one man's view is not reliable. But youth today appears to enjoy a certain freedom and flexibility that was not common in the more rigid days of our parents and grandparents. I even have the impression that there is less neuroticism among students now than among those of a generation ago. What is more, young people, I find, are not blind to the world changes that are occurring. Their apparent repression of the challenge is due largely to their bewilderment concerning proper paths to take. (And one has the feeling that our own statesmen in Washington are no less bewildered.) All in all, these are hopeful signs that should not be overlooked.

VALUES AND THE SCHOOL

Another hopeful sign is the fact that many teachers are asking, "What can we do to be helpful?" They know, and we all know, that the ability of the school to give training in values is limited. For one thing, the home is vastly more important. A home that infects the child with galloping consumption, that encourages only canned recreation and has no creative outlets, can only with difficulty be offset by the school. Another limitation lies in the fact that the school is ordinarily expected to mirror current social values and to prepare the child to live within the existing frame. It is an unusual school system and an unusual teacher who even *wish* to transcend the current fashions of value.

But assuming that we have an unusual school system and an unusual teacher, what values shall they elect to teach? If they do not choose to follow the prevailing fashions, what standards shall they follow? The ancient Romans were fond of asking, "Who will judge the judges?" and "Who will guard the guardians?" Can the guardians turn perhaps to standard discussions of "the aims of education"? Such discussions are numerous, abstract, and often dull. Their weakness, I feel, is their effort to formulate absolute goals, vistas of abstract perfection. The result is often a series of platitudes or generalizations so broad as to be unhelpful. Of course we want to develop "good citizenship"; we certainly want to "free the child's intellect." These and all other absolutes need to be reduced to concrete, stepwise processes before they can guide us in the strategy of teaching values.

The teacher must start with the situation as he or she finds it and in concrete instances sharpen the value-attributes of the lesson being taught. To a considerable extent, these value-attributes can be drawn from the codified wisdom of our nation. We cannot neglect the value of profitable production and high living standards, for all our vocational and professional education contribute to this end. But the codified wisdom of our unique society extends far beyond the obsession of today. Our values include also such matters as respect for civil liberties. Does the school accent this value? They include approval for individual initiative, for philanthropy, for compassion. And they imply much concerning civic duties that are the reciprocal of civic rights. What must we do to deserve our precious cornucopia of freedom? Vote? Yes. But voting does no good unless the voter is informed above the stereotyped level of the mass media. He must also pay taxes willingly. Do schools and colleges teach the young to pay a glad tax? I wonder. To me the most disturbing finding in *Youth's Outlook on the Future* lay in the elaborate talk about one's right to a rich, full life and in the almost total silence regarding one's duties.

I am saying that in the first instance teachers should choose the values they teach from the whole (not from a part) of our American ethos. Deep in our hearts we know, and most of the world knows, that our national values, derived, of course, from Judeo-Christian ethics, are about the finest mankind has yet formulated. In no sense are these values out of date, nor will they go out of date in the world of tomorrow. Yet many of them are badly rusted. Unless they are revitalized, however, our youth may not have the personal fortitude and moral implements that the future will require.

THE LARGER ANCHOR

Excellent as the American Creed is as a fountainhead of values, it does not contain them all. It says nothing explicitly, for example, about intellectual curiosity. And yet surely schools exist to augment this value. The most severe indictment of our educational procedures I have ever encountered is the discovery that a sizable percentage of graduates of our colleges after completing their formal education never afterward read a single book.

There are other important values that are not spelled out in our American Creed. I am thinking of those details of human relationships that make all the difference between boorishness and brotherhood in the human family. As our population increases, it becomes more and more important to teach the elements of the new science of human relations which go far toward smoothing the roughness of common life by leading us to respect effectively the integrity of the other fellow. I recall a teacher of English whose class was studying *The Merchant of Venice*. She turned a wave of incipient anti-Semitism in her class to a sound lesson in values. Shylock, she explained, was like the resentful, self-seeking portion of every person's nature. We are all potential Shylocks. But while self-love is prominent in all of us, we are so constructed that it need not be sovereign in our natures.

To return for a moment to the relation between home and school—the former, as I have said, is far more important. Recognizing this fact, some people say, "Well, let's leave the teaching of values to the home and to the church. Schools can't do much of anything about the matter."

This position is untenable. If the school does not teach values, it will have the effect of denying them. If the child at school never hears a mention of honesty, modesty, charity, or reverence, he will be persuaded that, like many of his parents' ideas, they are simply old hat. As they grow toward adolescence, children become critical of the teaching of both parents and the church. They are in a questioning stage. If the school, which to the child represents the larger outside world, is silent on values, the child will repudiate more quickly the lessons learned at home. He will also be thrown onto peer values more completely, with their emphasis on the hedonism of teen-age parties or on the destructiveness of gangs. He will also be more at the mercy of the sensate values peddled by movies, TV, and disk jockeys. What is more, some homes, as we have said, give no fundamental value training. In such a case, it is *only* in the school that the child has any chance at all of finding ethical anchorage.

This brings us to the hardest question: How does the teacher, the instructor, the professor, handle his assignment in the classroom? How is it possible to teach values, including the value of intellectual curiosity?

THE MEANING OF VALUE

Before tackling this question, we must pause to define what we mean by value. You will recognize that I am using the term psychologically, not in its objective philosophical sense. Values, as I use the term, are simply *meanings perceived as related to self*. The child experiences value whenever he knows that a meaning is warm and central to himself. Values, to borrow Whitehead's term, are "matters of importance" as distinct from mere matters of fact.

So much for definition. Now the hard-pressed teacher is given a solid substantive curriculum to teach. The curriculum in its original state consists of mere matters of fact. And on the number of facts absorbed the pupil's standing depends. It takes virtually all of a teacher's time to convey factual information and grade the pupil on his achievement. There is little time left to transmute these matters of fact into matters of importance, let alone teach all of the moral and social values we have thus far been discussing.

The curriculum itself is not, and should not be, a direct aid. Prescribed instruction in values would be laughed out of court. We have recently been bumped by Sputnik headforemost into core subjects. Get on with science, mathematics, language! Away with courses in folk-dancing, personal adjustment, and fudge-making! I agree that value-study has no place in curriculum planning, but not because it is a frivolous subject—rather, because it is a subject too hard and too subtle for curriculum makers.

Education for values occurs only when teachers teach what

they themselves stand for, no matter what their subject is. If I were to write a treatise on the teaching of values, I would give most of my emphasis to the moral pedagogy that lies in a teacher's incidental comments, to the *obiter dicta*. The hard core is central, but the hard core has a penumbra of moral significance. I mentioned the teacher of English who made a value-lesson out of Shylock. I recall also my college professor of geology who paused in his lecture on diatom ooze to say to us, "Others would not agree with me, but I confess that whenever I study diatoms, I don't see how anyone can doubt the existence of God because the design and behavior of these protozoa are so marvelous." Is it not interesting how we all recall the *obiter dicta* of our teachers, the penumbra of value they point out to us, surrounding the hard-core data? We remember them better than the subject matter itself.

Why does the student remember them so well? No current theory of learning seems able to tell us. I suspect it is because values, being matters of importance to the self, are always warm and central and ego-involved and therefore claim priority on our attention. The child, being value-ripe, cannot help being impressed when the teacher betrays excitement and enthusiasm for a mode of thought or for the content of the subject being studied. True, the youngster does not, and should not, adopt the teacher's values ready-made; but the teacher's self-disclosure leads the student to self-discovery.

What wouldn't we give if we could develop intellectual ardor in every child for hard-core subjects? Why is it that for most pupils arithmetic, spelling, physics, remain forever dull matters of fact and never become a meaning perceived as related to the self? One reason, I think, is that the weary teacher fails to convey his own sense of the importance of the subject to the student. If he did so, he would, as I have said, at least fix attention upon the value-potentiality of the subject.

Another reason perhaps is that not all of a teacher's *obiter dicta* are wholesome. Some, indeed, may be deeply damaging, though the teacher may be innocent of any such intent. Sometimes we hear incidental (but still attitude-forming) remarks like this one: "All right now, children. You have had a good time playing at recess; now settle down to your English lesson." Play is recognized as a matter of joyful importance. English, the teacher is saying in effect, is a mere routine matter of fact.

VALUES AND LEARNING

I think our educational psychology has been mostly wrong about the process of learning—or perhaps not so much wrong as woefully incomplete. At the beginning of his learning career, a young child cannot, of course, be expected to feel adult enthusiasm for the intellectual content of his studies. He does his work in the first instance to avoid a scolding or because he has a habit of obeying instructions. Soon he finds added incentive. The teacher—really in the role of mother—gives praise and love ("Susan, I am proud of you"). There is a great deal of such dependency in the learning situation. Love and social reward (as well as some fear of punishment) sustain the processes of attention and retention. When the child puts forth intellectual effort, he does so in order to obtain a gold star, commendation, or other symbols of love.

All these incentives are extraneous to the subject matter. The youngster does not learn it because it is a matter of importance. When he leaves school or college, he loses these extraneous supports. He finds his love relations directly; they are no longer a reward for intellectual effort. Hence, intellectual apathy sets in, and, distressing to say, no further books are read.

In such a case as this, intellectual curiosity was never tied to independence, only to extraneous supports. At some point in the schooling—and the earlier the better—intellectual activity should become not a secondhand but a firsthand fitting to the sense of self. At the beginning, all learning must be tied, perhaps, to specific reinforcements; but if the dependency is long continued, authentic curiosity fails to develop.

It would be going too far to put the blame for intellectual apathy onto our current teaching of educational psychology. Yet I am inclined to feel somewhat punitive about this matter. Psychology has not yet settled down to the problem of transforming matters of fact—whose acquisition current learning theories explain fairly well—into autonomous matters of importance—which they do not explain at all.

Our emphasis has been on learning by drill and by reinforcement. Such "habit acquisition" receives all the emphasis. But the learning theory involved postulates a continuing dependency relation (extraneous reinforcement). When the relation terminates, the habits of study simply extinguish themselves. I am surprised, therefore, that stimulus-response psychologists do not see this consequence of their own theory. Insofar as teachers employ an educational psychology of this order, they are not likely to break the dependency relation, which belongs properly only to the earlier stages of schooling.

Matters of importance, I strongly believe, are not acquired by drill or by reinforcement. They are transformations of habits and skills from the "opportunistic" layer of personality into the ego-system itself.[1] Once inside the ego-system, these habits and skills turn into true interests and utilize the basic energy, the basic spontaneity, that the organism itself possesses. They are no longer sustained as "operant conditionings" by outside rewards. The interest, now being the very stuff of life itself, needs no outer supports.

FUNCTIONAL AUTONOMY

I have called this process of transforming means into ends, of changing extrinsic values into intrinsic values, *functional autonomy*. Concerning this concept, I am often asked two questions: How do you define "functional autonomy, and how does functional autonomy come about"?

For a definition, I offer the following: Functional autonomy refers to any acquired system of motivation in which the tensions involved are no longer of the same kind as the antecedent tensions from which the acquired system developed. (If this definition seems too technical to be immediately helpful, see Chapter 10 of *Pattern and Growth in Personality*[2] for a more extended treatment of functional autonomy.) To answer the question of how functional autonomy comes about requires a more extended and technical discussion. I can only hint at the direction of my answer. Neurologists are gradually discovering a basis for what I would call "perseverative functional autonomy." I refer to the "self-sustaining circuits," "feedback mechanisms," and "central motive states" that are now commonly recognized to exist in the nervous system. This line of discovery, I find, provides a partial answer to the question. But I believe we have to go further and call on the concept of self. Values, we have said, are meanings perceived as related to the self. Functional autonomy is not a mere perseverative phenomenon; it is, above all, an ego-involved phenomenon. Besides admitting an opportunistic layer to personality, which is the exclusive concern of most current theories of learning, we have no choice but to admit also a "propriate" layer. It is in this layer that all matters of importance reside.

The goal of the educator, then is to shift the content of the subject he teaches from the opportunistic (matter of fact) layer to the propriate. But there is no sure-fire, mechanical strategy to use. The best general rule, one that John Dewey saw clearly, is to strive ceaselessly to integrate routine matters of fact into the growing experience system of the child himself. It would take a long treatise to specify various detailed strategies of teaching that help achieve this goal.

Let me focus on only one aspect of this topic, upon a common mistake that teachers make. I myself am a continual offender. It is to present students with our own carefully thought out conclusions when they themselves lack the raw experience from which these conclusions are fashioned.

This particular error is inherent, for example, in the lecture system. Instead of lecturing on comparative religion, for instance, it would be much better to require all students to attend services of worship that are unfamiliar to them. If raw experience is present, then perhaps a lecture may be effective. Much of the intellectual apathy we complain about is due to our fault of presenting conclusions in lieu of firsthand experience. To us, our well-chiseled conclusion, summing up a long intellectual struggle with a problem of knowledge or of value, seems like a beautiful sonnet. To the student, it may be gibberish.

The fallacy of giving conclusions holds both for subject matter and for values. A lad of 15 cannot profit from the fully fashioned philosophy of life of a man of 50. To register at all, a statement about values must fall precisely on his present growing edge.

Teaching, then, is not the art of offering conclusions, however hard won and valid they may be. No teacher can forcibly enter the students' proprium and plant a functionally autonomous motive. He can at best open channels of experience and, by his *obiter dicta*, sometimes lead the student to see the value-potential in the experience.

The theory of personality that we need to guide a more fully developed educational psychology will teach us something important about our basic verb "to educate." It will show us that only at the outset of learning is it a transitive verb. By drill, by reward, by reinforcement, the teacher does indeed educate the child—in matters of fact. But true maturity comes only when the verb is reflexive. For in matters of importance, where values lie, the growing individual alone can educate himself.

REFERENCES

1. Allport, G., *Becoming*, New Haven: Yale University Press, 1955.
2. ———, *Pattern and growth in personality*, New York: Holt, Rinehart, & Winston, 1961.

3. Gillespie, J., & G. Allport, *Youth's outlook on the future*, New York: Random House, 1955.
4. Goodman, P., *Growing up absurd*, New York: Random House, 1960.
5. Jacob, P., *Changing values in college*, New York: Harper, 1957.

IO

Crises in Normal Personality Development

THE RAW MATERIAL for this paper comes directly from students' autobiographical essays. (Over the years, I confess, I have leaned heavily upon this captive source of data. In several areas my research has been aided by such personal documents. I am thinking especially of the fields of religious attitudes, prejudice, youths' outlook on the future, as well as personal crises. I am grateful to these candid and cooperative captives.)

Like Chapter 9, this paper has a practical purpose and has been discussed especially with groups of college guidance specialists. It appeared in *Teachers College Record* in 1964.

† † †

There is one trick every teacher knows: When trapped in a state of ignorance throw the question back to the class. Without suspecting the teacher's predicament, bright students will often rescue him.

This is the strategy I employed to learn something about crises in normal personality development. I passed along the assignment to my class of 100 captive undergraduates, and they obligingly provided me, through their own autobiographical writing, with the insights that I articulate now. Parenthetically, let me say that in my opinion no teacher or counselor has the right to require intimate autobiographical documents from students. Yet when given a completely free choice, the large majority will choose to write in the autobiographical vein. For the few who would find the experience too threatening, it should not be prescribed.

INFLUENCE OF TEACHERS

First I shall report a minor investigation related to our main topic. I asked the hundred students, mostly sophomores and juniors, four questions with the results reported here. My first question was "Approximately how many different teachers at school and college have you had up to the present stage of your education?" The 100 respondents mentioned a total of 4,632 teachers. The three remaining queries were concerned with varying degrees of influence exercised by the teachers on the development of these students. With the percentages indicated as having played formative roles in student lives, the questions and their answers were as follows:

> How many teachers had a very strong or powerful influence on your intellectual or personal development? (8.5 per cent)
> How many others would you say had a reasonably strong, well-remembered influence? (14.8 per cent)
> How many do you remember only vaguely, or who seem to have had no substantial influence on your development? (76.7 per cent)

We are immediately struck by the fact that more than three-quarters of the teachers are remembered only vaguely and are credited with no appreciable influence, whether intellectual or personal. As teachers, we all know the shock of discovering how little impact we have had. A former student of mine brightened my day by remarking, "Years ago I took a course with you, but all I can remember about it is that the textbook had a blue cover." He grinned pleasantly while I shuddered inwardly.

Only about eight per cent of teachers are reported as having a very strong influence, and about 15 per cent are credited with a less strong but well-remembered influence. Another way of stating this finding is to say that the average teacher (assuming all teachers are equally effective) "gets through" to less than a quarter of the class, and exerts a really strong influence on not more than one student in ten.

VARIETIES OF INFLUENCE

Asked to tell when and in what way they were influenced the students give us three facts of special interest. First, about half of all their examples deal with experiences of intellectual awakening. For example,

> She encouraged me to read poetry and drama beyond the class assignment.
>
> In chemistry the instructor asked us why bubbles appeared overnight in a water glass. When we said we had never wondered about that, he told us that everyone must question even the most common and seemingly trivial things.

And about half of the examples deal with personal development:

> She made me see that others did not judge me as harshly as I was judging myself.
>
> He had so much warmth and humanity that I wanted to be like him.
>
> She seemed tough and disagreeable, but was so kind and helpful to me that I realized I must think twice before passing judgment on anyone.

A second insight, based on the large array of illustrative incidents, reveals the remarkably *casual* nature of the influence. In hardly any case could the teacher or counselor have known that what he was saying at a given moment would make a lasting impression upon the growing mind and character of the student. Elsewhere[1] I have argued that in teaching values and attitudes it is not the deliberately adopted curriculum that is effective; it is rather the *obiter dicta*, the parenthetical remark, the "little true things," and above all the example of the teacher that count. And what holds for teachers no doubt holds for the counselor, too.

Finally, and most relevant to my topic, is the finding that in elementary school there are few remembered influences of special strength. Apparently development is gradual at this time, and the teacher does not often bring a sudden and traumatic experience of "dawn" to the pupil. Only 12 per cent report any strong or even appreciable teacher influence in elementary school. Fully 88 per cent of the reports date the occurrences in high school (58 per cent) or in college (30 per cent, with the college years still incomplete).

So it is in middle and late adolescence where the role of the teacher is most vivid to the student. It is in this period, according to Erikson,[4] that the identity crisis is in the ascendance. The young person seems to be moving from past childhood into present adulthood in a jerky manner. Development is not continuous like a hill; rather, it is episodic like a flight of stairs. It is this episodic or crisis character of development that brings both challenge and opportunity to the guidance officer.

NATURE OF CRISIS

What precisely is a "crisis"? It is a situation of emotional and mental stress requiring significant alterations of outlook within a short period of time. These alterations of outlook frequently involve changes in the structure of personality. The resulting changes may be progressive in the life or they may be regressive. By definition, a person in crisis cannot stand still; that is to say, he cannot redact his present traumatic experience into familiar and routine categories or employ simple habitual modes of adjustment. He must either separate himself further from childhood and move toward adulthood, or else move backward to earlier levels of adjustment which may mean becoming disorganized, dropping out of school, escaping from the field, developing hostilities and defenses, and in general becoming a thorn in the flesh of the teacher, the parent, the counselor, the dean, and occasionally of the police. Sometimes, following a crisis, the adolescent will become stabilized anew after four or five weeks of severe disorganization; but in many cases the trauma retards development for a year or more, and may even leave a lifelong scar.

Turning now to my data, drawn from college undergraduates, we ask first about the phenomenology of crisis. What does it "feel" like to the student? Common is a sense of numbness and apathy. Upon entering college, the youth finds fewer strict role-prescriptions than at home. He is no longer tied to his domestic filial role, to the highly structured routine of high school, to his siblings, to his church connections, to his teen-age subcultures. He has left his possessions behind—his stamp collection, his television, his girl friends, his boy friends. All his familiar roles are in suspension. As one student writes,

> The complete freedom of college is itself a crisis. For the first time I live in close contact with people who are not members of my family. They don't even resemble people I have known before. They have different opinions, different origins, and different emotions. I feel numbed by it all.

Interestingly enough, this sense of hollowness does not necessarily have its maximum effect during the freshman year. The excitement of new scenes and especially frequent correspondence with and visits back to the hometown keep the silver cord intact. The student feels that he should prove to his parents, teachers, friends, that he can master the college environment and thus please them and win their approval as he has done in the past. The impending crisis has not yet overwhelmed him (or her—for what I am saying is as true for college girls as for boys).

It is the sophomore year that seems (from my data) to be the year of crisis *par excellence*. Suddenly it becomes no longer tolerable to live one's life for the edification of people "back home." The time has come for the child of the past to be separated once and for all from the adult of the present. Here are typical phenomenological statements of this stage of the crisis:

> I feel I have been dragged into something against my will.
> I feel like a rat in a maze.
> I want to be a law unto myself, but cannot.
> It seems suddenly that the decisions I make must be valid for the rest of my life.

> To shake off parental norms and values seems to me the
> most important thing I must do.

The life of the past and the life of the future seem suddenly
to be at cross purposes. There is often an intolerable feeling
of suspended animation. Recrystallization is not yet possible.
The youth is waiting still to make a choice of careers, a suitable marriage, and to find an integrative philosophy of life
which his diverse college courses are too discordant to supply.

APATHY AND ANXIETY

It is small wonder that apathy and a paralysis of will often
occur. But apathy is only a mask for anxiety. The whole
framework of life is disturbed. Whereas the majority of students contrive gradually to build a new framework in spite of,
or perhaps because of, the goals of anxiety, yet a large minority cannot cope with the situation unaided.

From my data, I would estimate that three-quarters are able
to take the progressive road in creating their new frame of
existence. About one-quarter cannot immediately do so. Proof
of this point is that the dropout rate during undergraduate
years is surprisingly high—over 20 per cent at Harvard, about
three-quarters of the cases representing voluntary withdraw-
als.[3] The dropouts present a special problem of guidance.
Blaine and McArthur[3] write,

> The drop-outs as a group ultimately do quite well if prop-
> erly handled. We attempt to establish a relationship, how-
> ever brief or tenuous, with these students, not so much to
> prevent their leaving school, but rather in the hope of giving
> them some insight into the determinants of their difficulties
> so that their dropping out can be ultimately converted into a
> meaningful constructive experience instead of mere failure.

After a year or two of constructive work elsewhere, the majority of voluntary dropouts return to college and graduate.
But they could not have met their crisis by remaining in the
environment that was the context of their conflict.

The regressive road is surprisingly common. Among eventual dropouts, but also among other students, we find such self-destroying behavior as quitting classes, a compulsion to do trivial things, playing bridge until four A.M., drinking bouts, feelings of unreality, fugues, and general debauchery. The candid documents received startle me a bit by the extent of plain juvenile delinquency among my innocent-appearing students:

> One student finding himself unable to handle his conflicts over choice of career and over friction with his roommate, indulged in plagiarism on a term paper in such a way that he would be caught and forcibly separated from college. In this case a wise instructor, catching him in the transgression, turned the occasion into constructive counseling, forgave the deed, and put the lad onto the progressive rather than regressive road.

Here I venture a theoretical digression. The problem, as I see it, is one of interiorizing motivation. To put it in a student's words: "I am fed up with having everybody else cheer me on. I want to work to please myself rather than others, but I don't know how to do it." This plaintive statement points to a serious dilemma in our educational process. In school, the child is rewarded and punished by good grades and bad grades. Even in college, As and Bs are pats on the back, Ds and Fs are punishments. To gain love, the student must read books and toe the academic line. Finally, he obtains his degree (which is a symbol of academic love) and is freed from this external form of motivation. What then happens?

We know that a shockingly high percentage of college graduates rarely or never read another book after receiving their bachelor's degree. Why should they? Their love now comes from their employer, their wife, their children, not from the approval of parents and teachers. For them, intellectual curiosity never became a motive in its own right. External rewards are appropriate props in early childhood. But we educators, being limited by current inadequate theories of

learning, do not know how to help the student free himself
from the props of reward and develop a functionally autonomous zeal for learning. With our slavish dependence on reinforcement theory, I think it surprising that we arouse as much
internal motivation as we do. In any event, we cannot be proud
of the many educational cripples who after graduation, lacking the routine incentive of college, sink into intellectual
apathy.

CRISIS AREAS

The counselor or teacher, of course, cannot wait for better
theories of learning. He is confronted here and now with
crises in the concrete. Four areas of conflict, judging from my
data, are especially common.

Intellectual crises. First, there are students whose problem
is one of intellectual malplacement. Among my cases, a large
number report that in primary and secondary school they
were too bright for their class. The penalty is one of boredom
lasting down into college work, which they still do not find
challenging enough for their abilities. At the same time, double promotions in elementary and high school are not a solution. To be placed with older children often creates social
difficulties far more serious than boredom. In fact, the evil
consequences reported from double promotion are so numerous that we should challenge this particular solution of the
bright child's dilemma.

The opposite type of intellectual crisis is also common. It
is the deep disturbance that often results in college from intensified competition. It is statistically impossible for most students to maintain the same relative superiority in college that
they enjoyed in high school. While this fact does not trouble
the majority, it is a critical experience for those who depend
on scholarship aid or who frame their self-image almost entirely in terms of scholarly preeminence. They are suffering
a severe narcissistic wound.

Specific inferiorities. A second area of crisis is the old, familiar "inferiority complex." Besides the sense of intellectual inferiority just described, we encounter deep disturbance due to physical handicaps or to plain physical appearance, with resulting shyness, loneliness, and misery. To be poor at athletics creates a crisis for males, probably more acute in high school than in college. To be a member of a minority group likewise creates an inevitable crisis somewhere along the line. Here again I suspect the major adjustments and defenses are prepared before the college age. Occasionally, the inferiority concerns guilt due to moral lapses. One student is still haunted by her dishonesty which enabled her to pass a certain course three years ago. She has felt miserable ever since about this critical experience and badly needs a means of expiation.

In this connection we may speak of religious crises. While they are uncommon in my sample, Havens[6] estimates that at any given time 12 per cent of college students have a critical concern, and sometimes acute crises, due to their religious conflicts. I suspect the concern is even more widespread, but since it pertains to one's whole ground of being, it is seldom configurated as a specific crisis at a given moment of time.

Another area, seldom mentioned but surely important, is the ideological crisis of modern society as a whole. Youth is inevitably worried, as are adults, by our uncertain future. Elsewhere I have discussed the withdrawal of American youth from their social and political context.[5] Both the earlier and present data show an almost exclusive concern among American youth with their own lives. Compared with autobiographies of youth in other cultures, the American documents are far more self-centered, more privatistic. They are too baffled to articulate their distress, and so take refuge in their private concerns.

SEX AND FAMILY

Sex conflicts. Needless to say, our candid discussions of crises frequently, in fact usually, report acute sex conflicts. Extremely common are breakups in boy-girl relationships which are usually taken as a disaster only slightly less fatal than the end of the world. Such breakups are so recently experienced that college students do not realize that they will, in spite of their present feelings, eventually make a good recovery.

We should face the fact that at least in the early years of college life crises in the sexual sphere are for the most part frankly genital in their reference. The biological drive is so powerful that the youth is concerned with it almost by itself. Its integration into mature love, into marriage, into career plans, into an embracing philosophy of life, exceeds his present capacity. He is likely to think that genitality by itself is maturity. Sexual gratification is frankly the aim, often with devastating consequences. At this stage of development, the students have much to say about sex and little to say about mature love.

Family conflicts. I have left until last the most pervasive area of conflict and crisis. I am referring, of course, to the situation that exists between every adolescent and his parents. It is not enough to say that adolescent rebellion against the parents is the rule. Of course it is; but my documents show that the whole history of the relationships from the time of earliest memories is important. Almost any irregularity in normal family life is felt bitterly and may trouble a student even into adulthood. A mother who is neglectful or self-centered, or perhaps overpossessive and neurotic, leaves traumatic traces in the child's life. A father who is ineffectual and weak, or cruel, or absent (if only for wartime service) leaves the child with a lasting feeling of protest.

One document of unusual maturity notes that many college students seem to need their parents as scapegoats. They find it comfortable to blame parents for their own shortcomings. Perceiving that their parents are not all-powerful, all-wise, and all-perfect, they can say, "Well, no wonder I am having a hard time growing up; they didn't raise me right." Thus, an adolescent, having no genuine ground for complaint, may yet soak himself in self-pity, not being mature enough to relate his restricted image of his parents to the totality of human nature—not yet ready to appreciate the fact that his parents, considering human limitations, may have done a good job. Even if the job was not especially good, the adolescent seems not yet able to appreciate his parents' good intentions as an important value in their own right. From talking with many parents, I hazard the hypothesis that normally it is not until the age of 23 that a child encounters his parents on a mature, adult-to-adult basis.

This brief account of crises emanating from the parent-child relationship leads me to a final point. My students were required to discuss their crises from the point of view of personality theory. They were free to employ any of the theories they were studying in my course. Most of them took Freud. (I may add that the reason was not because Freud was their instructor's favorite author.)

THE CONDITIONS OF THEORY

Now my observation is this: Their Freudian interpretations seemed to fit well if and when the family situation in early life was disturbed. When the father was absent or ineffectual, when the mother was notably aggressive, when there was deliberate sex stimulation within the family—in such cases, it seems that the Oedipal formula provides a good fit, together with all its theoretical accoutrements of identification, superego conflict, defense mechanisms, castration threats, and all the rest.

When, on the other hand, the family life is reasonably normal and secure, a Freudian conceptualization seems forced and artificial. If we say, by way of rough estimate, that 60 per cent of the students try a Freudian conceptualization of their own cases, about 10 per cent turn out to be wholly convincing and theoretically appropriate. The remaining 50 per cent appear to be somehow contrived and badly strained.

I am wondering whether the same ratio might be applicable to cases that come to counselors. If a counselor or a therapist approaches every client or patient with the preconceived belief that his life must fit a Freudian frame of conceptualization, he may win in a minority of the cases, but lose in the majority.

Even where a Freudian approach is clearly justified, exclusive adherence to it may distract the counselor from many significant developments within the life—for example, from the present functional significance of religious and aesthetic values, from the competence and interests that extend beyond the neurotic core, from the client's conscious plans for the future, and from his "will to meaning" and existential concern with life as a whole.

Every person concerned with guidance, or for that matter with teaching, needs as background some general theory of the nature of human personality.[2] Our tendency, I fear, is to draw our theories from the realm of illness and deviance. It is somehow tempting to apply psychiatric rubrics to all personalities, for psychiatric rubrics are vivid, incisive, dramatic, and easy. Our conceptual banners bear such sloganized concepts as Oedipal complex, character disorder, identity diffusion, schizoid, acting out, and maybe an array of dimensions drawn from the Minnesota Multiphasic Personality Inventory. All such concepts, of course, have their proper place. But personality theory for guidance and teaching needs also to be woven of less lurid fabrics.

Youth, whatever neurotic threads may lie in his nature, is busy with his realistic perceptions, with his gradual learning and quiet coping, with the slow extension of selfhood, with noncritical failures and successes, with developing a generic conscience and a personal style of life. Even in the throes of crisis, he seeks in undramatic ways to consolidate his gains and continue on the path of becoming. A theory of personality adequate to undergird the art of guidance will keep such nondramatic facts in mind. Crises in normal personality development are important, but so too is the slow growth of each youth's unique style of life.

REFERENCES

1. Allport, G. W., "Values and our youth," *Teach. Coll. Rec.*, 1961, *63*, 211–219.
2. ———, "Psychological models for guidance," *Harvard Educ. Rev.*, 1962, *32*, 373–381.
3. Blaine, G. B., & McArthur, C. C., *Emotional problems of the student*, New York: Appleton-Century-Crofts, 1961.
4. Erikson, E., *Childhood and society*, New York: Norton, 1950.
5. Gillespie, J. M., & Allport, G. W., *Youth's outlook on the future*, New York: Doubleday, 1955.
6. Havens, J., "A study of religious conflict in college students," *J. Sci. Stud. Relig.*, 1963, *3*, 52–69.

PART III

PREJUDICE IN PERSONALITY

II

Prejudice: Is It Societal or Personal?

SOME SOCIAL PSYCHOLOGISTS have a preference for theories that are "sociological" in nature, that is, that seek explanations in terms of group tradition, social structure, populational trends. Other social psychologists are inclined to seek causation at the "micro" level in the attitudes, habits, opinions of individual persons. Especially in the area of group conflict and prejudice is there a sharp divergence between these two forms of theorizing.

After exploring the case for each preferred approach, this paper finds a reconciliation possible through a closer study of the nature of conformity. Neither the individual nor the group type of explanation would be complete without an understanding of the conditions and nature of individual conformity with social norms.

Originally given in the Greenfield Center for Human Relations at the University of Pennsylvania, this paper was printed in the *Journal of Social Issues* in 1962.

† † †

History will surely record the year 1943 as the year in which American social science awakened to the challenge of ethnic conflict and prejudice. It was in that year that four of the largest cities of the United States—Philadelphia among them—suffered disastrous race riots.

Ever since 1943 there has been a high level of output in research and theory devoted to the understanding of causal factors in group conflict. Psychologists have focused their lens of scientific inquiry chiefly upon personality as a factor in ethnic prejudice.

But now some social scientists say that psychologists have been wasting their time; they even say that the efforts are harmful, since to focus upon personality is to lead away from the true dynamics of racial and ethnic relationships. Group conflicts, these critics warn, are group phenomena, to be understood only in terms of group theory and alleviated only through group action. In the sweep of group forces the personality of the single citizen is negligible. When all of us who today practice bigotry or brotherhood are gone from the face of the earth the forces making for brotherhood and bigotry will still remain.

THE SOCIETAL ARGUMENT

To be more specific: our critic argues as follows. America has had three major types of ethnic problems to solve: the white man's conflict with the native American Indian, with the Negro slave and his descendants, and the conflict between all resident Americans and new immigrant groups (Irish, Italians, Jews, Orientals, Mexicans, Puerto Ricans, and others). Each problem differs from the others in respect to its history, economic involvements, legal status, points of friction, and resulting behavior. The part played by any individual personality in these social networks is not appreciable. For psychologists to measure attitudes and record public opinion, or even to trace the impact of this or that experience of schooling or contact, is no more effective than to tap the barometer while a hurricane rages.

To be still more specific: the fact that our armed forces instituted overnight a policy of desegregating their units of service, without disturbance and in the face of unpropitious attitudes, shows how irrelevant individual personalities are. Similar is the evidence that comes from studies of segregation and desegregation in restaurants, department stores, motels, factories, and schools. Studies show that what people do in these situations seems to be almost independent of how they feel or what they think. Social setting is the prime factor. Segregationists act like integrationists where social prescription requires; integrationists behave like segregationists when it is socially appropriate to do so.

Where then must we look for a better guide for the purpose of understanding, predicting, and controlling ethnic relations? The answer, we are told, lies in the social network —in such impersonal forces as legislative enactment, managerial and executive regulation; in the power structure of a community, in police policy, in the self-interest of banking, industrial, and commercial establishments; in the historic opportunity structure, in pressure groups; perhaps most of all in long-term economic trends involving, for instance, the entrance of minorities into industry, their migrations, increasing education, and growing power as consumers. The proportion of a minority group in a community is likewise an important factor and has nothing to do with the personalities of particular individuals. Today we see an additional force at work, namely the pressure of outside world opinion upon our federal government, and in turn its pressure upon state and local officials.

To cap the argument for the overriding importance of historical, cultural, economic, and political forces, those who favor the societal approach can point to the Supreme Court decision of 1954. Unlike the Plessy-Ferguson decision of 1896 the more recent ruling did not say that we must change people before we change race relations. In the earlier Plessy-Ferguson decision the Court held that the Constitution was powerless against prejudice. We must wait for a change of attitudes, a conversion of the heart through long-term education, before we tamper with the social structure. Sharply reversing this logic, the 1954 decision said in effect personality is irrelevant. A social change can and shall be wrought without a prior effort to alter individual feelings.

The evidence in favor of the societal approach is impressive.[1] To take a single example: the rate at which schools in the border states have desegregated varies with the degree of urbanization and industrialization in constituent counties of the state, and with the proportion of Negroes in the population, and even with the percentage of white women who join the labor force.[2] None of these factors seems to depend upon the makeup of individual personalities.

Other studies show that hotelkeepers may refuse accommodations to Orientals, Negroes, or Jews if reservations are asked for by letter or over the telephone, but if the minority member arrives in person he may be received hospitably and accommodated. Customers, we know, may disapprove of stores hiring Negro salesmen, but at the same time they may courteously make purchases from Negro personnel. Conversely, the "gentle people of prejudice" may practice verbal brotherhood on Sunday, and discriminate on Monday. We teach this form of schizophrenia to our children. In the classroom they pledge allegiance to "one nation, indivisible, with liberty and justice for all." On the playground we expect them to divide the nation, denying liberty and justice to many.

Such are some of the reasons for the vigorous repudiation of feelings, attitudes, and personality as factors in group relations. Blumer writes, "The idea so current during the past decade that a racial relationship is sustained by individual feelings or attitudes must be recognized as puerile."[3] And Raab and Lipset declare flatfootedly, "Prejudiced attitudes do not predetermine prejudiced behavior."[4] And Rose writes, "Thus prejudice has little to do with intergroup relations."[5]

THE PERSONALITY ARGUMENT

But now it is time for the proponent of personality to strike back. His critics have called him in effect a "piddler," a "headshrinker," and an "attitude boy." He is tempted to retort "journalist!" "Marxist!" "togetherness boy!" But nothing will be gained from a professional brawl. The psychologist will do better to admit the impressive evidence in favor of the demographic, ecological, social-setting approach, and to reconcile this evidence as best he can with his own scientific outlook.

Take first the principal challenge. It is certainly true that prejudiced attitudes do not always lead to prejudiced behavior. It is equally true that a person with equalitarian attitudes may engage in unjust discrimination, especially if he lives in South Africa or in Mississippi. Behavior in the "questionnaire situation" may contradict behavior in the "real life situation." We often say one thing and do another; this is mankind's cherished privilege.

But here is the nub of the matter. No man would say anything at all, nor do anything at all, unless he harbored within himself—in his own personality—the appropriate habits, or expectancies, or mental sets, or attitudes—call them what you will. Some inner dispositions are causing him both to talk like an angel and act like a devil, or to talk like a devil and act like an angel. What else than this did Myrdal mean by "the American dilemma"? It is not only possible, but usual, for Americans to have within their personalities contrasting and conflicting attitudinal dispositions. Our critics, it seems to me, are asking us to discard personality as a factor in prejudice on no other grounds than that personality is very complex. And whoever thought that it was not?

Conflicting action tendencies are called into play according to the situation that exists. Our whole nervous system operates on the principle that there is a time and place for everything. We conceal our ailments from our friends and disclose them to our family. We may disapprove of Negro salesmen, but if we want to make a purchase badly enough we suppress our feelings. If the law is insistent and unambiguously enforced we accept school desegregation although some of our attitudes are not propitious. Please note, however, that we do so because another attitude takes command, namely, our customary docility if and when laws are strictly enforced.

Let me generalize my point. Between the external social forces and the overt behavior upon which our critics fix their attention, there lies, inevitably and forever, the mediation of single and definable personalities. Without them social forces would be mere phantasms.

It is true that we can, if we wish, take a long leap, as historians and sociologists are wont to do, from, say, the rate of urbanization to the rate of desegregation. But in so doing we are overlooking important links in the causal chain; we are playing leapfrog with the mediating personality. The true sequence is that the rate of urbanization in part reflects, and in part causes, the formation of certain habits, expectancies, and values (and the corresponding disruption of other habits, expectancies, and values) in individual lives. The final result is that individuals are more ready to accept desegregation than to resist it.

The critic may reply, well, why not play leapfrog with persons? If we can predict outcome from such variables as urbanization, density, voting behavior, and economic trends, why bother with the individual?

There are two answers. First, a full scientific explanation requires that proximal as well as distal causes be included in final accounting. Second, and more important, the predictions in terms of history, social forces, or situation are rough and often inaccurate. They are so because of the implicit assumption that social and economic forces always affect people in the same way, in other words, that personality is a constant in social change.

Here the phenomenon of deviant personalities haunts us. Nearly every pressure in Alabama was toward maintaining segregation, but a Martin Luther King arose to challenge the whole structure. The history of Little Rock would have been different if Governor Faubus had not had a trait of opportunism in his makeup. What of the toughness of Negro and white parents who suffer total social ostracism for their principles? And where do principles lie except inside the personality? An integrated high school in Clinton, Tennessee, was partly destroyed by dynamite at the hands of bigots whom the prevailing social forces toward integration had not been able to affect. Synagogues are bombed in areas where legal, economic, historical, situational forces frown heavily on such crimes. Personalities, we see, are not merely affected by history; they may *create* history.

But even where personality is a relative constant, that is to say, in cases where predictions in terms of social forces are fulfilled, the proximal cause still lies within personality. No custom can be maintained, no laws obeyed, and no social change can take place unless a large number of citizens possess attitudes of acquiescence and conformity. Unless many people are disposed to go along with the demands of tradition, legislation, industrialization, urbanization, economic expediency, or any other social force alleged to increase or decrease strain in ethnic relations, these social forces will have no effect at all. And so we conclude that all theories of social causation have as their unacknowledged silent partner the psychological fact of *conformity*.

Now the factor of conformity in personality is complex. An adequate analysis, I suggest, will have to examine the phenomenon on at least three levels.

First of all is our common disposition to prefer what is familiar to us. Maslow, for example, discovered that subjects who had previously encountered a Russian name felt that it was a prettier and better name than unfamiliar Russian names later presented to them.[6] Why? There seems to be no answer excepting to say with Lewin that "the familiar acquires positive valence"; or with Dewey that "the essence of routine is its own continuation." Children, of course, are addicts to the familiar. Only well-known foods, games, stories are desired. If you tell about the Big Bad Wolf, you will be corrected if you omit a single "huff" or a single "puff." Applying the point to our own problem, Stouffer found that 80 per cent of the ground crews of the air force during the war favored segregation of Negroes and whites in their branch of the service. But only 33 per cent of the Northern men and 66 per cent of the Southern said that it made any difference to them personally.[7] Apparently the only reason why many favored segregation was that it was the familiar practice. Why change anything? If segregation is the rule, then it is preferred; if integration, then that is the preference.

This kind of conformity, be it noted, is not deeply set in the core of personality. It satisfies no basic needs. The preference for the familiar is merely skin deep. Many people's prejudice and many people's tolerance are of this order. They feel no hate; nor do they have a stake in brotherhood. For them ethnic relations are simply not salient. I would estimate that fully a third of our population falls in this class. Their type of conformity makes them easy converts to a change in the social system. They will accept an executive order, a law if enforced, or an overnight change in social custom.

A second type of conformity runs deeper, based as it is upon emotional commitment to a way of life. Now a way of life often entails ethnic, caste, or class prejudice, but is something much broader. Thus a devout Hindu finds it easy to subscribe to the caste system, although his religion, which is his main allegiance, is a much more general value in his life. Similarly, a devotee of "the Southern way of life" conforms to *many* constituent practices. He goes to church faithfully, prizes hospitality, honor, and the purity of womanhood; and he favors military virtues, and is partial to fried chicken. He also believes in white supremacy, but only as a part of this preferred way of living. Such anti-Negro prejudice as exists (and, of course, it is never recognized as prejudice) is incident to an habitual and deeply satisfying value system.

To change conformity prejudice of this sort is not easy. In some cases it may be impossible to do so unless the total frame is destroyed or drastically refashioned. We do not like to have any single one of the strands of our lifeline severed. And yet there are exceptions. Many white Southerners have been able to disconnect their ethnic attitudes from their loyalty to the Southern way of life. They do so by resetting the ethnic attitudes in a different frame of loyalty: sometimes in a broader religious outlook, or in a sentiment of national pride or world-mindedness. The fact that such recentering occurs in some personalities once again challenges an oversimplified view of social, cultural, or regional causation.

A third type of conformity rests upon deep-rooted insecurity, upon status-dread. Many people, lacking inner strength, are overeager to conform to their chosen reference groups. "What will people say if I admit an African roomer?" asks the landlady in a college town. The suburban status-seeker wants no Jewish neighbor. The insecure boy in a fraternity blackballs the son of an immigrant. In these cases we are not dealing merely with the skin-deep conformer who goes along with whatever is the prevailing practice. The status-seeking conformist will always reject groups he considers inferior, whatever the prevailing social practice may be. He conforms not to the mores but to what he considers to be the uppercrust. To him mankind is forever arranged in a hierarchy. Even though the social pattern may prescribe equality he takes as his model only the superior breed. I once offered a piece of kosher wurst to my Irish landlady's dog. The landlady protested: "My dog is of good stock; he won't touch it." But the dog did!

THE AUTHORITARIAN PERSONALITY

At last then we come to the problem of the deeply rooted, prejudiced, character structure, to the so-called authoritarian personality. This concept, we know, was conjured into scientific existence in 1950, and has been alternately blessed and damned almost daily ever since.[8]

Let us first consider an emotional objection. We are told that the authoritarian personality as portrayed by its discoverers is immersed in a sticky molasses of value assumptions. Authoritarians are portrayed as "bad guys," nonauthoritarians as "good guys." Even the title of the chief measuring instrument, the F-scale, abbreviates the term "fascist," and this label alone is enough to condemn anyone who scores on the scale anything above absolute zero! The whole conception, it is said, is nothing more than statistical backscratching indulged in by moon-faced liberals. To this sort of complaint there is no reply except to say that scientific criticism should be made of sterner stuff. The fact that a social scientist undertakes to study values, and the fact that he himself possesses them, should not *ipso facto* discredit his research.

What is the alleged authoritarian character structure? It is thought to be a complex syndrome of personality traits, difficult to describe because there is no one central organizing feature. The pattern most certainly involves the status-dread type of conformity we have described—often called "authoritarian submission." With it goes the need for aligning oneself with a strong authority figure, and with a protective in-group. Present too are a strong nationalism, a subservience to existing institutions, conventionalism, rigid moralism, and a need for definiteness. Things are seen as black or white, as right or wrong, as pure or impure, as all good or all bad. There are no shades of gray, no tentativeness, no suspended judgment. The authoritarian seeks well-marked safety islands where he can resist the confusing crosscurrents of life in a democracy. A central theme is power. "We, the good people, must control them, the dangerous people." It is up to us to give to immigrants, to Negroes, what is good for them. And teachers should not worry about what children want, but teach them what is good for their souls—regardless.

A fuller account of the syndrome points to serious unconscious repression. While young people of the authoritarian cast usually profess loyalty and love for their parents, a bit of probing discloses large amounts of repressed hostility. The excessive moralism present in their behavior is really reaction formation, covering up unholy impulses. The fear authoritarians profess to have for Negro or Jewish aggression is merely a projection of their own hostile desires. Accusing other groups of immorality is a convenient displacement of one's own guilt. And so the story goes—for the most part in an approved Freudian manner. Early training is thought to be responsible for the development of this syndrome.

An important aspect of the authoritarian pattern is weakness in self-insight—a dullness that results from preoccupation with one's own immediate well-being, and from unawareness of the feelings of the other fellow. Perhaps the fault lies with parents who discourage the child's curiosity, who punish him severely for infractions against the code, or who give him only conditional love, so that he goes through life on guard lest he be rejected, and fearful lest others will take advantage of him. Whatever the cause may be, this insecurity, lack of insight, insensitiveness, do mark many personalities, and are central features of what we may call character-conditioned prejudice.

The existence of this authoritarian syndrome is established by many studies, and its close connection with autocratic ideology and with prejudice has been repeatedly demonstrated.[9] The formulation will undoubtedly remain as one of the major psychological contributions of this century.

But of course no concept is final or perfect in its original formulation. From the lively controversies of the past decade we shall have to accept two major emendations, and perhaps others—although here we have time to mention only two.

For one thing we now know of cases high in authoritarianism but displaying no hostility toward minority groups. On the contrary they are most favorably disposed. One man of this type denies that Negroes or Jews, Mexicans or Orientals, have any faults at all. At the same time this man is insensitive, insightless, and insecure—scoring high on all authoritarian measures. In his case there is partiality toward, or love prejudice for, out-groups.

This phenomenon was overlooked by the original authors of *The Authoritarian Personality*, but has been called to our attention by Rokeach, who believes that there is considerable dogmatism among people harboring "liberal attitudes." Communists are of this type. We must therefore allow for "authoritarianism of the left."[10]

The late Professor Stouffer often asked why we had so few studies of "prejudice against prejudice." He had in mind this same phenomenon: individuals who are as irrational, as intolerant, as lacking in balance as the more familiar bigot. The point is well taken, for we certainly find intemperate and exaggerated love prejudice just as we find intemperate and exaggerated hate prejudice. To accept this fact helps us to meet the charge that authoritarians are all "bad guys." It turns out that one can be authoritarian even if one's attitudes are on the side of the angels.

A second needed improvement comes about through the intensive critique given to the F-scale—the pencil and paper test usually employed in the diagnosis of authoritarianism. Here the Achilles heel has been found to lie in what is called a "response set." (And like hounds on a hunt psychologists love to worry the legendary heel of Mr. Achilles.)

The difficulty lies in the fact that every time you agree with an item on the F-scale you chalk up a credit toward authoritarianism. If you agree that "obedience and respect for authority are the most important virtues children should learn," ping! you score one! If you agree that "to a greater extent than most people realize, our lives are governed by plots hatched in secret by politicians," ping! you score another point for authoritarianism. In other words, all the items are unidirectional, so worded that agreement always signifies authoritarianism. Only by disagreeing with every item can you obtain a completely "democratic" score.

But suppose you are not at heart authoritarian at all, but merely an amiable and obliging soul who likes to agree with people, and who, perhaps to please the experimenter, says *yes* to every proposition. You may be suggestible but you are not necessarily authoritarian.

Strong criticism has been made of this artifact of response set, and in the hands of Couch and Keniston has led to an important contribution.[11] In an extensive research these investigators discovered that some people have a marked tendency to agree with almost any proposition, not only on the F-scale but on any and all scales, regardless of their content. Conversely, other people have a *contredisant* disposition. They disagree with practically every proposition, regardless of its nature. Couch and Keniston christen these types "Yeasayers" and "Naysayers."

Now the yeasayer turns out to have a fairly clear personality pattern. It is marked by weak ego-controls, by a tendency to seek quick gratifications, to act impulsively, and to seek change, novelty, movement, and by some open anxiety and jealousy. The naysayer by contrast is marked by excessive inhibition and strong and rigid ego-control. For our purposes the important point is that the yeasaying-naysaying scale has no significant correlation with the authoritarian scale. In other words, the present F-scale probably measures two unrelated traits. One is "pure authoritarianism"; the other an important but not relevant response set. Whether a yeasaying tendency if measured on many independent scales, as Couch and Keniston have done, will by itself correlate directly with prejudice we do not yet know. No relevant research has been done. If such a correlation is discovered then, to my mind, we shall have a fourth type of conformity entering into prejudice. We have already identified the skin-deep type that merely favors whatever is familiar; also the type that loves a certain way of life in which discrimination is an historic ingredient; and finally the status-dread type, leading often to a full-fledged authoritarian submission type. To these three we could—if my hypothesis holds—add the yeasaying type. Taken together they would give us an adequate psychological basis to explain how social forces act through individuals to maintain patterns of discrimination in society.

RECAPITULATION

Let us summarize our discussion thus far. In order to improve relationships within the human family it is imperative to study causes. One valuable and valid approach lies in an analysis of social settings, situational forces, demographic and ecological variables, legal and economic trends. I have called these "societal" causes.

At the same time, none of these social forces accounts for all that happens—in technical terms, for all the variance in group relations. Deviant personalities, if they gain influence, can hasten, alter, or retard social forces. What is more, these forces in and of themselves are of no avail unless they are channelized through the medium of conforming personalities. Hence to understand the full causal chain, we require a close study of habits, attitudes, perceptions, and motivation.

We have seen then that, in the main, two major psychological problems are involved: first, the nature of functional, need-fulfilling, character-conditioned bigotry (and of course its opposite, the tolerant and compassionate pattern of personality); and second, the phenomenon of conformity at various levels, whether deeply embedded or reflecting surface acquiescence.

In the field of ethnic relations these two aspects of personality, functional prejudice and conforming prejudice, are, to my mind, the two needed foci for psychological study.

But we must now add that prejudice never forms an isolated system within personality. No one possesses simon-pure, antiseptic, uncontaminated prejudice. It always has a setting within the personal life, just as do the opposite sentiments of equi-mindedness and human-heartedness.

This integration of prejudice with other parts of personality merits closer attention than it has as yet received. Perhaps we can best illustrate the point by brief reference to the interlocking of prejudice (or tolerance) with religion in the life of the individual.

RELIGION AND PREJUDICE

A few years ago some of us were startled, even shocked, by a persistent finding. People with church affiliation, it turned out, were on the average considerably more prejudiced than the unchurched. This finding caused cynics to chuckle and brought dismay to the clergy. Had thousands of years of exhortation been wasted? Could it be that atheists, agnostics, freethinkers were closer to the ideals of Judeo-Christian ethics than were churchgoers? Research showed that Jews as a group were more tolerant than Christians, but still less tolerant than those professing no affiliation at all. As between Catholics and Protestants it was a toss-up. Sometimes Protestants and sometimes Catholics stood higher in bigotry.[12]

Now a demographer might well let this finding stand as the last word that can be spoken regarding religion and prejudice. The psychologist, however, calls for a closer look.

His first step is to examine the *frequency* of church attendance against scores on prejudice scales. He finds—and nearly all studies confirm the point—that a curious curvilinear relation exists: frequent attenders, along with the total nonattenders, are most tolerant. It is *irregular* church attendance that correlates most highly with bigotry.[13]

This finding suggests that those who are truly devout, who take their religion as an obligation, and who attend worship every week or oftener have, for the most part, successfully interiorized their faith and live according to their creed. As for the totally unchurched, they seem somehow to have escaped those enticements to bigotry that lie in casual religion. Many secular traps beset casual religion, among them an invitation to clubbishness, to status-seeking through nominal membership, to a utilitarian exploitation of the church for personal ends. All of these inducements to bigotry are pitfalls for irregular attenders.

The distinction can be best expressed if we say that for the frequent attender religion seems to have "intrinsic" value. That is to say, he lives for his religion; its total creed (including love for his neighbor) is knit into the fabric of his personality. Human-heartedness for him is as essential as his belief in God. For the irregular attender, on the broad average, religion is more of an "extrinsic" value. It is something useful to his existence. It serves him; he does not serve it. For him religion confers status, provides sociability, pleasant excitement at Christmas and Easter, as well as comfort and support in time of trouble and bereavement. Nothing in the extrinsic religious orientation requires a surrender of pet prejudices. Indeed, a self-serving and exclusionist philosophy is actually encouraged.[14]

Support for this interpretation comes not only from studies of the frequency of church attendance. Additional studies show that church members who attend study groups for a closer perusal of the Bible and the faith are less prejudiced than those who attend only social clubs.[15] And research by W. C. Wilson shows that the extrinsic religious orientation can be measured by a questionnaire scale with some success, and that as measured it has a high correlation with ethnic prejudice.[16]

There are, of course, additional problems requiring study if we are to understand fully the intricate relationship between the religious aspects of personality and prejudice. Religious orthodoxy and theological fundamentalism have received much attention, usually with the result that traditionalism is, on the average, positively associated with prejudice.[17] To my mind the interpretation of this finding is not yet clear. Catholics, for example, hold a conservative theology and yet many of them are in the forefront of the fight for racial equality. I venture the opinion that theological belief is not itself a direct factor in prejudice. In all religious groups we find every degree of prejudice, from high to low. A fully interiorized, intrinsic faith, of whatever theological cast, makes for low prejudice; whereas an extrinsic religious orientation, be it orthodox or unorthodox, makes for high prejudice. Such is my hypothesis.

CHANGE IN PERSONALITY

One last word. It is said that human nature does not change; that one generation is pretty much like its predecessor. This statement is at best a relative truth. It may be that because of inborn temperament and traditional child training, the ratio of authoritarian character structure is fairly constant from generation to generation. If so, we shall always have an irreducible minimum of functional bigotry to reckon with. Or it may be argued that today's parents are, on the whole, inclined to avoid the harshness, fitfulness, and distrust that seem early to warp the child's relationships.

However this may be, there is one marked difference between personalities of today and of the future when compared with personalities of the past. The former are, and will be, much better educated. It is estimated that while the average educational attainment of the population in 1940 was eighth grade, by 1965 it will be twelfth grade.[18]

Of one thing we are sure: all relevant investigations show that on the average prejudice declines with higher education. A fairly safe quantitative estimation would be that people with college training are 40 per cent better informed on racial and ethnic matters than are people lacking college training. They are 20 per cent less given to folk beliefs and stereotypes. At the same time they are only 10 per cent more willing to associate with persons of minority status.[19] In other words, education seems to improve *rationality* far more than it creates *human-heartedness*. We can, if we wish, blame our educational program for its relative neglect of humane values. Or we can accept Rokeach's point that intimacy of relationship requires a high degree of congeniality in intellectual and cultural interests, and that this common ground is more likely to be found within a given economic, intellectual, and occupational level wherein few minority members are found.[20]

The fact that rationality is improving more rapidly than tolerance has an interesting consequence. Today we rarely hear that Negroes, Jews, Puerto Ricans, Orientals are an inferior breed of mankind, with a dangerously different kind of blood, and with innate proclivities to disease, aggressiveness, and immorality. Now we encounter far more often the genteel rationalizations for exclusion. "They prefer to be with their own kind," we say, or "They wouldn't be happy in our neighborhood." Most common of all: "I personally would welcome them, but I have to be considerate of my neighbors."

Yet even if we accept the lowest (10 per cent) finding, it is clear that our society now has a growing phalanx of human-hearted citizens, many of whom become leaders of the cause. If proof is needed we call attention to the enormous increase in the past 15 years of biracial committees, civic unity organizations, and associations for neighborhood amity.

Returning once again to theory, the demographer may point with glee to this statistical relationship between educational level and lessened prejudice. He would say, "See, the theory of social forces works." And so it does by and large.

But since I have the last word in the argument, I would insist that education in the abstract is of no avail. It is only when certain educational lessons are differentially perceived and incorporated into certain personalities that we find changes in certain attitudes and actions appropriate to certain situations. Only a closer and closer study of individual personalities will enable us to understand the intricate pathways that lead from abstract social forces to concrete personal acts.

CONCLUSION

I hope my argument is clear. Societal forces, taken in the round, are distal causal factors in group relations. From them one can predict, at least roughly, the course of integration and segregation, of accommodation and conflict. Statistics regarding churchgoing, educational level, power structure, historical trends, urbanization, law enforcement, and other similar factors are useful and relevant.

At the same time, the intervening factor of personality is ever the proximal cause of human conduct. Conformity is the missing link that explains why and how societal forces eventuate into patterns of acceptance or discrimination—so far as they do so. And there are various levels and types of conformity in the structure of personality.[21] Insofar as societal predictions fail it is because they overlook the nonconformist, deviant, morphogenic aspects of personal behavior—of which there are many.

There are no good reasons for professional rivalry and backbiting among social scientists preferring one approach or the other. They can and should be blended in our outlook.[22]

NOTES

1. Some of this evidence, as well as the argument against the "personality" approach and in favor of the "social setting" approach will be found in the following sources. A. Rose, "Intergroup relations vs. prejudice: pertinent theory for the study of social changes," *Social Problems*, 1956, *4*, 173–176. H. Blumer, "Recent research on racial relations: United States of America," *Internat. Soc. Sci. Bull.*, 1958, *10*, 403–447. E. Raab and S. M. Lipset, *Prejudice and Society*, New York: Anti-Defamation League, 1959.
2. T. F. Pettigrew and M. R. Cramer, "The demography of de-segregation," *J. Social Issues*, 1959, *15*, 61–71.
3. H. Blumer, *op. cit.*, p. 437.
4. E. Raab and S. M. Lipset, *op. cit.*, p. 11.
5. A. Rose, *op. cit.*, p. 176.
6. A. H. Maslow, "The influence of familiarization on preference," *J. Ex. Psychol.*, 1937, *21*, 162–180.
7. S. A. Stouffer *et al.*, *The American Soldier: Adjustment During Army Life*, Princeton: Princeton Univ. Press, 1949, Vol. 1, p. 579.
8. T. W. Adorno, Else Frenkel-Brunswik, D. J. Levinson, R. N. Sanford, *The Authoritarian Personality*, New York: Harper, 1950.
9. By now the bibliography on the authoritarian personality runs to over a thousand titles. See: R. Christie and Peggy Look, "A guide to published literature relating to the authoritarian personality," *J. Psychol.*, 1958, *45*, 171–199. Some of the evidence regarding its composition and demonstrated relation to prejudice is contained in G. W. Allport, *The Nature of Prejudice*, Cambridge: Addison Wesley, 1954, Chaps. 25 and 26.

10. M. Rokeach, "Political and religious dogmatism: an alternative to authoritarian personality," *Psychol., Monogr.*, 1956, *70*, Whole No. 425.

11. A. Couch and K. Keniston, "Yeasayers and Naysayers: agreeing response set as a personality variable," *J. Abnorm. & Soc. Psychol.*, 1960, *60*, 151–174.

12. See, for example: R. K. Young, W. M. Benson, W. H. Holtzman, "Change in attitudes toward the Negroes in a Southern university," *J. Abnorm. & Soc. Psychol.*, 1960, *60*, 131–133; M. Argyle, *Religious Behavior*, Glencoe, Ill.: Free Press, 1959, pp. 83–85; M. Rokeach, *The Open and Closed Mind*, New York: Basic Books, 1960; R. W. Friedrichs, "Christians and residential exclusion: an empirical study of a northern dilemma," *J. Soc. Issues*, 1959, *15*, 14–23.

13. See, for example: G. Shinert and C. E. Ford, "The relation of ethnocentric attitudes to intensity of religious practice," *J. Educ. Sociol.*, 1958, *32*, 157–162; A. L. Rosenblum, "Ethnic prejudice as related to social class and religiosity," *Sociol. & Soc. Res.*, 1958, *43*, 272–275; also, R. W. Friedrichs, *op. cit.*, R. K. Young, W. M. Benson, W. H. Holtzman, *op. cit.*, and M. Argyle, *op. cit.*

14. For a fuller discussion of intrinsic and extrinsic religious values in relation to prejudice see: G. W. Allport, "Religion and prejudice," in *Personality and Social Encounter*, Boston: Beacon, 1960, Chap. 16.

15. See: R. W. Friedrichs, *op. cit.* (p. 19); and G. W. Allport, "The nature of prejudice," *op. cit.* (p. 452).

16. W. C. Wilson, "Extrinsic religious values and prejudice," *J. Abnorm. & Soc. Psychol.*, 1960, *60*, 286–288.

17. See, for example: D. J. Levinson, "The intergroup relations workshop: its psychological aims and effects," *J. Psychol.*, 1954, *38*, 103–126; also, W. E. Gregory, "The orthodoxy of the authoritarian personality," *J. Soc. Psychol.*, 1957, *45*, 217–232; T. C. Keedy, "Anomie and religious orthodoxy," *Sociol. & Soc. Res.*, 1958, *43*, 34–37.

18. D. J. Bogue, *The Population of the United States*, Glencoe, Ill.: Free Press, 1959, p. 340.

19. See, for example: Babette Samelson, "Does education diminish prejudice?" *J. Soc. Issues*, 1945, *1*, 11–13; C. H. Stember,

"The effect of education on prejudice against minority groups," *Research Reports*, Sept. 1960, New York: Amer. Jewish Committee.

20. M. Rokeach, *The Open and Closed Mind, op. cit.*
21. See, for example, H. C. Kelman, *Social Influence and Personal Belief*, New York: Wiley, 1962.
22. See T. F. Pettigrew, "Social psychology and desegregation research," *Amer. Psychol.*, 1961, *16*, 105–112.

12

Prejudice and the Individual

WHEN the *American Negro Reference Book* was prepared the editor solved the problem of the "sociological" vs. the "psychological" approach by asking different authors to handle each in separate articles. The present paper considers prejudice as an attitude held by an individual and examines the many conditions that bear upon this formation within the personality.

In a sense this article may prove to be a useful condensation of much that I have written in books and articles concerning the nature of prejudice. For permission to reprint the piece I am grateful to the *American Negro Reference Book* (J. P. Davis, ed.), Prentice-Hall, 1966.

† † †

We here consider prejudice as a psychological condition lodged in single individual minds. To understand the total psychosocial complex of prejudice we need also to take into account situational and societal factors. The present article is one of a trilogy. The reader should consult also *Prejudice and the Situation* and *Prejudice and Society* in this *Handbook*.

DEFINITION AND EXTENT OF PREJUDICE

There are two ingredients in any prejudiced state of mind: (a) a feeling of favorableness or unfavorableness which in turn is (b) based on unsupported judgment. While some prejudice can be *pro*, or "love prejudice" (as when we think too well of our own group), the ethnic attitudes that cause most social concern are *con*, or "hate prejudice."

A scholastic definition states that hate prejudice is "thinking ill of others without sufficient warrant." An equivalent slang definition says "prejudice is being down on something you are not up on." Whatever wording we prefer, there is always an element of inadequate knowledge or false judgment in prejudice; if not, then we are dealing with a well-grounded dislike, not with prejudice. If a criminal gang threatens my safety my fear and hatred of it are not prejudice; but if I say that no ex-convict can be trusted, I am overgeneralizing and am therefore prejudiced. Examples are legion. An Oxford student said, "I despise all Americans, but I have never met one I didn't like." "Every Jew will cheat you if he gets a chance." "Negroes are a violent lot; they carry razors." "Puerto Ricans are ignorant." "I couldn't trust any white man."

It should be added that overgeneralized prejudgments of this sort are prejudices only if they are not reversible when exposed to new knowledge. A person (e.g., a child) can start with a misconception about Jews, Negroes, Puerto Ricans; but if he changes his mind when new evidence comes along he was not really prejudiced, only misinformed. Prejudices are inflexible, rigid, and erroneous generalizations about groups of people.

Discrimination and prejudice. While discrimination ultimately rests on prejudice, the two processes are not identical. Discrimination denies people their natural or legal rights because of their membership in some unfavored group. Many people discriminate automatically (e.g., in using a labeled waiting room) without being prejudiced; and others, the "gentle people of prejudice," feel irrational aversion, but are careful not to show it in discriminatory behavior. Yet in general discrimination reinforces prejudices, and prejudices provide rationalizations for discrimination. The two concepts are most distinct when it comes to seeking remedies. The corrections for discrimination are legal, or lie in a direct change of social practices; whereas the remedy for prejudice lies in education and the conversion of attitudes. The best opinion today says that if we eliminate discrimination, then—as people become acquainted with one another on equal terms—attitudes are likely to change, perhaps more rapidly than through the continued preaching or teaching of tolerance.

Generality of prejudice. While some people are prejudiced against one group only, it is more common to find that if a person is bigoted in regard to one nationality, race, or religion, he is likely to be bigoted regarding all "out-groups." He feels safe only within the narrow confines of his own familiar circle. It is this finding that argues most cogently for regarding prejudice as rooted in personal character structure.

How widespread is prejudice? Research suggests that perhaps 80 per cent of the American people harbor ethnic prejudice of some type and in some appreciable degree. Only 20 per cent of the people are, in Gandhi's terms, "equiminded" or completely democratic in all their attitudes.[1] Widespread though ethnic prejudice is, there is good reason to believe that in the United States it is declining year by year. One example may be given. A cross-section of the population responded to the question, "Do you think Negroes are as intelligent as white people—that is, can they learn things just as well if they are given the same education and training?" In 1946, 60 per cent of the Northern white population answered "yes," and the figure rose in 1956 to 82 per cent. The rise among Southern whites for the same decade was from 33 per cent to 59 per cent.[2]

ORIGINS OF PREJUDICE

While some animals have an instinctive aversion to others, this is not true among species that are cross-fertile. Human beings of all races can (and do) mate and procreate. There is therefore no reason to assume that instinctive aversion exists between ethnic and racial groups. A young child may be frightened by a person of unfamiliar color or appearance, but ordinarily this fear lasts only a few moments. It is well known that young children will play contentedly together whatever their race or national origin. Thus since prejudice is not in-born but acquired, the question is: what are the chief factors in the complex process of learning?

Some prejudice is deliberately taught by parents. Children obediently learn the lesson, as in the case of the little girl who asked her mother, "What's the name of those children I am supposed to hate?" The parent may pass on prejudice by punishing a child for his friendliness to minority groups. A child thus punished may acquire a conditioned aversion to members of the out-group. Sometimes the teaching is subtler. Even to a four-year-old dark skin may suggest dirt; and since he is repeatedly warned to keep clean, he may develop an avoidance for dark-skinned people.

Tags are powerful factors in learning. Most children learn the emotional force of words long before they know the meanings of the words. An angry first grader once called his white teacher a "nigger." She asked him what "nigger" meant. He replied, "I don't know, but you're supposed to say it when you're mad." Before the child has knowledge of the meaning of Jap, Jew, nigger, Pollak, and similar labels, he senses the potency of the negative feeling-tone behind these labels. Derogatory chatter in the home may thus dispose a child of six or eight to "think ill of others without sufficient warrant."

Much prejudice is *caught* rather than directly *taught*. The whole atmosphere of child training may be subtly decisive. Thus a child who is sometimes rejected, sometimes loved, who is punished harshly or capriciously, who does not know unconditional trust at home—such a child grows up "on guard." Unable to depend emotionally upon his parents, he enters school with a suspicious, fearful attitude toward people in general, and especially toward those who have an unfamiliar appearance, and (to him) odd and threatening ways of talking, or worshiping, or behaving. Although we cannot make the assertion with finality, it seems likely that the major factor in predisposing a child toward a lifetime of prejudice is this rejective, neglectful, harsh, or inconsistent style of preschool training.[3]

As the child grows older additional factors may create or intensify prejudice. Around the age of 8 or 10 he goes through a period of fierce identification with his family. Whatever the family is, is "right" (whether it be Catholic, Jewish, white, Negro, Scotch Irish, or Hottentot). By comparison all other groups are of doubtful status and merit. At this point the church and the school have the opportunity of teaching the child the concept of reciprocity and basic equality among human groups. The lesson is difficult to learn, because as adolescence approaches the child seeks personal security and a new identity in his peer groups which usually are of his own color, class, and neighborhood. If adolescents are friendly with out-groups they risk a diffusion and loss of their own precarious identity.[4] To build up a sense of personal importance they often persecute out-groups. *The West Side Story* is an epic of this gang-age phenomenon.

Occasionally prejudice is formed on the basis of a single emotional trauma. A certain youngster who was chased by a Chinese laundryman felt ever after a terror of Orientals (a clear case of overgeneralizing from a single experience). Such traumatic origins are relatively rare. But we see that throughout childhood and youth there are many opportunities for irreversible and unfavorable belief systems to become set.

PSYCHODYNAMICS

However prejudice is learned it takes root in a personality because it meets certain basic needs or cravings. It works for the person, and may be a pivotal factor in the economy of his life.

Need for categorization. All mortals require simplified rubrics to live by. We think of school teachers, or physicians, of blind people, of Russians, or of ex-convicts, as homogenous groups. All Orientals, we perceive as mysterious (though many are not); we regard all weeds as inedible (though some are nutritious). Thus our thinking seems to be guided by a law of least effort. If I reject all foreigners (including the United Nations), I simplify my existence by ruling out the troublesome issues of international relations. If I say "all Negroes are ignorant," I dispose of 14 million more people. If I add "Catholics only know what the priest tells them," I eliminate 40 million more. With the conviction that Jews will skin me alive, I discard another 5 million. Labor unions I exclude by calling them "pirates." Intellectuals are simply "long-haired communists." And so it goes. My wife is simplified when I invoke these stereotyped rejections. With the aid of aversive categories I avoid the painful task of dealing with individuals as individuals. Prejudice is thus an economical mode of thought, and is widely embraced for this very reason.

Anxiety and the need for security. A major source of prejudice is the sense that one's security and status are threatened. One fears for one's job, for one's home, especially for one's prestige. American culture is enormously competitive, and so we find ourselves keenly fearful of our rivals. Downwardly mobile people on the whole are more prejudiced than people who hold a stable social position.[5] Now in cold logic it is very seldom that any minority group actually threatens the well being, safety, or equity of our lives, but we nontheless perceive them as the cause of our distress. Racist agitators play upon this anxiety. The easiest idea to sell anyone is that he is better than someone else, and that this someone else must be kept "in his place" so that we may enjoy our own position of superiority.

Scapegoating. When things go wrong we find it convenient to blame others. Since Biblical times it has been known that a scapegoat relieves our own sense of failure or guilt. We say it is the Jews who are keeping us from a promotion, or the migration of Negroes that takes away available jobs. Or we may vaguely blame our failures or discomforts upon "the politicians." Few people take blame upon themselves. They are quick to adopt an extrapunitive ego-defense.

Sexual conflict. A peculiarly deep complex is found in accusations that out-groups (especially Negroes) are immoral. Simply because they are "forbidden fruit" many white people find Negroes sexually attractive; much miscegenation has been the result. Since looseness of morals is condemned, the white person may exonerate himself from his web of desire, fantasy, and guilt, by projecting it upon the Negro male, who, he says, is sexually aggressive—at heart a rapist. In Germany, Hitler accused the Jews of all manner of sexual irregularities; in the United States, it is the Negro who is the projection screen (the "living inkblot") for one's own frightening id-impulses.

The authoritarian pattern. To summarize these, and other similar emotional needs, trends, and twists that enter into the psychodynamics of prejudice, psychologists have formulated the concept of "authoritarianism."[6] It says that a person who is basically insecure, anxious, sexually repressed, suffering from unresolved Oedipal conflicts with his own parents, given to projection—such a person will develop a rigid, conventional, hostile style of life. Ethnic prejudice fits into this character syndrome. This formulation has been widely studied and debated. Just how to define it in detail is a matter of dispute, but most scholars believe that it contains an important truth. People having this syndrome are "functional bigots" whose whole style of life is hostile, fearful, rejective of out-groups. Such people need prejudice and are ready to follow a demagogue who focuses all this latent hate upon some ethnic target.

CONFORMITY

Although the authoritarian pattern clearly exists, we must not assume that it accounts for all prejudice. What we call "conformity prejudice" springs from the tendency of people to yield to local custom and to the legends and ideology of their own class.[7] If bigotry is in the air, they are bigots; if tolerance is customary, they are tolerant. Perhaps half of our population can be considered to be in this middle range. Since prejudice is to some degree prevalent, especially in the Southern regions of the United States, this half of the population can be expected to go along with the existing biases.

What we have called the authoritarian syndrome accounts for about the same amount of prejudice in both Northern and Southern states, but there is much more conformity prejudice in the South.[8]

VICTIMIZATION

Those who are victims of prejudice cannot be indifferent to their plight; they must constantly defend themselves from discomfort or insult. One study states that 50 per cent of Negroes say that when they are with a white person they expect him "to make a slip and say something wrong about Negroes."[9] Even when not expecting an insult, a minority group member must ordinarily plan his life within a racial or ethnic frame of reference.

Besides this chronic sensitization to the problem, additional psychological reactions to victimization may be noted; among them, withdrawal and apathy, slyness and cunning, clowning, rejection of one's own group—or quite the reverse, forming closer in-group ties—resignation, neuroticism, sympathy with other minorities, and enhanced striving and militancy.[10] Of course not all members of a minority group will show all of these types of response.

REDUCING PREJUDICE

Someone has said that it is easier to smash an atom than a prejudice. In the case of deep-dyed functional bigots this verdict may be true. And yet change in prejudice does occur, and has clearly occurred since World War II in America. Prejudiced attitudes change when it makes sociological, economic, and personal sense to change them. Not all people are incurably blind to their own illogical and harmful ways of thinking. Education combats easy overgeneralizations, and as the educational level rises we find reduction in stereotyped thinking.[11] Also we know that increased self-knowledge and personal insight reduce prejudice.[12] Education for mental health works in this direction. Furthermore, militant protests call attention to needed reforms and win the sympathy of potentially democratic citizens. Various measures of prejudice have been invented to help follow these trends, even the subtle factor of human-heartedness within the population.[13]

All progress toward the reduction of prejudice will be met by vociferous resistance from the functional bigots. And yet, even when violence flares up, the trend is unmistakable. Antidiscrimination laws, revised school curricula and effective desegregation, raising of educational levels, open discussion and enlightenment, nonviolent protests that focus attention and win sympathy—all these, and other forces, are working in a single direction. Let the reader also keep in mind the fact that the problem we are here discussing has had in the past 20 years more attention and intelligent study among people of goodwill than in all the millennia of human history previously. Recent research on ethnic prejudice has been remarkably rich and informative,[14] and shows clearly that the forces of social science are strongly arrayed in the battle against bigotry.

NOTES

1. G. W. Allport, *The Nature of Prejudice*, New York: Doubleday Anchor Books, 1958, p. 77.
2. Bettelheim and M. Janowitz, *Social Change and Prejudice*, Glencoe, Ill.: Free Press, 1964, p. 11.
3. D. B. Harris, H. G. Gough, W. E. Martin, "Children's ethnic attitudes: II, Relationship to parental beliefs concerning child training," *Child Development*, 1950, *21*, 169–181. Also, D. P. Ausubel, *Ego Development and the Personality Disorders*, New York: Grune and Stratton, 1962.

4. B. Bettelheim and M. Janowitz, *op. cit.*, p. 57.
5. *Ibid.*, pp. 29–34.
6. T. W. Adorno, E. Frenkel-Brunswik, D. J. Levinson, and R. N. Sanford, *The Authoritarian Personality*, New York: Harper, 1950.
7. G. W. Allport, "Prejudice: Is it societal or personal?" *Journal of Social Issues*, 1961, *18*, 120–134.
8. T. F. Pettigrew, "Regional differences in anti-Negro prejudice," *Journal of Abnormal and Social Psychology*, 1959, *29*, 28–36.
9. R. M. Williams, Jr., *Strangers Next Door*, New York: Prentice-Hall, 1964, p. 47.
10. G. W. Allport, *The Nature of Prejudice*, New York: Doubleday Anchor Books, 1958, Chapter 9.
11. C. H. Stember, *Education and Attitude Change*, New York: Institute of Human Relations Press, 1961. Also, H. G. Stetler, *Attitudes Toward Racial Integration in Connecticut*, Hartford: Commission on Civil Rights, 1961.
12. R. M. Jones, *An Application of Psychoanalysis to Education*, Springfield, Ill.: Charles C. Thomas, 1960.
13. H. Schuman and J. Harding, "Sympathetic identification with the underdog," *Public Opinion Quarterly*, 1963, *27*, 230–241.
14. B. Berelson and G. A. Steiner, *Human Behavior: an Inventory of Scientific Findings*, New York: Harcourt, Brace & World, 1964.

13

The Religious Context of Prejudice

IT IS A STRIKING PARADOX that religion, in certain respects, fosters and increases prejudice, and yet, in other respects, reduces and negates prejudice. This paper examines the conditions that distinguish the pro-prejudice from the anti-prejudice influences inherent in religion. These influences are grouped under three rubrics: the theological, the sociocultural, and the psychological.

The paper may be regarded as propaedeutic to much empirical research that does in fact establish the dual force of religion—toward making and toward unmaking prejudice.

The paper was delivered to a conference at the Princeton Theological Seminary, and was published both in the *Graduate Journal* of the University of Texas (Vol. 7, 1966) and in the *Journal for the Scientific Study of Religion* (Vol. 5, 1966).

† † †

Two contrary sets of threads are woven into the fabric of all religion—the warp of brotherhood and the woof of bigotry. I am not speaking of religion in any ideal sense, but, rather, of religion-in-the-round as it actually exists historically, culturally, and in the lives of individual men and women, the great majority of whom (in our land) profess some religious affiliation and belief. Taken in-the-round, there is something about religion that makes for prejudice, and something about it that unmakes prejudice. It is this paradoxical situation that I wish to explore here.

It is a well-established fact in social science that, on the

average, churchgoers in our country harbor more racial, ethnic, and religious prejudice than do nonchurchgoers. Needless
to say, this fact is both surprising and distressing to thoughtful
religionists. Many public opinion surveys, as well as intensive
investigations establish this finding.[1] The finding is always the
same: it is secularism and not religion that is interwoven with
tolerance. In S. A. Stouffer's words, "More churchgoers are
intolerant of . . . nonconformity . . . than nonchurchgoers." And this relationship holds when "education, age, region,
and type of community also are taken into account."[2]

Although we do not know whether this correlation holds
for other lands, or for past centuries, we can assume that it
does. At least we know that most persecutions and inquisitions
of the past, especially the vicious and shameful, have occurred
within religious contexts.

One can become immediately defensive and argue that today, as in the past, many (perhaps most) battlers for civil
rights, for social justice, for tolerance and equi-mindedness—
in short, for brotherhood—have been religiously motivated
and fortified by religious doctrine. The array of such spiritual
heroes is long; it would include Christ himself and many followers: Tertullian, Pope Gelasius the First, Raymond Lully,
who dared oppose both the Crusades and the rising Inquisition, Cardinal Cusa, Sebastian Castellio, Schwenkfeld and the
Irenicists; and, in this country, Roger Williams, John Wool-
man, and modern figures such as Father John La Farge, Martin
Luther King, and an expanding army of religiously motivated
workers for civil rights. Gandhi, a non-Christian, was also religiously motivated. It is further possible to point to recent
pronouncements from nearly every major religious body stating in golden words its stand for racial justice and brotherhood.

All this evidence is convincing; but it does not cancel the
fact that members of Christian churches in this country are,
on the average, more bigoted than nonchurchgoers. Since the
evidence on both sides is incontestable, we are surely con-

fronted with a paradoxical situation which requires careful analysis in order to unravel the contrary sets of threads.

The needed analysis can follow three lines of inspection, corresponding to the three religious contexts which seem to me to contain the seeds of bigotry:

1. The theological context
2. The sociocultural context
3. The personal-psychological context

WHAT IS PREJUDICE?

Before entering upon our analysis it is well to pause for a moment to ask what we mean by prejudice. At what point do our justifiable predilections, beliefs, and convictions spill over into prejudice?

The clearest answer, I think, comes from Thomistic philosophy which defines prejudice very simply as "thinking ill of others without sufficient warrant." Such is a definition of "prejudice against," what Spinoza calls "hate prejudice." There is, of course, a condition of "thinking *well* of others without sufficient warrant" (as we sometimes do concerning our own children)—Spinoza's "love prejudice."

By this definition of hate prejudice (the type that concerns us here), we identify two ingredients: a negative feeling or attitude, and a failure of rationality. A particularly ugly example is the illogic of the Ku Klux Klan rabble rouser who justified the killing of Negro children in Birmingham on the grounds that if one kills rattlesnakes one doesn't care whether they are old rattlers or young. Or take a person who was once cheated by a Jew and thereupon turns anti-Semite. Here, also, is a clear case of "insufficient warrant." Sometimes the situation is subtler, as with the rabbi who had vigorously fought against the McCarthy concept of guilt by association, but who judged Kennedy unfit to be President on the basis of a medieval papal encyclical.

Here we should recall that in many regions of human life we learn through harsh experience not to think or act without sufficient warrant. Our scientific work, our family budgets, our jobs, our health require a measured calculation of warranted cause-and-effect relationships. But in other regions of our life there is little if any objective monitoring of our activities or beliefs. Religion is one such region; our view of our fellow man is another. Both of these contexts of living are particularly prone to unwarranted assumptions.

A more recent attempt to define prejudice proceeds in a different way. It takes off from certain ideal values affirmed by our democratic society. It declares that prejudice is a departure from three different sets of ideal norms. Since prejudice is ordinarily a matter of gross and unwarranted overgeneralization, it departs from the norm of *rationality* (just as the Thomistic definition says). Since prejudice often leads to segregation, discrimination, and denial of rights, it is a departure from the norm of *justice*. And, finally, since it entails contempt, rejection, or condescension, it is a departure from the norm of *human-heartedness*.[3] This threefold definition somewhat amplifies the Thomistic, but is not inconsistent with it.

I am not saying that it is always possible to ticket a given state of mind as clearly prejudiced or unprejudiced. As in all of our mental life, there are borderline conditions. My argument is simply that there are attitudes that are unwarranted, unjust, and insensitive; and that these attitudes may all be, in varying degrees and for varying reasons, interlocked with their possessor's religious life.

THE THEOLOGICAL CONTEXT

We now come to the theological context of prejudice. Although I have little competence in the field I venture to suggest that, while plentiful supports for brotherhood are found in nearly all systems of theology, these systems also contain three invitations to bigotry. In the past all three have led to prejudice, injustice, outrage, and inquisition. Even today the peril exists, although it is greatly lessened.

First, the doctrine of *revelation* has led, and can still lead, a religion to claim exclusive possession of final truth concerning the destiny and end of man, as well as sole authority and means for interpreting that end. Held rigidly, this position regards the teaching of other religious and philosophical formulations as a threat to human salvation. Saint Augustine declared that where truth is known men have not the right to err. Within the Protestant tradition heresy was for a long time a capital crime. Menno Simons, the Anabaptist, reinterpreted Saint Paul's injunction to "judge nothing before the time, until the Lord shall come." It meant, he said, "none may judge unless he have the Judging Word on his side."[4]

The General Court of Massachusetts decreed in 1647 that "No Jesuit or spiritual or ecclesiastical person (as they are termed), ordained by a pope of the see of Rome, shall henceforth come into Massachusetts. Any person not freeing himself of suspicion shall be jailed, then banished. If taken a second time he shall be put to death." If the law has not been repealed, 3,200 Catholic clergy in Massachusetts are there illegally.[5]

Most theologians today, of course, take a far softer position, agreeing in effect with Bishop Lesslie Newbigin, who writes, "We must claim absoluteness and finality for Christ and His finished work; but that very claim forbids us to claim absoluteness and finality for our understanding of it."[6] Firm faith in revelation is not incompatible with tentativeness and tolerance in our attempts to interpret this faith to mankind. From the practical point of view, this leniency is not different from the "fallibilism" of Charles Peirce and John Dewey, who held that the best society is one that remains open and encourages all men to search with equal freedom for satisfying truths.

Whatever the reasons may be, persecutions deriving from rigid interpretations of divine revelation have largely vanished. Today's religious wars—and we still have them—between Moslem and Hindu, between Buddhist and Catholic, are largely due to traditional economic and ethnic hostilities wearing convenient religious tags.

The second theological goad to bigotry (likewise more common in the past than in the present) is the doctrine of *election*. The frenzied battle cry of the Crusades, *Deus vult*, the more recent *Gott mit uns*, the very concepts of God's chosen people, of God's country, have all conferred sanctions for persecution and cruelty. The infidel is accurst; so, too, the black children of Ham. In speaking to the Jews, Saint Chrysostom said, "God hates you." The doctrine of election divides the ins from the outs with surgical precision. Since God is for the ins, the outs must be excluded from privileges, and, in extreme cases, eliminated by sword or by fire.

Such divinely sanctioned ethnocentrism is decreasing; ecumenism, its polar opposite, is in ascendance. It seems that the principal active residue of prejudice based on the doctrine of election is the racial bigotry of South Africa and our own South, where we find lingering doctrinal justification for keeping the descendants of Ham in the position of drawers of water and hewers of wood.

The third and last theological peril has by now virtually disappeared. I speak of *theocracy*—the view that a monarch rules by divine right, that the Church is a legitimate guide for civil government; or that a legal code (perhaps based, as in early New England, on the Ten Commandments), being divinely ordained, is inviolable on the pain of fierce punishment or death. No theological idea has caused so much persecution and suffering in both the Old World and the New as have the various versions of theocracy. By virtue of its control over civil government, ecclesiastical whims based on doctrines of revelation and election could be translated into immediate and cruel sanctions.

Theocracy, we now know, disappeared soon after this country adopted the First Amendment to its Constitution, guaranteeing religious liberty and the separation of church and state. Historians have claimed that this achievement is America's principal contribution to civilization.[7]

What I have been saying is that, for all its stress on compassion, theology itself has been far from blameless. It has encouraged bigotry in thought, in word, and in deed. At the same time this particular context of prejudice, prominent in the past, has undergone marked relaxation, and may be destined to vanish.

THE SOCIOCULTURAL CONTEXT

Since the average churchgoer has only vague intimations of theology, it seems farfetched to search for the roots of his prejudices in their theological context—especially since, as we have seen, the pathogenic elements in theology are disappearing. But if theological influences in daily life are diminishing, sociocultural influences in religion are increasing. What are the sociocultural factors in religion that predispose the churchgoer to prejudice?

If we stand off and look at our contemporary social edifice, we note that without doubt religion is one of its pillars; but, also, that a parallel pillar is built of the clichés of secular prejudice. Where would our social structure be if most people didn't believe in "my country right or wrong," in the superiority of Western culture, in the prevailing social stratification and earmarks of status, in the moral superiority of people with ambition over people without ambition—which means, in effect, in the moral superiority of privileged over unprivileged classes—in the evils of miscegenation, in the backwardness of immigrants, and in the undesirability of deviants? Secular prejudice is a pillar of a functioning society.

Now pillars must be well matched. Religion, therefore, finds itself peculiarly tailored to the nationalistic, class, and ethnic cleavages and outlooks that sustain the prevailing social order. It is a conservative agent, rather than an agent of change. A striking instance is the extent to which German Catholicism capitulated to the political and cultural demands of Nazi pressure.[8]

The phenomenon is also clearly visible at the parish level. By and large every congregation is an assemblage of like-minded people, each congregation representing the ethnic, class, and racial cleavages of society, over and above denominational cleavages. Churches exclude Jews, and synagogues exclude Christians. Protestants and Catholics keep apart in their religious subcommunities. Negro churches are peculiarly isolated in tradition and in function.[9] Sects affirm values held by the less-educated working classes; churches foster congenial middle-class values. The fact that many parishioners leave their group when Negroes or other deviants are admitted shows that, for them, ethnic and class values hold priority over religious values. Church membership for them is primarily a sociocultural significance, a matter of class and caste—a support for their own ethnocentrism.

Here we find a key to our riddle. The reason churchgoers on the average are more prejudiced than nonchurchgoers is not because religion instills prejudice. It is rather that a large number of people, by virtue of their psychological makeup, require for their economy of living both prejudice and religion. Some, for example, are tormented by self-doubt and insecurity. Prejudice enhances their self-esteem; religion provides them a tailored security. Others are guilt-ridden; prejudice provides a scapegoat, and religion, relief. Still others live in fear of failure. Prejudice provides an explanation in terms of menacing out-groups; religion promises a heavenly, if not terrestrial, reward. Thus, for many individuals, the functional significance of prejudice and religion is identical. One does not cause the other; rather, both satisfy the same psychological needs. Multitudes of churchgoers, perhaps especially in times of social anomie and crisis, embrace both supports.

According to this line of reasoning, we assume that non churchgoers, on the whole, have less psychological need for prejudice and for religion. Their philosophy of life, whatever it is, seems self-contained, requiring no direct reliance on these two common social supports.

Here, then, in broadest outline, is an explanation for the troublesome correlation we find between churchgoing and bigotry. We need, however, to look much more closely at both data and theory in order to sharpen our understanding of the religious context of prejudice.

First, we must remind ourselves that there are churchgoers *and* churchgoers. Today 63 per cent of the population claims formal religious affiliation, a figure far larger than in earlier decades. Also, we recall the common poll finding that as many as 96 per cent of the American people say they believe in God. Religion seems to be neither dead nor dying.

But here we need to draw an immediate distinction between two polar types of religious affiliation, as Will Herberg and Gerhard Lenski have done.[10] Some religious groups and many individuals stress the sociocultural factor in membership. The result is a "communal" type of affiliation. For example, many Jewish congregations and Negro Protestant groups provide an important communal service quite apart from their specifically religious functions. Herberg and Lenski both argue that Americans are turning increasingly to their religious groups for the satisfaction of the communal identification and need to belong. Paradoxically, it can be said that Americans are becoming more religious while at the same time they are becoming more secular.

In *all* religious groups we find parishioners whose interests are primarily communal. Affiliation is in fashion; it provides status for some, a gossip center for others, a meeting place for the lonely, entertainment for the disengaged, and even a good way to sell insurance. One study reports that 80 per cent of members indicated they are more concerned about a comfortable life on earth than about other-worldly considerations, and 54 per cent admit that their religious beliefs do not have any effect on the way they conduct their daily affairs.[11]

The type opposite to "communal" is "associational" which includes those members whose involvement is primarily for purposes of religious fellowship. Comparing these types revealing differences emerge. To give one example: Lenski finds that among Detroit Catholics whose communal involvement is high and whose associational involvement low, 59 per cent favor segregated schools; whereas among Catholics whose associational involvement is high and whose communal involvement low, only 27 per cent favor segregated schools—a difference of thirty-two percentage points between the religiously oriented and the communally oriented churchgoers. A significant trend in the same direction is found also among Detroit Protestants.[12]

Thus, we see that one type of churchgoer tends to be prejudiced; another type relatively unprejudiced. To my mind, it is precisely here that we find the analytic tool we need to solve our problem. Soon I shall return to this mode of analysis and to several relevant supporting researches.

Meanwhile, let me say that a sociological or historical scholar could point to many additional relationships between religion as a cultural institution and prejudice. For one thing, almost every religious group has been a target for hostility. The fierce anti-Catholicism in the United States during the nineteenth century was certainly in large part a mask for the workingman's resentments against the flood of immigration from Ireland, and later from Italy and other Catholic countries. Not only was there vague uneasiness about the curious folkways of these foreigners, there was growing fear of the power of the cities where they settled. Rural nativism focused upon ecclesiastical visibility as a target, likewise upon the Jew who was also an identifiable foreigner.

A different line of sociological interest deals with the ideological differences among Protestant, Catholic, and Jew; and sometimes between Negro and white churches. Lenski, for example, argues that the communications networks, being relatively limited to the adherents of the same faith, facilitate the development and transmission of distinctive political and economic norms and outlooks.[13] In short, religious groups favor provincialism and a compartmentalization of living. Since immigration has virtually ceased, the socioreligious community is becoming a substitute for ethnic groupings, and we must accordingly expect many of the prejudices formerly supported in ethnic terms to be sustained in socioreligious communities. The drift he sees is toward a more compartmentalized society where the heightened sense of religious group loyalty will lead to a lessened sense of responsibility toward those outside. Lenski's research establishes the fact that there are appreciable differences (independent of social class) that mark the political and social attitudes of the major religious groups and affect their images of one another. The Jews, for example, turn out to be the least critical of other groups, but at the same time to suffer the severest criticism from them.

Virtually all of the studies of religion and social conflict are focused on the demographic level. That is to say, trends are found to be true of certain groups taken as a whole. The spirit of capitalism, says Max Weber, is built into Protestantism and not into Catholicism. Negro religion is, by and large, a religion of protection and protest; Jews, having most to lose through violations of the First Amendment, are its strongest supporters. Churches guard middle-class values; sects, working-class values.[14]

All such analyses are, of course, useful as background to the study of the religious context of prejudice. And, yet, I feel that they fail to reach the heart of the matter. They focus upon religion as a sociocultural phenomenon, that is to say in its communal aspects, and overlook its place in the personal life. Both religion and prejudice are intensely personal states of mind. To understand their inherent relationships (whether positive or negative) we have to examine the psychological composition of individual people.

The Personal-Psychological Context

There are, as we have observed, churchgoers *and* churchgoers. Now what is the simplest possible distinction between them? Well, some attend frequently and regularly, some only on occasion or rarely. Offhand, this distinction may seem to be purely demographic—the "regulars" versus the "irregulars." But, in reality, the process of forming the habit of regular attendance, or the state of mind that lets weather, circumstance, and mood determine attendance clearly depends on personal motives and attitudes. True, there is a tendency for Protestants to attend less regularly than Catholics, although much more regularly than Jews. In Detroit among self-styled Protestants, 30 per cent go to church every Sunday, 20 per cent between one and three times a month, 30 per cent only occasionally, 14 never.[15] But, for our purposes, the important consideration is that each major religious group has its nuclear and its marginal members in terms of attendance. The outer fringe of the marginal groups consists of those who attend exceedingly rarely—as someone has said, only thrice in a lifetime: once when they were hatched; again when matched; and, finally, when dispatched.

Now, many investigations have shown that regular and frequent church attenders harbor, by and large, less ethnic and racial hostility than do members who are casual about their attendance. An illustrative study is one made by E. L. Streuning whose data come from nearly 900 faculty members in a large Midwestern university.[16] Besides obtaining scores on a prejudice scale, he learned what their habits were regarding church attendance. Almost a third never attended church at all, and they had a low prejudice score (14.7). Many attended once a month, and, for these, the average prejudice score nearly doubled (25). This finding immediately confirms our earlier statement that nonchurchgoers are less prejudiced than churchgoers—or at least than casual churchgoers. The prejudice scores of those attending once, twice, or three times a month were also high. For weekly attenders, the score fell, and it continued to fall rapidly for those whose attendance ranged from five to eleven or more times a month. For the last group (eleven or more a month), the average score of 11.7 was significantly lower even than for the nonattenders.

In these data we clearly perceive what is called a curvilinear relation: nonattenders and frequent attenders having low prejudice scores; intermediate attenders, high.

This evidence fits well with Lenski's distinction between communal and associational religion. Frequent attendance is not required to maintain nominal membership or to derive the benefits of communal contact. On the other hand, a religiously motivated person who seeks spiritual association is drawn with greater regularity and frequency to the church's fellowship. An imposing array of studies supports this finding and interpretation.[17]

The lives of many marginal attenders, it seems, are regulated in a fitful way by what we may call "religious tokenism." A token of churchmanship is all they need—an occasional anchorage against the gusts of fate. Tokenism, while superficial, may be fiercely important. Its devotees may incline to see in the Supreme Court ruling against prescribed prayers in public schools a menacing threat. Religion resides in a symbol. One Southern politican complained that while the Supreme Court ushered Negroes into the public schools it ushered God out—as though God dwells in a token.

While the data on frequency of church attendance and its relation to prejudice are revealing, they do not tell us directly about the nature of the personal religious sentiment that provides the context for prejudice, nor about the nature of the contrary sentiment that engenders tolerance, fair play, and humane regard.

To take this additional step, we borrow from axiology the concepts of *extrinsic* value and *intrinsic* value. The distinction helps us to separate churchgoers whose communal type of membership supports and serves other (nonreligious) ends from those for whom religion is an end in itself—a final, not instrumental, good.

The distinction clearly overlaps with that drawn by Father Joseph Fichter in his study of the urban Catholic parish.[18] What he calls the "marginal" and "modal" parishioner corresponds fairly well to our extrinsic type. What he calls the "nuclear" parishioner—who orients his life wholly by the full doctrine of the Church—is essentially our intrinsic type. For our purposes, it is important to note that Father Fichter assigns only 10 per cent to the intrinsic or nuclear group. Unless I am mistaken, the ratio is roughly what we would find in the average congregation of any Christian (and perhaps Jewish) parish.

Every minister knows and laments the preponderance of the extrinsic type. Some such parishioners find self-expression in managing investments, arranging flowers, running bazaars, in simply avoiding loneliness. They have no true association with the religious function of the Church. Others do, to varying degrees, accept the spiritual ministry, but remain dabblers because their connections are determined exclusively by mood or by crisis. Many extrinsics do, of course, have religious needs, but they feel no obligation to attend church regularly nor to integrate religion into their way of life. Lenski, we have seen, regards compartmentalization as the chief mark of religion today. It is something for an occasional Sunday morning, for High Holy Days, or for moments of crisis. Since its function is to serve other needs, we call it an extrinsic value in the personal life.

While most extrinsics are casual and peripheral churchgoers, a few are ideological extremists. With equal fervor, they embrace some political nostrum along with the tenets of some religious (usually fundamentalist) sect. In such cases religious extremism is found to be ancillary to a prejudiced philosophy of life. I am thinking here of the right-wing groups whose ardent desire is to escape from the complexities of modern life. They do not seek so much to preserve the *status quo* as to return to a former, simple small-town or agrarian way of life where individual achievement and responsibility are the only virtues. God has an important role in this ideology as a dispenser of rewards for individual achievement. Modern life threatens this idyll; immigrants threaten it;

Negroes, Jews, Catholics are seen as menacing. Extreme right ideology invariably harbors this sort of bigotry; and its supporting religion justifies and rationalizes the prejudice, often through the selection of congenial scriptural passages.

The same phenomenon is seen, though less often, in ideologies of the extreme left. Ralph Roy has pointed to cases of clergy who justify hatred of the wealthy, expropriation, and extreme left-wing policies by one-sided scriptural interpretations.[19]

Thus, while there are several varieties of extrinsic religious orientation, we may say they all point to a type of religion that is strictly utilitarian: useful for the self in granting safety, social standing, solace, and endorsement for one's chosen way of life. As such, it provides a congenial soil for all forms of prejudice, whether racial, national, political, or religious. Since extrinsic religion predominates among churchgoers we have an explanation for our riddle.

By contrast, the intrinsic form of the religious sentiment regards faith as a supreme value in its own right. It is oriented toward a unification of being, takes seriously the commandment of brotherhood, and strives to transcend all self-centered needs. Dogma is tempered with humility, and in keeping with the Biblical injunction the possessor withholds judgment until the day of the harvest. A religious sentiment of this sort floods the whole life with motivation and meaning. Religion is no longer limited to single segments of self-interest.[20]

While many of the intrinsically religious are pietists and express their religion chiefly by being good neighbors, others are of a militant stripe. Were not Saint Francis, John Wesley, Mahatma Gandhi—was not Christ himself—intrinsically religious; and were they not all zealous beyond the bounds of moderation? Yes, there are intrinsic as well as extrinsic zealots. We can usually distinguish between them: the latter group having ulterior motives of personal or political advantage; the former being fired only by a conviction that the kingdom of God should be realized on earth.

AN EMPIRICAL APPROACH

Up to now we have been speaking chiefly in theoretical terms concerning the religious context of prejudice. And I have been moving the argument closer and closer toward a psychological analysis of the situation, with the claim that in the last analysis both prejudice and religion are subjective formations within the personal life. One of these formations of religion (the extrinsic) is entirely compatible with prejudice; the other (the intrinsic) rules out enmity, contempt, and bigotry.

With the proposition stated in this way, an empiricist will ask, "Can we not test it? After all, you have simply stated an hypothesis at the speculative level. Do not all hypotheses need empirical verification before they can be accepted?"

In a series of investigations, my students and I have undertaken this very task. There is not time to describe the studies in detail. Essentially, they consist of using two questionnaires with assorted groups of churchgoers. One undertakes—and I apologize for the audacity—to determine to what extent a given parishioner holds an extrinsic or an intrinsic view of his religion. As an example, a person who agrees with the following propositions would receive scores indicating an *extrinsic* orientation:

> The purpose of prayer is to secure a happy and peaceful life.
> The Church is most important as a place to formulate good social relationships.

A person would be credited with an *intrinsic* orientation if he subscribed to such statements as the following:

> I try hard to carry my religion over into all my other dealings in life.
> Quite often I have been keenly aware of the presence of God or the Divine Being.

There are twenty-one items in the scale, which enables us to locate each subject on a continuum from consistently extrinsic to consistently intrinsic. There are also a number of subjects who are inconsistent in the sense that they endorse any and all propositions favorable to religion, even though these propositions are contradictory to one another.

A second questionnaire consists of a valid measure of prejudice.[21] It deals primarily with the extent to which the subject favors discriminatory practices and segregation.

In brief, the findings, not yet published, support the hypothesis that the extrinsic religious orientation in personality is indeed the context of prejudice. The intrinsic orientation is the matrix of tolerance. An additional interesting finding is that those subjects who are inconsistent—who grasp at any and all statements favorable to religion, regardless of their logical consistency, are the most prejudiced of all. Thus, it seems that the religious context for bigotry lies both in the extrinsic and in the muddle-headed types of religious sentiment. Only the consistent intrinsic type (a small minority) escapes.[22]

It is clear that these investigations, still in progress, tend to confirm demographic and sociological studies that we have also reviewed. Further, I believe, they are compatible with our theological analysis, since it is clear that communal and extrinsic religion can draw strong support from the doctrines of revelation, election, and theocracy, which, as we have seen, provide the theological context of prejudice, so far as such exists.

We can hope that this convergence of theological, sociological, and psychological analysis will lead to a further cooperation between behavioral and religious disciplines. We can also hope that our findings, when understood by clergy and laity, may lead to a decrease in bigotry and to an enhancement of charity in modern religious life.

If I were asked what practical applications ensue from this analysis, I would, of course, say that to reduce prejudice we need to enlarge the population of intrinsically religious people. There is no simple formula, for each personality is unique and is stubbornly resistant to change. Yet, precisely here lies the pastor's task, his opportunity, and his challenge.

NOTES

1. T. W. Adorno *et al.*, *The Authoritarian Personality*, New York: Harper and Bros., 1950; M. Rokeach, *The Open and Closed Mind*, New York: Basic Books, 1960; G. W. Allport and B. M. Kramer, "Some Roots of Prejudice," *Journal of Psychology*, 1946, *22*, 9–39; R. M. Williams, Jr., *Strangers Next Door*, Englewood Cliffs, N.J.: Prentice-Hall, 1964; S. A. Stouffer, *Communism, Conformity and Civil Liberties*, Garden City, L.I., N.Y.: Doubleday, 1955.
2. Stouffer, *op. cit.*, p. 147.
3. Cf. Howard Schuman, "Sympathetic Identification with the Underdog," *Public Opinion Quarterly*, 1963, *27*, 230–41. Additional reports in preparation.
4. Menno Simons, "A Foundation and Plain Instruction of the Saving Doctrine of Christ," *On the Ban: Questions and Answers, 1550*, trans. I. D. Rupp, Lancaster, Pa.; Elias Barr, 1863.
5. This and similar instances of theologically induced intolerance are presented in G. W. Allport, "Religion and Prejudice," *The Crane Review*, 1959, *2*, 1–10. See also Gustavus Myers, *History of Bigotry in the United States*, New York, Random House, 1943.
6. Lesslie Newbigin, "The Quest for Unity Through Religion," *Journal of Religion*, 1955, *35*, 17–33.
7. Leo Pfeffer, "Freedom and Separation: America's Contribution to Civilization," *Journal of Church and State*, 1960, *2*, 100–111.
8. See Gunter Lewy, *The Catholic Church and Nazi Germany*, New York: McGraw-Hill, 1964. Also, Gordon C. Zahn, *German Catholics and Hitler's Wars*, New York: Sheed and Ward, 1962.
9. J. R. Washington, *Black Religion*, Boston: Beacon Press, 1964.
10. Will Herberg, *Protestant, Catholic, Jew*, Garden City, L.I., N.Y.: Doubleday, 1955; Gerhard E. Lenski, *The Religious Factor*, Garden City, L.I., N.Y.: Doubleday, 1961.

11. Earl Raab (ed.), *Religious Conflict in America*, Garden City, L.I., N.Y.: Doubleday Anchor Books, 1964, p. 15.

12. Lenski, *op. cit.*, p. 173.

13. *Ibid.*, p. 303.

14. Analyses at this demographic level are plentiful. See, *e.g.*, Robert Lee and Martin E. Marty (eds.), *Religion and Social Conflict*, New York: Oxford University Press, 1964.

15. Lenski, *op. cit.*, p. 35.

16. E. L. Streuning, *The Dimensions, Distributions and Correlates of Authoritarianism in a Midwestern University Faculty Population*, unpublished Ph.D. dissertation, Purdue University, 1957.

17. W. H. Holtzman, "Attitudes of College Men toward Non-segregation in Texas Schools," *Public Opinion Quarterly*, 1956, *2*, 559–69; J. G. Kelly, J. E. Ferson, and W. H. Holtzman, "The Measurement of Attitudes toward the Negro in the South," *Journal of Social Psychology*, 1958, *48*, 305–317; R. W. Friedrichs, "Christians and Residential Exclusion: An Empirical Study of a Northern Dilemma," *Journal of Social Issues*, 1959, *15*, 14–23; Melvin M. Tumin, *Desegregation*, Princeton, N.J.: Princeton University Press, 1958; R. M. Williams, Jr., *Strangers Next Door*, Englewood Cliffs, N.J.: Prentice-Hall, 1964.

18. J. H. Fichter, S.J., *Social Relations in the Urban Parish*, Chicago: University of Chicago Press, 1954.

19. R. L. Roy, "Conflict from the Communist Left and the Radical Right," *Religion and Social Conflict*, pp. 55–68.

20. For further discussion of the extrinsic and intrinsic types see G. W. Allport, "Behavioral Science, Religion, and Mental Health," *Journal of Religion and Health*, 1963, *2*, 187–97; also, *Personality and Social Encounter*, Boston: Beacon Press, 1960, Chapter 16; also, *The Nature of Prejudice*, Reading, Mass.: Addison-Wesley, 1954, Chapter 23.

21. Devised by J. S. Harding and Howard Schuman, in preparation.

22. G. W. Allport and J. M. Ross, "Personal Religious Orientation and Prejudice," *Journal of Personality and Social Psychology* (in press).

14

Personal Religious Orientation and Prejudice
(*with J. Michael Ross*)

WHEREAS THE PREVIOUS PAPER dealt with three factors within the structure of religion that make for prejudice, the present paper concentrates on the psychological factors alone. The concept of *extrinsic* vs. *intrinsic* religion, discussed in Chapter 8, turns out to be pivotal for understanding why there are so many "gentle people of prejudice" in our churches and at the same time so many battlers for civil rights.

This paper makes a number of references to related pieces of research. Taken all together they help one to see that modern social psychology, inventing and utilizing new tools of social science, is able to lift age-old problems (like religion and prejudice) from the morass of speculation into the light of analytical truth.

The publication of this paper was in *The Journal of Personality and Social Psychology* (Vol. 5, 1967).

† † †

Previous psychological and survey research has established three important facts regarding the relationship between prejudiced attitudes and the personal practice of religion.

1. On the average, church attenders are more prejudiced than nonattenders.

2. This overall finding, if taken only by itself, obscures a curvilinear relationship. While it is true that most attenders are *more* prejudiced than nonattenders, a significant minority of them are *less* prejudiced.

3. It is the casual, irregular fringe members who are high in prejudice; their religious motivation is of the *extrinsic* order. It is the constant, devout, internalized members who are low in prejudice; their religious motivation is of the *intrinsic* order.

The present paper will establish a fourth important finding —although it may properly be regarded as an amplification of the third. *The finding is that a certain cognitive style permeates the thinking of many people in such a way that they are indiscriminately pro-religious and, at the same time, highly prejudiced.*

But first let us make clear the types of evidence upon which the first three propositions are based and examine their theoretical significance.

CHURCHGOERS ARE MORE PREJUDICED

Beginning the long parade of findings demonstrating that churchgoers are more intolerant of ethnic minorities than non-attenders is a study by Allport and Kramer (1946). These authors discovered that students who claimed no religious affiliation were less likely to be anti-Negro than those who declared themselves to be Protestant or Catholic. Furthermore, students reporting a strong religious influence at home were higher in ethnic prejudice than students reporting only slight or no religious influence. Rosenblith (1949) discovered the same trend among students in South Dakota. *The Authoritarian Personality* (Adorno, Frenkel-Brunswik, Levinson, & Sanford, 1950, p. 212) stated that scores on ethnocentrism (as well as on authoritarianism) are significantly higher among church attenders than among nonattenders. Gough's (1951) findings were similar. Kirkpatrick (1949) found religious people in general to be slightly less humanitarian than nonreligious people. For example, they had more punitive attitudes toward criminals, delinquents, prostitutes, homosexuals, and those in need of psychiatric treatment. Working with a student population Rokeach (1960) discovered nonbelievers to

be consistently less dogmatic, less authoritarian, and less ethnocentric than believers. Public-opinion polls (as summarized by
Stember, 1961) revealed confirmatory evidence across the
board.

Going beyond ethnic prejudice, Stouffer (1955) demonstrated that among a representative sample of American
church members those who had attended church within the
past month were more intolerant of nonconformists (such as
socialists, atheists, or communists) than those who had not
attended. It seems that on the average religious people show
more intolerance in general—not only toward ethnic but also
toward ideological groups.

Is this persistent relationship in any way spurious? Can it be
due, for example, to the factor of educational level? Many
studies show that people with high education tend to be appreciably less prejudiced than people with low education.
Perhaps it is the former group that less often goes to church.
The reasoning is false. Sociological evidence has shown conclusively that frequent church attendance is associated with
high socioeconomic status and with college education (Demerath, 1965). Furthermore, Stouffer's study found that the intolerant tendency among churchgoers existed only when
educational level was held constant. Struening (1963), using
as subjects only faculty members of a large state university
(all highly educated), discovered that nonattenders were on
the average less prejudiced than attenders. These studies assure
us that the association between churchgoing and prejudice is
not merely a spurious product of low education.

Turning to the theoretical implications of these findings,
shall we say that religion in and of itself makes for prejudice
and intolerance? There are some arguments in favor of such a
conclusion, especially when we recall that certain powerful
theological positions—those emphasizing revelation, election
(chosen people), and theocracy (Allport, 1959, 1966)—have
throughout history turned one religion against another. And
among *sociological* factors in religion we find many that make

for bigotry. One thinks of the narrow composition of many religious groups in terms of ethnic and class membership, of their pressure toward conformity, and of the competition between them (see Demerath, 1965; Lenski, 1961). It does seem that religion as such makes for prejudice.

And yet it is here that we encounter the grand paradox. One may not overlook the teachings of equality and brotherhood, of compassion and human-heartedness, that mark all the great world religions. Nor may one overlook the precept and example of great figures whose labors in behalf of tolerance were and are religiously motivated—such as Christ himself, Tertullian, Pope Gelasius I, St. Ambrose, Cardinal Cusa, Sebastian Castellio, Schwenkfeld, Roger Williams, Mahatma Gandhi, Martin Luther King, and many others, including the recently martyred clergy in our own South. These lives, along with the work of many religious bodies, councils, and service organizations would seem to indicate that religion as such *unmakes prejudice*. A paradox indeed.

THE CURVILINEAR RELATIONSHIP

If religion as such made *only* for prejudice, we would expect that churchgoers who expose themselves most constantly to its influence would, as a result, be more prejudiced than those who seldom attend. Such is not the case.

Many studies show that frequent attenders are less prejudiced than infrequent attenders and often less prejudiced even than nonattenders. Let us cite one illustrative study by Struening (1963). The curvilinear trend is immediately apparent in Table 1. In this particular study nonattenders had lower prejudice scores than any group, save only those devotees who managed to attend 11 or more times a month. Without employing such fine time intervals other studies have shown the same curvilinear trend. Thus, in *The Authoritarian Personality* (p. 212) we learned that in 12 out of 15 groups "regular" attenders (like nonattenders) were less prejudiced than

TABLE 1

CHURCH ATTENDANCE AND PREJUDICE AMONG
FACULTY MEMBERS OF A MIDWESTERN
UNIVERSITY

Frequency of attendance (times per mo.)	N	Prejudice score
0	261	14.7
1	143	25.0
2	103	26.0
3	84	23.8
4	157	22.0
5–7	94	19.9
8–10	26	16.3
11 or more	21	11.7

Note.—From Struening (1957).

"seldom" or "often" attenders. Employing a 26-item Desegregation Scale in three separate studies, Holtzman (1956) found the same trend as shown in Table 2. If more evidence for the curvilinear relationship is needed, it will be found in community studies made in New Jersey (Friedrichs, 1959), North Carolina (Tumin, 1958), New England (Pettigrew, 1959), and Ohio and California (Pinkney, 1961). One could almost

TABLE 2

CHURCH ATTENDANCE AND PREJUDICE AMONG STUDENTS
IN THE BORDER STATES

	1956 study % intolerant	Mean score on D scale	
		1958 study	1960 study
Nonattenders	37	41.3	38.1
Once a mo.	66	48.5	51.4
Twice a mo.	67	50.6	48.4
Once a wk. or oftener	49	44.5	44.3

Note.—Adapted from Holtzman (1956), Kelley, Ferson, and Holtzman (1958), Young, Benson, and Holtzman (1960).

say there is a unanimity of findings on this matter. The trend holds regardless of religion, denomination, or target of prejudice (although the case seems less clear for anti-Semitism than for prejudice against other ethnic groups).

What are the theoretical implications? To find that prejudice is related to frequency of church attendance is scarcely explanatory, since it may reflect only formal behavior, not involvement or commitment to religious values. And yet it seems obvious that the regular attenders who go to church once a week or oftener (and several studies indicate that oftener than once a week is especially significant) are people who receive something of special ideological and experiential meaning. Irregular, casual fringe members, on the other hand, regard their religious contacts as less binding, less absorbing, less integral with their personal lives.

At this point, therefore, we must pass from external behavioral evidence into the realm of experience and motivation. Unless we do so we cannot hope to understand the curvilinear relationship that has been so clearly established.

EXTRINSIC VERSUS INTRINSIC MOTIVATION

Perhaps the briefest way to characterize the two poles of subjective religion is to say that the extrinsically motivated person *uses* his religion, whereas the intrinsically motivated *lives* his religion. As we shall see later, most people, if they profess religion at all, fall upon a continuum between these two poles. Seldom, if ever, does one encounter a "pure" case. And yet to clarify the dimension it is helpful to characterize it in terms of the two ideal types.

Extrinsic Orientation

Persons with this orientation are disposed to use religion for their own ends. The term is borrowed from axiology, to designate an interest that is held because it serves other, more ultimate interests. Extrinsic values are always instrumental and utilitarian. Persons with this orientation may find religion useful in a variety of ways—to provide security and solace, sociability and distraction, status and self-justification. The embraced creed is lightly held or else selectively shaped to fit more primary needs. In theological terms the extrinsic type turns to God, but without turning away from self.

Intrinsic Orientation

Persons with this orientation find their master motive in religion. Other needs, strong as they may be, are regarded as of less ultimate significance, and they are, insofar as possible, brought into harmony with the religious beliefs and prescriptions. Having embraced a creed the individual endeavors to internalize it and follow it fully. It is in this sense that he *lives* his religion.

A clergyman was making the same distinction when he said,

> Some people come to church to thank God, to acknowledge His glory, and to ask His guidance. . . . Others come for what they can get. Their interest in the church is to run it or exploit it rather than to serve it.

Approximate parallels to these psychological types have been proposed by the sociologists Fichter (1954) and Lenski (1961). The former, in studying Catholic parishioners, classified them into four groups: the dormant, the marginal, the modal, and the nuclear. Omitting the dormant, Fichter estimated in terms of numbers that 20 per cent are marginal, 70 per cent modal, and less than 10 per cent nuclear. It is, of course, the latter group that would most closely correspond to our conception of the "intrinsic." Lenski distinguished between church members whose involvement is "communal" (for the purpose of sociability and status) and those who are "associational" (seeking the deeper values of their faith).

These authors see the significance of their classifications for the study of prejudice. Fichter has found less prejudice among devout (nuclear) Catholics than among others (see Allport,

1954, p. 421). Lenski (1961, p. 173) reported that among Detroit Catholics 59 per cent of those with a predominantly "communal" involvement favored segregated schools, whereas among those with predominantly an "associational" involvement only 27 per cent favored segregation. The same trend held for Detroit Protestants.

The first published study relating the extrinsic-intrinsic dimension directly to ethnic prejudice was that of Wilson (1960). Limiting himself to a 15-item scale measuring an extrinsic (utilitarian-institutional) orientation, Wilson found in 10 religious groups a median correlation of .65 between his scale and anti-Semitism. In general these correlations were higher than he obtained between anti-Semitism and the Religious-Conventionalism Scale (Levinson, 1954). From this finding Wilson concluded that orthodoxy or fundamentalism is a less important factor than extrinsicness of orientation.

Certain weaknesses may be pointed out in this pioneer study. Wilson did not attempt to measure intrinsicness of orientation, but assumed without warrant that it was equivalent to a low score on the extrinsic measures. Further, since the items were worded in a unidirectional way there may be an error of response set. Again, Wilson dealt only with Jews as a target of prejudice, and so the generality of his finding is not known.

Finally, the factor of educational level plays a part. Wilson used the California anti-Semitism scale, and we know that high scores on this scale go with low education (Christie, 1954; Pettigrew, 1959; Titus & Hollander, 1957; Williams, 1964). Further, in our own study the extrinsic subscale is negatively correlated with degree of education ($r = -.32$). To an appreciable extent, therefore, Wilson's high correlations may be "ascribed" to educational level.

At this point, however, an important theoretical observation must be made. Low education may indeed predispose a person toward an exclusionist, self-centered, extrinsic, religious orientation and may dispose him to a stereotyped, fearful image of Jews. This fact does not in the least affect the functional relationship between the religious and the prejudiced outlooks. It is a common error for investigators to "control for" demographic factors without considering the danger involved in doing so. In so doing they are often obscuring and not illuminating the functional (i.e., psychological) relationships that obtain (see Allport, 1950).

Following Wilson the task of direct meaurement was taken up by Feagin (1964) who used a more developed scale—one designed to measure not only extrinsic orientation but also the intrinsic. His scales are essentially the same as those discussed in a later section of this paper. In his study of Southern Baptists Feagin reached four conclusions: (*a*) Contrary to expectation, extrinsic and intrinsic items did not fall on a unidimensional scale but represented two independent dimensions; (*b*) only the extrinsic orientation was related to intolerance toward Negroes; (*c*) orthodoxy as such was not related to the extrinsic or intrinsic orientation; (*d*) greater orthodoxy (fundamentalism of belief) did, however, relate positively to prejudice.

Taking all these studies together we are justified in assuming that the inner experience of religion (what it means to the individual) is an important causal factor in developing a tolerant or a prejudiced outlook on life.

Yet, additional evidence is always in place, and new insights can be gained by a closer inspection of the rather coarse relationships that have been established up to now.

THE PRESENT STUDY

We wished to employ an improved and broader measure of prejudice than had previously been used. And since direct measures of prejudice (naming the target groups) have become too sensitive for wide use, we wished to try some abbreviated indirect measures. Further, we wished to make use of an improved Extrinsic-Intrinsic scale, one that would give reliable measures of both extrinsic and intrinsic tendencies in a person's religious life. For these reasons the following instruments were adopted.

Social Problems Questionnaire

This scale, devised by Harding and Schuman (unpublished;[1] see also Schuman & Harding, 1963, 1964), is a subtly worded instrument containing 12 anti-Negro, 11 anti-Jewish, and 10 anti-other items (pertaining to Orientals, Mexicans, and Puerto Ricans). The wording is varied so as to avoid an agreement response set.

Indirect Prejudice Measures

Six items were taken from Gilbert and Levinson's (1956) Custodial Mental Illness Ideology Scale (CMI). Example: "We should be sympathetic with mental patients, but we cannot expect to understand their odd behavior. a) I definitely disagree. b) I tend to disagree. c) I tend to agree. d) I definitely agree."

Four items are related to a "jungle" philosophy of life, suggesting a generalized suspiciousness and distrust. Example: "The world is a hazardous place in which men are basically evil and dangerous. a) I definitely disagree. b) I tend to disagree. c) I tend to agree. d) I definitely agree."

In all cases the most prejudiced response receives a score of 5 and the least prejudiced response, 1. No response was scored 3.

From Table 3 we see that while the indirect measures have a positive correlation with each other and with direct measures the relationship is scarcely high enough to warrant the substitution of the indirect for the direct. The high correlations between prejudice for the three ethnic target groups once

[1] J. Harding and H. Schuman, "Social Problems Questionnaire," Cornell University.

TABLE 3

INTERCORRELATIONS BETWEEN FIVE MEASURES
OF PREJUDICE

	Anti-Jewish	Anti-Other	Jungle	CMI
Anti-Negro	.63	.70	.20	.25
Anti-Jewish		.67	.24	.31
Anti-Other			.33	.36
Jungle				.43

Note.—$N = 309$.

again illustrate the well-established fact that ethnic prejudice tends to be a broadly generalized disposition in personality.

Religious Orientation Measure

The full scale, entitled "Religious Orientation," is available from ADI.[2] It separates the intrinsically worded items from the extrinsic, gives score values for each item, and reports on item reliabilities. In all cases a score of 1 indicates the most intrinsic response, a score of 5, the most extrinsic. While it is possible to use all 20 items as one continuous scale, it will soon become apparent that it is often wise to treat the two subscales separately. A sample item from the extrinsic subscale follows: "What religion offers me most is comfort when sorrows and misfortune strike. a) I definitely disagree, 1. b) I tend to disagree, 2. c) I tend to agree, 4. d) I definitely agree, 5." A sample item from the intrinsic subscale: "My religious beliefs are what really lie behind my whole approach to life. a) this is definitely not so, 5. b) probably not so, 4. c) probably so, 2. d) definitely so, 1."

[2] The full Religious Orientation scale has been deposited with the American Documentation Institute. Order Document No. 9268 from ADI Auxiliary Publications Project, Photoduplication Service, Library of Congress, Washington, D.C. 20540. Remit in advance $1.25 for microfilm or $1.25 for photocopies and make checks payable to: Chief, Photoduplication Service, Library of Congress.

SAMPLE

While our sample of six groups of churchgoers shows some diversity of denomination and region, it is in no sense representative. Graduate-student members of a seminar collected the 309 cases from the following church groups: Group A, 94 Roman Catholic (Massachusetts); Group B, 55 Lutheran (New York State); Group C, 44 Nazarene (South Carolina); Group D, 53 Presbyterian (Pennsylvania); Group E, 35 Methodist (Tennessee); Group F, 28 Baptist (Massachusetts).

We labeled the groups alphabetically since such small subsamples could not possibly lead to valid generalizations concerning denominations as a whole. All subjects knew that they were invited to participate as members of a religious group, and this fact may well have introduced a "proreligious" bias.

GROSS RESULTS

If we pool all our cases for the purpose of correlating religious orientation with prejudice, we discover that while the findings are in the expected direction they are much less impressive than those of previous studies, especially Wilson's.

Correlations with Extrinsic Subscale

Since Wilson employed an extrinsic scale similar to ours, we first present in Table 4 our findings using this subscale and the

TABLE 4
CORRELATIONS BETWEEN EXTRINSIC SUBSCALE
AND PREJUDICE

Anti-Negro	.26
Anti-Jewish	.21
Anti-Other	.32
Jungle	.29
CMI	.44

Note.—$N = 309$.

various measures of prejudice. Whereas Wilson found a correlation of .65 between his extrinsic and anti-Semitic measures, our correlation falls to .21. In part the reason no doubt lies in certain features of Wilson's method which we have criticized.

Correlations with Combined Extrinsic-Intrinsic Scale

From the outset it was our intention to broaden Wilson's unidirectional (extrinsic) measure to see whether our hypothesis might hold for the total scale (combined scores for the 11 extrinsic and 9 intrinsic items). As Table 5 shows, matters do

TABLE 5
CORRELATIONS BETWEEN TOTAL EXTRINSIC-
INTRINSIC SCALE AND PREJUDICE

Anti-Negro	.26
Anti-Jewish	.18
Anti-Other	.18
Jungle	.21
CMI	.17

Note.—$N = 309$.

not improve but seem to worsen. The logic of combining the two subscales is of course to augment the continuum in length and presumably enhance the reliability of the total measure. It soon became apparent, however, that subjects who endorse extrinsically worded items do not necessarily reject those worded intrinsically, or vice versa. It turns out that there is only a very low correlation in the expected direction between the two subscales ($r = .21$). Obviously at this point some reformulation is badly needed.

REFORMULATION OF THE APPROACH

Examination of the data reveals that some subjects are indeed "consistently intrinsic," having a strong tendency to endorse intrinsically worded items and to reject the extrinsically worded. Correspondingly others are "consistently extrinsic." Yet, unfortunately for our neat typology, many subjects are provokingly inconsistent. They persist in endorsing any or all items that to them seem favorable to religion in any sense. Their responses, therefore, are "indiscriminately proreligious."

The problem is essentially the same as that encountered by the many investigators who have attempted to reverse the wording of items comprising the F-scale, in order to escape an unwanted response-set bias. Uniformly the effort has proved to be frustrating, since so many subjects subscribe to both the positive and negative wording of the same question (see Bass, 1955; Chapman & Bock, 1958; Chapman & Campbell, 1959; Christie, 1954; Jackson & Messick, 1957).

An example from our own subscales would be: "My religious beliefs are what really lie behind my whole approach to life" (intrinsic). "Though I believe in my religion, I feel there are many more important things in my life" (extrinsic).

The approach used by Peabody (1961) offers us a model for analyzing our data in a meaningful way. Peabody administered both positive and negative F-scale items to subjects at two different testing sessions. By comparing each individual's responses to the same question stated positively at one time and in reverse at another he was able to separate out those who were consistently pro or anti toward the content of authoritarian items. But he found many who expressed double agreement (or disagreement) with both versions of the same question. Table 6 applies Peabody's paradigm to our data.

TABLE 6
FOUR PATTERNS OF RELIGIOUS ORIENTATION

	Agrees with intrinsic choice	Disagrees with intrinsic choice
Agrees with extrinsic choice	Indiscriminately proreligious	Consistently extrinsic in type
Disagrees with extrinsic choice	Consistently intrinsic in type	Indiscriminately antireligious or nonreligious[a]

[a] Not found in present sample.

In assigning our 309 cases to these categories we employed the following criteria.

Intrinsic type includes individuals who agree with intrinsically worded items on the intrinsic subscale, and who disagree with extrinsically stated items on the extrinsic subscale. By the scoring method employed these individuals fall below the median scores on both subscales.

Extrinsic type includes individuals who agree with extrinsically stated items on the extrinsic subscale, and who disagree with items on the intrinsic subscale. By our scoring method these individuals all fall above the median scores on both subscales.

Indiscriminately proreligious includes those who on the intrinsic subscale score at least 12 points less than on the extrinsic subscale. (This figure reflects the fact that a subject gives approximately 50 per cent more intrinsic responses on the intrinsic subscale than we should expect from his extrinsic responses to the extrinsic subscale.)

Indiscriminately antireligious or nonreligious includes those who would show a strong tendency to disagree with items on both subscales. Since nonchurchgoers are excluded from our samples, such cases are not found. (Some pilot work with markedly liberal groups indicates that this type does exist,

TABLE 7
PERCENTAGE OF EACH RELIGIOUS TYPE IN
EACH SUBSAMPLE

Religious group	N	Consistently intrinsic	Consistently extrinsic	Indiscriminately proreligious
A	(94)	36	34	30
B	(55)	35	36	29
C	(44)	36	39	25
D	(53)	32	30	38
E	(35)	31	29	40
F	(28)	39	39	22

however, even among members of "religious" organizations.) Table 7 gives the percentage of the three types.

RESULTS OF THE REFORMULATION

The five measures of prejudice were analyzed by a 6 (Groups) × 3 (Religious Types) analysis of variance. Table 8 presents

TABLE 8
PREJUDICE AND RELIGIOUS ORIENTATION

Target of prejudice	Mean prejudice score			
	Intrinsic type $N = 108$	Extrinsic type $N = 106$	Incon- sistent type $N = 95$	F ratio
Anti-Negro	28.7	33.0	36.0	8.6**
Anti-Jewish	22.6	24.6	28.9	11.1**
Anti-Other	20.4	23.3	26.1	10.9**
Jungle	7.9	8.7	9.6	8.4**
CMI	10.2	11.8	13.4	20.4**

Multivariate analysis of variance

Source of variation	F ratio	df
Religious type (A)	5.96***	10,574
Sample groups (B)	3.19***	25,668
A × B	1.11*	50,1312

*$p > .25$.
**$p > .001$.
***$p > .0005$.

the overall effects for religious types for each of the five measures of prejudice. The multivariate analysis of variance indicates that there is both a significant difference between the three types of religious orientation and between the six subsamples in the level of prejudice.[3] Examination of the

[3] The multivariate F reported here is Wilk's lambda (Anderson, 1958). Statistical computations are summarized by Bock (1963) and programmed for the IBM 7090 by Hall and Cramer (1962). The univariate tests to be reported are adjusted for unequal Ns to obtain orthogonal estimates according to mathematical procedures described in Hall and Cramer.

means shows two trends: (*a*) The extrinsic type is more prejudiced than the intrinsic type for both direct and indirect measures; (*b*) the indiscriminate type of religious orientation is more prejudiced than either of the two consistent types. Statistically all these trends are highly significant.

We note especially that the scores of the indiscriminate type are markedly higher on all measures than the scores of the intrinsic type. Corresponding F ratios for paired comparisons range from 8.4 for the jungle scale to 20.4 for the CMI scale. The differences between the indiscriminate and extrinsic types are smaller. For the anti-Jewish and CMI scales these differences are, however, beyond the .005 level; for the anti-other and jungle scales, at the .05 level. For the anti-Negro the difference falls below significance.

The relationship between the indiscriminately proreligious orientation and prejudice receives support (see Table 9) when

TABLE 9
DEGREES OF INDISCRIMINATENESS AND AVERAGE
PREJUDICE SCORES

Target of prejudice	Moderately indiscriminate $N = 56$	Extremely indiscriminate $N = 39$	F ratio
Anti-Negro	35.4	37.9	.97
Anti-Jewish	28.0	30.1	.90
Anti-Other	24.9	28.2	3.25*
Jungle	9.5	10.2	1.11
CMI	10.2	14.6	3.99*

*$p > .05$.

we compare subjects who are *moderately* indiscriminate with those who are *extremely* indiscriminate. (In the first group the scores on the intrinsic subscale average 16 points lower than on the extrinsic subscale; whereas the extreme cases average 23 points less on the intrinsic than on the extrinsic subscale.)

The discovery that the degree of indiscriminateness tends to relate directly to the degree of prejudice is an important finding. It can only mean that some functional relationship obtains between religious muddleheadedness (for that is what indiscriminate scores imply) and antagonism toward ethnic groups. We shall return to this interpretation in the concluding section of this paper.

RESULTS FOR SUBSAMPLES

It would not be correct to assume that the variance is distributed equally over all the subsamples, for it turns out that the denominational groups differ appreciably in prejudice scores and in religious type, as Tables 10 and 11 indicate.

TABLE 10
ANTI-NEGRO PREJUDICE: MEAN SCORES ON SOCIAL PROBLEMS SCALE

Religious group	Intrinsic type	Extrinsic type	Indiscriminate type	Group M
A	27.4 (34)	34.8 (32)	32.2 (28)	31.4 (94)
B	27.2 (19)	32.3 (20)	31.9 (16)	30.4 (55)
C	22.4 (16)	36.2 (17)	35.0 (11)	30.9 (44)
D	35.5 (17)	28.7 (16)	42.5 (20)	36.1 (53)
E	40.5 (11)	35.5 (10)	43.0 (14)	40.1 (35)
F	22.6 (11)	27.9 (11)	28.7 (6)	26.0 (28)
Type M	28.7 (108)	33.0 (106)	36.0 (95)	32.5 (309)

Analysis of variance

Source of variation	df	MS	F ratio
Religious type (A)	2	1077.8	8.6**
Religious group (B)	5	952.2	7.6**
A × B	10	251.1	2.0*
Error (w)	291	125.6	

*$p > .10$.
**$p > .001$.

It is true that when we combine subsamples all the trends are in the expected direction, but troublesome exceptions occur for single groups as indicated by the nearly significant interaction effects. The most troublesome contradictions appear in relation to the anti-Negro measures based on the Harding-Schuman scale. Table 10 discloses certain sore points, even though the average trend over all the subsamples is in the predicted direction.

For Groups A, B, and C we note that the indiscriminate type is slightly less prejudiced than the extrinsic type, and for Groups D and E the extrinsic type seems actually less prejudiced than the intrinsic. (Groups D and E are consistently more troublesome than other subsamples, perhaps because of some salient racial issue in the local community. It will be noted that both these groups are considerably more anti-Negro than the other subsamples.)

By way of contrast we present in Table 11 the results for the short (five-item) CMI scale. With the exception of the indiscriminate type in Group F, the progression of scores is pre-

TABLE 11

INDIRECT (CMI) MEASURE OF PREJUDICE

Religious group	Intrinsic type	Extrinsic type	Indiscriminate type	Group M
A	11.2 (34)	12.4 (32)	13.6 (28)	12.3 (94)
B	10.1 (19)	10.8 (20)	13.4 (16)	11.3 (55)
C	9.5 (16)	12.2 (17)	12.6 (11)	11.3 (44)
D	10.6 (17)	11.4 (16)	14.8 (20)	12.4 (53)
E	8.6 (11)	12.9 (10)	13.6 (14)	11.8 (35)
F	9.2 (11)	10.7 (11)	9.2 (6)	9.8 (28)
Type M	10.2 (108)	11.8 (106)	13.4 (95)	11.9 (309)

Analysis of variance

Source of variation	df	MS	F ratio
Religious type (A)	2	255.0	20.4**
Religious group (B)	5	36.5	2.9*
A × B	10	15.3	1.2
Error (w)	291	12.5	

*$p > .05$.
**$p > .001$.

cisely as expected. Each subsample shows that the intrinsic type is less prejudiced toward the mentally ill than the extrinsic type, and the extrinsic type is less prejudiced than the indiscriminately proreligious.[4]

Returning in a different way to the original question of whether consistent extrinsic and intrinsic orientations make for prejudice and for tolerance, respectively, we shall now examine this matter in each subsample separately. Inspection of the mean scores and variance for the total scale indicates that we are dealing with a relatively narrow range of variation. To minimize the effect of a narrow range of scores and skewed distributions, we used Kendal's (1955) tau as a measure of degree of relationship between prejudice and consistent religious orientation. The results are given in Table 12. While the correlations are not high (14 are significant in the expected direction), only one (in the troublesome Group E) is significant in the reverse direction.

[4] If we apply a more severe test, asking whether *all* differences between groups are significant, we find the following results. In four of the six groups (in both Tables 10 and 11) the extrinsic type is significantly more prejudiced than the intrinsic. Likewise in four out of six groups (Table 10) and five out of six (Table 11), the indiscriminate type is significantly more prejudiced than the intrinsic. However, in only two of the six groups (in both Tables 10 and 11) is the indiscriminate type significantly more prejudiced than the extrinsic.

TABLE 12

CORRELATIONS BETWEEN COMBINED EXTRINSIC-INTRINSIC
RELIGIOUS SCORES (FOR CONSISTENT SUBJECTS) AND
PREJUDICE (KENDAL'S TAU)

Religious group	Anti-Negro	Anti-Jewish	Anti-Other	Jungle	CMI
A	.31***	.26***	.24***	.14*	.19***
B	.19*	.13	.15	—.05	.03
C	.32***	.17*	.35***	.14*	.28***
D	—.12	.05	—.09	.03	.11
E	—.24*	—.11	—.13	.26*	.46***
F	.39***	.13	.25*	—.01	.24*

*$p > .10$.
**$p > .05$.
***$p > .01$.

EDUCATIONAL DIFFERENCES

Computing the actual years of schooling for all groups we find that the indiscriminate type has significantly less formal education than the intrinsic cases ($p > .005$, $F = 18.29$), and somewhat less than the extrinsic type ($p > .10$, $F = 2.89$). Comparing extrinsic with intrinsic types we find that the former has finished fewer years of schooling ($p > .10$, $F = 3.45$). (Oddly enough the groups with highest average education are D and E, which also displayed the highest anti-Negro and anti-Semitic prejudice—perhaps because of particular local conditions.)

In our survey of earlier studies we saw that educational level is often a factor in the various relationships discovered between religion and prejudice. We have also argued that demographic factors of this sort should not be allowed to obscure the functional (psychological) analysis that the data call for. Granted that low education makes for indiscriminate thinking, the mental confusion that results from low education may have its own peculiar effects on religious and ethnic attitudes.

SUMMARY AND INTERPRETATIONS

At the outset we stated three propositions that seem to be firmly established: (*a*) Churchgoers on the broad average harbor more ethnic prejudice than nonchurchgoers; (*b*) in spite of this broad tendency a curvilinear relationship in fact exists; (*c*) the intrinsically motivated churchgoers are significantly less prejudiced than the extrinsically motivated. Our present research supplies additional strong support for the second and third of these propositions.

To these propositions we add a fourth: *churchgoers who are indiscriminately proreligious are more prejudiced than the consistently extrinsic, and very much more prejudiced than the consistently intrinsic types.*

The psychological tie between the intrinsic orientation and tolerance, and between the extrinsic orientation and prejudice, has been discussed in a series of papers by Allport (1959, 1963, 1966). In brief the argument holds that a person with an extrinsic religious orientation is using his religious views to provide security, comfort, status, or social support for himself —religion is not a value in its own right, it serves other needs, and it is a purely utilitarian formation. Now prejudice too is a "useful" formation: it too provides security, comfort, status, and social support. A life that is dependent on the supports of extrinsic religion is likely to be dependent on the supports of prejudice, hence our positive correlations between the extrinsic orientation and intolerance. Contrariwise, the intrinsic religious orientation is not an instrumental device. It is not a mere mode of conformity, nor a crutch, nor a tranquilizer, nor a bid for status. All needs are subordinated to an overarching religious commitment. In internalizing the total creed of his religion the individual necessarily internalizes its values of humility, compassion, and love of neighbor. In such a life (where religion is an intrinsic and dominant value) there is no place for rejection, contempt, or condescension toward one's fellow man. Such is our explanation for the relationship between extrinsic religion and prejudice, and between intrinsic religion and tolerance.

Our present task is to discover, if we can, some similar functional tie between prejudice (as measured both directly and indirectly) and the indiscriminately proreligious orientation. The common factor seems to be a certain cognitive style. Technically it might be called "undifferentiated thinking," or excessive "category width," as defined by Pettigrew (1958). Rokeach (1960) notes the inability of the "dogmatic" mind to perceive differences; thus, whereas some people distinguish in their thinking and feeling between Communists and Nazis, the undifferentiated dogmatist has a global reaction (cognitive and emotional) toward "Communazis."

We have no right, of course, to expect all our subjects to make discriminations exactly corresponding to our own logic. Nor should we expect them to read and respond to every item on the Extrinsic-Intrinsic scale according to its full meaning as intended by the investigators. Perhaps we should be gratified that two-thirds of our cases can be safely classified as "consistent" (i.e., having about the same strength of disposition toward an extrinsic or intrinsic orientation across most of the items). These consistent cases, as we have seen, support the hypothesis with which we started. It is the remaining (indiscriminate) one-third of the cases which obscure the trend (or diminish its statistical significance).

In responding to the religious items these individuals seem to take a superficial or "hit and run" approach. Their mental set seems to be "all religion is good." "My religious beliefs are what really lie behind my whole life"—Yes! "Although I believe in my religion, I feel there are many more important things in my life"—Yes! "Religion is especially important to me because it answers many questions about the meaning of life"—Yes! "The church is most important as a place to formulate good social relationships"—Yes!

There seems to be one wide category—"religion is OK." From the way in which the scale is constructed this undifferentiated endorsement can be the product of an agreement response set. Our inconsistently proreligious may be "yeasayers" (Couch & Keniston, 1960). But if so, we are still dealing with an undifferentiated cognitive disposition. We recall likewise that the inconsistent cases have a lower level of formal education than the consistent cases. This factor also is relevant to the formation and holding of overwide categories.

But why should such a disposition, whatever its source, be so strongly related to prejudice, in such a way that the *more* undifferentiated, the *more* prejudiced—as Table 9 shows?

The answer is that prejudice itself is a matter of stereotyped overgeneralization, a failure to distinguish members of a minority group as individuals (Allport, 1954, Chaps. 2, 10). It goes without saying that if categories are overwide the accompanying feeling tone will be undifferentiated. Thus, religion as a whole is good; a minority group as a whole is bad.

It seems probable that people with undifferentiated styles of thinking (and feeling) are not entirely secure in a world that for the most part demands fine and accurate distinctions. The resulting diffuse anxiety may well dispose them to grapple onto religion and to distrust strange ethnic groups. The positive correlation between the jungle items and other prejudice scales (Table 3) is evidence for this interpretation.

Our line of reasoning, readers will recognize, is compatible with various previous contributions to the theory of prejudice. One thinks here of Rokeach's concept of dogmatism; of Schuman and Harding's (1964) discovery of a "confused" type in their study of the relation between rational consistency and prejudice; of the same authors' work on sympathetic identification (1963); of studies on the dynamics of scapegoating, the role in insecurity, of authoritarian submission, of intolerance for ambiguity, and of related concepts.

All in all, we conclude that prejudice, like tolerance, is often embedded deeply in personality structure and is reflected in a consistent cognitive style. Both states of mind are enmeshed with the individual's religious orientation. One definable style marks the individual who is bigoted in ethnic matters and extrinsic in his religious orientation. Equally apparent is the style of those who are bigoted and at the same time indiscriminately proreligious. A relatively small number of people show an equally consistent cognitive style in their simultaneous commitment to religion as a dominant, intrinsic value and to ethnic tolerance.

One final word: our research argues strongly that social scientists who employ the variable "religion" or "religiosity" in the future will do well to keep in mind the crucial distinction between religious attitudes that are *intrinsic, extrinsic,* and *indiscriminately pro.* To know that a person is in some sense "religious" is not as important as to know the role religion plays in the economy of his life. (The categories of *nonreligious* and *indiscriminately antireligious* will also for some purposes be of central significance, although the present research, confined as it is to churchgoers, does not employ them.)

REFERENCES

Adorno, T. W., Frenkel-Brunswik, E., Levinson, D. J., & Sanford, R. N., *The authoritarian personality*, New York: Harper, 1950.

Allport, G. W., review of S. A. Stouffer, E. A. Suchman, L. C. De Vinney, S. A. Star, & R. W. Williams, Jr., *The American soldier*, Vol. 1, *Adjustment during Army life. Journal of Abnormal and Social Psychology*, 1950, 45, 168–173.

———, *The nature of prejudice*, Reading, Mass.: Addison-Wesley, 1954.

———, "Religion and prejudice," *The Crane Review*, 1959, 2, 1–10.

———, "Behavioral science, religion, and mental health," *Journal of Religion and Health*, 1963, 2, 187–197.

———, "Religious context of prejudice," *Journal for the Scientific Study of Religion*, 1966, 5, 447–457.

———, & Kramer, B. M., "Some roots of prejudice," *Journal of Psychology*, 1946, 22, 9–39.

Anderson, T. W., *An introduction to multivariate statistical analysis*, New York: Wiley, 1958.

Bass, B. M., "Authoritarianism or acquiescence," *Journal of Abnormal and Social Psychology*, 1955, 56, 616–623.

Bock, R. D., "Programming univariate and multivariate analysis of variance," *Technometrics*, 1963, 5, 95–117.

Chapman, L. J., & Bock, R. D., "Components of variance due to acquiescence and content in the F-scale measure of authoritarianism," *Psychological Bulletin*, 1958, 55, 328–333.

Chapman, L. J., & Campbell, D. T., "The effect of acquiescence response-set upon relationships among the F-scale, ethnocentrism, and intelligence," *Sociometry*, 1959, 22, 153–161.

Christie, R. C., "Authoritarianism re-examined," in R. C. Christie & M. Jahoda (eds.), *Studies in the scope and method of the authoritarian personality*, New York: Free Press of Glencoe, 1954. Pp. 123–196.

Couch, A., & Keniston, K., "Yeasayers and naysayers: Agreeing response set as a personality variable," *Journal of Abnormal and Social Psychology*, 1960, 60, 151–174.

Demerath, N. J., III, *Social class in American Protestantism*, Chicago: Rand McNally, 1965.

Feagin, J. R., "Prejudice and religious types: A focused study of southern fundamentalists," *Journal for the Scientific Study of Religion*, 1964, *4*, 3–13.

Fichter, J. H., *Social relations in the urban parish*, Chicago: University of Chicago Press, 1954.

Friedrichs, R. W., "Christians and residential exclusion: An empirical study of a Northern dilemma," *Journal of Social Issues*, 1959, *15*, 14–23.

Gilbert, D. C., & Levinson, D. J., "Ideology, personality, and institutional policy in the mental hospital," *Journal of Abnormal and Social Psychology*, 1956, *53*, 263–271.

Gough, H. G., "Studies in social intolerance: IV," *Journal of Social Psychology*, 1951, *33*, 263–269.

Hall, C. E., & Cramer, E., *General purpose program to compute multivariate analysis of variance on an IBM 7090*, Washington, D.C.: George Washington University Biometric Laboratory, 1962.

Holtzman, W. H., "Attitudes of college men toward non-segregation in Texas schools," *Public Opinion Quarterly*, 1956, *20*, 559–569.

Jackson, D. H., & Messick, S. J., "A note on ethnocentrism and acquiescence response sets," *Journal of Abnormal and Social Psychology*, 1957, *54*, 132–134.

Kelly, J. G., Ferson, J. E., & Holtzman, W. H., "The measurement of attitudes toward the Negro in the South," *Journal of Social Psychology*, 1958, *48*, 305–317.

Kendal, M. G., *Rank correlation methods* (2nd ed.), London: Griffin, 1955.

Kirkpatrick, C., "Religion and humanitarianism: A study of institutional implications," *Psychological Monographs*, 1949, *63* (9, Whole No. 304).

Lenski, G., *The religious factor*, Garden City, N.Y.: Doubleday, 1961.

Levinson, D. J., "The inter-group workshop: Its psychological aims and effects," *Journal of Psychology*, 1954, *38*, 103–126.

Peabody, D., "Attitude content and agreement set in scales of authoritarianism, dogmatism, anti-Semitism and economic conservatism," *Journal of Abnormal and Social Psychology*, 1961, *63*, 1–11.

Pettigrew, T. F., "The measurement and correlates of category width as a cognitive variable," *Journal of Personality*, 1958, *26*, 532–544.

———, "Regional differences in anti-Negro prejudice," *Journal of Abnormal and Social Psychology*, 1959, *49*, 28–36.

Pinkney, A., *The anatomy of prejudice: Majority group attitudes toward minorities in selected American cities*. Unpublished doctoral dissertation, Cornell University, 1961.

Rokeach, M., *The open and closed mind: Investigations into the nature of belief systems and personality systems*, New York: Basic Books, 1960.

Rosenblith, J. F., "A replication of 'Some roots of prejudice,'" *Journal of Abnormal and Social Psychology*, 1949, *44*, 470–489.

Schuman, H., & Harding, J., "Sympathetic identification with the underdog," *Public Opinion Quarterly*, 1963, *27*, 230–241.

———, & ———, "Prejudice and the norm of rationality," *Sociometry*, 1964, *27*, 353–371.

Stember, H. C., *Education and attitude change*, New York: Institute of Human Relations Press, 1961.

Stouffer, S. A., *Communism, civil liberties, and conformity*, Garden City, N.Y.: Doubleday, 1955.

Struening, E. L., "Antidemocratic attitudes in a Midwest university," in H. H. Remmers (ed.), *Anti-democratic attitudes in American schools*, Evanston: Northwestern University Press, 1963. Ch. 9.

Titus, H. E., & Hollander, E. P., "The California F scale in psychological research: 1950–1955," *Psychological Bulletin*, 1957, *54*, 47–64.

Tumin, M., *Desegregation: Resistance and readiness*, Princeton: Princeton University Press, 1958.

Williams, R. M., *Strangers next door: Ethnic relations in American communities*, Englewood Cliffs, N.J.: Prentice-Hall, 1964.

Wilson, W. C., "Extrinsic religious values and prejudice," *Journal of Abnormal and Social Psychology*, 1960, *60*, 286–288.

Young, R. K., Benson, W. M., & Holtzman, W. H., "Changes in attitudes toward the Negro in a Southern university," *Journal of Abnormal and Social Psychology*, 1960, *60*, 131–133.

Extrinsic-Intrinsic Religious Orientation

THE ITEMS employed in the present research are listed separately for the extrinsic subscale and for the intrinsic. In actual use, of course, they are interspersed (to avoid agreement response-set).

In both subscales the items are scored in such a way that scores of 4 or 5 indicate an extrinsic orientation, while scores of 1 and 2 indicate an intrinsic orientation. If an item is omitted it receives a score of 3.

While the scores of the 20 items may be summed (with high totals indicating an extrinsic orientation), it is probably well, as the present research demonstrates, to obtain separate scores for the two subscales in order to distinguish cases that are "indiscriminately pro-religious" from those that are consistently extrinsic or intrinsic.

In parentheses following the statement of each item the reader finds the correlation of the item with the total subscale score.

Inquiry Concerning Social and Religious Views

The following items deal with various types of religious ideas and social opinions. We should like to find out how common they are.

Please indicate the response you prefer, or most closely agree with, *by writing the letter corresponding to your choice in the right margin.*

If none of the choices expresses exactly how you feel, then indicate the one which is closest to your own views. If no choice is possible you may omit the item.

There are no "right" or "wrong" choices. There will be many religious people who will agree with all the possible alternative answers.

Extrinsic Subscale

1. What religion offers me most is comfort when sorrows and misfortune strike. (.49)
   - a) I definitely disagree   1
   - b) I tend to disagree   2
   - c) I tend to agree   4
   - d) I definitely agree   5

2. One reason for my being a church member is that such membership helps to establish a person in the community. (.47)
   - a) definitely not true   1
   - b) tends not to be true   2
   - c) tends to be true   4
   - d) definitely true   5

3. The purpose of prayer is to secure a happy and peaceful life. (.51)
   - a) I definitely disagree   1
   - b) I tend to disagree   2
   - c) I tend to agree   4
   - d) I definitely agree   5

4. It doesn't matter so much what I believe so long as I lead a moral life. (.39)
   - a) I definitely disagree   1
   - b) I tend to disagree   2
   - c) I tend to agree   4
   - d) I definitely agree   5

5. Although I am a religious person I refuse to let religious considerations influence my everyday affairs. (.31)
   - a) definitely not true of me   1
   - b) tends not to be true   2
   - c) tends to be true   4
   - d) clearly true in my case   5

6. The church is most important as a place to formulate good social relationships. (.44)
   - a) I definitely disagree   1
   - b) I tend to disagree   2
   - c) I tend to agree   4
   - d) I definitely agree   5
7. Although I believe in my religion, I feel there are many more important things in my life. (.32)
   - a) I definitely disagree   1
   - b) I tend to disagree   2
   - c) I tend to agree   4
   - d) I definitely agree   5
8. I pray chiefly because I have been taught to pray. (.31)
   - a) definitely true of me   5
   - b) tends to be true   4
   - c) tends not to be true   2
   - d) definitely not true of me   1
9. A primary reason for my interest in religion is that my church is a congenial social activity. (.33)
   - a) definitely not true of me   1
   - b) tends not to be true   2
   - c) tends to be true   4
   - d) definitely true of me   5
10. Occasionally I find it necessary to compromise my religious beliefs in order to protect my social and economic well-being. (.18)
   - a) definitely disagree   1
   - b) tend to disagree   2
   - c) tend to agree   4
   - d) definitely agree   5
11. The primary purpose of prayer is to gain relief and protection. (.50)
   - a) I definitely agree   5
   - b) I tend to agree   4
   - c) I tend to disagree   2
   - d) I definitely disagree   1

Intrinsic Subscale

1. I try hard to carry my religion over into all my other dealings in life. (.39)
   - a) I definitely disagree   5
   - b) I tend to disagree   4
   - c) I tend to agree   2
   - d) I definitely agree   1

2. Quite often I have been keenly aware of the presence of God or the Divine Being. (.44)
   - a) definitely not true   5
   - b) tends not to be true   4
   - c) tends to be true   2
   - d) definitely true   1

3. My religious beliefs are what really lie behind my whole approach to life. (.50)
   - a) this is definitely not so   5
   - b) probably not so   4
   - c) probably so   2
   - d) definitely so   1

4. The prayers I say when I am alone carry as much meaning and personal emotion as those said by me during services. (.30)
   - a) almost never   5
   - b) sometimes   4
   - c) usually   2
   - d) almost always   1

5. If not prevented by unavoidable circumstances, I attend church. (.47)
   - a) more than once a week   1
   - b) about once a week   2
   - c) two or three times a month   4
   - d) less than once a month   5

6. If I were to join a church group I would prefer to join (1) a Bible Study group or (2) a social fellowship. (.49)
   - a) I would prefer to join (1)   1

    b) I probably would prefer (1)   2

    c) I probably would prefer (2)   4

    d) I would prefer to join (2)   5

7. Religion is especially important to me because it answers many questions about the meaning of life. (.28)

    a) definitely disagree   5

    b) tend to disagree   4

    c) tend to agree   2

    d) definitely agree   1

8. I read literature about my faith (or church). (.41)

    a) frequently   1

    b) occasionally   2

    c) rarely   4

    d) never   5

9. It is important to me to spend periods of time in private religious thought and meditation. (.58)

    a) frequently true   1

    b) occasionally true   2

    c) rarely true   4

    d) never true   5

PART IV

PERSONS

15

The Personalistic Psychology of William Stern[1]

THE HISTORY of psychology is pretty much a matter of the theorizing of individual men. Unlike the natural sciences there is little accumulation of consecutive fact that seems to build an objective body of knowledge regardless of the subjective world view of single theorizers. The type of psychology one chooses to follow reflects inevitably one's philosophical presuppositions about human nature.

William Stern is perhaps the only psychologist to call his systematic philosophical-psychological position "personalistic." Probably the rigidity of his formulations has discouraged others, even kindred thinkers, from adopting this label.

In Germany before the time of Hitler, Stern had considerable influence, presenting, as he did, one of the principal wholistic or structural approaches to human personality—nonassociational, nonatomistic. As one of his students, I find my own thinking considerably influenced by him, although I am selective in my borrowing from his large personalistic canvas.

This biographical account is composed of two earlier expository papers, and is here reprinted from a book edited by Benjamin Wolman and entitled, *The Historical Roots of Contemporary Psychology*, Harper and Row, 1957.

† † †

William Stern was both a pioneer and a systematizer in psychology. His mind was one of the first to range several of the special fields that are now familiar territory. He will be remembered especially for his sure-footed explorations in differential psychology, forensic psychology, psychotechnics, child psychology, and intelligence testing. But he will be remembered likewise and, I think, with increasing renown for his theoretical system of personalistic psychology wherein he ordered his manifold research, and which, in turn, he incorporated within his comprehensive philosophic doctrine of Critical Personalism.

Stern's life—in spite of his last five troubled years of exile—was remarkable for its orderliness of purpose. Already at the age of nineteen he had planned the intellectual road that he would travel, and, never doubting, he pursued it to the day of his death.[2] His every act seemed an efficient expression of his dominant purpose. He worked eagerly, without lost motion, keeping throughout his lifetime a distinctive boyish zeal and optimism. His own enthusiasm made him an effective teacher, and his well-ordered life was reflected in the high morale of the two institutes that he directed.

THE MAN AND HIS ACCOMPLISHMENTS

Born on April 29, 1871, in Berlin, (Louis) William Stern lived in that city until he was twenty-five years of age. In his third semester in the University he began to study with Ebbinghaus, a fact which decided his training and his career. Yet the influence of Lazarus and of Paulsen, with whom he likewise studied, led him to an early decision that he must transcend the naturalistic views of Ebbinghaus and work out for himself a fuller and less limited conception of proper scope of psychological science. Even in his doctoral dissertation, *Die Analogie im volkstümlichen Denken* (1893), he attempted a synthesis of cultural and experimental science, blending, as it were, the teachings of Lazarus and of Ebbinghaus.

Before going to Breslau as Privat Dozent in 1897—at the invitation of Ebbinghaus who had moved there in 1894—Stern worked for five years upon his experimental monograph, *Psychologie der Veränderungsauffassung* (1898). In this work we find an account of his invention, the *Tonvariator*, and likewise one of the earliest discussions of the "conscious present." Treating the perception of change in many sense modalities, the work foreshadows, though none too clearly, the purely phenomenological descriptions of the Gestalt school. It begins to break with the "constancy hypothesis" and may fairly be ranked as an early expression of the *Strukturbegriff*. Yet, in this work the interpretation of the nature of structure is lacking. The author only vaguely felt the need for a substantial agent which he might designate as the cause and the carrier of perceptual change. The Person was not yet discovered. The logical completion of this early monograph was not reached until thirty-seven years later in his paper, *Raum und Zeit als personale Dimensionen* (1935).

Before his promotion in Breslau to the post of *ausserordentlicher Professor* in 1907, Stern manifested his originality to its fullest extent. The first seven years of this century were for him a period of true genius. In rapid succession there appeared his pioneering books and monographs in five virgin fields of psychology. (1) *Über Psychologie der individuellen Differenzen* was published in 1900, and in it the author declared, fulsomely perhaps but nonetheless prophetically, that individuality would be the problem of the twentieth century. The book was completely rewritten in 1911 under its more familiar title, *Die differentielle Psychologie*. (2) *Zur Psychologie der Aussage* appeared in 1902, followed by two volumes of the *Beiträge zur Psychologie der Aussage*. It is interesting to note that his last public lecture delivered in New York City in December 1937 dealt with this same problem in relation to trial procedure at law. (3) The child studies likewise began at this time. Children's interest in their school work, their manner of reporting, and the accuracy of their testimony first engaged his attention. There followed soon an account of the case of Helen Keller, and the two famous monographic studies based upon observation of his three children, written in collaboration with his wife, Clara Stern, *Die Kindersprache*

(1907) and *Errinerung, Aussage und Lüge in der ersten Kindheit* (1908). (4) Applied psychology was christened and presented to the psychological public in a brochure entitled *Angewandte Psychologie* (1903). In this publication he likewise advanced the concept of *psychotechnics* (eleven years before Münsterberg appropriated it and brought it to fame). In 1906 (with the help of his student Otto Lipmann) Stern founded the *Institut für angewandte Psychologie* in Berlin and shortly thereafter the *Zeitschrift für angewandte Psychologie* (1907). Stern remained codirector of the *Institut* until 1916 and coeditor of the journal until 1933. (5) In 1900 he began to work on the foundations of his Critical Personalism, choosing definitely in that year the title for his first volume and doing much of the writing. His first philosophical publication (1903) was an article considering the second law of thermodynamics in its significance for mental science, controverting the pessimistic deductions that Von Hartmann had drawn. To the same period belongs the first publication of his system, Volume 1 of *Person und Sache: Ableitung und Grundlehre* (1906).

Thus between the ages of 29 and 35, while still a Privat Dozent, Stern fashioned with marked sureness of touch new views and new methods in four important departments of psychology—differential, forensic, child, and applied; and at the same time accomplished the initial, and therefore most creative portion of his theoretical system.

His work in child psychology, for which he is best known in America, soon grew beyond the bounds of the diary method. He became interested in more exact methods of study, and undertook to introduce into Germany the new movement of intelligence testing. His influential book, *Die psychologischen Methoden der Intelligenzprüfung und deren Anwendung an Schulkindern* (1912) was twice later rewritten. It was in this work that the concept and first formulation of the I.Q. were advanced. Soon followed another notable book, written from the normative and developmental point of view, *Psychologie der frühen Kindheit bis zum sechsten Lebensjahre* (1914). This volume found its way into several editions both in German and in English.

In 1915 Ernst Meumann died in Hamburg. Stern immediately became his successor as editor of the *Zeitschrift für pädagogische Psychologie*, and in 1916 his successor as professor of philosophy, psychology, and pedagogy at the *Kolonialinstitut* and director of the psychological laboratory that Meumann had founded. After the war the demand for new universities, caused by the return of the soldiers, led to the transformation of the colonial institute into a full-fledged university. In this transformation Stern himself played a strategic and leading part.

At Hamburg the interest in child psychology spread in a practical direction, partly to satisfy the demands of the local school system. Valuable researches are to be found in the *Hamburger Arbeiten zur Begabungsforschung*. The Institute soon became a well-known center for research in educational and vocational psychology. All the while fruitful researches in psychotechnics, legal psychology, and experimental psychology were continuing. In 1925–1928 Stern gave considerable attention to the study of puberty and adolescence, planning to extend his treatment of child psychology through these ages. Several miscellaneous papers mark this period in addition to the monograph, *Anfänge der Reifezeit* (1925), containing a psychological analysis and commentary on the diaries of a boy from his twelfth to his fifteenth year. This work takes on special interest when the reader comes to realize that the anonymous writer of the diaries and the commentator are one and the same person. Stern as boy and Stern as man were too much alike to make complete disguise possible!

The story of the Hamburg Institute (1916–1933) is told by Stern himself in four reports.[3] The last is an ominous *Schlussbericht* (1933), hastily written under the shadow of Hitler, but as ever an orderly and workmanlike report, winding up the affairs of an active, democratic, and renowned center of psychological research.

The story of his last five years serves best of all to reveal his character. His first asylum was in Holland, where he worked doggedly on his last and most comprehensive volume, *Allgemeine Psychologie auf personalistischer Grundlage*. Unable to issue it in Germany, he found for it a Dutch publisher (1935). With this writing completed, he joined the trek of exiled German scholars to America, accepting a position as lecturer and later as professor at Duke University (1934–1938). Though he had visited America twice before (once for the celebrated conference at Clark in 1909, and a second time for the IX International Congress at New Haven in 1929), he spoke little English and was entirely unfamiliar with American educational practices. Courageously, he and his gifted wife, who was his close collaborator since their marriage in 1899, set to work to master a new language and a new way of life. Besides teaching at Duke he gave occasional lectures in Eastern colleges and taught in the Harvard summer school in 1936. He held two honorary degrees from American educational institutions (Clark, 1909, and Wittenberg, 1928). America had been good to him, and so with bright prospects here he undertook the task of refashioning his personal and professional life. His chief desire was to introduce personalistic psychology into America, to counteract, as he said, the "pernicious" influence of his earlier invention, the I.Q. In February 1938 he was deeply gratified by the appearance in America of the translation (by Howard D. Spoerl) of his comprehensive text, *General Psychology from the Personalistic Standpoint*. For his next work he planned a new volume on child psychology. Suddenly, in the night of March 27, his work was ended, his prospects over. He died, without warning, of coronary occlusion.

Stern had the completest confidence in psychology, never doubting its firm position among the sciences nor its practical value for mankind. He had equal confidence in his own mission as a leader in theoretical and applied work. Consistent with this self-confidence were his ease and dignity of manner and his fluency and lucidity of expression. These qualities, combined with the vivacity and enthusiasm of which I have spoken, gave him a prominent place in public gatherings. He was a gifted conciliator. When tempers were frayed in debate, when awkward pauses followed an awkward scene, or when the occasion called for friendly remarks, it was he who could be relied upon for the right word easily spoken. Though fully conscious of his prerogatives as a German professor, and vocal about the merits of his own work, he was at the same time responsive to the thought of others and patient and kind in all his personal relations.

Unlike many philosopher-psychologists, Stern held to the end of his life his interest in the detailed problems of general psychology. His philosophical work may be said to have been completed with the publication of his *Wertlehre* (1924) or perhaps with the short volume, *Studien zur Personwissenschaft* (1930). In his last years he returned (with only a slightly relaxed grasp) to the finer details of general psychological analysis. His final text covers much the same ground as any modern text. The difference, however, lies in its tireless locating of every fragment and fact within its proper personalistic niche. For him all difficulties were resolved in the Person. This concept, and this concept alone, he thought, could provide the substantiality, the causality, and the individuality required in every mature psychological analysis.

It troubled him relatively little that his formulations ran counter to the trend of the times, particularly in American thought. Intellectually he lived largely in a world of his own making, and he believed so intensely in the liberating powers of personalistic thought that he had faith in its ultimate acceptability to others. He simply could not believe that psychologists would dwell for long within the narrow cells that they had created for themselves by a prior act of freedom. Any system other than personalistic, he felt, makes a travesty of the very mind that created it. Thinking in this vein Stern became a monumental defender of an unpopular cause. And what of that? he would ask. Are there not fashions and fashions in psychological theory? The personalistic way of thought will yet have its day, and its day will be long and bright.

THE PERSONALISTIC SYSTEM

Very few psychologists have succeeded in writing a comprehensive, full-bodied and systematic interpretation of their science. To do so requires that the author find a place for all the discordant fragments of research gathered under diverse points of view; and also that he face up to and resolve the troublesome antinomies of mental life. Determinism and freedom, dualism and monism, mind-in-general and mind-in-particular—all these and other fundamental issues call for a solution (or at least for a clear statement of position) if a psychologist aspires to be a systematist. True systematists are rare; Stern was one. His ambition was to place all psychological detail under his own philosophical tent. We watch the process as we read the three volumes of *Person und Sache* whose first editions appeared in 1906, 1918, 1924 respectively. Helpful too are *Studien zur Personwissenschaft*, 1930, and *Psychology from the Personalistic Standpoint*, 1938 (Macmillan).

The Method. The first thing to understand about Professor Stern's approach is that he offers a direct, straightforward analysis of mental life. In the manner of most scientists in the past he believes that by fixing one's gaze directly upon the course of nature, nature's own categories and cleavages will eventually appear.

The argument against this direct method is that it seems solipsistic; it fails in the test of social agreement. No two people, it is said, have the same interpretative insight. Their various accounts of nature have been likened to the slicing of a cheese. Each person slices it differently, and then declares that everyone else's cuttings fall in the wrong place. But did

Galileo, Newton, or Darwin do any differently? Their data, drawn from observation and experiments were verifiable; so too are Stern's. Their theoretical interpretations attempted to tell something about the course of events occurring in the depths of nature. Stern's interpretations are of the same order. All of them undoubtedly made errors in their slicing, but so far as we can tell they are for the most part only errors of *approximation* which subsequent scientists can correct. The direct method, naïve though it may be, is the most fruitful.

Although he is untroubled by the hypercritical methodologies of today, Stern uses most of the common safeguards of science. Observation and experimentation are employed for the data they will yield, but to his data he applies understanding, interpretation, and orderly arrangement; and he is much bolder about it than most psychologists of today are willing to be. He adopts the findings and some of the procedures of "exact" (elementaristic) psychology but only on the basis of an entirely different theoretical assumption, namely, that *everything mental is at the same time personal, and everything personal is either a totality or a part of a totality.*

At the outset this assumption of functional wholeness creates a serious difficulty for personalistic psychology (as it does for Gestalt and all other modern structural theories). Stern states the difficulty as follows: "As soon as we name anything and thus assign it to some definite psychological category, it is no longer the same thing that it was before; it acquires a peculiar rigidity and fixity that cannot be ascribed to mind itself." And yet science (including general psychology) is possible only by virtue of abstraction which substitutes for the complex pattern of relationships that obtain within the personality a different, purely conceptual system of relationships that have no organic connection with one another.

Being forced to adopt this familiar method of abstractive analysis, Stern plunges into the use of methodological dimensions much as any other psychologist would do. In fact, he has probably more polarities, more resulting dimensions, and makes a more intensive use of dialectic than any other psychological author. Yet there are two *differences*. Never is the reader allowed to forget that the procedure is artificial, that it is not an end in itself, but is merely a tool for disclosing *aspects* of personal existence. There is constant reversion to the primary fact of the total personal organization. The second difference is even more significant. The dimensions that are chosen are dictated by the primary assumption that the person is the locus of every mental event. They are for the most part utterly unlike any dimensions ever used in psychological analysis hitherto. For example, there are such strikingly personal dimensions as depth-surface, embeddedness-salience, reactivity-spontaneity, nearness-remoteness, genuineness-disingenuousness, expectancy-retrospect, subjectivity-objectivity. Unlike most dimensional analyses these are not merely empirical constructs of the laboratory. They are dimensions dictated by the datum. It is not the hobby of the experimenter that is being located with their aid, but the personal experience of the subject himself.

Psychology as a Branch of Personalistics.

> The person is a living whole that is individual, unique, goal-directed, self-contained, yet open to the world around him. He is capable of having experience.

Of all the properties of the person mentioned in this definition, that of experience is the least indispensable. The person is *complete*, whereas experience is *fragmentary*. And yet it is the province of psychology to deal with this very fragment. It is for this reason that psychology is not coextensive with personalistics; it is a narrower discipline, defined as the *science of the Person considered as having experience or as capable of having experience*.[4] Experience and the capacity for experience are only a portion of personal existence. Since the latter is rooted not only in experience, but in the biosphere and in the sphere of objective values as well, there is need for a more comprehensive philosophical discipline of personalistics of which psychology is only a part.

The Person-World Dimension. However unified and self-contained the person may be in the metaphysical sense, he is actually open at every moment to the surrounding world. He acts upon and is acted upon by the environment; a tension always exists. When the tension is most acute there is a resultant state of consciousness. The most important of all facts about consciousness is that it is graded; sometimes it stands out, as it were, against the diffuse background of personal life. It is *salient* (*abgehoben*). Whenever we are acutely aware of objects or of our own states there is this sharpness. At other times, as in states of feeling, consciousness is embedded (*eingebettet*) more deeply; there is less clearness, less salience. Salience represents an act of pointing, a directedness of the person toward something that at the moment has special significance for him. The more salient an experience, the greater is its objective meaning; the more embedded, the greater is its subjective meaning. Complete embeddedness is of course unconsciousness. The minimal threshold represents the first degree of salience; and all the thresholds familiar to psychophysics are, when interpreted, so many boundaries of the personal significance of the world.

According to Stern, Gestalt psychology with its sharp studies of perception deals too exclusively with salient experience, neglecting the no less important sphere of embedded experience which by its very nature constitutes an *Ungestalt*. Embeddedness of experience is marked particularly within the province of vital processes. For instance, the experiences produced through the lower senses, viz., through smell, taste, and the organic modalities, are characteristically embedded. Vision and audition on the contrary, because of their superior capacity for making contacts with the outer world, usually yield salient experiences; touch is in this respect an intermediate modality. Experience is embedded likewise when it is empathic, when it is introceptive (nonsalient adoption of surrounding cultural values), or when it bears a "physiognomic" correspondence to the surrounding events in the environment.

Monism. Psychophysical neutrality, which is Stern's solution of the body-mind problem, is, of course, not altogether original with him. Any double-aspect hypothesis in effect refers body and mind to a common underlying substratum; they are two sides to the same shield. But generally the shield itself has not been considered of any psychological significance. It is generally only the mutual conformity of the two sides of the psychophysical shield that interests the psychologist (as in isomorphism). But for Stern this conformity, though always present, is of much less importance than the shield itself. The shield is none other than the tangible, psychologically important *person*. Mental phenomena and bodily processes are properties of the person, but the person himself is not a passive theater for the play of psychophysical events; he is their true generator and carrier, and regulator. There are no specific mental or physical elements that are isolable and stable enough to form *between themselves* a direct relationship independently of the person. This is the weakness of parallelism, and of isomorphism as well.

That the person is the locus and generator of every psychophysical event is not merely a tautological proposition for science. For, with the aid of this person, new light is cast on virtually every problem. The monism is not therefore like most current monisms simply a denial of the dualism of mind and body. It is a constructive monism, increasing rather than decreasing the range of problems that can come within the field of psychology. A remarkable feature of the personalistic doctrine is the immensely broadened range of categories that it is able to offer to the psychological investigator, otherwise crippled by monisms and dualisms that place restrictions on the scope of problems admitted to good standing in psychology.

Dynamic, Purposive (goal-directed), and Voluntaristic Emphasis. Unlike most American psychologists who are critical and sparing of their motivational concepts, selecting the minimum with which to work, Stern has use for them all;

instinct, impulse, motive, need, disposition, goal-striving, urge, interest, inclination, wish, will, drive, and even the more inchoate principles of entelechy and "personal energy"—all find their place in his system.

But to say that personalistic psychology is dynamic and purposive does not sufficiently characterize it, for there is at the same time an additional flavor of voluntarism. This flavor does not arise merely from the fact that the terms *Will* and *Volition* appear constantly in the book, for in German psychology they have a more generic connotation than in America. In this country these terms terrify most psychologists because they bring to mind the problem of freedom with which the psychologist finds himself utterly unable to deal. Professor Stern has no respect for the taboo on Will, but rolls up his sleeves and attacks the problem from all sides. The result is the voluntarism to which I have alluded. The person is not merely a reactive creature, the product of biological adaptation to the environment. He is likewise creative; he has, besides his equipment of biological needs, for example, a need for thinking which is but one reflection of his capacity for *spontaneous* as well as *reactive* behavior. Stern cannot be classed as a mere evolutionist nor as an organismic psychologist, for these doctrines stress only the biological unity of the reactive (not the creative) organism.

The author's frank admittance of volition to good standing in his psychological domain leads him to treat a number of problems that many psychologists never recognize: problems of intention, attempt, effort, and especially that characteristically human ability of conscious planning for the future.

The tendency of the living organism to preserve and advance its own life is taken for granted in personalistics. Inorganic substance may under certain circumstances seem reactive much as living creatures are, but there remains an unbridgeable gap. All the important domains of life—vital functions, experience, and introception (the adoption, creation, and enhancement of values)—are denied to inanimate nature. These domains reflect *spontaneity* as well as *reactivity*.

But personalistics is not a biological vitalism, because the *human* person is to be distinguished from the *animal* person. The latter, to be sure, possesses vital functions and rudimentary conscious functions (experiential), but the sphere of introception is completely denied to lower animals. Human beings have two poles to their life of experience: *vitality* and *value;* animals one pole alone, *vitality*. The theory then is not a biologism. Nor does it merely reiterate, in the manner of Driesch, a somewhat hollow principle of vitalism, for each page of the entire book is in effect a documentation and definition of the distinctive vital and value properties of the human being.

SOME DETAILED APPLICATIONS

The best way to indicate the value of personalistic theory for the problems of general psychology is to suggest a few typical applications. But, we are warned, "since all special fields of experience may be understood only with reference to the totality of the person, they are bound up with one another and interfused in such a way that any sequence of treatment remains arbitrary."

Perception. The historic category of "sensation" receives as scant treatment in personalistic psychology as it does in Gestalt theory, for "sensation" is not only an elementaristic conception but is nonpersonal as well. Both schools agree that it is only at the level of sensory perception that problems become psychological. In spite of this initial agreement personalistic psychology deviates widely from the Gestalt approach. Stern fears that if Gestalten are made the true fundamental phenomena in perception and endowed, as it were, with their own laws (e.g., "self-distribution") the danger of a new elementarism arises; for then the Gestalten themselves may be regarded as elements out of which all mental activity is composed, just as was formerly true of sensations. For Stern there can be no Gestalt without a person who forms Gestalten

(*Keine Gestalt ohne Gestalter*). On occasion, of course, the Gestalt is dominated by features of external constraint; the objective stimulus situation determining by its very definiteness of boundaries the type of salience that arises in experience; but even here the significance of the phenomenal Gestalt is invariably its relevance to the person in his intricate process of adaptation to the complexity of the world. In the last analysis Gestalten require some active participation of the person himself; they are never self-sufficient. It depends upon *me*, for example, whether I arrange the ticking of my watch into three-part or four-part rhythm, or see the cloud in the sky as a menace or as a negligible factor on the day of a picnic.

Furthermore, not every experience is salient; the category of *Ungestalt* (embeddedness) is quite as important as is the category of *Gestalt*. Its significance is especially apparent in the domain of feeling, with which Gestalt psychology is ill-equipped to deal. In various respects, then, the boundaries of personalistics are wider than those of Gestalt theory.

Both theories are much interested in the phenomena of intersensory perception. The personalistic approach holds that experience mediated by the separate modalities is "dissociated" from the nonspecific total perception that is deeply embedded in the person, and originally represented by a state of diffuse feeling. "Sharpness," for example, in smell, taste, hearing, and touch is not to be explained by the association of various specific sensations. It is a prior total experience that under certain conditions may become ascribed primarily to one modality or another. The Gestalt theory of course does not take into account the unifying substratum of the person, nor does it imply as does Stern's theory a genetic process of differentiation among modalities.

The experiences of space and time are admirable instances of intersensorial perception. There are no special "spaces" for each sensory modality, but only one personal space. The locality and volume of a tone may seem to be a spatial experience of a predominantly auditory nature, but space *in* which these impressions exist is not a sound space, but *my* space, the same space that is the common ground of my visual and tactual experiences as well.

Without doubt the recasting of the experiences of space and time is one of the most original features of personalistic psychology, sustained and convincing in its development. What impersonalistic psychology is able, for example, to give an intelligible setting to the fact that my seatmate in the plane is distant from me while the friend toward whom I am riding is already near me? The essence of space and time, psychologically considered, is their *personal relevance*. Events are distant when they lack such relevance; near when they possess it. The synthesis of space and time is likewise possible on the basis of personalistic theory, for there is at the center of my experience the feeling of *here-and-now*, an unanalyzable blend of space-time.

Memory. Memory too brings up the problem of personal time which, of course, is much more irregular than the unidimensional schema of objective time. Thus, a segment of life that is ten years behind me may be far nearer to me subjectively than the period two years ago; or vice versa, some act that I performed yesterday may today appear incomprehensible to me, a totally foreign element in an otherwise continually unfolding past.

The significance of memory is found in the midposition that it occupies in personal life between the function of instinct (the conservational factor) on the one hand and the function of intelligence (the progressive factor) on the other. Memory conserves the past, providing salient features of experience for the present in the service of future goals. It is thus not merely a matter of reactivated traces. Without memory each present state would be self-sufficient and rigid; having lost its connection with the total person, it would be meaningless. Salient experience (e.g., perception) must continually be embedded in the life of the person through the function of memory in order to acquire vital significance and utility. The image, for example, is more deeply embedded than the perception, and for that reason has a more personal content.

In most acts of memory remembrance of self and remembrance of the outer world are not differentiated; even attempts at critical analysis never give a wholly separate picture of what occurred in the world around us and what occurred in ourselves. The entire episode has become embedded in the substratum of personal existence. It is for this reason that objective recall never possesses complete fidelity. Testimony in a court of law is seldom fully trustworthy.

Thought. Personalistic psychology readily finds a suitable place for all facts known concerning imagery, insight, attitude, fantasy, and intelligence. It arranges these facts, however, under teleological principles. Thought takes place whenever our personal world seems insecure, that is, whenever occasions arise that cannot be taken for granted; herein its functions differ from instinct, habit, or memory. Thought has survival value; it facilitates adjustment. But that is not all. Thought is not merely reactive; it is spontaneous and creative as well. It reaches out, as it were, *looking* for trouble. The person not only adapts in a passive sense, but, having the capacity for self-development, for asserting himself against the world, he has therefore an active *need* for thought.

There is a special role assigned to precategorial thinking and to fantasy. Purely objective and rational thinking is brittle and artificial. It is so salient that it is ever in danger of becoming depersonalized. It is *too* objective; it is far from life, and lacks *understanding*. The most comprehensive and adequate products of thought, the works of art, religion, literature, and metaphysics, are a result of embedded experience that comes from feeling, from empathy, and from "physiognomic" understanding quite as much as from sharply salient, rational analysis.

Fantasy, dreams, and play fit readily into the personalistic system, for they reflect in various ways the restorative, anticipatory, creative, and symbolic functions of which the person is capable.

Feeling. Since of all types of experience feeling is "nearest to the person" one would expect personalistic psychology to be most productive in this province. And it is. The dimensions that it uses are exceedingly numerous, and more distinctions are turned up than other schools of psychology ever dreamed of. Wundt's tridimensional framework is made to look like a bony scarecrow.

Although all feelings are embedded, some are relatively more salient than others, i.e., some pertain to objects, some to self; some are near and some distant in their reference (e.g., terror vs. grief). There are feelings of expectancy and of retrospect, of alienation from the world (anxiety) and of harmony with it; there are feelings of familiarity, of unfamiliarity, of premonition and recollection; there are positive and negative feelings toward the future (hope and dread). There are feelings of success and of failure, of the expansion or of the negligibility of the self (as in various aesthetic experiences); of preparation for action or reflection after action. Some feelings are broad, some narrow, some intense or weak, some lasting or temporary. They possess depth or shallowness, genuineness or disingenuousness, seriousness or playfulness; they may pertain to cultural or to vital functions, and may lead to adaptive action or to expressive action. All these are recognized and used in addition to Wundt's dimensions, pleasure and unpleasure, strain and relaxation, and excitement and calm.

The author finds no difficulty in fitting known facts concerning affectivity into his system. Full recognition, for example, is given to the principle of "affective equilibrium," the phenomenon of the relativity of feeling. As all experimentalists now admit feelings depend very largely upon a state of contrast, and contrast is exclusively an intrapersonal relationship, and therefore a typical personalistic concept.

The category of feeling includes emotional seizure and

states of passion, as well as mood, temperament, and the emotional toning of objects. All feeling has a formless character; it is *Ungestalt*. It occupies a middle position between that which is perfectly embedded in the personal life (utterly habitual or instinctive) and that which is sharp and salient (clearly intellectual or volitional). It is transitional between the unconscious realm of smooth running vital activities and the state of acutely voluntary conduct. Feeling often precedes salient thought or action; it represents a period of preparation. For example, the adolescent with his turbulent emotions and moods will later develop the more salient volitional consciousness required for his sexual, vocational, and social adaptations. Feeling also exists when conduct has been completed, and the experience is subsiding through the affectively toned period of retrospect into oblivescence.

PERSONALISTICS AND SELF PSYCHOLOGY

In America the closest counterpart of Stern's system of thought is the Self Psychology of M. W. Calkins. For Calkins the Self is a *given* that cannot be defined. (Definition requires a *class* to which an object may be referred. The Self being entirely *sui generis*, belongs to no class.) The principal characteristics of the Self, however, are identifiable, and they turn out to be characteristics that Stern likewise recognizes as highly central in the Person. The Person, like the Self, is *persistent;* it *changes* as it develops; it is *unique;* it is *many-sided;* it is the *groundwork of all its own experiences;* and it is *related to its physical and social environment.*[5]

Stern, however, does not share Calkins' belief that all of these characteristics are immediately experienced. An exaggeration of the role of self-awareness is a feature of Calkins' system, and springs naturally from her body-mind dualism. The Self, she says, is not made of body-mind; rather it *is* mind, and *has* a body. The Person, on the other hand, is psychophysically neutral. Human personality cannot be characterized as *mental* because mind in turn must be defined in terms of its significance within and in the service of the Person. The Person, to be sure, is sometimes sharply aware of itself, sometimes dimly (or even wrongly) aware, and sometimes totally unaware. Personal unity, however, is not endangered by this fitful course of consciousness. Calkins sought her support almost entirely from introspective evidence; for Stern the person is an inescapable postulate; not immediate experience alone, but all evidence, of whatever type it may be, points to its central position.

CRITIQUE

Let us consider the charges that are leveled against the personalistic system by its critics.

(1) *It is solipsistic. Comment:* It is true that the author spent many long years weaving together his experiments and observations into a single view of the psychological universe. To an operationist, of course, it is scientifically meaningless to have a coherent view of the psychological universe, or of any other universe. One should view only such portions of it as other people may agree with him about. Hence personalistics will be regarded as solipsistic—a *Weltanschauung* of one man only. To this charge there are two possible lines of defense. One might say, the application of operational criteria to restricted parts of the system, and eventually perhaps to some of the more inclusive concepts is not impossible. In part this answer seems acceptable. But a number of the personalistic categories (e.g., those of feeling) inevitably rest upon the evidence of immediate experience. As such they become operationally weak. Then there is the conceptual unification of the system as a whole for operationism to scorn. When this point is reached, I suspect the author might have to reply "so much the worse for operationism. There are tasks of synthesis for science more significant than the piddling regress of operationism. If mine is a solipsistic view of life, so too are all *Weltanschauungen,* and whether they get agreement or not,

psychologists, like all other philosophers, cannot and will not live without them."

(2) *It is common sense*. There is something about the selection of the person for central emphasis that seems both self-evident and question-begging. In other words, personalistics is a kind of common sense characterized by its obviousness and by its *petitio-principii*. *Comment:* In stressing the person, the author with remarkable directness calls psychologists back from their wanderings and confronts them with their forgotten man. Is it necessarily a deficiency in a system if it accepts the datum that everyone (excepting psychologists) would agree is the property par excellence of psychology? Personalistics takes pride in the fact that it is *lebensnah*, and therefore in a better position than other psychologies to codify and refine common sense. Furthermore, the concept of the person is more than the name of a self-evident datum; it furnishes unexpected aid in recasting many thorny problems of a metaphysical and epistemological order, among them the relation between body and mind and between conscious and unconscious mental activity.

The charge of question-begging is more intricate. To select some one disposition or state for analysis from the total person, then to proceed with the analysis up to a point, and then to refer the disposition or state back to the person, saying that only in the light of the total personality can it be interpreted, does seem to be somewhat of a circular process. And yet, if the person is the sole authentic point of reference, to what other source of explanation or clarification can a state be referred? If the person is *ex hypothesi* both origin and terminus, is it truly circular to depart and arrive by the same door?

If one agrees with Stern that in a peculiar sense the person is real, and that analyses merely employ artificial constructs, one cannot consistently object to this procedure. Yet I for one confess that I wish there were less frequent emphasis upon the totality of the person. One example might be given.

Stern's trenchant criticisms of intelligence testing are well known, and all the more significant because of the part he himself played in the testing movement. Yet his frequently abrupt dismissal of the test-result and his haste to embed it within the total person does, I think, blind him somewhat to the merits of a reliable test score; its significance often reaches further than he admits. The same may be said of his impatience with any sustained attempt to explore personality at the level of traits, attitudes, and dispositions. Even though it is true that the person is not divisible, progress comes not from reiterating this fact, but from finding some level of analysis that does the least possible violence to the structure of personality (e.g., a concept of *personal disposition* that in a sense epitomizes the whole person), and following it to the bitter end before returning to the totality.

(3) *It is formalistic.* In personalistics the polarities and the resulting dimensions are almost bewildering. E. G. Boring has pointed to the possibility of infinite dimensions in psychological analysis, but only in personalistics does one seem to encounter them all. *Comment:* To be sure, the author uses a great many abstractive dimensions, but he uses them only as temporary aids; they are not intended to be true divisions of the person; they simply disclose aspects under which he may be viewed. Furthermore, he tends on the whole to use dimensions of maximum personal significance (such as depth-surface, nearness-remoteness, retrospect-prospect). And yet he does not always do so. Thus his account of motivation might be improved by a logic of truly personal (characterological) traits, attitudes, interests to replace the universal dimensions of need, instinct, and drive.

The method is not merely dimensionalistic; it is dialectical as well. There is often a thesis and antithesis; the opposition is overcome by synthesis. This characteristic of personalistics is more apparent in Stern's philosophy than in his psychology. But there are instances of it in the psychology as well. One example will serve. The doctrine of Convergence holds that forces from within the organism and forces from without may *converge* to form new states in the person: the stimulus converges with disposition, the environment converges with heredity. Although this concept has been taken over by some American psychologists, it is not, I think, a psychological doctrine at all. The "forces" of the environment are so different in kind from the "forces" of the dispositions that true convergence is unthinkable. All that happens is that the environment furnishes stimulus situations or provides models for conduct, which in turn provoke processes of change within the person. Although Professor Stern would no doubt agree with this interpretation of the meaning of "convergence," the fact remains that the term itself is a product of dialectic and does not (like "learning," "suggestion," "imitation," or "resolution of conflict") refer to purely psychological functions.

It is important to understand the reason for Stern's use of dialectic. It does not spring, as in Hegel, from an abstract idealism or from an a priori conception of logical necessity, but rather from the incessant flow and ebb of personal existence itself; the individual is ceaselessly striving and resting, approaching and avoiding, responding and causing others to respond. To exist at all means to struggle, and in every conflict there are contrasting poles and an eventual resolution of some sort. The formalistic use of dialectic, therefore, has its basis in the very nature of the person himself. And yet I cannot feel that every personal event requires such dramatic representation. The gradual growth of—let us say—an attitude can be characterized without stressing the ideal extremes between which it might in principle, but does not in practice, oscillate. I am not here questioning the prevalence of conflict in personal life, nor am I rejecting altogether Stern's use of contrasts and dialectic. I am suggesting merely that I think the method is on occasion overworked.

(4) *Common dimensions cannot account for personal uniqueness.* Even though Stern criticizes the isolation of a single dimension (e.g., the I.Q.) from the personality as a

whole, he implies that all personalities, however unique, are in fact woven from the same common threads. *Comment:* An example would be his handling of motivation. He employs the customary rubrics of instinct, drive, and need, assigning essentially the same motives uniformly to all persons. Thus, for example, he speaks of a universal drive of men to broaden their intellectual horizons. Is there in fact any such universal need, even granted that it might have myriad forms of expression? Isn't Stern here manufacturing a uniform dimension out of the behavior of a relatively small population of intellectuals?

It is an odd fact that Stern does not go to the logical conclusion of personalistic reasoning, and say that the dynamics of each life are in the last analysis unique. He does not say that we need idiographic (or morphogenic) methods that will enable us to discover where in fact the cleavages and tensions in a given life fall. While dimensions (common traits) may be useful for comparing one personality with another, they are always approximate. Stern does not perceive the need for morphogenic methods which focus on one individual alone as a population of unique events arranged in a unique pattern.[6] On one occasion when I confronted Stern with this particular criticism his eyes twinkled while he replied, "Oh no, there is such a thing as being *too* personalistic." I persist in my conviction that Stern in employing throughout his system uncritically a plethora of common dimensions, was not genuinely consistent with his own goals. Or perhaps I should say that individuality and uniqueness as a problem did not intrigue Stern as deeply as did the simple substantive fact of personhood. The unity of the person impressed him more deeply than did his uniqueness.

STERN'S INFLUENCE

Stern was an innocent victim of Hitler's blind rage against *Judentum.* After hastily writing his *Schlussbericht* for the Hamburg Institute, to which I have already referred, he and his wife fled first to Holland and then to America. A son and a daughter likewise escaped to America; another daughter, after serving in Germany as long as possible to rescue Jewish children from the wrath, fled to England and later settled in Israel. Two of Stern's closest professional associates (Dr. Martha Muchow and Dr. Otto Lipmann) were political suicides. Just at the time when he might be consolidating his influence in Germany (at the age of 63) every anchor was lost. His major psychological book, *Allgemeine Psychologie auf personalistischer Grundlage,* had to be printed in Holland. All his other books, if not burned, were allowed to go out of print. The new generation of students grew up without knowledge of Stern's monumental work, and after World War II there was little remaining of his influence. One of his students, Professor Curt Bondy, likewise a fugitive in America, did return to Hamburg after the war, and for more than a decade worked toward reestablishing Stern's Institute.

Yet it is questionable whether, if conditions had remained normal in Germany, Stern would have founded a school of personalistic thought. For all his alertness and boyish friendliness he lived intellectually pretty much in a world of his own making. His line of thought was *sui generis,* having the flavor of the nineteenth century "myth in the grand style." The younger generation was about to clamor for operationism, physicalism, mathematical models. At least such was the situation in America where he lived too short a time to win disciples. In Germany the postwar fashion was stratification theory (*Schichtentheorie*) which had the merit of accounting in terms of personality layers for the appalling regressive degradation which the Hitler era had provoked.

To be sure, Stern's students were spread around the world —his Institute had an international reputation. I have mentioned Bondy, who eventually returned to Hamburg. There were also Vučić (Jugoslavia), Katzenstein (Brazil), Klüver and myself (United States), and many others. Some of these have acknowledged Stern's inspiration in their work. But one cannot claim that there is today either in Germany or internationally a school of personalistic psychology. The movement known as personalistic philosophy in America, centered at Boston University and at the University of Southern California, acknowledges a limited kinship with Stern, but no causal connection.[7]

The most we can say is that Stern's many students borrowed rays from his "star." And that their students in turn have absorbed some of the same light. The influence is most evident when certain specific topics are under discussion, such as the I.Q., the psychology of testimony, early childhood, cloud pictures as a projective method.

Today the personalistic system as a whole is nowhere intact, although I suspect its rays may increasingly have powers of penetration. The time may come when psychologists will be less afraid than they now are to delve into problems of personal emotion (lest they seem emotional), or into the study of sentiments (lest they appear sentimental), or into the riddles of personhood (lest they become personal). When this time comes Stern's influence may again grow.

NOTES

1. In preparing this chapter I have drawn freely upon my two previous papers: "William Stern: 1871–1938," *American Journal of Psychology,* 1938, *51,* 770–774; and "The personalistic psychology of William Stern," *Character and Personality,* 1937, *5,* 231–246.

2. In 1926 when he had reached what he called a "provisional resting point" (after the appearance of the third and final volume of *Person und Sache,* his system of Critical Personalism) Stern wrote his intellectual autobiography which was published in both German and English (*Die Philosophie der Gegenwart in Selbstdarstellung,* ed. by Raymond Schmidt, 1927, 129–184; *A History of Psychology in Autobiography,* I, ed. by C. C. Murchison, 1930, 335–388). This source, though stressing Stern's philosophical work at the expense of his psychological, gives the best picture of Stern as man and

thinker. Its bibliography, however, is by no means complete, listing only 36 selected titles up to 1926 (twelve years before his death). The *Psychological Register*, III, 1932, lists 95 titles for the same period; and 29 additional titles (1927–31). From 1931–37 the *Psychological Abstracts* lists 15 titles. The total thus becomes 139 published articles and books including a few translations and basic revisions.

3. "Das Psychologische Laboratorium der Hamburgischen Universität," *Zsch. f. Päd. Psychol.*, *23*, 1922, 161–196; "Aus dreijähriger Arbeit des Hamburger psychologischen Laboratoriums," *ibid.*, *26*, 1925, 289–307; "Das Psychologische Institut der Hamburgischen Universität in seiner gegenwärtigen Gestalt," *Zsch. f. ang. Psychol.*, *39*, 1931, 181–227; "Aus den letzten Arbeiten des psychologischen Instituts der Hamburgischen Universität, *ibid.*, *45*, 1933, 397–418.

4. A remarkable similarity exists between this definition of psychology and Titchener's. The latter wrote, "*Psychology is the study of experience considered as dependent on some person.*" How could such similar definitions lead their authors into diametrically opposed courses? The only explanation seems to be that Titchener paid no further attention to the second part of his definition after he wrote it. For him the dependence was purely rhetorical; for Stern it is the most significant fact in all of science.

5. Calkins, Mary W., *Psychological Review*, 1917, *24*, 279–300.

6. Cf. G. W. Allport, "The general and the unique in psychological science," *Journal of Personality*, 1962, *30*, 405–422.

7. Knudson, A. C., *The philosophy of personalism*, Cincinnati: Abingdon Press, 1927, pp. 25ff.

16

The Productive Paradoxes of William James

UNDOUBTEDLY WILLIAM JAMES is the most respected and most loved of all psychological writers. The respect that he commands is not due to a firm texture of philosophical-psychological theory, for his position is loose and, as the present paper shows, full of paradoxical assertions. The respect he wins is partly for the brilliance of his insight into mental processes and partly for his candor and honesty in recognizing the inconsistencies that do in fact mark our mental operations. Fortunately for James he was able to handle these inconsistencies to his satisfaction within the hospitable framework of his theories of pragmatism and pluralism.

This paper was written as a tribute at the centenary of his birth, and printed in the *Psychological Review* in 1943.

† † †

It takes the whole of us to spell the meaning out completely. W. J.

A few years ago, on a hot afternoon in August, a foreign student walked slowly up the path to Emerson Hall, and spoke to a man on the doorstep. "I have just arrived from Syria," he said, "and wish to study where William James taught. Could you tell me, please, if this is the place? And could you direct me to his grave, so that I may visit it?" I report this incident while we are celebrating the one-hundredth anniversary of William James's birth because it seems to me to memorialize in a simple way the respect and the affection in which inquiring minds, the world over, still hold his spirit and his genius.

Yet, whatever tributes we pay to the radiance of his personality and to his accomplishments, it is nonetheless true that James, like other historic figures of equal stature, grows legendary in the course of time. Few psychologists under the age of forty-five, I venture to say, have read the *Principles* from cover to cover, or the *Varieties*, or even *Talks to Teachers*. Still fewer are conversant with his philosophical writings. All of them, to be sure, can quote from James—who cannot? —but not many have voyaged with him into the obscurer reaches of his thought as attentively as he himself once voyaged with Louis Agassiz to the dark country of the Amazon.

One reason, no doubt, is that two shattering world wars divide the epoch of James from the present. It is more than catastrophe, let alone to bind the insights of half a century ago one can do to keep pace with modern social and intellectual with those of the precarious present.

But there is, I think, a more specific reason why modern psychologists are inclined to do obeisance to James's name while avoiding the details of his thought. The reason is that today's reader is frankly bewildered. At first, led along by lucidity and inspiration, he finds himself assenting eagerly to a great many discrete observations, as arresting in their brilliance as anything he ever encountered. But soon he comes upon propositions that contradict one another and do violence to his sense of syllogism. The further he reads, the more the contradictions pile up, and his discomfort becomes acute. In reading the *Principles* he probably feels as Bertrand Russell felt in reading *Pragmatism*—as if he were taking a bath in water which heated up so imperceptibly that he didn't know when to scream.

After wrestling with the sporadic and episodic character of James's thought, Santayana concluded that James merely "made raids" upon philosophy. There are many who would also say that he made only raids upon psychology, and would add, that, insofar as he applied scientific standards at all, most of them are now to be regarded as primitive and as dated. At the same time, the *Principles,* published fifty-two years ago, remains far more penetrating about human behavior and seems more alive than most textbooks published within the past year. Presenting, as it does, the perennial problems of the human mind so sincerely, so modestly, so truly, the passing of years can do nothing but confer upon it the verdict of classic.

But it is not with James's insight, nor with his inspiring personal qualities that we are here concerned. It is rather with the basic contradictions that mark his psychological thought.

THE PERSISTENT RIDDLES OF PSYCHOLOGY

In the course of his professional life, every psychologist encounters a sphinx who asks of him six riddles:

(1) How is the mind you study related to its body? The *psychophysical* riddle.

(2) Are the objective methods you by preference employ suited to the subjective facts that are your ultimate data? The riddle of *positivism.*

(3) How do you account for such integration and unity as the human personality manifests? The riddle of the *Self.*

(4) Why is it that, in spite of your postulate of strict determinism, you half-believe, and nearly always act on an hypothesis of indeterminism? The riddle of *free will.*

(5) Why is it that the old laws of mental connection, going back to Aristotle, seem sometimes adequate and sometimes inadequate in accounting for the organization of higher mental processes? The riddle of *association.*

(6) Why is it that, after making your analyses of mental states, you are unable to find in the sum total of them any close approximation of the way mental life is uniquely and individually presented in nature? The riddle of *individuality.*

Of every passing psychologist these questions are asked. Many refuse to answer, muttering impatiently, but not convincingly, that important questions are merely semantic. It is true that some psychologists linger long over one or another of these puzzles, but William James lingered over all six. He agonized over them; he proposed a solution to each, and more often than not he landed squarely in the middle of a paradox.

THE RELATION BETWEEN MIND AND BODY

In his chapter on "The Automaton Theory" he first made a clear and persuasive case for radical reflexology, that is to say, for holding to the physiological level of discourse consistently, and for regarding consciousness after the manner of Huxley, merely as the steam whistle which accompanies the work of the locomotive engine, without ability to exert any causal influence upon the machinery itself. James pointed to the aesthetic and scientific superiority of his epiphenomenal position. But in the second half of the same chapter he repudiated the automatism view, regarding it as an "unwarrantable impertinence in the present state of psychology" (10, I, p. 138). The automaton analogy, he maintained, is too simple, too one-sided. Particularly is it unable to answer the obvious question: why, if consciousness doesn't count, are we conscious at all? Is not consciousness capable of "bringing a more or less constant pressure to bear in favor of those of its performances which make for the most permanent interests of the brain's owner"? (10, I, p. 140). Is it not capable of selectively reinforcing one of the various possible tendencies to action? Does it not make for survival, and is it not at any given moment "a fighter for ends"? (10, I, p. 141).

He was particularly impressed by the fact that consciousness is intense only when nerve processes are hesitating. "Where indecision is great, as before a dangerous leap, consciousness is agonizingly intense" (10, I, p. 142). Why? Is it, as the epiphenomenalists say, merely because friction in antagonistic nerve pathways engenders much heat? What a worthless invention of nature that would be, unless the consciousness resulting from such conflict has at least a limited causal efficacy of reinforcing the favorable possibilities and repressing the unfavorable or indifferent ones. Now, to claim that consciousness may at times enter into the causal chain is to advocate the interactionistic view of the body-mind relation, a classic expression of which occurs in the passage where he insists that an examination of the properties of consciousness shows that they are "exactly such as we might expect in an organ added for the sake of steering a nervous system grown too complex to regulate itself" (10, I, p. 144).

But he did not follow up this brief and brilliant defense of interactionism with consistent application. Only a few aspects of his psychologizing demand this dualism, notably his doctrine of the Fiat, of a subliminal cosmic consciousness, his defense of psychic research, and his numerous moral exhortations to better living. On the contrary, in most areas of his psychological thinking, James accepted the implications of physiological determinism scrupulously. So much so that Durkheim actually berated him for being a materialist, drawing attention to James's insistence that retention is not a fact of a mental order at all, but purely physiological, and to his belief that mental images are "exactly matched" to brain states (5). Perry thinks of James as a consistent psychophysical parallelist:

> He recognized an obligation to find a physiological correlate for every state or function of mind, and to confine psychological speculation within the bounds of physiological probability. Nothing is more striking than the fidelity with which James carried out this method, in his treatment of association, habit, emotion, will, perception, and other topics. Furthermore, he used physiological hypotheses to extend and supplement, as well as to explain, the processes of consciousness (20, II, p. 76).

Perry, I think, exaggerates the fidelity with which James kept to the physiological anchorage in his theories, even though he did defend the parallelistic position (only forty pages beyond his championship of interactionism!). By keeping to parallelism, he said, "our psychology will remain positivistic and nonmetaphysical" (10, I, p. 182). Yet sensing his own predicament he argued that this shall be merely a "provisional halting place," and that some day things must be "more thoroughly thought out." In another connection, weary of body-mind disputes, he impatiently exclaimed, "such arguments as these can eat each other up to all eternity" (10, I, p. 134).

And so we find James expounding various alternative solutions to the body-mind problem. Carried away by his own persuasiveness he adopted these solutions seriatim, unabashed by his own inconsistency. By turns he was parallelistic, epiphenomenalistic, and interactionistic. William McDougall, attempting to gain support in James's writing for his own interactionist position, found what he was looking for but found also flat contradictions. "Could anything," asked the aggrieved McDougall, "be more perverse!" (17, p. 362).

POSITIVISM AND PHENOMENOLOGY

John Dewey has argued that the natural trend of James's thought, and the bulk of his writings, squares directly with a biological and situational behaviorism (4). And Edman has said James gave "the original impulsion" toward treating of existences in terms of movement and of knowledge in terms of operation (6). On the other hand, Boring insists that James was a phenomenologist (2). Dewey and Edman see James in the camp of modern objectivism; Boring billets him with the subjectivists. The truth is that James moved from tent to tent, as if driven now by his own tough-mindedness, and now by his own tender-mindedness. In his positivistic moods, however—and this is a point of some importance—it was Mach rather than Bridgman whom he most closely resembled.

He admired the tireless grubbing of the German experimentalists, and tried in his way to imitate it. Rigor in method was his ideal. Over and over in his letters we find it expressed:

The more we can steer clear of theories at first, the better.
. . . *"Facts"* are what are wanted (9, I, p. 250).

I want now if possible to write something serious, systematic,
and syllogistic; I've had enough of the squashy popular-lecture
style . . . (20, II, p. 338).

I actually *hate* lecturing; and this job [the Hibbert Lectures,
A Pluralistic Universe] condemns me to publish another book
written in picturesque and popular style when I was settling
down to something whose manner would be more *strengwis-
senschaftlich, i.e.,* concise, dry, and impersonal (20, II, p. 583).

If his tastes were rigorously tough-minded on Tuesdays,
Thursdays, and Saturdays, pointing as Dewey and Edman
insist in the direction of behaviorism and positivism, they
seem more exuberantly natural on Mondays, Wednesdays,
Fridays, and Sundays when he wrote his phenomenological
passages.

Many persons nowadays seem to think that any conclusion
must be very scientific if the arguments in favor of it are all
derived from twitching of frogs' legs—especially if the frogs
are decapitated—and that, on the other hand, any doctrine
chiefly vouched for by the feelings of human beings—with
heads on their shoulders—must be benighted and superstitious
(20, II, p. 30).

The most interesting and valuable things about a man are his
ideals and overbeliefs (12, p. xiii).

Individuality is founded in feeling; and the recesses of feeling,
the darker, blinder strata of character, are the only places in
the world in which we catch real fact in the making, and
directly perceive how events happen, and how work is actually done (11, p. 501–502).

As soon as we deal with private and personal phenomena
as such, we deal with realities in the completest sense of the
term (11, p. 598).

As the years went by he shifted his emphasis more and
more from the positivistic empiricism to which he himself had
given such impulse, and defended that special form of sub-

jectivism which he chose to call "radical empiricism" (15).[1]

Radical empiricism has never become integrated with modern psychology. It might have served as the foundations for an American school of phenomenology, but it did not. Instead, the examination of the intent and constitution of experience was left largely to Husserl and his associates in Germany, and their work has only recently been taken up in this country as a foundation for a somewhat synthetic psycho-phenomenology.[2]

What is radical empiricism, and what are its neglected implications for psychology? It is a tentative theory of knowledge, admitting all experiences of fact as hypotheses to be verified in the course of future experience. Immediacy of understanding is given a more sympathetic hearing than is customary among present-day psychologists. The opposition between James's phenomenology and modern operationism is clearly stated by Perry:

> He [James] differs from the positivists in his insistence that acquaintance is also knowledge. He further insists that both conceptual and operational knowledge are dependent on knowledge by acquaintance. They are the best possible knowledge in the majority of cases, but they are, nonetheless, a second best. Concepts and operations are substitutes for immediacy, but they are qualified substitutes in so far as they are expectations of immediacy. Concepts are abstracted from experience; or, if they are pure conventions, they derive their meaning from their power, through association and agreement, to suggest experience. An operation may be substituted for any given object, when it would be appropriate to the presence of that object. Concepts and operations may be provisionally verified in terms of other concepts and operations; but their ultimate verification occurs only when an experience is as was expected, or when *what* was conceived or assumed in practice is realized in immediacy (19, p. 68).

For all the impetus James gave to biological and situational behaviorism, toward the end of his life he reversed his emphasis. Instead of holding, as behaviorism does, that conscious report is valid if it is equated with objectifiable and operation-

ally communicated propositions, he would maintain that an
experiment or an operation is valid if it confirms the expectations of direct experience. Immediacy is the essence of psychological truth.

THE SELF

In the 1880's, while James was writing the *Principles*, discussions of the unity of mental life were prevalent. James himself
felt that the British associationists with their mind-stuff theory
had left out the conditions of coherence in the individual mental life. Somewhere, he contended, the effects of the manifold
brain processes must combine to account for the spearhead of
purposes that characterize the living being. While tussling
with this problem, he spoke impatiently to himself, asking
"Why on earth doesn't the poor man say the Soul and have
done with it?" (10, I, p. 180). And so he boldly said Soul, and
(for the moment) *meant* Soul; but he didn't have done with it.

This postulate which seemed the most satisfactory hypothesis in Chapter VI of the *Principles* becomes a "complete super-
fluity" in Chapter X. In fact he argued, throughout most of
the book, that a sufficient guarantee of such unity and integration as a given mind possesses is to be found in the over-
lapping of memories, the cumulative character of thought,
each successive moment of which appropriates the thought of
preceding moments, and in the interpenetration of states of
feeling and cognition.

The famous chapter on "The Consciousness of Self" starts
off with a dazzling descriptive account of the empirical aspects of man's material and social selves. Thereafter it settles
down to the dreary grind of considering arguments for and
against a Pure Ego (or Knower). Deciding against a self-
active agent of this order, he concluded that

> the passing thought itself is the only *verifiable* thinker, and its
> empirical connection with brain-process is the ultimate known
> law (10, I, p. 346).

Yet there is another strain in his exposition. There are arguments that, taken by themselves, might lead to a thoroughgoing personalistic or self-psychology. Calkins actually dated the origin of her self-psychology from James's enthusiastic elevation of the personal consciousness to the supreme place in psychology (3, p. 31). And the following passage states the case as strongly as any personalist could desire:

> It seems as if the elementary psychic fact were not *thought* or *this thought* or *that thought*, but *my thought*, every thought being *owned*. Neither contemporaneity, nor proximity in space, nor similarity of quality and content are able to fuse thoughts together which are sundered by this barrier of belonging to different personal minds. The breaches between such thoughts are the most absolute breaches in nature. . . . On these terms the personal self rather than the thought might be treated as the immediate datum in psychology. . . . No psychology, at any rate, can question the *existence* of personal selves. The worst a psychology can do is so to interpret the nature of these selves as to rob them of their worth (10, I, p. 226).

One might make much of James's prophetic remark that psychology at its worst interprets the nature of these selves in such a way as to rob them of their worth. It would be easy to argue that psychology, especially since the time of James, has done its worst. But, ironically enough, James himself is partly to blame. In the chapter on "Self-consciousness" we encounter a completely sensationalistic reduction of the Self from the introspective point of view:

> . . . the *"Self of selves," when carefully examined, is found to consist mainly of the collection of these peculiar motions in the head or between the head and throat. . . . I feel quite sure that these cephalic motions are the portions of my innermost activity of which I am most distinctly aware . . . our entire feeling of spiritual activity, or what commonly passes by that name, is really a feeling of bodily activities whose exact nature is by most men overlooked* (10, I, pp. 301f.).

Although James used both introspective evidence and reductionist reasoning (at times) to get rid of the Self conceived as Knower and as Subject, he never argued directly
against the Self as a teleological unity, as the center of striving, as the dynamic aspect of personality. Indeed there are
numerous references to the fact that the whole import of
higher mental processes is to advance private purposes. Every
moment of consciousness is a "fighter for ends" (10, I, p.
141). It is *interest* that guides attention, *purposes* that determine meanings, and, above all, *belief* that makes life the energetic thing that it is. And yet, to the very end a teleological
writer, he seems bent perversely enough on exhibiting purposive striving as brain pulsations, and belief (in part at least)
as a cluster of sensations.

In passing one must remark the fact that the famous chapter on "Habit" is not consistent with James's concept of a
purposive Self endowed with a selective consciousness. According to the doctrine of habit, any deed, however casually
performed, is counted and stored up in the nerve cells to be
used against us on Judgment Day. But this mechanistic view
is contradicted in the chapter on "Attention," where we read
that

> an object once attended to will remain in the memory whilst
> one inattentively allowed to pass will leave no traces behind
> (10, I, p. 427).

Effort and interest are here made the guides of conduct. The
ball and chain logic of habit, for all its dramatic appeal, really
plays only an isolated and eccentric role in James's thought.

While considering the conditions of unity in mental life, and
the different meanings this conception had for James, we
make note of his doubly unorthodox view of the *unconscious*.
He took positions so extreme that we can scarcely find their
counterpart in psychology before or since his time, and the
two positions he adopted were diametrically opposed. In the
Principles he argued against unconscious mental states, whether

of the order postulated by von Hartmann, by Schopenhauer, by the British empiricists, or by the German experimentalists. Unconscious states, he claimed, are unnecessary assumptions; what they are alleged to represent are mere physiological processes, or else nothing at all (10, I, pp. 162–176). Yet in the *Varieties* he defended the hypothesis of a "subliminal consciousness." Below the level of self-conscious awareness he envisioned a silent but accessible region wherein the Self is extended. Our conscious egos are like tiny islets which dot a vast Pacific, each the abode of a luxuriant personal life, and each apparently isolated from its neighbors. In reality we are but the peaks of a submerged continent, and, when in rare moments we reach out under the surface, we may lay hold of nonsensory knowledge, of religious truth.

> . . . there is a continuum of cosmic consciousness, against which our individuality builds but accidental fences, and into which our several minds plunge as into a mother-sea or reservoir (16, p. 204).

Whatever merits this postulate may have as an explanation of mysticism and psychic occurrences, it clearly runs counter to his own earlier denial of a nonphysiological unconscious.

The man who wrote on Starbuck's questionnaire that he did not pray, because he felt foolish when he did so, and who was not in a professing sense a religious man, nevertheless argued repeatedly and extravagantly for the pragmatic legitimacy of religious faith. "Every sort of energy and endurance, of courage and capacity for handling life's evils," he insisted, "is set free in those who have religious faith. For this reason the strenuous type of character will on the battlefield of human history always outwear the easy-going type, and religion will drive irreligion to the wall" (12, p. 213). Perhaps the most important thing to be noted about James's view of religion is his rare ability to shake off the shackles of literal-mindedness with which most psychologists contemplate this area of experience. In his letters he summed it up,

. . . although all the special manifestations of religion may
have been absurd (I mean its creeds and theories), yet the life
of it as a whole is mankind's most important function (9, II,
p. 127).

Always a bit perverse, he could not let the matter rest there.
Even if religion be mankind's most important function, he
advised his students,

After taking a bath in religion come out and take another
bout with philosophy (20, II, p. 354).

And then, with a touch of his cosmic humor, he wrote,

Of all the vanities, when you come to look penetratingly at
them, lectures on the philosophy of religion by mortal men
may take the first prize (20, II, p. 355).

FREEDOM AND DETERMINISM

James's well-known recipe for getting out of bed on a cold
morning is to lie long enough for the feeling of conflict to dis-
appear, when suddenly the impulsive idea, "Hollo! I must lie
here no longer," draws the laggard to his feet. Ideomotor behavior of this sort is not, in the strict sense of the word,
volitional at all; but it—along with reflexes and habits—accounts for many activities that are ordinarily considered volitional. Remaining, however, is a large class of acts, true acts
of will, which puzzled him deeply. To explain them he developed another of his most unorthodox hypotheses, the hypothesis of the *Fiat*. Later psychologists have not admitted the
existence of a distinctive "feeling of effort" upon which the
introspective evidence for the Fiat hinges. It is this feeling,
says James, that segregates simple ideomotor activity from true
will. By denying the existence of this differential psychologists
have contrived to equate will with the determining tendency
or even with subvocal verbal conditioning. But for James,

. . . the whole drama of voluntary life hinges on the amount
of attention, slightly more or slightly less, which rival motor
ideas may receive (10, I, p. 453).

The Fiat, or element of consent, comes in when the neutralization of the antagonistic and inhibitory idea is required. Assuming, as the ideomotor theory does, that all representations of movement tend in some degree to evoke the actual movement, there must be times when contradictory and mutually exclusive movements are simultaneously innervated. It is under such conditions of conflict that selection, reinforcement, inhibition are achieved through an output of effort which succeeds in keeping the "selected idea" uppermost. The power to keep the selected (usually the more repugnant) idea uppermost *is* the will. When this is done, then ideomotor action takes care of the rest, the sustained idea issues automatically into action. It is, therefore, in the realm of attention that the effortful will-act takes place.

Will is related to character through the fact that what need to be controlled are the instinctive and hedonistic impulses which so frequently are antisocial. Character has to do with sustaining noninstinctive motives and with the deliberate negation of hedonism: thus character can be attained only through the exercise of will.

Now, it is only occasionally that will enters as a determinant of behavior.

> Sometimes the bare idea is sufficient, but sometimes an additional conscious element, in the shape of a Fiat, mandate, or express consent, has to intervene and precede the movement (10, II, p. 522).

Nor is will needed when ordinary *interest* is a guide.

> If one must have a single name for the condition upon which the impulsive and inhibitive quality of objects depends, one had better call it their *interest*. "The interesting" is a title which covers not only the pleasant and the painful, but also the morbidly fascinating, the tediously haunting, and even the simply habitual, inasmuch as the attention usually travels on habitual lines, and what-we-attend-to and what-interests-us are synonymous terms (10, II, pp. 558f.).

In passing I remark how odd it seems that this class-concept of *interest* should have had so little influence upon subsequent systematic psychology. James offers us a simple structural unit for human motivation; but psychologists have persistently overlooked it in their search for what they consider to be "more basic" motivational units: drives, needs, instinctual energies. And yet there is much to be said for the proposition that *interests*, developed and matured beyond the basic level of biological striving, are in fact the prime movers of human conduct.[3]

But we have drifted away from our discussion of the Fiat. That this conception is dualistic, mentalistic, interactionistic there can be no doubt.

Volition is a psychic or moral fact pure and simple, and is absolutely completed when the stable state of the idea is there (10, II, p. 560).

> *To sum it all up in a word, the terminus of the psychological process in volition, the point to which the will is directly applied, is always an idea. . . . The only resistance which our will can possibly experience is the resistance which such an idea offers to being attended to at all* (10, II, p. 567).

James admitted that there are strict limitations to the powers of the Fiat. It cannot override instincts or habits that are too strong. It cannot extend itself in directions where there are no possibilities of action. No one can by mere effort of attention speak Chinese without previous training, or hold himself to work beyond the limits of his endurance. But our limits are far wider than we customarily realize (13). And our accomplishments can exceed by far our ordinary output. The great problem of the voluntarist, James clearly saw, is to discover the limits of freedom. If we are not totally free, as obviously we are not, then just how free are we?

> Decisions with effort merge so gradually into those without it that it is not easy to say where the limit lies (10, II, p. 575).

James knew that he was unable to answer the question "How free are we?" But he risked a margin of true volition.

In this matter where scientific and moral postulates are at war, and where objective proof simply is not to be had, the pragmatic justification for casting one's lot with the indeterministic hypothesis is that it releases energies and avoids the tempting rationalizations in which the determinist can indulge, letting himself slip always into the channel of least resistance and regarding this slothful course as the only one possible. Provided it is not indiscriminate or extreme, a belief in freedom has—who can deny it?—benign consequences.

Perceiving the predicament that his vote for freedom creates for much that he himself had written in the *Principles*, James took a singularly lame way out. He said that psychology, as a science, can safely postulate determinism even though free will be true. It can leave freedom in a realm before which "science simply stops."

The trouble with this solution is that psychology by not taking freedom into account, if freedom is a fact, must of necessity give a distorted view of human conduct. If the power to keep the selected idea uppermost is an authentic power, then why bury our scientific heads and refuse to face it? James seems to advocate precisely the ostrich policy for others which he himself refused to adopt. He personally was too hungry for a comprehensive view of human nature to leave out so important a capacity as the Fiat. In fact, without it, he believed that the physicalistic analogies pursued by psychologists are "intensely reckless," but yet he invited the recklessness of the determinists to persist.

It is safe to say that the aversion which some later psychologists have felt toward James is grounded chiefly in his own lapses from the position of strict determinism. The effect of these lapses is to weaken, in their minds, his integrity as a scientist. But do his critics themselves never lapse from strict determinism? Do they never assume in themselves or in others the possibility of "keeping the selected idea uppermost"? Do they never in good faith praise or blame? Do they never bank on the value of marshaling or expending effort? The significant thing about James is that he wrestled openly with his contradictory hypotheses, admitted his inconsistencies in practice, and finally threw his lot with the larger and more comprehensive view.

ASSOCIATION

Next we call attention to James's predicaments in respect to the traditionally central law in psychology—the law of association. His chapter on this topic in the *Principles* is not itself unorthodox.[4] To be sure he preferred the physiological language of *brain states* to the mentalistic language of *ideas*, but for the most part he merely summed up and reinforced the dogmas of his associationistic predecessors. Even his repudiation of *ideas* was in line with the tendency of the times, and, if anything, made him appear a more thoroughgoing connectionist and prophet of behaviorism.

Take, for example, his treatment of association by *similarity*. The brightest minds, he contended, are known for their ability to perceive remote similarities through what he called their "electric aptitude for analogy." Humdrum minds associate by a more routine and predictable redintegration. But in either case the same principle of association is involved, namely that in two contexts there are aroused some partially identical elements. In simple redintegration large portions of identical nerve tracts underlie both the primary and the associated thought; whereas in association by similarity, lesser quantities of identical nerve tracts are called upon. But similarity not less than redintegration is a matter of partial identity (10, I, p. 579).

But turning back at this point to the chapter on "The Stream of Thought," commonly regarded as the most characteristic Jamesian chapter, we find him denying the stability of traces which his own associationistic theory requires, and we encounter a denial of the possibility of partial identity:

It is out of the question, then, that any total brain state should identically recur. Something like it may recur; but to suppose it to recur would be equivalent to the absurd admission that all the states that had intervened between its two appearances had been pure nonentities, and that the organ after their passage was exactly as it was before (10, I, p. 234).

If identities are never identical, how then, we must ask him, can similarity be a matter of partial identity?

In recent years it has become customary to assert that James anticipated portions of Gestalt theory, and Gestalt theory as everyone knows is antiassociationistic. His repudiation of elementarism is often cited (10, I, pp. 145–182), likewise his interest in relations and in the transitive parts of the stream of consciousness which seem to anticipate Gestalt as clearly as did the *Gestaltqualitäten* postulated by von Ehrenfels (10, I, pp. 243–248). James also may be said to have anticipated Wertheimer's conception of insight (10, I, p. 590; II, p. 676).

Yet, in crediting him with all these anticipations of antiassociationism, we repeat that in much of his own writing James was himself an undeniable associationist. Once again the enthusiasm of the moment carried him along. Characteristically he stated the position favored in a particular context so strongly and so persuasively that both he and the reader lose sight of his previous commitments.

INDIVIDUALITY

James is most frequently classed as a functionalist, but it is important to note the context in which he submitted somewhat reluctantly to this label. Surprisingly enough he equated the *functional* with the *clinical* points of view.

We habitually hear much nowadays of the difference between structural and functional psychology. I am not sure that I understand the difference, but it probably has something to do with what I have privately been accustomed to distinguish as the analytical and the clinical points of view in psychological observation . . . the clinical conceptions, though they may be vaguer than the analytic ones, are certainly more adequate, give the concreter picture of the way the whole mind works, and are of far more urgent practical importance. So the "physician's attitude," the "functional psychology" is assuredly the thing most worthy of general study today (13, pp. 1f.).

In the present day we do not think of functionalism as identical with the concrete, clinical approach to psychology. Indeed functionalism is generalized or nomothetic, whereas the clinic approach is individualized or idiographic (8, p. 1). But by whatever name we designate the intensive study of the individual, William James was its champion:

> Surely the individual, the person in the singular number, is the more fundamental phenomenon, and the social institution, of whatever grade, is but secondary and ministerial (16, p. 102).

> . . . in every concrete individual, there is a uniqueness that defies all formulation. We can feel the touch of it and recognize its taste, so to speak, relishing or disliking, as the case may be, but we can give no ultimate account of it, and we have in the end simply to admire the Creator (16, pp. 109f.).

He maintained in the *Principles* that he has

> expressly avoided the outward appearance of doctrine and system, the definitions, classifications, subdivisions and multiplication of technical terms, because I know that these things tend to substitute an artificial schematism for the living reality with which I wished to bring my reader into direct concrete acquaintance (20, II, p. 53).

Yet for all his predilection for concrete acquaintance, for all his sparkling use of case studies, for all the brilliance of his descriptions of experience-in-the-round, seasoned with quotations from perceptive novelists, travelers, and artists, still he was both a generalizer and an abstractionist. In nearly every chapter of his writings he aimed at the discovery of universal laws of mental life uncomplicated, if possible, by the perturbations of idiosyncrasy.

One might say that for him each mental state was like a landscape, which could be appraised with the eyes of an artist and by an artist faithfully represented in all its complexity and fullness, or which could be cut with the analytical knife and reduced to the cleavages familiar to science. But it is not enough to say that James was both artist and scientist, surveying the scene now with the idiographic lens and now with the nomothetic. He did more than that. In his own unique way— and here, I believe, is where the kernel of his genius lies—he attempted to *combine* both modes of perception, a most difficult undertaking indeed. Life to him was indeed a clinic, but the cases he examined blended instantly with his theories and his laws, which in turn added the increment of scientific knowledge to the richness of immediate acquaintance. The result in his hands was a vital grasp on both the concrete and the abstract aspects of his subject. By comparison the grasp obtained by the exclusively analytical or the exclusively descriptive psychologist seems one-sided and partial.

EXPLAINING THE PARADOXES

If, in keeping with the modern passion for genetic origins, we seek to trace the background of these inconsistencies, many possibilities lie before us. The influence of his father William repeatedly and lovingly acknowledged. Of the intellectual atmosphere the father created, Henry James, Jr., has written,

> The literal played in our education as small a part as it perhaps ever played in any, and we wholesomely breathed inconsistency and ate and drank contradictions. The presence of paradox was so bright among us . . . that we fairly grew used to allow from an early time, for the so many and odd declarations we heard launched, to the extent of "happily discounting them" (8, p. 216).

The atmosphere of brilliant paradox and lawless metaphor undoubtedly formed early habits that became second nature, intensified possibly by a modicum of father-identification.

In his late twenties, we know, James was excessively moody,

and even preoccupied with thoughts of suicide. But during the darkest days he never lost for long his tenacious interest in the world around him. The end of his melancholia came with a sudden belief in the freedom of the will, gained upon reading Renouvier. We may perhaps speculate that the coexistence of depression and hope, of melancholy and the will to believe gave him a temperamental sense of the simultaneous reality of good and evil, of thesis and antithesis, of life and death. That these moody opposites impressed him we know from his remark to his father in 1873 when he was 31 years old,

> Bless my soul, what a difference between me as I am now and as I was last spring at this time! Then so hypochondriacal and now with my mind so cleared up and restored to sanity. It's the difference between death and life (9, I, p. 169).

Relevant as such genetic speculations may be, they are not sufficient to explain the significance of the contradictions found in his mature thought. The fruit of his productive years is nourished by more than the husks of his past. James himself was not a geneticist, and if analyzing himself today would, I think, not encourage the backward or historical view. Let us say rather that paradox somehow fitted his mature style of work, reflecting faithfully his own mature philosophy of life. It is, after all, the mature life-philosophy by which grown-up men and women normally live.

What I mean may be illustrated by referring to a relatively minor contradiction in his theory of emotions. On one page we read the statement,

> Refuse to express a passion, and it dies. Count ten before venting your anger, and its occasion seems ridiculous (10, II, p. 463).

But three pages later,

> . . . if tears or anger are simply suppressed . . . vengeful brooding may replace a burst of indignation; a dry heat may consume the frame of one who fain would weep, or he may, as Dante says, turn to stone within (10, II, p. 466).

Our first impulse is to say, "Why doesn't he make up his mind? Does refusal to express an emotion lead to its suppression with hurtful consequences, or does it not?" On second thought, we yield and say "James is right on both counts: sometimes an emotion whose expression is blocked leaves harmful tension; sometimes it doesn't, and we simply do not know the factor that differentiates the two occasions." James didn't know and we do not know. Under such circumstances is it better to present only one alternative in order to have a consistent theory of emotional inhibition, or to present both, and to appear inconsistent? In many minor instances, as the one just cited, perhaps James did not realize his own contradiction, but seeing the matter in a different light at different moments his honesty compelled him to state the facts. Honesty of report was to him a virtue far higher than consistency.

Regarding some of his major paradoxes he was fully aware. To James Ward he wrote,

> Yes I *am* too unsystematic and loose! But in this case [the writing of the *Briefer Course*] I permitted myself to remain so deliberately on account of the strong aversion with which I am filled for the humbugging pretence of exactitude in the way of definition of terms and description of states that has prevailed in psychological literature.[5]

He said, in effect, consistency is a luxury we cannot yet afford. It often takes two opposed views to cut into a subject, just as a pair of scissors requires two opposed blades. Why not, then, let the science of mind be as vague, as many-sided, as contradictory as its subject? (10, I, p. 6).

Now a paradox implies that two conflicting ideas find their reconciliation in an inclusive proposition that resolves the conflict between them. When the philosopher says, "This is the best of all possible worlds, and everything in it is a necessary evil," he implies that rightly understood the apparent contradiction is resolved in a larger and self-consistent doctrine of good and evil. But in James we are not dealing with smart rhetorical paradoxes, but rather with assertions widely sepa-

rated by text, each of which seems true enough in separate
contexts but irreconcilable when juxtaposed. Such a situation
as this would make no trouble for the true dialectitian, who
tells us how to gather together a thesis and an antithesis and
view them both as a species of eternal truth. But James scorned
dialectics, especially the fatted and verbose methodology of
Hegel. He was offended by the arrogance of any forced
monism, preferring by far to leave his thesis and antithesis
dangling free. He would express the truth in hard words today, and tomorrow a contrasting truth in words equally hard,
risking error and self-contradiction:

> So far as a man stands for anything, and is productive or
> originative at all, his entire vital function may be said to deal
> with maybes. . . . It is only by risking our persons from one
> hour to another that we live at all (12, p. 59).

Insofar as his paradoxes can be resolved, it is in the method
of pragmatism, the metaphysics of pluralism, and the episte-
mology of radical empiricism that we must seek the synthesis.
To him the universe seemed but loosely joined, "filled with
copulas." The word "and" abounds, trailing along, he said,
after every sentence that is spoken (14, p. 231). In such a universe we must expect mind to be many things, and truth to be
many-sided. Perhaps this line of thought does not really provide a solution for all his paradoxes. Indeed, his philosophy, we
are often told, simply multiplies our difficulties, for it too is
fraught with paradoxes. Yet this much seems to be true: the
general design of his philosophy was the only one possible
that could comprehend his paradoxical assertions in psychology, and that could express adequately his deepest conviction
that the study of mind is unfinished business, and that any attempt to proceed upon narrow and exclusive assumptions is
sheer arrogance.

He was definitely unwilling to buy consistency if it cost
him an ounce of his own integrity. He must faithfully report
his insights. If it seemed to him that men had great reserves of
hidden energies, that a moral equivalent for war could be

found, that mystical experiences had beneficent effects, that psychical research was a legitimate activity, he said so. And he would not refrain from saying so because such assertions would fail to square with physiological, positivistic, or behavioral premises which at moments likewise seemed valid. Objectivity and fact have their place in the scientist's view but so too have the affirmations of the believing scientist which enter into the total matrix of fact.

> Reason deals with consistencies only, truth with consistencies *plus* facts; belief is itself a part of fact and a part-maker of fact, life includes all these elements and rolls reason along in its flood—enveloping it, not enveloped by it (20, II, p. 559).

Thus it is the general design of James's thought and the texture of his personality that soften and absorb his contradictions. Pluralism, tychism, radical empiricism were his own ultimate labels for his philosophical outlook. These are wholly congruent with his dominant trait of essential modesty. To his nature presumption and intellectual arrogance were totally alien. Pragmatism, the doctrine that we must appraise a theory according to its purely practical consequences, leads to the embracing of contradictory propositions whenever these in turn lead to equally beneficent results, as in a pluralistic universe they often do. Tychism, or the admission of chance, may be distasteful to the scientist, but by admitting the occurrence of chance he becomes a chastened and more open-minded observer of the world about him.

THE SIGNIFICANCE OF JAMES'S PARADOXES
FOR PSYCHOLOGY TODAY

In many respects psychologists of the present day resemble James. Like him they distrust apriorism in mental science, and are, for the most part, content to work on their many-sided subject matter in mosaic fashion, resisting the tempting lures of unification offered by rationalism and by dialectics. Like him, they are opposed to any form of self-deception, holding aloof especially from the authoritarian superstitions of racial and class prejudice. As a group they are internationally minded, distinctively liberal, and genuinely devoted to the interests of humanity. Furthermore, they share James's optimistic view that human nature is improvable, that wars are avoidable, and that a more inclusive democracy is possible.

Where the difference lies, I think, is in the lessened width of their horizon. As the years went by James included more and more within his conception of mental science. He wrote,

> . . . our science is a drop, our ignorance a sea. Whatever else be certain, this at least is certain—that the world of our present natural knowledge *is* enveloped in a larger world of *some* sort of whose residual properties we at present can frame no positive idea (12, p. 54).

It was his passion to face up to all phenomena of mental life, and to exclude none. He made room in his psychology not only for the possible contributions of psychic research, phrenology, and mysticism, but he opened channels that would admit to the domain of psychology the "big fears, loves, and indignations" of mankind and the penetrating appeal of "the higher fidelities, like justice, truth, or freedom" (12, p. 211). And he wanted psychologists to confront the fundamental moral fact that by their own theories of human nature they have the power of elevating or degrading this same human nature. Debasing assumptions debase the mind; generous assumptions exalt the mind. His own assumptions were always the most generous possible. The contrast between the expanding horizons of James and the constricting horizons of much recent psychology has been vigorously expressed by Perry:

> James's psychology was, therefore, by deliberate intent, and not by inadvertence, an omnibus psychology, in which any psychologist of today can find some of his affirmations and none of his negations. James did, it is true, seek to be in a sense "positivistic." But the positivism of James was almost the precise opposite of the doctrine which now passes by that name. Contemporary positivism closes all doors but one,

while James's positivism opened all doors and kept them open (19, p. 79).

In the titanic world struggle now going on psychology is learning what James knew so well, the wisdom of leaving doors open. In recent months psychologists by the hundreds have left their laboratories, and shaking off the crust of custom, have entered the struggle where the "big fears, loves, and indignations" of mankind are at large, where men are savage in the cause of evil or savage in the cause of good, where "the higher fidelities" have come into their own. Long ago James pointed out that a mere spectator's judgment is likely to be wrong. Discarding their habits of spectatorship psychologists are participating, and in so doing, are opening more doors of the human mind than they have ever previously taken account of. They are confronting William James face to face, for with him they are now struggling to comprehend humanity's will to believe, to marshal and release the energies of men, and to search out the moral equivalent of war. If psychologists help to make the peace they will do well to remember his words:

> The course of history is nothing but the story of men's struggles from generation to generation to find the more and more inclusive order. Invent some manner of realizing your own ideals which will also satisfy the alien demands—that and that only is the path of peace (12, p. 174f.).

The message of James for psychology today is this: narrow consistency can neither bring salvation to your science, nor help to mankind. Let your approaches be diverse, but let them in the aggregate do full justice to the heroic qualities in man. If you find yourselves tangled in paradoxes, what of that? Who can say that the universe shall not contain paradoxes simply because he himself finds them unpalatable? To accommodate the whole of human experience keep layers of space and air and vision in your scientific formulations.

When his father was upon his death bed, James, then in Europe, wrote him a touching farewell:

All my intellectual life I derive from you; and though we have often seemed at odds in the expression thereof, I'm sure there's a harmony somewhere, and that our strivings will combine (9, I, p. 219).

Had he written a valedictory to his profession I feel sure it would have contained the selfsame words. In the pluriverse of mental science, where we stumble at thresholds, William James, the lover of humanity and of truth, would admonish us to mutual respect and a larger breadth of outlook:

I'm sure there's a harmony somewhere, and that our strivings will combine.

BIBLIOGRAPHY

1. Allport, G. W., "The use of personal documents in psychological science," New York: Social Science Research Council, 1942. Bulletin, No. 49. Pp. xix–210.
2. Boring, E. G., "Human nature *vs.* sensation: William James and the psychology of the present," *Amer. J. Psychol.*, 1942, *55*, 310–327.
3. Calkins, M. W., in Murchison, C. C., *A history of psychology in autobiography*, Worcester: Clark Univ. Press, Vol. I, 1930. Pp. 31–62.
4. Dewey, J., "The vanishing subject in the psychology of James," *J. Phil.*, 1940, *37*, 589–599.
5. Durkheim, E., "Représentations individuelles et représentations collectives," *Rev. Metaphys.*, 1898, *6*, 274–302.
6. Edman, I., "William James; 1842–1942," *The Nation*, 1942, *154*, 67–68.
7. Grattan, C. H., *The three Jameses*, New York: Longmans, Green & Co., 1932. Pp. xi+376.
8. James, H., *A small boy and others*, New York: Scribner's Sons, 1914.
9. ———, (ed.) *The letters of William James*, Boston: Atlantic Monthly Press, 1920, Vol. I, pp. xx+348; Vol. II, pp. xii+382.
10. James, W., *Principles of psychology*, New York: Henry Holt, 1890. Vol. I, pp. 689; Vol. II, pp. 704.
11. ———, *Varieties of religious experience*, New York: Longmans, Green & Co., 1902. Pp. xii+534.

12. ———, *The will to believe, and other essays*, New York: Longmans, Green & Co., 1897. Pp. xvii+333.
13. ———, "The energies of men," *Phil. Rev.*, 1907, *16*, 1–20.
14. ———, *The pluralistic universe*, New York: Longmans, Green & Co., 1909. Pp. iv+405.
15. ———, *Essays in radical empiricism*, New York: Longmans, Green & Co., 1912. Pp. xiii+283.
16. ———, *Memories and studies*, New York: Longmans, Green & Co., 1912. Pp. 411.
17. McDougall, W., *Body and mind*, London: Methuen & Co., 1911.
18. Perry, R. B., *General theory of value*, New York: Longmans, Green & Co., 1926. Pp. xvii+702.
19. ———, *In the spirit of William James*, New Haven: Yale Univ. Press, 1938. Pp. xii+211.
20. ———, *The thought and character of William James*, Boston: Little, Brown & Co., Vol. I, 1935, pp. 824; Vol. II, 1936, pp. 786.

Notes

1. It seems probable that this shift was due in part to his wrestling at the turn of the century with autobiographical case studies in the course of preparing the *Varieties*. He grew to respect these documents which set forth the intense personal experiences of "the most religious people in their most religious moments." Such experiences, though virtually inaccessible to outsiders, were, he felt, of undoubted authenticity and should be admitted as belonging to the very core of psychological subject matter.
2. The journal, *Philosophy and Phenomenological Research*, was founded in 1940.
3. The influence of James's concept of interest has been greater on educational practice (progressive education) and on philosophy (*cf.* 18) than upon psychology.
4. With the exception of his insistence upon the role of interested attention and volition in holding fast to selected elements in the course of an otherwise mechanical train of association (10, I, pp. 572, 594).
5. In Wundt's passion for perfect consistency he sensed a "terrible flavor of humbug" (20, II, p. 96).

17

Dewey's Individual and Social Psychology

JOHN DEWEY stands second only to William James in giving American psychological science its characteristic stamp of activism, functionalism, and problem solving. As everyone knows it was particularly in the educational process that Dewey's psychological conceptions became effective. So diversified were his interests (in logic, politics, ethics, education) that it is not correct to claim him exclusively for the field of psychology. It is rather as a social theorist that the present paper presents his psychologically relevant work. *The Library of Living Philosophers*, where this paper appeared in 1939, gave Dewey an opportunity to reply to the several contributions. In his reply Dewey said that he judged my exposition and critique to be sound and acceptable.

† † †

John Dewey's productive years span almost exactly the lifetime of modern scientific psychology. Born in 1859, his formative period coincided with the formative period of the New Psychology. In 1882, just three years after the founding of the first psychological laboratory, he began to write on topics of mental science—at first with a broad philosophical touch, but soon also with a concreteness better fitted to the aspirations of a young science. His distinguished work continues into the present, and taken as a whole constitutes a remarkable story of intellectual leadership over a period of more than fifty years.

Although we are interested here only in Dewey's psychological work, it is impossible to trace its development entirely apart from the course of his philosophical thought. He himself assigns his psychology to a subordinate position. Primarily he is concerned with the *norms* of experience and conduct; with their psychological machinery he has less to do. Yet, at the same time, so close is the dependence of his philosophy upon the actual conduct of living men that he finds himself frequently forced to deal with psychological principles. Thus psychology constitutes a necessary and prominent support to his philosophical thought. It is in this light that we must describe and evaluate it.

I. EARLIEST PSYCHOLOGICAL WORK

Dewey's first psychological work consisted of a group of papers wherein he attempted to gain for himself a surer understanding of the concept of *experience*. In the *Andover Review* he expounded at the age of twenty-five the New Psychology with reference to the implications of laboratory researches for a philosophy of experience. Dewey observed that the new science was willing to throw itself upon experience, making "no attempts to dictate to this experience, and tell it what it *must* be in order to square with a scholastic logic."[1]

Yet experience, he felt, is not a matter of mere sensational impressions. The sensationalistic views of the so-called empirical psychologists he rejected as a species of peculiarly degrading anthropomorphism, an anthropomorphism which sets up "the poorest elements of its own feeling, a sensation, and reverences that as its own and the universe's cause."[2] We shall never account for experience, Dewey insisted, by referring it to something else. Sensation is not prior to consciousness or knowledge; it is but a consequent that depends upon experience. In the fullness of experience, which is our starting point, we find a fusion of subject and object.[3] Psychology does not deal with mere subjective states minus the object world, because both subject and object are contained within the experiential whole; they cannot be characterized separately. It is the work of psychology to determine the relations of subject and object as they arise *within* consciousness.

One sees here the powerful influence of Hegel. Dewey

named the position he was defending "absolute idealism," and his critic Hodgson added a bit crisply that if such transcendentalism is to be admitted as psychology, then Dewey should in simple fairness label it "psychology: human *and divine*."[4]

As one might expect, *Psychology*, Dewey's textbook of 1886, was caught in the same turmoil of ebbing transcendentalism and upsurging positivism. The text supports the older rationalistic, soul psychology, on the one hand, and the newer sensory and reaction psychology, on the other. Introspection is the preferred method. Sensation is important, though not all-important. The researches of Helmholtz, Hering, Volkmann, Stumpf, and Wundt are faithfully recorded. Habit—lightly touched—is a matter of successive associations that tend with repetition to become somehow simultaneous. Reaction-forms are described, and there are other adumbrations of the functional psychology to come. It is because of these features that Brett characterizes the text as "the first gray dawn of that tomorrow for which the psychology of the American colleges was waiting."[5]

At the same time the text still invokes the Soul to assist in the psychologizing. The unity of mental life must be accounted for, and Dewey saw no way to obtain unity excepting through the activity of the self, defined, a bit circularly, as "the activity of synthesis upon sense."[6] Attention, for example, is "the activity of self in combining units." Apperception "organizes the world of knowledge by bringing the self to bear upon it." Eight years later Dewey would regard the unifying self as a useless redundancy, accounting in other terms for such unity as mind achieves; but in 1886 he was still far from this position.

II. FUNCTIONALISM

It was James's *Principles* that helped lift Dewey from the fence where his early writings had precariously perched him. So assured was James in his endorsement of the positive premises of the new psychology that his younger colleague felt encouraged to abandon transcendental psychology for good and all in favor of a more earthy functionalism.[7]

But Dewey was no blind follower. He quickly perceived inconsistencies in James that needed to be remedied, as well as insights that merited expansion. Immediately following the publication of the *Principles* came Dewey's heaviest concentration on the special problems of psychology.

In 1894 he reported a minor observational study on the language of a young child, stressing characteristically the importance of its predicative character. Even though nouns prevail in the child's vocabulary, their predicative significance in the child's striving for better contact with his environment must not be overlooked.[8]

At the same time the James-Lange theory of emotions engaged his attention. He perceived a contradiction between Darwin's theory of emotion as *expression* and James's theory of its *peripheral* origin during acts of adjustment. The opposition he resolved by demonstrating that expression itself is a mode of adaptation. Emotion follows an interference with a smoothly coordinated tendency to action. It occurs only when there is a temporary struggle among habits and partial inhibition. Its origin is indeed peripheral, as James says, but its significance for survival and its relation to the situation of the total organism at the moment are compatible with Darwin's views. A significant concept introduced in these papers on emotion is that of *interest*. Interest, Dewey maintains, is the antithesis of emotional seizure, existing only when an adjustment is well coordinated, when conflict—and hence emotion—are virtually absent.[9]

So whole-hearted is his conversion to the functional position that Dewey accuses James of faint-heartedness. In particular it is the self, with which Dewey had such deep concern in 1886, that he is now bent on ruling out of court. With James's *Fiat* he will have nothing to do; not even the mildest endorsement of indeterminism is allowable. The individual and his actions are one, says Dewey. There are concrete attitudes,

habits, desires, ideas, and ignorance; but there is no ego behind these states. There is no call to recede into the ego to
explain will, any more than to explain consciousness. If James
can dispense with the Pure Ego in thought, he should dispense likewise with the Pure Mover in conduct. "If the stream
of thought can run itself in one case, the stream of conduct
may administer itself in the other."[10]

In a similar vein Dewey criticizes Baldwin's theory of effort.[11] Effort is not, as Baldwin says, "consciousness of opposition between what we call self and muscular resistance." There
is for Dewey no longer any self separate from musculature.
Effort now is viewed merely as "the critical point of progress
in action arising whenever old habits are in process of reconstruction or of adaptation to new conditions." Nor is attention
any longer one of the capacities of selfhood; it does not cause
the sense of effort. It *is* the sense of effort.

By 1894, then, we see that Dewey has repudiated completely both the substance and the shadow of soul psychology.
He will have nothing more to do with an active self, as knower
or as effective agent in will; nor does he see any need for the
passive self, preserved by Calkins, as the unique ground for all
experience. Dewey insists upon the seamless character of experience. To be aware of oneself is merely a part of the total
circuit of awareness. It is an event belonging to a larger whole.
No need to postulate a substantive person as carrier and locus
of a circuit.[12]

We come now to the most important psychological paper
of the nineties and probably, so far as psychology is concerned, Dewey's most influential essay, "The Reflex Arc Concept in Psychology."[13] Having abandoned the remote
unifying agency from his conception of mental life, he is looking around for a new guarantee of consecutiveness and coherence in behavior. He finds at hand the concept of the reflex
arc, recently borrowed by psychology from physiology. But
on examination he rejects it, for it makes activity "a patch-
work of disjointed parts, a mechanical conjunction of unallied
processes."[14]

A burn does not merely induce us to jerk our finger from the flame. It brings not only a withdrawal reflex but at the same time affects the ocular perception of the inviting flame in such a way that its stimulating character is forever changed. Or, we turn our head to catch a whisper. Is the act thus completed? No, our response is as closely related to the sound that is now becoming effective as it was to the unintelligible sound that served as the first stimulus. The stimuli of both the beginning and the end situation belong to the same act. Every reaction is a circuit, leading to a redistribution of stress and tension. Adjustment is not a matter of response to a stimulus but of reestablished rapport within one's environment.

III. HABITS

Dissatisfied with the reflex arc, Dewey felt his way toward a unit that might better express the circuit character of all behavior. Twenty-six years after his attack upon the reflex arc he finally proposed *habit* as the unit most suitable for psychology to employ.

Habit was not a new concept in Dewey's thinking. On the contrary, it had always been a favorite with him. But in his early years he seemed content with the traditional definition in terms of the fusion of successive associations into one simultaneous pattern. Then came the brilliant and melodramatic chapter by James that set a fashion hard to break. Though James, no less than Dewey, was a believer in an open universe and in man's capacity to modify his behavior step by step, James was never troubled by the excessive rigidity he ascribed to habit. But Dewey, always more consistent than James, saw the consequences of this view and never subscribed to the ball-and-chain conception.

He sought rather in his doctrine of habit to represent both the lag that is characteristic of human behavior and of social custom, and at the same time the adaptability and range of equivalence found in conduct. Habit, he also felt, should be credited with a dynamic or motivational character. When between 1917 and 1922 he decided to dispense with instincts, the need for a dynamic unit, one that should be "assertive, insistent, self-penetrating" became all the more urgent.[15]

In the following passage Dewey characterizes habit as he now conceived it, setting it against the traditional view established by James and the elder associationists:

> While it is admitted that the word habit has been used in a somewhat broader sense than is usual, we must protest against the tendency in psychological literature to limit its meaning to repetition. This usage is much less in accord with popular usage than is the wider way in which we have used the word. It assumes from the start the identity of habit with routine. Tendency to repeat acts is an incident of many habits but not of all. A man with the habit of giving way to anger may show his habit by a murderous attack upon someone who has offended. His act is nonetheless due to habit because it occurs only once in his life. The essence of habit is an acquired predisposition to *ways* or modes of response, not to particular acts except as, under special conditions, these express a way of behaving. Habit means special sensitiveness or accessibility to certain classes of stimuli, standing predilections and aversions, rather than bare recurrence of specific acts. It means will.[16]

Habits, though elements of behavior, are not independent of one another; the exercise and development of one affects all. Were it not so, our acts would be "simply a bundle, an untied bundle at that."[17] Character could not exist. It is the consecutiveness and consistency among habits, achieved through a gradual process of selection, that constitute character. But be it noted that the selection occurs only through modifying surrounding conditions, not by fiat or will. Selection, or choice, becomes effective when the organism learns to cooperate with environmental conditions in a deliberative manner; deliberation being nothing more than "an experiment in making various combinations of selected elements of habits and impulses, to see what the resultant action would be like if it were entered upon. Deliberation and will are a matter of trial acts executed incipiently in imagination not in overt fact."[18]

Here Dewey's conception of habit leads into his philosophy of morality. Indeed it is in the interests of ethics that the doctrine of habits was evolved. It has a decidedly deductive cast. It is not advanced with experimental evidence, nor is it compared in any detail to similar units, especially *attitudes*, proposed by other psychologists.[19]

Dewey's conception of habit is not altogether successful; it is neither explicitly defined nor consistently employed. To give one example of inconsistency: after stating that repetition of acts is not the essential fact of habit Dewey later declares that "with habit alone there is a machine-like repetition, a duplicating recurrence of old acts."[20] To add to the confusion we are told that habit covers "the very make-up of desire, intent, choice, disposition which gives an act its voluntary quality."[21] Because he ascribes so many contradictory attributes (variability and stability, lag and progress, compulsiveness and choice) to the habit mechanism, psychologists have failed to adopt Dewey's account of it in detail. But the conception has had its influence nonetheless.

IV. MOTIVE

To understand sympathetically Dewey's psychology of motivation it is necessary to grant his primary assumption that the first need of the organism is to live and to grow. What man wants is not so much the satisfaction of separate autochthonous drives as a way of controlling the environment in relation to the diversified and almost limitless array of goals involved in the life process. Even though our first wants are determined by what our body calls for, we soon come to want the instruments of satisfaction of these wants for their own sakes. Means and ends seldom are as sharply distinguished as instinct psychologists would have us believe. Even in primitive agricultural societies man does not define his end to be the satisfaction of hunger as such.

Agriculture is so complicated and loaded with all kinds of technical activities, associations, deliberations and social divi-

sions of labor, that conscious attention and interest are in the
process and its content. Even in the crudest agriculture,
means are developed to the point where they demand attention on their own account.[22]

This quotation, written twenty years before the publication
of *Human Nature and Conduct*, contains the essence of Dewey's later doctrine of motivation. Man, so Dewey is convinced,
quickly loses sight of his simple original impulses. Motives are
vastly more numerous than instincts—"as numerous as are
original impulsive activities multiplied by the diversified consequences they produce as they operate under diverse conditions."[23]

He has no use for sex, hunger, anger, or fear, treated as if
they were "lump forces, like the combustion or gravity of old-
fashioned physical science."[24]

Even in the cases of hunger and sex, where the channels of
action are fairly demarcated by antecedent conditions (or
"nature"), the actual content and feel of hunger and sex, are
indefinitely varied according to their social contexts. Only
when a man is starving, is hunger an unqualified natural impulse.[25]

The treatment of sex by psychoanalysts is most instructive,
for it flagrantly exhibits both the consequences of artificial
simplification and the transformation of social results into
psychic causes.[26]

Nor is Dewey well disposed toward the simple and sovereign motivational forces advanced by the simplicist social
scientists.

We have no generalized will to power, but only the inherent pressure of every activity for an adequate manifestation.[27]

Egoism holds no appeal:

The fallacy consists in transforming the (truistic) fact of
acting *as* a self into the fiction of acting always *for* self.[28]

Hedonism is equally deceptive. The utilitarians are as far off
as any other instinct-mythologists.

> Of all things [future pleasures and pains] lend themselves least readily to anything approaching a mathematical calculus.[29]

The present, not the future, is ours. And in the present we find that our motives are nothing more than impulses viewed as constituents of habit. Impulses never exist by themselves. The primary fact in conduct is the habit. It is our habits that enable us to live—or someone else's habits, as in infancy where the first determiners are parental habits. By the time the young child's impulses rebel at parental regulation, he has his own habits of self-regulation.

Only when impulses are acute and not taken care of in the ordinary habitual channels do they become actually decisive and prepotent in conduct, pivots upon which the reorganization of activities turns, giving new directions to old habits and reshaping them.

Impulses like stimuli are only mediative. Having once provoked a response, their own nature is altered. This back reference of experience into impulse is simply an extension of Dewey's doctrine of the evolving stimulus-response circuits with which he sought (in 1896) to replace the concept of the reflex arc. Motives like all other units of behavior are constantly changing.[30]

The critique of Dewey's motivational psychology takes various forms. McDougall is a sharp critic of its lack of incisiveness.[31] He objects that one cannot discover just how much dynamic force Dewey intends to ascribe to habit. Some habits Dewey clearly regards as mechanical, automatic, and as auxiliary to other forms of motivation. Other habits are "energetic and dominating ways of acting," "assertive, insistent, self-perpetuating." They are "propulsive" and moving always toward some end. Criteria are lacking for distinguishing between a habit that is motivational and one that is passively instrumental.

Further, some psychologists, McDougall among them, are dissatisfied with the secondary role assigned to impulse and instinct. According to Dewey impulse arises only when habits prove inadequate to the perpetual task of coming to terms with the environment. Habits blocked engender impulse; but impulse is serviceable only for the restructuration of habits. And impulses are never twice the same. Such constant evolving and interweaving, stressing now habit and now impulse, is fatally opposed to all attempts at psychological classification. The traditional thing to do is to erect a systematic psychology of motivation upon the hypothesis of one simple and sovereign motivational force, or upon an assumption of a plurality of separate instincts, drives, desires, or wishes; it is even possible to handle compounds, fusions, and hierarchies of motivational forces, together with their conditioning and modification so long as these motivational forces are named and defined. But when Dewey, or anyone else, proposes to take away the anchorage of fixed categories and fixed mechanisms, the possibility of conceptual manipulation disappears and the science of human nature seems built not upon solid rock but upon shifting sand.

Yet Dewey's path may be that of wisdom. The desire to classify and to standardize motivational forces is perhaps an instance of wholly misguided taxonomic enterprise. Psychology may have to resign itself to the admission that motivation *is* unique, that no two habit systems, no two sets of impulses, no two ends-in-view are identical in different people. Regrettable as it may seem from the point of view of nomothetic science, there may be no escape from this conclusion. Dewey's picture of motivation may lack the incisiveness of McDougall's, Freud's, Kempf's, or Murray's, yet he may perceive more clearly than they the infinite variety of ways in which man can accomplish his primary task of adapting and growing within the surrounding world.

Although the picture of evolving motives, changing step by step as proximate goals are reached, successfully challenges the easy classifications of dynamic psychology, it leads at the same time to an exaggeration of change within any given individual. Dewey's stress on evolving goals and evolving mechanisms takes his attention away from the stability of organization in the individual personality. It is all to the good to conclude that motives are not uniform within the species, that they grow with experience, and that they exist independently of their origins, involving peculiar blends of habit, impulse, and thought; but it is not helpful to be left without any way of conceiving the patterning of motives within personality over a range of years. He seems not to have asked himself how long-lived an interest may be, or how enduring a habit. Nor has he considered the variable range that thoughts and impulses may have and still retain the same essential significance for the individual. He deals, in short, more adequately with the progressive shifts in personality than with its stability of structure.

V. THOUGHT

The problems of thought, or, as he now prefers to say, the problems of inquiry,[32] have always been for Dewey a matter of major concern. We have already called attention to his doctrine that "thought is born as the twin of impulse in every moment of impeded habit." Its function is to increase the meaning of the present experience and lead to novel solutions beyond what is possible through merely impulsive or routine (habitual) action. Yet thought is more ephemeral than either impulse or habit: "unless it is nurtured, it speedily dies, and habit and instinct continue their civil warfare."[33] Left to itself without training, thought accomplishes nothing. Without training it is unable to resist the idols and inadequate beliefs that beset every state of perplexity. Rapid, comforting solutions, the product of untrained thought—sentimental, romantic, self-justifying fantasies—serve only to blunt the misery of the moment. Emotional disturbance, even though it is the original incentive to thought, is at the same time the chief cause of unwarranted belief and conviction. "Nothing is so easy to fool as impulse and no one is deceived so readily as a person under strong emotion."[34]

Dewey's treatment of thought is thoroughgoing in its functionalism. Thought is always *mind in use*. It is not a matter of images, *Bewusstheiten*, or postures of consciousness. It is rather active search for coherent meaning serviceable to practical activity. Thought is an instrument virtually equated with intelligence. Both are the means by which we foresee the future, giving our next action order and direction.[35]

Although Dewey assigns intellect an instrumental role, auxiliary to impulse and habit, he gives it more significance than do the true antirationalists.

> Impulse is primary and intelligence is secondary and in some sense derivative. There should be no blinking of this fact. But recognition of it as a fact exalts intelligence. For thought is not the slave of impulse to do its bidding. . . . What intelligence has to do in the service of impulse is to act not as its obedient servant but as its clarifier and liberator. . . . Intelligence converts desire into plans. . . .[36]

What he says of intelligence and thought is equally true for judgment, deliberation, reflection, and reason. They all have one and the same function: to restore that balance which because of changing internal and external conditions is constantly interfered with in spite of all habit can do. Such a totally functional view leaves no room for fine distinctions between the various higher mental processes. They are all functionally equivalent. Dewey disdains the subleties of *Denkpsychologie*. Even in *How We Think* (1910) there is no mention of the flood of introspective studies coming from the German and American laboratories of that time. He early lost interest in structural psychology. Apperception, the texture of ideas, the fusion of percepts, the feeling of relation, vanished from his writings. He cares only about the use of the states and processes of consciousness in the service of education for straight thinking. For this reason Dewey's writings on thought are not a systematic contribution to the psychology of the higher mental processes. His nearest approach to an orderly analysis is the widely quoted five-fold steps in reflective thinking: (i) a felt difficulty; (ii) its location and definition; (iii) suggestion of possible solution; (iv) development by reasoning of the bearings of the suggestion; (v) further observation and experiment leading to its acceptance or rejection, that is, the conclusion of belief or disbelief.[37]

The *Logic* (1938) adds little to the psychological analysis of thought, even though it regards psychology as "more directly concerned with the focal center of initiation and execution of inquiry than are other sciences."[38] But just what psychology has to contribute is not explained. We do, however, find in the *Logic* two developments that have important bearings on psychological theory and practice. One is the author's complete repudiation of the dualistic position.

Although in the *Logic* Dewey does not free himself from subjective terminology, he is quite certain that terms like thought, judgment, idea, suggestion, and reason can be interpreted in objective ways. He writes, "I am not aware of any so-called merely 'mental' activity or result that cannot be described in the objective terms of organic activity modified and directed by symbols-meaning, or language, in its broad sense."[39] The subject or self vanishes, and in its place Dewey establishes the "biological-cultural human being." The felt needs and perplexities of this biological-cultural being are not to be viewed as subjective; they arise because "the situation is inherently doubtful." It is not a hunger drive, for example, that leads to searching behavior but rather a whole problematic situation in which the organic imbalance of hunger plays an interdependent part with all other phases of the situation: "The habit of disposing of the doubtful as if it belonged only to *us* rather than to the existential situation in which we are caught and implicated is an inheritance from subjectivistic psychology."[40]

It is true that possible solutions present themselves as *ideas*, "but an idea is merely an organic anticipation of what will happen when certain operations are executed under and with respect to observed conditions."[41] The organism is caught in an indeterminate situation requiring some transformation for the organism's own welfare. Then follows a progression of finer discriminations and better objective relationships, until a balanced condition ensues. The resolution of indeterminate situations suggests Köhler's principle of requiredness, and the reduction of the problem to what is objectively accessible—the methodological procedure—recalls contemporary operational behaviorism.

The second concept in the *Logic* of special significance for psychology is that of the "situation." Suggestive as it is of the "field" of Gestalt theorists, "situation" has considerably broader reference. It is more than a mere perceptual field. Psychologists err in treating perception in an isolated way, apart from many other effective parts of the situation. "In actual experience, there is never any such isolated singular object or event; *an* object or event is always a special part, phase, or aspect, of an environing experienced world—a situation."[42] And Dewey goes so far as to deny the capacity of psychology to study the nature of a problematic situation in its entirety.

One of the failures of perception psychology is its neglect of the economic and political conditions that are important factors in many, if not most, of the indeterminate conditions that we are striving to resolve. Perceptually we are usually unaware of such important influences as these. The cultural and social sciences recognize them, and psychology would do well to allow more generously than it does for the unconscious influence upon conduct of our status, our memberships, and the times in which we live.

With its operational and Gestalt flavor, and with its acceptance of situational and cultural determinism, the *Logic* brings Dewey's general philosophy of human behavior to mature expression, but adds little to the narrower psychology of thought.

VI. EDUCATIONAL PSYCHOLOGY

The secret of Dewey's great devotion to education lies in his conviction that no man ever realized his potentialities merely by being left alone. If democracy is, as he believes, the most advanced way of community living, it must be continually born anew in every generation, for man's original nature by no means leads to the spontaneous exercise of the powers of inquiry and self-reorganization that is demanded by democratic life. A set of cheap and easy absolutes may satisfy adherents of a totalitarian state but not of democracy. The authentic democrat takes fright at the appearance of rigid formulations set for the guidance of his conduct. He is satisfied only with an educational policy that keeps the mind limber, and enables it to participate in its own destiny. Especially objectionable are those psychological theories that set fixed limits to the capacity of human beings for self-improvement. A rigid doctrine of instinct, for example, may be used to discourage educational progress and so lead to the defeat of the democratic ideal of participation by all. Even the conception of the constant I.Q. savors of conservative aristocracy.

Among psychological theories that lead to educational stagnation Dewey attacks imitation. There is, of course, no instinct of imitation, and if imitativeness is encouraged in the child by routine drill, it inhibits his power to remake old habits. Drill at best generates skill in a *particular* performance. In itself it does not lead to new perceptions of bearings and connections. The environment constantly changes, and since this is so any stereotyped way of acting may become disastrous at some critical moment. A vaunted, highly trained skill may then turn out to be merely a gross ineptitude. Learning must bring with it capacity for constant adaptation. Every skill should be transferable, every hypothesis tentative, every channel of thought versatile in its combination and intercommunication with other channels; for education is that "reconstruction or reorganization of experience which adds to the meaning of experience, and which increases ability to direct the course of subsequent experience."[43]

A properly formulated psychology will inevitably work hand in hand with the instrumental ideal of education. True psychology is itself "a conception of democracy," for it believes in the efficacy of training, of communication, participation and action, as ways of changing human conduct. It does not deal with absolutes. Rather, it proceeds step by step, asking what the organism is going to do next. And it marches hand in hand with the ethics of instrumentalism asking what it is *better* to do next.

Psychology provides the teacher with tools for discrimination and analysis. She cannot deal with a total, unanalyzed personality. She needs instruments of discernment to confront a personality in the forming. Specifically, psychology must tell the teacher what stimuli shall be presented to the sense organs to obtain a desired result; what stable complexes of associations may be created; what coordinations and adaptations can be evoked and what their effect will be. Hence the application of psychology to education is the only way of achieving particular ends within the broadly conceived ethical goal of democracy and self-realization.

The close linkage between psychology and education is a long-standing conviction with Dewey. As early as 1889 he entitled his "Introduction to the Principles and Practice of Education" *Applied Psychology.*[44] And in 1895 in *The Psychology of Number* he again insisted that only a knowledge of psychology will supply education with the conditions which will enable psychical functions to mature and to pass into higher stages of integration.

The true purity of psychology as a science exists only in its application, never apart from it. If psychology is not actively concerned with education, or health, or adaptive thought, or social relations, then it has no reason for being. To be a science lockstitched with life is the highest tribute Dewey can pay psychology. He has only scorn for the snobbish notion that applied knowledge is somehow less worthy or less desirable than pure knowledge.

Yet Dewey does not fall into the trap of psychologism. He does not regard psychology as all-powerful and all-inclusive. It cannot, for instance, supply us with our *ideals* for education, nor can it test the *correctness* of thought nor the *value* of conduct. But it can give us a definite base line from which to measure ethical claims by telling whether ideals are attainable, and how to go about attaining them.

All these considerations lead Dewey to foster the closest and friendliest relations between education and psychology. He sees psychology as an infant science, perhaps offering little as yet to the cause of sound pedagogy. But great is his faith that ultimately the psychology of functional and organic development will expand, dealing more adequately than now with progressive adaptations within complex situations. Such a psychology will implement and advance immeasurably the aims of education and therewith the aims of democracy itself.

VII. SOCIAL AND POLITICAL PSYCHOLOGY

As early as 1899 Dewey made the striking observation that the system of postulates and theories that one adopts in psychology is likely to be politically conditioned.[45] In particular the estimate people place upon the significance of individuality varies according to the political frame within which psychology is written. An aristocracy sees the individual as unimportant unless the individual is of the higher classes. Apologists for the *status quo* draw support from psychological doctrines that declare human nature to be virtually unalterable.[46] In present times Dewey could find additional proof for his contention in the psychological dicta of the National Socialist and Communist ideologies. His recognition of the ideological factor, it should be noted, antedates the work of Mannheim and other *Wissenssoziologen*.

So important to Dewey are the political consequences of psychological theory that he takes considerable pains to discredit social psychologies that seem to him undemocratic in their orientation. He does not combat these theories by marshaling contradictory evidence but repudiates them frankly upon the basis of their ideological affiliations. What Dewey wants is a psychology compatible with democracy and he rejects any mental science having contrary implications. His opposition to the theory of fixed instincts, to the French school of Imitation, to Durkheim's school of the collective mind, can be understood on this ground, likewise his suspiciousness of capacity psychology and his discrediting of the intelligence quotient.

Other concepts are equally uncongenial to him. He has little use for Wundtian folk-psychology, since it employs the rubrics of introspective psychology. In fact, introspective categories, he holds, are the chief cause for the backwardness of social psychology.[47] Interestingly enough, he rejects the dualism of introspective psychology partly for its political implications.

> Those who wish a monopoly of social power find desirable the separation of habit and thought, action and soul, so characteristic of history. For the dualism enables them to do the thinking and planning, while others remain the docile, even if awkward, instruments of execution. Until this scheme is changed, democracy is bound to be perverted in realization.[48]

Dewey compels even a metaphysical postulate to give way unless it is democratically oriented.

To complete his list of rejections, Dewey discounts all social psychology that neglects the outside forces that play upon the organism. For unless we believe in the potency of the environmental situation, it does no good to press for social reform. Even in 1917, when he favored the hypothesis of instincts, he insisted that instincts become real events only when they are related to the situation. Besides instinct or impulse the rubrics of social psychology must include many others— habit, discrimination, thought, coordination, adaptation, and custom. Custom is particularly significant, for it supplies the inescapable framework of conception within which individual thinking is compelled to move.[49]

Custom is the first teacher of habits, and it is the primary duty of social psychology to illuminate the ways in which customs shape habits, and with them desires, beliefs, and purposes. Social psychology rests, of course, directly upon the biological or functional psychology that the previous pages have described. Both begin with the living organism engaged in some act, some coordination. When this coordination is interrupted, when an inadequate habit is broken up, we have the possibility of new coordination, novel conduct, effected through impulse, discrimination, attention, association, and thought. This brief formula sets the problems for individual psychology, but whenever custom plays a part in the new coordination, or when other individuals are involved, social psychology is called for.

Some of the special problems of social psychology arise when new coordinations are frustrated and the reconstruction of habits prevented. In such a case emotion rises like a tide. Perhaps this emotion will be diverted into side channels of substitute habits and disperse itself aimlessly. But perhaps it will rise higher and be met by corresponding emotions in other people. There may result a wave of enthusiasm for some reform, or a violent reaction against some threatening novelty. In any case the conditions of the so-called mob mind are fulfilled. The crowd and mob come into existence because of a disintegration of habits which releases impulses that can be manipulated by skilled demagogues and by propaganda.

Far more stable than the crowd or the mob are the group, the club, the political party. It is this level of human association that interests Dewey particularly, for it is here that the public exists and democratic activity is achieved.

The *Public and Its Problems* sets forth the broad framework of a system of political psychology, much as does Hobbes' *Leviathan*, Rousseau's *Social Contract*, or McDougall's *Group Mind*. But Dewey's views agree with none of his predecessors. He rejects all time-honored conceptions of the common will, the Sovereign People, the group mind, and the Great Society. Political groupings, he insists, have no superpersonal character. Nor are they based upon social instincts. Wants, choices, and purposes are diverse acts of single human beings, not springing from any native social propensity.

A public, instead of being a mystical entity or the expression of social instinct, is nothing but the by-product of social activity between individuals. So long as A and B have direct private transactions no public is involved. But let the consequences of their transactions extend beyond their own lives, affecting the lives and welfare of others, and a public, based on common interest, springs into being. In itself such a public is unorganized and formless, comprised merely of common segments of certain individuals' interests. One public is created by the existence of motor cars, another by the existence of schools, another by the practice of taxation. As soon as officials are elected, or in some other way recognized, the formless public becomes organized. The officials themselves, of course, are single beings, but they exercise special powers designed to protect the common interests of the members. A comprehensive public articulated and operating through officers who are expected to subordinate their private interests for the good of all, is a State.[50]

Unfortunately the same forces which have brought about our form of democratic state have brought about conditions which impede the effective practice of democracy. Technology alone has created *many* publics, with conflicting interests. Each of us is a member of many unrelated, and sometimes even antagonistic groups. For us to elect an official who represents *all* of our diversified interests is impossible. We do not even *understand* the vast industrial and economic enterprises with which we are related in we know not how many ways, and for that reason do not know even in what direction our interests lie. Our so-called popular elections often express nothing more than the will of a certain group of financial forces, propagandists, or selfish leaders. There results an "eclipse of the public." Democracy becomes ineffective.

These observations of the plight of an "inchoate and unorganized" democratic public lead Dewey to plead for the invention of new ways of securing full expression of the wants and interests of whole personalities. Free discussion concerning public policy will help; information on matters now reserved for the expert alone will also help. We need education to free us from stereotyped emotional habits centering around signs and symbols, to give us greater latitude of communication. Freedom of communication is especially needed.

Dewey's picture of the ineffective functioning of democracy is realistic and sorrowful. Probably few will question its correctness, and all believers in democracy will subscribe to his proposed educational remedies. He is never more convincing than in his repeated demonstration that the improvement of the methods and conditions of debate, discussion, and deliberation are necessary for the support of democracy. Each public must become a participant public, every member helping to shape its destiny. Becoming active within the publics to which we belong, we find our own well-being.

It is here, however, that one serious difficulty arises. Does Dewey himself see the inherent contradiction that exists between his advocacy of the community of *whole* individuals as the ideal unit of public organization, and his hope to harmonize the *segmental* types of public based upon common but highly specialized interests? The latter type of public, as he admits, is an abstraction derived from the separation of one partial segment of life from the remainder of that life. A single individual may belong to many, many publics. His interests as an individual are not truly fulfilled by his being partially included in multiple groups. If a given citizen is, say, a veteran, a "dry," a believer in free trade, a broker, a motorist, a home owner, an urbanite, a pacifist, how shall he vote to gain total inclusion for his pattern of interests? Or what groups shall he join that will bring unity into his life? As complications develop under modern conditions, total inclusion of the personality in specialized publics becomes increasingly difficult to achieve.[51] In a simple, primitive community such inclusion may conceivably be accomplished, but not under the complex conditions of modern society.

The question is then how to reconcile personality as an ethical end with the inevitable increase in the number of special publics that include mere segments of the personality and never the whole. In advocating the face-to-face community Dewey is on solid enough ground; but such a totally inclusive community cannot be achieved by the multiplication of partial publics separated in space. More and more vigorous participation in the segmental activities of a democratic state will not achieve unity for the individual. The problem is a serious one and it remains, in spite of Dewey's efforts, unsolved.

VIII. CONCLUSION

What is the nature of John Dewey's influence on modern psychology? That an answer is not to be sought in conventional directions is clear from our present survey. He is not a laboratory psychologist; there is no record of his conducting a controlled experiment, nor devising nor administering a psychological test. In his bibliography we had only one minor and now forgotten observational study (on infant language). He has not dealt clinically with single cases. He has created no systematic classifications to guide psychologists in their researches, nor has he founded a well-defined school of psychology. Though he spends much time in evaluating psychology, he makes no use of the accumulated researches in its archives. He is thus not an historian nor a bibliographer. He does virtually none of the things that present-day psychologists are supposed to do.

Yet he writes extensively on the very subjects that psychologists are interested in, and he has fashioned his views into a coherent scheme. Is he then a systematist? Many psychologists would say no, for the system Dewey offers is of such nature that it lacks fixed points of reference. It is elusive and difficult to grasp. The reciprocal interpenetration of impulse, habit, and thought, the continuous relating of these functions with the properties of the environment, which in turn is regarded as continuously evolving in terms of the properties of *both* the organism and the environment *as* related—such a flux of processes and events makes it difficult for the psychologist to gain a familiar hold. He finds it much easier to redact his observations into the fixed categories of behaviorism, Freudianism, hormic psychology, or even the elder categories of structuralism and simple Jamesian functionalism. Evolving circuits may indeed be, as Dewey insists, the course of mental life, but spiraling processes make orderly analysis in terms of separate variables impossible. Unless situations remain fixed and can be relied upon to recur, how can the psychologist plot those definite functions that are said to constitute scientific law, or having plotted them how can he apply them to ever-novel situations?

But Dewey is unmoved by such criticism. To those who wish to work only with fixed categories and isolable variables he replies:

> When we assume that our clefts and bunches represent fixed separations and collections *in rerum natura*, we obstruct rather than aid our transactions with things. We are guilty of a presumption which nature promptly punishes. We are rendered incompetent to deal effectively with the delicacies and novelties of nature and life.[52]

It is this warning, repeated with all manner of variations in his writings, that constitutes one secret of Dewey's influence. He has taught his readers to be wary of "clefts and bunches." His insistence upon the complete process of coordination leads them to be suspicious of the fragments produced by neat analysis. When the laboratory wheels turn and the knives cut, and some exuberant investigator holds up an excised segment of behavior for acclaim, Deweyites are not edified. They know that true statements cannot be made about fragments snatched from their natural context. They have little use for a psychology that isolates separate functions within the total course of experience, and prefer a thoroughgoing organismic psychology, preferably one that has a strong social emphasis.

It is another mark of Dewey's influence that he has made psychological propositions indispensable to philosophy. Morals, for him, deal with aims as they are tied to wants, habits, and choice; and wants, habits, and choice are whatever

psychology says they are. Logic is the science of inquiry, but
the act of inquiry can proceed only according to psychological canons. Art is experience, but experience must be revealed
by a study of typical attitudes and habits which psychology
identifies. Politics too depends upon psychological discoveries
concerning the nature of communication, discussion, and
persuasion. At every step education likewise must employ
psychological rubrics and rules. The whole pragmatic philosophy of proximate goals, next steps, "ends that are literally
endless" must tie in at every point with a psychology that
treats the successive stages of organic conduct. Dewey's own
interests are primarily normative, but he constantly exposes
his norms to the actualities of human conduct. It is because
he does so that one feels that psychology has a part to play
in human progress. Human betterment becomes plausible and
practicable, and psychology receives recognition and bound-
less encouragement.

Finally, deep and far-reaching significance lies in Dewey's
perception of the inherent relation between psychology and
democracy. Psychology is in essence the science of democratic
living:

> The cause of modern civilization stands and falls with the
> ability of the individual to serve as its agent and bearer. And
> psychology is naught but the account of the way in which
> individual life is thus progressively maintained and reorgan-
> ized. Psychology is the attempt to state in detail the machin-
> ery of the individual considered as the instrument and organ
> through which social action operates.[53]

Psychology studies progressive mental adaptation; democracy is the means of achieving that adaptation. The two must
go hand in hand. Both have to do with human experiments in
living. While psychology provides the knowledge with which
to make democracy effective, democracy provides the congenial, progressive, beneficial frame in which psychology can
be productive.

In 1939 Dewey's perception is seen for its true brilliance. It is true beyond shadow of doubt that within no other frame than democracy does psychological inquiry proceed with even a relative freedom, and equally true that the perils and weakness of democracy are to a large extent psychological in origin and must be psychological in cure. The times have caught up with Dewey. We realize at last what he has long contended, that without democracy psychology cannot succeed, and without psychology democracy will surely fail.

NOTES

1. "The New Psychology," *Andover Review*, 1884, *2*, 268.
2. "Psychology as Philosophic Method," *Mind*, 1886, *11*, 169.
3. "The Psychological Standpoint," *Mind*, 1886, *11*, 1–19.
4. S. H. Hodgson, "Illusory Psychology," *Mind*, 1886, *11*, 488.
5. G. S. Brett, *A History of Psychology*, 1921, Vol. 3, 261.
6. "On Some Current Conceptions of the Term 'Self,'" *Mind*, 1890, *15*, 58–74.
7. Another influence doubtless was Dewey's growing interest in education. His *Applied Psychology* (1889) demonstrated to him the urgent need for a less formalistic psychology of will. Habit, interest, and adjustment were the concepts he needed, and these he could not evolve so long as he treated will in the manner of Hegel or Herbart.
8. *Psychol. Rev.*, 1894, *1*, 63–66.
9. *Psychol. Rev.*, 1894, *1*, 553–569; *ibid.*, 1895, *2*, 13–32. McDougall has questioned Dewey's claim that emotion comes merely from the clash of habits. For McDougall, of course, emotion accompanies the operation of primary instincts, whether or not a state of frustration exists. It is therefore fully present in interests. *Amer. J. Sociol.*, 1924, *29*, 657–676.
10. "The Ego as Cause," *Philos. Rev.*, 1894, *3*, Ftn. 340f.
11. "The Psychology of Effort," *Philos. Rev.*, 1897, *6*, 43–56.
12. At about this time Dewey rejects also the sharp distinction then prevailing between functional and structural psychology. The problem of psychology, he says, is the total course of experience in the individual mind. The distinction between structuralism and functionalism seemed to him about as reasonable "as a division of botanists into rootists and flowerists."

("Psychology as Philosophic Method," Berkeley: *Univ. Chronicle*, 1899.) Yet in spite of this stricture Dewey's own stress was so consistently upon the stream of consciousness and so seldom upon its states that he must be classified with the functionalists.

13. *Psychol. Rev.*, 1896, *3*, 357–370.
14. *Ibid.*, 358.
15. The dates represent the publication of "The Need for a Social Psychology," *Psychol. Rev.*, *24*, 266–277, and *Human Nature and Conduct*, respectively.
16. *Human Nature and Conduct*, 41f.
17. *Ibid.*, 38.
18. *Ibid.*, 190.
19. Here we have an example of the isolationism that afflicts Dewey's psychology. Granted that relatively little work had been done in 1922 upon the perplexing problems of units of personality, still there were many contacts that he could have made with profit.
    Present-day readers of Dewey will do well to check his doctrine of habit against other comparable concepts. See W. McDougall, "Tendencies as Indispensable Postulates of all Psychology," Paris: *Proc. XI Internat. Congress of Psychology*, 1937; likewise G. W. Allport, "Attitudes," *Handbook of Social Psychology*, Worcester: Clark University Press, 1935, Ch. 17; also *Personality: A Psychological Interpretation*, New York: Holt, 1935, Chs. 9–12.
20. Cf. *Human Nature and Conduct*, 42 and 180.
21. Dewey and Tufts, *Ethics*, revised edition (1932), 181.
22. "Interpretation of Savage Mind," *Psychol. Rev.*, 1902, *9*, 217–230.
23. *Human Nature and Conduct*, 122.
24. *Ibid.*, 150.
25. *Ibid.*, 153.
26. *Loc. cit.*
27. *Ibid.*, 141.
28. *Ibid.*, 136.
29. *Ibid.*, 203.
30. The consequences for ethics of this doctrine of evolving circuits is important. It follows that "good" conduct can never

twice be the same. Only if impulse and habit were rigid to the point of immobility could exactly the same good ever recur. Since impulse and habit are in reality ever-changing, we must conclude that "ends are, in fact, literally endless, forever coming into existence as new activities occasion new consequences." *Human Nature and Conduct*, 211. The good is a matter of rectifying *present* trouble through the cooperation of habit, impulse, and thought. Trouble is eternally fresh trouble, and "good" solutions are forever new.

31. *Amer. J. Sociol.*, 1924, *29*, 657–676.
32. Cf. *Logic*, 21.
33. *Human Nature and Conduct*, 171.
34. *Ibid.*, 255.
35. Here we must comment on Dewey's lack of interest in *capacity* psychology. Intelligence testing concerns him not at all. *Anyone* is capable of thinking and so improving his adaptations and mastery within his environment. A pupil labeled as hopeless, he points out, may react in a quick and lively fashion when the thing in hand seems to him worth while. He has likewise written, "Barring physical defect or disease, slowness and dullness in all directions are comparatively rare." (*How We Think*, 35.) There is no homogeneous faculty of thought nor any uniform power of intelligence that would, because of differential possession, make education for some pupils unnecessary and for others worthless. In short, individual differences in capacity are of far less consequence than is the fact that everyone can be taught to think more effectively than he does.
36. *Human Nature and Conduct*, 254f.
37. *How We Think*, 72.
38. *Logic*, 36.
39. *Ibid.*, 57.
40. *Ibid.*, 106.
41. *Ibid.*, 109.
42. *Ibid.*, 67.
43. *Democracy and Education* (1916), 89.
44. J. A. McLellan was coauthor of both *Applied Psychology* and *The Psychology of Number*.
45. "Psychology as Philosophic Method," Berkeley: University

Press, 1899. Reprinted as "Consciousness and Experience" in *The Influence of Darwin on Philosophy and Other Essays* (1910), 242–270.

46. "The ultimate refuge of the standpatter in every field, education, religion, politics, industrial, and domestic life, has been the notion of an alleged fixed structure of mind. As long as mind is conceived as an antecedent and ready-made thing, institutions and customs may be regarded as its offspring." *Psychol. Rev.* (1917), *24*, 273.

47. "The Need for Social Psychology," *Psychol. Rev.* (1917), *24*, 271.

48. *Human Nature and Conduct*, 72.

49. It should be noted that in his most recent book, the *Logic*, Dewey widens his concept of framework to include not only custom, but also physical conditions such as soil, sea, mountains, climate, tools, and machines. Conduct is only in part determined by subjective wants, beliefs, and skill, and only in part by the social frame of custom. Both in turn are conditioned by physical phenomena and their laws. By stressing here physical and ecological factors, Dewey diminishes proportionately the place he would give to psychology in accounting for social life. Indeed, he says explicitly that his broadened account of the nature of the surrounding situation is "fatal to the view that social sciences are exclusively, or even dominantly, psychological." *Logic*, 492.

50. *The Public and Its Problems*, 67.

51. This dilemma as found in Dewey's political philosophy has been discussed at length by F. H. Allport, *Institutional Behavior*, 1933, Chap. 5.

52. *Human Nature and Conduct*, 131.

53. "The Significance of the Problem of Knowledge," in *The Influence of Darwin on Philosophy and Other Essays* (1910), 302.

18

Karl Bühler

THIS SHORT PAPER is in fact a belated book review. In the
1960's it seemed to several Americans that the psychological
contributions of Karl Bühler—before Hitler a prominent professor at the University of Vienna—were not widely enough
appreciated in America. It seemed a good idea to gather together a variety of expository tributes so that his career as a
whole might be appreciated.

Die Krise der Psychologie, published in German in 1927
and again in 1965, has been unwisely neglected by American
psychologists. It gives an authoritative picture of psychology
in German-speaking countries during the highly productive
first quarter of the twentieth century. It is too important a
book to be overlooked.

This review is contained in the memorial symposium printed
in the *Journal of General Psychology*, Vol. 75, 1966.

† † †

One wonders why some of the most important psychological
treatises in the German language have remained untranslated
for decades. One thinks, for example, of Fechner's *Psycho-
physik*, of Brentano's *Psychologie vom empirischen Stand-
punkt*, and of the work here under review, Bühler's *Die Krise
der Psychologie*. The last named was published in 1927,
reissued in 1929, and again in 1965. Recently I have heard
rumors that all three of these neglected classics are now in
process of belated translation. I hope the rumors become
realities.

Die Krise is a landmark in the history of psychology, presenting as it does a perspective on the pre-Hitler golden age of German-Austrian psychological theory. The author expounds and evaluates the major antiassociationist movements that followed the decline of Machian sensory positivism. First came the *Denkpsychologie* of the Würzburger (to which Bühler himself contributed). Psychoanalysis followed closely in time. Both movements, so different in other respects, agree that mental processes run their course under dynamic management and not by virtue of mechanical connection. Besides these two movements the author surveys the theories of *Verstehen*, of *Gestalt*, and of kindred concepts of structure, as well as his own work on language and some of Charlotte Bühler's work on child development; but chiefly it is the presuppositions, logic, and fruitfulness of the standard theories that are the center of attention.

The author's effort is directed toward the fashioning of a systematic eclecticism. "*Raum für alle hat das grosse Haus der Psychologie*" (p. 142). He rejects no school *in toto*, but rather sifts and selectively accepts distinctive contributions of the various schools. He turns against a theory only when it seems to him to be guilty of overplaying its hand. The term "crisis" refers to the pretense of each single school of thought that it alone has a monopoly of truth. Actually no single school gives the needed balance in dealing with the three basic characteristics of human conduct: *inner experience, meaningful behavior*, and their relation to *culture* (19, p. 29). Psychoanalysis neglects the social and cultural context; the *Geisteswissenschaften* are one sided in their commitment to an Hegelian mentalism; behaviorism, in rejecting the Delphic admonition to "know thyself," adheres too exclusively to external observation of behavior (usually meaningless unless related to inner experience).

Bühler is perhaps weakest in his evaluation of American behaviorism. He cites only the work of H. S. Jennings and of E. L. Thorndike, who are scarcely typical of the movement. J. B. Watson he does not mention. More regrettable is the omission of certain quasi-behavioristic currents in American thought that he would have found highly congenial, notably the social psychology of John Dewey, Charles Cooley, and of George Herbert Mead.

An adequate science of psychology will of course deal with behavior, but always within the context of inner experience and social relevance.

To make clear what he means by these three aspects, the author draws on his own famous theory of the three functions of language. When all is said and done, language is the most representative function of mind. It entails the expression of inner states, it is heavily cultural and has social consequences, and it has representational (symbolic) significance. Sign, signal, and symbol are all involved (19, p. 75). Roughly these functions correspond to behavior, culture, and experience.

A central concept in this connection is *Steuerung* (steering) which is virtually identical with the master key of cybernetics, invented a decade or two later. "Wherever a truly common life exists, it must entail a mutual steering of meaningful behavior among the members of the social unit" (19, p. 50). Such is the function of language; and such, too, is the nature of psychological activity in general. Bühler sums up his argument syllogistically: if language has the three irreducible aspects, and if language is wholly a psychological phenomenon, then psychology as a science must be broad enough to handle all three aspects (19, p. 58).

In order to fashion a psychology adequate to experience-behavior-culture, one must deal with the functioning of systems (*Systemsteuerung*). To understand this functioning requires a basic comprehension of *structure*, of meaning (*Sinn*), and of goal (*Zweck*) (19, p. 65). Again we find that certain schools of thought stress one but not all of these interlocking attributes of system.

All schools of thought accept the concept of *structure*. Bühler regards Dilthey as its prophetic sponsor and quotes his pronouncement of 1894: "All psychological thinking rests on the principle that in grasping the whole we are enabled to interpret and define details" (19, p. 106). While Bühler is basically in agreement with Dilthey, he fears that exclusive emphasis on structure may limit the theories to a merely homeostatic or equilibrium concept of the functioning of systems. Structure needs to be infused with meaningful directedness. *Sinn* and *Zweck* must also be provided in any fully adequate theory of system. The term *Sinn* is not easy to translate. It derives from an old high German word "sinan" that signifies "going forth with a goal in view." The English term "meaning" falls short. Only by joining sense and purpose with structure can any psychological totality be understood (19, p. 137).

The author presents a sympathetic but cautious endorsement of *Verstehen*. He finds that the positions of Dilthey and Spranger rest almost exclusively on the Hegelian objective mind. While it is true that any form of psychological understanding must recognize cultural context, still Bühler would not rule out organic (physiological) processes of individual behavior as important aspects of the whole that is to be understood.

Freud is praised for seeing the inadequacy of his own pleasure principle. Since satiation is the end result of every gratification of instinct, there must be something "beyond the pleasure principle." Unfortunately Freud embraces the dismal hypothesis that a repetition-compulsion regulates conduct that is not specifically drive-induced, and he goes on to postulate a vague Thanatos that ultimately beckons man over the hill. Had Freud looked more closely he would have found beyond the pleasures of drive-satisfaction the more pervasive pleasures of sheer functioning (*Funktionslust*) and of creative activity (*Schaffensfreude*), such as are met in play, in art, and in all rhythmic activity. Repetition-compulsion is wholly inadequate to represent the ongoing, free-functioning, creative, and playful conduct that marks much of human development.

Here, as elsewhere in the book, we note the prophetic quality in *Die Krise*. Bühler's attack on Freud's meager motivational formulae and his own postulation of functioning and productive pleasure clearly anticipate recent theorizing in terms of exploration, arousal, conflict-free activity, competence, and kindred concepts which taken together add up to post-Freudian ego-psychology.

Freud, unfortunately, was a *Stoffdenker*, unable to think in terms of pattern, Gestalt, form, or productivity. Always Freud stresses content, composition, the structural fabric of mental life that incessantly repeats and recurs. There is no adequate feeling for the *Formwille* (proactive tendency) that marks normal mental life. Play is a good example. The playing child is not concerned with drive-satisfaction but with rhythm and rules and the completion of Gestalten. Bühler remarks that Freud and Gestalt theory stand at opposite poles (19, p. 178).

The theory of play leans toward that of Groos who sees it as preparation for the future (in animals as well as in children). Some degree of teleology is inescapable, for in play as in most activity one senses the operation of the *produktives Gegenwartsprinzip*. A particularly interesting observation is that the child does most of his learning, including the learning of language, in connection with play. It is therefore not reinforcement or drive reduction that anchors learning, but rather the location of the learned event in the ongoing stream of functioning. Something is learned if it fits into the presently active pattern.

For Karl Bühler joy in creative activity is one of life's chief assets and principal values. As Hubert Rohracher says in his introduction to the 1965 edition, the reader often discerns this creative joy in Bühler's own brilliantly freewheeling engagement with the psychological theories of his day. This engagement proves to be prophetic of many developments in present-day psychology—including information theory, cybernetics, cognitive theory, ego-psychology, and the humanistic "third force." The volume therefore is of distinctly current interest. One hopes that a worthy translation soon will become available.

19

The Genius of Kurt Lewin

HISTORY MAY JUDGE Kurt Lewin to be the most original thinker in psychology during the present century. Many of his novel concepts quickly became coin of the psychological realm: aspiration level, detour, valence, quasi-need, barrier, group atmosphere, social perception, and many others. Since his death twenty years ago, his influence has somewhat waned, but his contributions still merit close attention. The present tribute was presented at a memorial meeting shortly after his death and printed in the *Journal of Personality*, Vol. 16, 1947.

† † †

In the words of the poet, genius is "heaven born and seldom seen." Perhaps because it is so, psychologists, busily burdened with the mundane and the average, have given the subject little attention. Our most fruitful approach to date has been in terms of the intelligent quotient; but its insufficiency is evident when we consider the work of a man whose originality seems to remove him from all comparison scales. We do not know what Kurt Lewin's I.Q. may have been, but this measure if known would not be relevant to an understanding of the unique pattern of his accomplishment.

Greatness seems always to beget controversy. In psychology the most controversial figure in our times is Freud, incomparably the most original and important. After Freud, we think of McDougall and Kurt Lewin, both influential systematists, and for that very reason controversial. McDougall had the disadvantage of defending a dualism and nativism that were caught in the ebbing tide of intellectual fashion. Lewin had the advantage of rising with the flood tide of configurationism and an awakening social conscience. If less controversial than McDougall, he was yet rejected by a small minority of psychologists, for the most part rigid methodologists and mathematicians, who were offended by his latitudinarian incursions into their domain.

Although we have little empirical guidance in the matter, I venture to suggest certain conditions that seem always in the case of genius to converge. I do not pretend that these are the sufficient conditions of genius, but only that they seem to be some of the necessary conditions.

1. In the first place, the work of a genius seems always marked by a certain *intellectual solitude*.

It sounds strange to say that Kurt Lewin, who was surely the most affable and friendly of men, was in any respect solitary. Yet we mark his avoidance of the well-worn paths of psychological science, and his apparent compulsion to strike off by himself. I recall spending much time with him discussing the concept of attitudes, trying to persuade him to accord it a more systematic place in his theoretical doctrine. Others, I know, urged him to import into his system various psychoanalytic concepts. Characteristically he gave the petitioners a most considerate hearing and declared there was much truth in their argument, but then he would plead in his peculiarly winning manner, "Now, you don't mind do you, if I represent the same phenomenon in a slightly different way?" Whereupon, more often than not, he would draw a Jordan curve. His restless intelligence seemed continuously to put forth pseudopods to engulf the thought of the other. But the prize, once grasped, was forthwith assimilated into the parent body of field theory.

In no respect was his intellectual solitude asocial. On the contrary, more than most original thinkers, he exposed himself to the benefits of social facilitation. While deriving much stimulation from others he sparked back with ideas in such a lively and radiant manner that inevitably he won a circle of followers who for a time constituted a closely knit team of like-minded investigators. Yet Lewin had no desire to found a separate school of psychology, and—in spite of the originality of his thought and the devotion of his youthful collaborators—finally succeeded in avoiding the trap of separatism. The phrase "Lewin and his students" was heard more often during the few years immediately preceding and following his immigration to America in 1932 than during the last decade of his life. As his own interests branched out into industrial psychology and public service, and as his students took up important positions in war research, in clinics, and in community life, we heard less about an "inner circle" and felt more widely in our national and professional life the wholesome impact of their work. Furthermore, many Lewinian concepts that at first seemed esoteric came soon to saturate the discourse of standard psychology. The dynamic power of unfinished tasks, escape from the field, the level of aspiration, differentiation, the detour are a few of the many concepts that general psychology today has widely adopted.

When he took cognizance of the work of others, his response, as I have said, was an urge to reshape this thought into his own expanding system. Some methodologists with a similar urge show themselves intolerant and snappish in dealing with their opponents. Lewin was never ungracious, nor did he feel the compulsion to single out villains whom he might ridicule and deride in order to highlight the superiority of his own thought. When he felt it necessary to condemn class theory in order to clarify the merits of field theory, he took as the representative villain nothing more personal than "the Aristotelian mode of thought."

2. Without the solitude that brings detachment from the folkways there could be no marked *originality*, which, of course, is the central attribute of genius. Though of necessity Lewin built with the psychological, sociological, and mathematical blocks that he found available, the structure that he erected is startling in its originality.

The problem that has most perplexed psychological scientists is that of relatedness, of the interdependence of parts within a whole. It is precisely this problem to which Lewin devoted himself. In Lippitt's words, "Although his life line could be analyzed in terms of many themes, I believe the most persistent and central was his continuous scientific study of the mysteries of interdependence in the successful functioning of individual personality, of group life, and of science as an ongoing operation made up of many subparts."[1] At various times psychology has tried to handle problems of interrelatedness with the aid of correlational methods, including factor analysis, with the postulation of habit hierarchies and integration, with the concept of form-qualities, with profiles. The Gestalt movement carried with it the stronger assertion that interdependence is in reality a matter of wholeness and not of relations. But in the fields of personality and social behavior, the Gestalt movement provided no concepts as useful and as embracing as Lewin's twofold representation of the person as a differentiated region, and as a point region in his life space.

To trace the history of any department of science rapidly is a dangerous thing, for epochs intertwine and each age has its dissenting voices. But in order to indicate the nature of Lewin's originality in the field of social psychology, let me suggest that this discipline has come through three fairly distinct epochs, and now, thanks largely to him, is entering a fourth, more promising, period of development.

For many hundreds of years, and extending into the present century, we have had simplicist systems of social theory. All these systems were rationally evolved, with no more empiricism to support them than the selective perceptions of their authors. One mental mechanism, or a narrowly conceived cluster of mechanisms, a kind of *deus ex machina*, underlay the social theories of Hobbes, Comte, Mill, Spencer, Bagehot, Tarde, Le Bon, Ross, McDougall, and many other writers whose principal work was published prior to 1910.

There followed the individualistic era, ushered in with Mc-Dougall's simple and sovereign doctrine of instincts. The individual was the center of the social universe. This emphasis led to the period of experimentation that dealt with social influence upon the sensory and higher mental processes of individuals. Behaviorism aided the conception by fragmenting the environment into an infinite number of conditioned stimuli to act as instigators to an infinite number of reflex tracts. In the midst of this period McDougall attempted to escape from the solipsism he himself helped create by postulating a "group mind" in close analogy to the individual mind. The very term "group mind" as used by him, and by many of his predecessors, betrays preoccupation with the individual model. It was for other reasons, however, that the concept was rejected. It was not in line with the extreme pluralism of the period; it was not fruitful experimentally; it was stained with European metaphysics. The individualistic era was principally a time when the methods and concepts of experimental psychology were in the ascendancy and when individual mental operations, interpreted with the aid of statistical method, were held to explain adequately all social behavior. Freudianism with its highly individualistic emphasis was easily assimilated into this line of thought.

Two decades ago a reaction set in when both sociologists and anthropologists spoke up vigorously concerning the importance of status, role, caste, and pattern, and of the significance of the *situation*, both immediate and remote, in determining present conduct. To be sure, sociologists and anthropologists had been speaking in these terms for many years, but it was not until the departmental walls in our universities were weakened that their voices were heard by psychologists across the corridor. There came a time when many of the same psychologists who had been speaking in individualistic terms swung to the other extreme. It became fashionable for them now to talk in terms of patterns of culture, to assert that personality is naught but man's social stimulus value, and to solve the mysteries of character by invoking the mores of the "upper-upper" or the "lower-middle."

To some extent the influence of all three of these periods is persisting today, especially of course, of the third period. But it is at this point that we are beginning to sense the significance of the Lewinian influence which represents a better-balanced fusion of the individualistic and social emphasis. At first sight, we are inclined to brush aside Lewin's favorite formula, $B = f(P, E)$, as a truism. Has not every psychologist from the beginning of time agreed that it is always the dynamics of the person and the dynamics of the environment that unite to determine behavior? Probably so—with their lips. But even while we agree in principle, individualists among us insist that P must dominate the scene, with the past history of the person assuming the all-determining role. Culturalists among us strive to minimize P and to exalt E. Lewin points to the middle course, and advises that we resolve our dispute by taking the situational field as it is viewed by the participants themselves. When we do so we find that culture patterns, caste, role, and status are indeed decisive in conduct, but only insofar as these categories of social structure are actually transmuted into effective forces within the behavioral environment, through the needs and perceptual processes of the individual.

"Systems under tension" are the whole story, not the cultural stimuli that we think ought to be operating, nor the past habits that might be supposed decisive. The present tensions include the psychological past so far as it is in fact relevant to present behavior; they contain likewise all cultural and environmental pressures to which the person is in fact responding. This conceptual approach, we know, has fruitful application to an immensely wide variety of problems, ranging from the person acting as a member of a small face-to-face group to the class of nations.

I do not believe the predictive power of field-theoretical formulations has been compared experimentally with the predictive power of individualistic and cultural formulations. If it were, we might well find Lewin's superiority in prediction demonstrated, for the simple reason that he is able to take more parameters simultaneously into account. During the war, whenever our paths crossed, I made it a practice to ask his predictions. I now wish I had kept a record of his remarkable accuracy. His only substantial blunder, I believe, was his failing to foresee the Battle of the Bulge and its delaying effect on the end of the war. In November 1944 sensing the intensification of the field forces then at work, he predicted the total collapse of Germany not later than February 1945. VE Day actually came in May. I mention this astuteness, not, of course, as validation of his general theories, but because I do believe long experience thinking in terms of fields did sharpen his perception of the manifold and interrelated happenings in the complex world about him.

Returning to the fourth period of social psychology which seems now to be emerging, we ask what its leading characteristics are. First, it reflects a better-balanced view of the combined operation of the personal and social determinants of conduct. Second, it has the ability to handle simultaneously more variables, historical and contemporaneous, than before. Thirdly, as a result, it displays heightened skill in dealing with actual full-bodied group phenomena. These improvements, I submit, are due more to the work of Kurt Lewin than to the work of any other single social scientist.

His originality ascends high into the realm of theory even while it digs deeply into the practical. Inventor of "topological" and "vectorial" psychology, he is also the inventor of "action research." To his mind, though not always to the minds of others, the two were inseparable. He himself tells how his early experimental findings in his research on association drove him to recognize that the central datum in psychology is the "system under tension." For the last twenty-five years of his life he felt compelled both to conceptualize in formal terms the forces and directions and displacements involved in such systems, and to explore them in their concrete manifestations. Virtually all of his researches, he said, grew out of "certain theoretical expectations." "They have been designed to prove or to disprove certain assumptions."[2] Systematist that he was, he sought the continuity of phenomena from the smallest experimental detail to the properties of hodological space. I do not believe that the time has come to pass judgment upon his bold venture into geometric formalism. If its merits are finally established, Lewin will have moved us far toward the unification of psychological and mathematical science. If not, his audacity will inspire some genius of the future. Columbus, we recall, did not in his voyages of discovery reach the mainland of America. His followers did.

Even with our present limited perspective we know how much richer we are through Lewin's legacy of brilliant concepts experimentally derived. I have mentioned the Zeigarnik effect, the level of aspiration, differentiation, detour, escape from the field. We might add to the list: time perspective, cognitive structure, levels of reality, barrier, rigidity, satiation, life space, marginal affiliation, group decision, and still others. Most of these concepts are his own invention; where they are not, it was his work that established them as standard tools for psychological theorizing.

3. Along with intellectual solitariness and originality, we must list a negative aspect of genius, ordinarily overlooked in discussions of the subject. Poincaré spoke of the long periods of fallowness and confusion that lay between his bursts of insight. All who knew Kurt Lewin learned to pay close attention to his lively stream of speech. Often it seemed confused. But it was a rare conversation when the listener did not take away at least one idea of power and brilliance, even though the discourse to which he listened may have been neither orderly nor consecutive. In his writing Lewin was more lucid, but even here his strength lay in the total impact of his communication rather than in quotable phrases or crisp climax. He may have been handicapped when, in middle age, he was forced to adopt a new language as a medium for his

complex thought. But the situation seems not to have been markedly different in his German days. The story is told of an American student in Berlin who asked a German student how to translate *Aufforderungscharakter* into English. The student replied, "Search me; I can't even translate it into German."

4. *Hard work* is an ingredient of genius. The capacity of great scientists and artists to labor inhumanly long hours is legendary. We cannot yet calculate the ratio of inspiration and of perspiration that enters into productive careers. Lewin was remarkably energetic and apparently tireless. Especially in the last years of his life, his deep concern for the state of the world led him to spend his vitality upon numerous committees, government research projects, in lecturing and community service, carrying these activities in addition to his teaching, writing, directing of research, money raising, and administration.

5. From a list of the determinants of genius one dare not omit the *situational factor*, least of all since it is the determinant upon which Lewin himself would chiefly insist. His first two published works appeared during World War I. One of these, like the early studies of the Gestalt psychologists, dealt with perception, specifically with camouflage and the war landscape. The other adumbrated his later interest in motivation, expressing, as it did, deep dissatisfaction with the associationism of Ebbinghaus and G. E. Müller. The world came to know him through the brilliant series of twenty studies published between 1926 and 1930 in the *Psychologische Forschung* under the general title of *Untersuchungen zur Handlungs-und Affekt-Psychologie*. Easily the most exciting event of the International Congress of Psychology in 1929 at New Haven was Lewin's simple but instructive film that showed an eighteen-month-old child learning to sit down on a stone. To some American psychologists this ingenious film was decisive in forcing a revision of their own theories of the nature of intelligent behavior and of learning. Other Lewinian

films from this German period are classics of the same order. During the 1920's we could certainly call him a dynamic psychologist, a child psychologist, an experimentalist, but not yet a social psychologist.

The macabre events of history forced him to seek refuge in this country. Their effect upon him was to shift his interest vigorously to the field of social relations. Shortly before he died I asked him how and when he first became interested in the psychological problems of democracy. He told me that this interest was a direct result of his centering his life space in America. Throughout his earlier years he had concerned himself with liberal thought, with progressive education, with the philosophy of politics. But in retrospect he saw that German liberalism was marked by abstract discussion and unproductive effort. It was an illuminating experience for him to see democracy in action in the United States and to ponder the reasons why it functioned more successfully here than in Germany. He said to me, "I was deeply impressed by the open, easy-going give-and-take of American life. I became convinced that the American ideals are the best ideals for human society. I am now a citizen of the United States." He set for himself the task of learning the conditions under which group discussion leads to wholesome action, and the principles involved in delegating responsibility so that each individual may grow through participating in his own destiny.

The first productions in the final period of his life were brilliant contributions to the vexing subject of ethnic and national differences.[3] Soon afterward he inaugurated the renowned experiments upon autocratic and democratic group atmospheres. The world-situation set for him his problems. America provided him the opportunity to work on them, the appreciation that means incentive, and the criticism that corrects. Yet the situational factor, auspicious and determinative though it was, would not have been effective unless it had acted upon a humane and gifted individual, abounding in energy, in compassion, and in zeal for discovery. His own past history, including the suffering of his fellow Jews, was an important element in the situation. Behavior, verily, is a function of the environment *and* the person.

6. A final mark of genius is *tenacious devotion to one or more nonhedonistic values*. We are accustomed to celebrate the single-mindedness of the scientific genius in his pursuit of truth. But in recent painful years we have learned that truth lone is an insufficient value for human survival. In social psychology, for example, it is not enough to find out why people in national groups behave as they do. We have suddenly come to realize that we must discover how they may learn to behave better. (For unless they soon behave better, there may be no groups to study or no science to do the studying.) Kurt Lewin did not hesitate to make the required value judgment. To him the better life meant always the democratic life, the humane life, the humorous and kindly life. As a truth-seeker we honor him; but as a humanist, whole-souled in his loyalty to the values of democracy—which he claimed to have found among us—we remember him with special gratitude and affection.

NOTES

1. R. Lippitt, "Kurt Lewin, 1890–1947; Adventures in the exploration of interdependence," *Sociometry*, 1947, *10*, 87. This reference likewise contains a bibliography of Lewin's writings.
2. A self-told account of the development of his researches and theories is contained in *Studies in topological and vector psychology: I*, Iowa City: University of Iowa Press, 1940.
3. "Psychosociological problems of a minority group," *Charact. & Pers.*, 1935, *3*, 175–178; "Some social psychological differences between the United States and Germany," *Charact. & Pers.*, 1936, *4*, 265–293.

20

The Spirit of Richard Clarke Cabot

THIS BRIEF MEMORIAL is not, of course, a complete biography of the highly versatile and creative Dr. Cabot. Selected are only a few facts concerning his philanthropic activity which led eventually to the founding of the modern movement for clinical training of the clergy and thus to the more enlightened practice of pastoral counseling.

One reason for including the paper in this series is that Cabot (like Stern) was one of my teachers who to a considerable degree influenced my outlook. In 1966 Harvard announced the founding of a new professorship, the Richard Clarke Cabot chair in Social Ethics, and appointed me as the first incumbent. This fact in itself indicates that many of my own interests have continued the tradition of the Harvard's former Department of Social Ethics, of which Dr. Cabot was chairman during the days of my graduate study and of my first instructorship. The paper appeared in the *Journal of Pastoral Counseling*, Vol. 20, 1966.

† † †

To me, it seems especially appropriate on this happy occasion to call to mind a personality who gave radiant impetus to the movement we know as "clinical training of the clergy." To me, the Johnson Fellowship embodies not only the fine spirit of its donors, but also the spirit of Richard Clarke Cabot.

The dates of this remarkable man's life were 1868–1939. I knew him quite well during the last eighteen years of his life, and have had the privilege of serving as an executive trustee of some of his imaginative benefactions.

He was a Boston Brahmin, a professor at the Harvard Medical School, also Chairman of the Department of Social Ethics at Harvard. Like his pupil and younger colleague, Paul Dudley White, he was the most renowned cardiologist of his day.

But, in spite of the dignity of his status, he was a rebel and, therefore, a controversial figure. Although an idealist and visionary, he was also a very shrewd and practical fellow, fortunately possessed of enough financial means to carry through some of his experimental ideas.

Around 1904, for example, he felt distressed by the treadmill operations of the Outpatient Department at Massachusetts General Hospital. As one instance, he noted that a scrubwoman came time after time to receive help with her badly affected hands. The remedies they gave her did no good because she had to scrub floors for a living. From this and similar experiences, he came to realize that the Outpatient Clinic could not achieve its goal unless it had an auxiliary service to rely on—a department that would help the scrubwoman change her job. Hence in 1905 he founded, largely through his own means, Medical Social Service at Massachusetts General Hospital, which proved to be one of the truly great inventions in the course of medical history.

He also felt that medical men, especially students, had too little recreation and diversion. He, accordingly, founded a chorus of medical men. And from it, he developed his famous band of Christmas Eve carolers, which he led all around Beacon Hill. What could be more eccentric than a perambulating, singing doctor?

Even more radical was his introduction of Clinical Case Conferences in teaching medical interns and residents. He would take a medical record of a deceased patient, but without the autopsy report. Reading it with his students, he would hazard an opinion as to the precise cause of the patient's death, predicting what the autopsy would show. Very often he was correct, but not infrequently he made a bad blunder. What was revolutionary was his willingness to expose his ignorance or errors of judgment to young students. His courage, of course, did not endear him to his senior colleagues, but did win the admiration from his juniors. Some form of the Clinical Case Conference is now a standard procedure not only at Massachusetts General Hospital, but in many, perhaps most, teaching hospitals around the world.

In all of these activities, we note his devotion to the welfare and uniqueness of the individual person. As years went by, he became more and more absorbed with the physical, social, moral integrity of the individual human being. It was the potentiality for growth in the person that fascinated him, even in sick, handicapped, or dying persons.

Medical Social Service, he soon felt, was not really reaching the soul of the person, especially in times of crisis—perhaps before an operation, or in terminal illness. Only spiritual counsel could help, and so, with his characteristic creativeness, he inaugurated a Protestant chaplaincy at Massachusetts General Hospital, for years paying the salary of the chaplain from his own pocket. But this work, begun with Russell Dicks and David Hunter, led to the obvious need for training others in ministering to the sick. Hence, at Massachusetts General Hospital and at Andover-Newton Theological School, he helped establish programs of clinical training for the clergy. He did not foresee that his idea, backed by further financial support from his trustees, would lead ultimately to the widespread movement that now exists—practically a required course in all good theological seminaries.

Let me mention just one additional revolution that he engineered. Deeply interested in social work, he was president both of the local and national associations of social work. On many occasions he put a brutal question to social workers: "How do you know that you are doing any good?" This uncomfortable query holds a bold challenge for us today. "Does clinical counseling do any good?" he would ask. "Don't be pious about your efforts. Evaluate them in terms of the growth of your clients." His main project at the end of his life was the Cambridge-Somerville Youth Study, designed to see whether early delinquency in boys could be treated so as to prevent criminal careers. An historic experiment resulted—inconclusive, perhaps—but nonetheless a model and challenge for the future.

While not a man of great wealth, he wanted to leave such property as he had to foster the growth of creative individuals at critical and crescent moments in their careers. Let me read from a memorandum accompanying his will. It gives the flavor of his own forthright, clearheaded, style of expression.

> . . . I want my property to back men and their causes, but not causes or institutions uncontrolled by men or women of the right kind.
>
> By the "right kind of men or women" whose plans and causes I want to back, I mean the spiritual successors of the line of saints and heroes whose names I give below: Jesus Christ, Saint Augustine, St. Francis of Assisi, Tolstoi, Pasteur, Lincoln, Phillips Brooks, Jane Addams, Josiah Royce, Ella Lyman Cabot. These persons have in common the desire to see the human soul blossom in its individual and deepest nature, through its relationship to God and to His creatures.
>
> These persons were ready for the most part to use institutions of government, education, or religion so far and so long as these institutions served God and man better than they would be served in noninstitutionalized ways. But these persons knew all institutions to be fragile and man-made things, easily perverted so as to cumber the earth and blight the soul.
>
> So, I hope my property may be tied up to no institution except so far and so long as the control of persons of the saintly and heroic type (as suggested in my list) is effective in those institutions.
>
> . . . I want to help no man or cause that is opposed to the spirit of Christ, as my trustees conceive it to have existed in the list of persons above.
>
> (Signed) *Richard C. Cabot*

Cabot was a great admirer of Tolstoy and of Gandhi. And Gandhi was an admirer of Cabot. William Ernest Hocking tells how he saw at Gandhi's Ashram Cabot's book *What Men Live By* (this title, of course, is borrowed from Tolstoy). "Work, play, love, and worship," says Cabot, "are the values whole men live by."

Each person, including the poor scrubwoman in the Outpatient Clinic, should be allowed full opportunities for growth, should be respected, loved, and dealt with as a whole person, and not fragmented by professionalism or institutionalism.

Richard Clarke Cabot was deeply religious, theologically a liberal (a Unitarian of King's Chapel). To him, it was always the person, seeking his place in the context of God's creation, that was his central concern. And so among his own creative and pioneer labors, I am sure that he would place the continuing development of pastoral counseling high on his list of priorities.

He was one of the leading spirits whose vision fostered the movement which we are tonight celebrating and which is symbolized in the generous and farsighted gift of Professor and Mrs. Paul Johnson.

21

An Autobiography

WE CLOSE THIS VOLUME by pointing the finger directly at the author, asking him to account, as well as he can, for his own choice of pathways and bypaths in the wide territory of psychology.

No problem is more challenging than the degree and manner to which the structure of a person's thought reflects his own personal life history. Given a certain start in life and a certain environmental impetus, must a life evolve a certain cognitive content and style?

The following autobiographical essay does not, of course, answer this question. It does, however, present a selective intellectual history wherein I have stressed the events and experiences that seem to me most central in their bearing upon my research and theory.

† † †

Bergson held that every philosophic life pivots on a single "personal idea," even though the attempt to express this idea never fully succeeds. This dictum, savoring as it does of idealism and romanticism, is alien to the Lockean image of man that dominates Anglo-American psychology. And yet I confess I am attracted to this proposition. It seems to state in a broad way a testable hypothesis.

One might say that my own personal idea is to discover whether such broad hypotheses concerning the nature of man are empirically viable—at least as viable as the associationistic and reactive hypotheses that today govern the American psychological outlook. Although I suspect that Bergson exaggerates the potential unity of human personality, I also think that he, as well as other Leibnitzian, neo-Kantian, and existential writers, sets a challenge to empirical psychology; and that something should be done to test these views. The philosophy of man and the psychology of man should be brought to confront one another.

Let me suggest some relevant empirical questions. How shall a psychological life history be written? What processes and what structures must a full-bodied account of personality include? How can one detect unifying threads in a life, if they exist? The greater part of my own professional work can be viewed as an attempt to answer such questions through piecemeal and stepwise research and writing. If my theoretical writings exceed in bulk my output of research, it is because of my conviction that significant, not trivial, questions must be posed before we lose ourselves in a frenzy of investigation.

In 1940 I assigned my Harvard seminar the problem "How shall a psychological life history be written?" The seminar included the following members: Jerome Bruner, Dorwin Cartwright, Norman Polansky, John R. P. French, Alfred Baldwin, John Harding, Dwight Fiske, Donald McGranahan, Henry Riecken, Robert White, and Freed Bales. I mention their names because it seems to me that while these scholars have pursued diversified and distinguished careers, much of their subsequent creative work has been broadly relevant to the topic of the seminar.

We did not succeed in our self-imposed task. It is true that we designed a set of rules and composed cases to fit the rules, but at the end we were distressed by the hollowness of the product. Our abortive rules were never published, yet from the seminar issued several important published researches, some of them summarized in my monograph *The Use of Personal Documents in Psychological Science* (1942).

I still do not know how a psychological life history should be written. And here I am, faced ironically enough with the assignment of writing my own psychological vita. Lacking a method I shall have to bumble along as best I can, hoping that psychologists of the future will learn how such an assignment should be carried through.

1897–1915

Every autobiographer finds his own genealogy of captivating interest and knows that his family relationships are of highest explanatory importance. But the reader is likely to find the same material dull—something to be tolerated because it *ought* to be relevant. The writer has great difficulty showing the reader just *what* is relevant, and *where* and *why*. He himself does not know how to separate primary formative influences in his heredity and early environment from those that are of minor or negligible significance. My own account will be as brief as possible.

Father was a country doctor who learned his profession after a career in business and after having a family of three sons. I, the fourth and last of the family, was born November 11, 1897, in Montezuma, Indiana, where my father had set up his first medical practice. My mother and I were, I believe, his first patients. Soon afterward he moved his practice to Streetsboro and to Hudson in Ohio. Before I started school he moved again to Glenville (Cleveland), where I had the advantage of twelve years of sound and uninterrupted schooling.

Since my brothers were considerably older (Harold, nine years; Floyd, seven years; Fayette, five years) I fashioned my own circle of activities. It was a select circle, for I never fitted the general boy assembly. I was quick with words, poor at games. When I was ten a schoolmate said of me, "Aw, that guy swallowed a dictionary." But even as an "isolate" I contrived to be the "star" for a small cluster of friends.

Our family for several generations had lived in rural New York State. My paternal grandfather was a farmer, my maternal grandfather a cabinetmaker and Civil War veteran. My father, John Edwards Allport (born 1863), was of pure English descent; my mother, Nellie Edith Wise (born 1862), was of German and Scottish descent.

Our home life was marked by plain Protestant piety and hard work. My mother had been a school teacher and brought to her sons an eager sense of philosophical questing and the importance of searching for ultimate religious answers. Since my father lacked adequate hospital facilities for his patients, our household for several years included both patients and nurses. Tending office, washing bottles, and dealing with patients were important aspects of my early training. Along with his general practice my father engaged in many enterprises: founding a cooperative drug company, building and renting apartments, and finally developing a new specialty of building and supervising hospitals. I mention his versatility simply to underscore the fact that his four sons were trained in the practical urgencies of life as well as in a broad humanitarian outlook. Dad was no believer in vacations. He followed rather his own rule of life, which he expressed as follows: "If every person worked as hard as he could and took only the minimum financial return required by his family's needs, then there would be just enough wealth to go around." Thus it was hard work tempered by trust and affection that marked the home environment.

Except for this generally wholesome foundation, I cannot identify any formative influence of special importance until after my graduation from Glenville High School in 1915, at which time I stood second highest in a class of 100. Apparently I was a good routine student, but definitely uninspired and uncurious about anything beyond the usual adolescent concerns.

Graduation suddenly brought up the problem of further schooling. Wisely my father insisted that I take a summer to learn typing at a business college—a skill I have endlessly prized. During this period my brother Floyd who had graduated from Harvard in 1913 suggested that I apply there. It was late to do so, but I was finally admitted after squeezing through the entrance tests given in Cambridge in early September. Then came an experience of intellectual dawn.

1915–1924

Did ever a Midwestern lad receive a greater impact from "going East to college"? I doubt it. Almost overnight my world was remade. My basic moral values, to be sure, had been fashioned at home. What was new was the horizon of intellect and culture I was now invited to explore. The undergraduate years (1915–1919) brought a welter of new influences.

First and most important was the pervading sense of high standards. Harvard simply assumed, or so it seemed to me, that excellence should prevail. At the first hour examinations I received an array of D's and C's. Profoundly shattered, I stiffened my efforts and ended the year with A's. As a prize I was awarded a *detur* (what might that be?) in the form of a de luxe edition of *Marius, the Epicurean* (who was he?). In the course of fifty years' association with Harvard I have never ceased to admire the unspoken expectation of excellence. One should perform at the highest level of which one is capable, and one is given full freedom to do so. Although all my courses were valuable to me, my focus was soon directed toward psychology and social ethics. Taken together these two disciplines framed my later career.

Münsterberg, looking like Wotan, was my first teacher in psychology. My brother Floyd, a graduate student, was his assistant. From Münsterberg's guttural lectures and from his textbook *Psychology: General and Applied* (1914), I learned little except that "causal" psychology was not the same as "purposive" psychology. The blank page dividing the two corresponding sections of the textbook intrigued me. Could they not be reconciled and fused? I wondered. Harry Murray had also started to study with Münsterberg. In "What Should Psychologists Do About Psychoanalysis?" (1940), he reports that he was so revolted by the chill of Münsterberg's approach that he fled to the nearest exit, thereby retarding by several years the choice of his later profession. Meat for me was poison for Murray. The question arises then: What is a "good" teacher? I drew nourishment from Münsterberg's dualistic dilemma as well as from his pioneer work in applied psychology.

Soon I found myself taking courses with Edwin B. Holt, Leonard Troland, Walter Dearborn, and Ernest Southard. Experimental psychology I took with Herbert Langfeld and my brother. Between times and out of hours I gained much from my brother's more mature reflections on the problems and methods of psychology. He invited me to serve as a subject in his own researches on social influence. Münsterberg had persuaded him to follow the Moede tradition and discover the differences resulting from the performance of tasks in groups and alone.

World War I dislocated my program only slightly. As an inductee in the Students' Army Training Corps I was allowed to continue my courses (with sanitary engineering and map-making added). Even at our training camp I prepared, with Langfeld's encouragement, reports on psychological aspects of rifle practice. Although my contribution was sophomoric, the assignment was beneficial. The Armistice was signed on my twenty-first birthday, November 11, 1918. Demobilization and a return to my chosen program followed rapidly. At commencement, 1919, I received my A.B. degree, and Floyd received his Ph.D.

A final line of undergraduate influence came through my studies in the Department of Social Ethics, chiefly with James Ford, and especially from the accompanying field training and volunteer social service which heavily engaged my interest. All through college I conducted a boys' club in the West End of Boston. At various times I did volunteer visiting for the Family Society and served as volunteer probation officer. During one summer I held a paid job with the Humane Society of Cleveland; during another I worked for Professor Ford as field agent for the registration of homes for war workers in crowded industrial cities of the East. At the Phillips Brooks House I held a paid job as executive of the committee to assist foreign students and as secretary of the Cosmopolitan Club. All this social service was deeply satisfying, partly because it gave me a feeling of competence (to offset a generalized inferiority feeling) and partly because I found I liked to help people with their problems.

This social service interval reflected my search for personal identity. It blended also with my attempt to achieve a mature religious position. Like many undergraduates I was in the process of replacing childhood conceptions of doctrine with some sort of humanitarian religion. A few years later, however, I reacted against this essentially Unitarian position because it seemed to me that to exalt one's own intellect and affirm only a precarious man-made set of values cheapened the whole quest. Humility and some mysticism, I felt, were indispensable for me; otherwise I would be victimized by my own arrogance. Arrogance in psychological theorizing has always antagonized me; I believe it is better to be tentative, eclectic, and humble.

My two lines of study gradually merged into an important conviction. If one were to do effective social service, one needed a sound conception of human personality. Sound theory must underlie application. This conviction was clearly expressed later in my Ph.D. thesis, which was titled "An Experimental Study of the Traits of Personality: With Special Reference to the Problem of Social Diagnosis." This, of course, was an early formulation of the riddle. How shall a psychological life history be written?

After graduation I had no clear idea what I should do. Vaguely I felt that social service administration might be a better line for me than teaching. But an opportunity came to give teaching a trial. For one year I taught English and sociology at Robert College in Constantinople during the last gasp of the Sultan's reign (1919–1920). I greatly enjoyed the year

—its freedom and novelty and sense of achievement. When by cable I was offered a fellowship for graduate study at Harvard I knew that teaching was not such a bad career for me, and I accepted the opportunity. Two life-long friendships were formed at Robert College—one with the family of Dean Bradlee Watson, who later became professor of dramatic literature at Dartmouth and our son's godfather; the other with Edwin Powers, later Deputy Commissioner of Correction for the Commonwealth of Massachusetts.

En route from Constantinople to Cambridge, an event of pungent significance occurred, namely, my one and only encounter with Sigmund Freud. I have told the story many times but it must be repeated, for it had the character of a traumatic developmental episode. My brother Fayette was at that time in the United States trade commission in Vienna. It was during the period of Hoover relief activities. My brother invited me to stop for a visit.

With a callow forwardness characteristic of age twenty-two, I wrote to Freud announcing that I was in Vienna and implied that no doubt he would be glad to make my acquaintance. I received a kind reply in his own handwriting inviting me to come to his office at a certain time. Soon after I had entered the famous red burlap room with pictures of dreams on the wall, he summoned me to his inner office. He did not speak to me but sat in expectant silence, for me to state my mission. I was not prepared for silence and had to think fast to find a suitable conversational gambit. I told him of an episode on the tram car on my way to his office. A small boy about four years of age had displayed a conspicuous dirt phobia. He kept saying to his mother, "I don't want to sit there . . . don't let that dirty man sit beside me." To him everything was *schmutzig*. His mother was a well-starched *Hausfrau*, so dominant and purposive looking that I thought the cause and effect apparent.

When I finished my story Freud fixed his kindly therapeutic eyes upon me and said, "And was that little boy you?"

Flabbergasted and feeling a bit guilty, I contrived to change the subject. While Freud's misunderstanding of my motivation was amusing, it also started a deep train of thought. I realized that he was accustomed to neurotic defenses and that my manifest motivation (a sort of rude curiosity and youthful ambition) escaped him. For therapeutic progress he would have to cut through my defenses, but it so happened that therapeutic progress was not here an issue.

This experience taught me that depth psychology, for all its merits, may plunge too deep, and that psychologists would do well to give full recognition to manifest motives before probing the unconscious. Although I never regarded myself as anti-Freudian, I have been critical of psychoanalytic excesses. A later paper entitled "The Trend in Motivational Theory" (1953) is a direct reflection of this episode and has been reprinted, I believe, more frequently than any other of my articles. Let me add that the better balanced view of motivation expressed in later neo-Freudian, ego psychology is more to my taste.

Back at Harvard I found that the requirements for the Ph.D. degree were not stiff (not nearly stiff enough); and so with only two years' additional course work, a few examinations, and the thesis, I qualified for this degree in 1922 at the age of twenty-four. McDougall had joined the staff and was one of the readers of my thesis, along with Langfeld and James Ford. During this period Floyd, an instructor, was editing Morton Prince's *Journal of Abnormal and Social Psychology*. I helped him with the work, thus making an early acquaintance with the journal I myself was later to edit (1937–1948).

During this period I suffered from vocational misgivings. Unlike most of my student colleagues I had no giftedness in natural science, mathematics, mechanics (laboratory manipulations), nor in biological or medical specialties. Most of the psychologists I admired had competence in some adjuvant field. I confessed my misgivings about my fitness to Professor

Langfeld. In his laconic way he remarked, "But you know there are many branches of psychology." I think this casual remark saved me. In effect he was encouraging me to find my own way in the humanistic pastures of psychology.

But did I have enough courage and ability to develop my deviant interests? No other psychologist, at least at Harvard, seemed to be interested in social values as an academic problem nor in developing a lifelike psychology of personality. Indeed the available relevant work included not much more than a few early studies by June Downey (Wyoming), Walter Fernald (Concord Reformatory), and R. S. Woodworth (Columbia), who during the war had devised his "Personal Data Sheet," an early pencil-and-paper personality test. I believe that my own thesis was perhaps the first American dissertation written explicitly on the question of component traits of personality. It led to my maiden publication (with my brother) entitled "Personality Traits: Their Classification and Measurement" (1921). In this connection I may add that I suspect my own course given at Harvard in 1924 and 1925, titled "Personality: Its Psychological and Social Aspects," was probably the first course on the subject offered in an American college.

Standing at a frontier was a somewhat alarming business. The climax of my conflict came in connection with my single encounter with Titchener. I had been invited to attend the select gathering of his group of experimentalists, which met at Clark University in May 1922, just as I was finishing my thesis. After two days of discussing problems in sensory psychology Titchener allotted three minutes to each visiting graduate to describe his own investigations. I reported on traits of personality and was punished by the rebuke of total silence from the group, punctuated by a glare of disapproval from Titchener. Later Titchener demanded of Langfeld, "Why did you let him work on that problem?" Back in Cambridge Langfeld again consoled me with the laconic remark, "You don't care what Titchener thinks." And I found that I did not.

The whole experience was a turning point. Never since that

time have I been troubled by rebukes or professional slights directed at my maverick interests. Later, of course, the field of personality became not only acceptable but highly fashionable. But, although the field itself became legitimate, my own theoretical position was not always approved.

I have implied that my graduate years at Harvard were not particularly productive intellectually. They did, however, lead to two benefits over and beyond the degree. Within the congenial circle of graduate students I found my future wife, Ada Lufkin Gould, a Boston girl, who, after taking her master's degree, worked in the field of clinical psychology. Our interests were closely parallel. I was also awarded by Harvard a Sheldon Traveling Fellowship, which gave me two years in Europe. For me these years were a second intellectual dawn.

The German tradition in psychology was still strong in America, although Germany itself had been flattened by World War I and inflation. It was only natural for me to head for Germany. William James and E. B. Titchener had immortalized in their textbooks the Teutonic foundations of our science, and my own teachers had studied there. From Harvard philosophers R. B. Perry and R. F. A. Hoernle, I had gained further respect for German thought.

I was not prepared, however, for the powerful impact of my German teachers who included the aged Stumpf and Dessoir, the younger Max Wertheimer, Wolfgang Köhler, and Eduard Spranger in Berlin, and in Hamburg, William Stern and Heinz Werner. A fellow student was Heinrich Klüver, who helped me with my halting German, and who has remained a cherished friend ever since even though our paths of psychological interest have diverged.

At that time Gestalt was a new concept. I had not heard of it before leaving Cambridge. It took me some weeks to discover why my teachers usually started their two-hour lectures with a castigation of David Hume. Soon I learned he was the natural whipping boy for the German structural schools of thought. *Ganzheit* and *Gestalt*, *Struktur* and *Lebenformen*,

and *die unteilbare Person* were new music to my ears. Here
was the kind of psychology I had been longing for but did
not know existed.

Of course I realized that romanticism in psychology could
poison its scientific soil. (I myself had been brought up in the
Humean tradition.) At the same time it seemed to me that the
high quality of experimental studies by the Gestalt school,
the original empirical investigations at Stern's Institute, and the
brilliance of the Lewinian approach (which I came to know at
second hand) gave safe anchorage to the kinds of concepts
that I found congenial.

Thus Germany gave me support for the structural view of
personality that I had pieced together for myself. For the
American Journal of Psychology I wrote a brief *Bericht*,
"The Leipzig Congress of Psychology" (1923), outlining the
various German movements that reflected the *Strukturbegriff*:
Gestalt, Stern's *Personalistik*, Krueger's complex qualities, and
the school of *Verstehen*. From Stern in particular I learned
that a chasm exists between the common variety of differential
psychology (which he himself had largely invented along with
the concept of the I.Q.) and a truly personalistic psychology
that focuses upon the organization, not the mere profiling, of
an individual's traits.

I became acquainted also with German doctrines of types.
Among them were the elaborate speculations and investigations of E. R. Jaensch on eidetic imagery. I ventured to repli-
cate some of his work a year later while in Cambridge, England.
Three papers resulted: "Eidetic Imagery" (1924), "The
Eidetic Image and the After-image" (1928), and "Change and
Decay in the Visual Memory Image" (1930). Later I was
horrified by Jaensch's prostitution of his scientific work to
provide psychological underpinning for Nazi doctrine. His
paranoid efforts explained to me some of the weaker portions
of his earlier eidetic theory.

The year in England was spent largely in absorbing my
German experiences. Professor Frederic Bartlett was courte-

ous in providing me with facilities for work. Ivor A. Richards invited me to contribute a paper on "The Standpoint of Gestalt Psychology" to *Psyche* (1924); but I confess I chiefly ruminated on my German year and enjoyed myself by studying Faust with Professor Breuel.

Thus did my years of formal training come to an end. A cable from Professor Ford offered me an instructorship in social ethics at Harvard to begin in the fall of 1924. Besides taking over his course on social problems and social policy, I was invited to offer a new course in the psychology of personality—a pioneer enterprise.

1924–1930

Temperamentally I am a bit of a worrier, and for this reason I prepared my courses with conscientious thoroughness. When my chairman, Dr. Richard Cabot, implied that my platform manner "lacked fire" I tried to add animation to substance in my teaching. Ada and I were married in 1925, and for forty years she has had to tolerate the strain that marks all my preparations.

Our son Robert Bradlee was born in 1927 after we had moved to Dartmouth College. He later became a pediatrician, and it pleased me to find myself sandwiched between two generations of physicians.

Profoundly important professional friendships resulted from my first two years of teaching at Harvard. The first was with Dr. Richard Cabot, who held a double professorship at Harvard in cardiology and in social ethics. He proved to be a man of remarkably forthright social conscience. At the top of his field in medicine, he somehow found time to establish medical social service, to write many lucid volumes in medicine and in ethics, and to stir undergraduates profoundly with his uncompromising teaching of his own Puritan brand of ethics. Himself a wealthy Boston Brahmin, Cabot followed a theory and practice of philanthropy that appealed directly to my own sense of values. He believed as strongly as I in the integrity of each individual human life and would give financial and spiritual assistance when he felt he could aid in another's growth at some critical and crescent moment. (In 1936 he gave me support so that I could take a semester of free time to complete my book *Personality: A Psychological Interpretation*, 1937.) Gradually I became involved in his projects, inheriting after his death the general supervision of the Cambridge-Somerville Youth Study (Powers and Witmer, 1951). Likewise he asked me to be a trustee of the Ella Lyman Cabot Trust which has continued year by year to carry through his own philanthropic conception of "backing persons with projects." In connection with this Trust I have been associated with Dr. Cabot's famous successor, Dr. Paul Dudley White, and with other friends in a unique and highly congenial philanthropic activity.

My second friendship was formed with Edwin G. Boring who had come to Harvard while I was studying abroad. Fearing that my appointment in social ethics might remove me from psychology proper, I asked Boring if I could assist him in his introductory course, the famous Psychology 1. He agreed to the arrangement, and so I gained some experience teaching sections in experimental psychology (but not in arranging demonstrations, at which I should certainly be a failure). With Boring's encouragement I wrote further on imagery (1928). Acquaintance with a man of such amazing strenuosity and profound personal integrity, such deep historical erudition, and meticulous standards was, and is, a great influence and a major gratification in my career.

Less intimate, but likewise influential, was my contact with William McDougall. I assisted him as well as Boring in his elementary course. Needless to say, the two courses were in marked contrast. Although I admired McDougall for his vigor and independence, I harbored all the prevailing anti-McDougall prejudices. I deplored his doctrines of instinct, interactionism, and the group mind (all of which I, like most other Americans, only half understood). Although Germany had converted me from my undergraduate semifaith in behaviorism, I felt that McDougall's antagonism to the prevailing American psychological creed went too far. His solution to the causal-purposive problem seemed as dualistic as Münsterberg's, and no more satisfactory. At the same time I was fully exposed to his point of view and found it became more persuasive in later years. McDougall always had a bad press in America. In spite of his forensic gifts, his British style of polemic diminished his effectiveness. After about seven years at Harvard he moved to Duke University where he continued his monumental heresies until his death in 1938. To Duke he brought my other teacher and friend, William Stern, a Hitler fugitive who outlived McDougall by two years. He also provided a haven for Rhine and his parapsychological research, once again exhibiting his independence of the prevailing psychological ethos.

My brother had left Harvard for the University of North Carolina before my instructorship began. Besides our joint article we published "A Test for Ascendance—Submission" in 1928. This was a scale to measure dominant and submissive tendencies (one of the earliest pencil-and-paper personality tests). Apart from these two papers we never collaborated, even though we have occasionally helped each other with criticism. The truth, of course, is that our psychological views diverged. His *Social Psychology* (1924) was too behavioristic and too psychoanalytic for my taste. While our later works on political and social attitudes and on prejudice were similar in orientation, his theories became more positivistic, more monistic, and in a sense more interdisciplinary than my own. Floyd was a stricter logician and more systematic in his use of method than I. It should also be said that he had artistic, musical, and manual giftedness that I lacked. Over the years we pursued our own ways, but because of our common and unusual surname and divergence of points of view we managed to confuse students and the public. Were there one or two Allports?

It is clear to me now that the common quality in Stern,

McDougall, Boring, Cabot, and my brother is a fierce personal and professional integrity. Unconsciously no doubt I have drawn much encouragement from them in pursuing my own personal idea in the face of contrary fashion.

To this list of senior intellectual mentors and friends I must add the name of Pitirim A. Sorokin, whom I met when he came to Harvard in 1930 to head the Department of Sociology (to replace Social Ethics). Later I dedicated my book *Becoming* (1955) to this colleague of powerful erudition and blazing conviction. How he maintained his own moral and intellectual integrity during the Russian Communist Revolution he himself tells in his autobiography, *A Long Journey* (1964). In comparing my life with his I realize how sheltered my own career has been.

Another influential figure has been my amiable and supportive colleague Harry A. Murray. Our fields of interest lie so close together that by unspoken agreement we allow a "narcissism of slight differences" to keep us in a state of friendly separation. I derive from Murray a great deal of stimulation and encouragement.

Somewhat later, in the 1940's, I met Peter A. Bertocci, now Bowne Professor of Philosophy at Boston University, devoted to the personalist school of thought and well read in psychological theory. Over the years we have had frequent amiable arguments in and out of print. While he approves the general trend of my thought, he would like me to subscribe to an agent-self and to a larger measure of voluntarism. On these issues I demur, but I deeply prize his philosophical monitoring and his friendship.

An offer from Charles Stone at Dartmouth now broke my connection with Harvard for a period of four years. In Hanover I found myself in a pleasant and more relaxed atmosphere, free to pursue my own inclinations. I helped with the general introductory course and taught both social psychology and personality. During summer sessions I generally returned to teach at Harvard. The Baker Library during the long win-ter days at Hanover provided me with German journals so that I could keep abreast of thinking in typology, Gestalt, and *Verstehen*. Ever since the days of my thesis I had been haunted with the idea that I should write a general book on personality. Hanover gave me an opportunity to read and to think about this project. As one product, I might mention my first professional paper offered at the IX International Congress, held at Yale in 1929. It was titled "What Is a Trait of Personality?" (1931). The problem of the structure of personality was already much on my mind. (I resumed the theme thirty-six years later in a lecture to the APA in 1965, acknowledging my Distinguished Scientific Contribution Award. I titled it "Traits Revisited.")

Among my Dartmouth undergraduate students were Hadley Cantril, Henry Odbert, Leonard Doob, all of whom followed me to Harvard for their Ph.D. degrees. When McDougall left Harvard there was a gap in the area of social psychology. During 1928 Boring invited me to return as assistant professor, but it was September 1930 before I entered upon this final academic assignment. It is obvious to the reader that I had from 1915 a deep attachment to Harvard—an infatuation that has continued to this day.

1930–1946

Back in Cambridge the frenzy began. In Hanover I had started an editorial connection with the *Psychological Bulletin*, being responsible for survey articles in the field of social psychology, and I had formed the habit of reading the *Psychological Abstracts* from cover to cover (a habit soon extinguished by competing stimuli). All in all I felt fairly familiar with the then current field of general psychology and so enjoyed colloquia and luncheon discussions with my colleagues: Boring, Pratt, Beebe-Center, Chapman, Murray, White, and others. Graduate students in social psychology formed a band we called "The Group Mind." For some years we met to discuss one another's research programs in the fields of attitudes, expressive behavior, propaganda, and radio. Philip Vernon came from England for a time and brought a tornado of initiative. With him I was able to work out two investigations of lasting significance: *Studies in Expressive Movement* (1933) and *A Study of Values* (1931). Both of these projects rested upon my own German background but were sparked by Vernon's energy. *A Study of Values* was an attempt to establish empirically the six primary dimensions of personal values defined by Eduard Spranger, my Berlin teacher: the theoretical, economic, aesthetic, social, political, and religious. The resulting test, although unconventional in many ways, has shown astonishing vitality over the years. Gardner Lindzey assisted with a revision in 1951 and again in 1960. It is my contention that a measuring instrument in the field of personality is far better if based on good a priori analysis than if based on factorial or other adventitiously achieved dimensions.

My mention of Vernon and Lindzey leads me to a warm and grateful acknowledgment of the happy collaboration I have enjoyed with many of my students. My joint publications (see the bibliography in *The Person in Psychology*) include as coauthors, besides Vernon and Lindzey, the names of Hadley Cantril, Henry Odbert, Leo Postman, Jerome Bruner, Bernard Kramer, James Gillespie, Thomas Pettigrew, and a dozen others. I can only hope they have shared my satisfaction in our joint labors.

Psychology was a rapidly growing subject in the 1930's. The social emphasis was suddenly enhanced by the impact of world events: the depression, the rise of Hitler, the threat of war, and other fractures in the social edifice. There were relatively few social psychologists. Thus a host of responsibilities came my way. The Social Science Research Council and National Research Council wanted me for committees. The *Journal of Abnormal and Social Psychology* wanted me as editor. After Boring had successfully piloted a final break between philosophy and psychology at Harvard, he wanted me to assume chairmanship of the now finally independent Department of Psychology. Lashley joined the department, and I was promoted to the third permanency on the staff (1937). Astonishing to me was my election as president of the American Psychological Association for the year 1939.

But for me the event of chief significance in this decade was the publication by Holt of *Personality: A Psychological Interpretation* (1937). This book, as I have said, had been "cooking" in my head since my graduate days. My ambition was to give a psychological definition of the field of personality as I saw it. My vision, of course, was influenced by my encounters with social ethics, Anglo-American empiricism and German structural and personalistic theories. I wanted to fashion an experimental science, so far as appropriate, but chiefly I wanted an "image of man" that would allow us to test in full whatever democratic and humane potentialities that he might possess. I did not think of man as innately "good," but I was convinced that by and large American psychology gave man less than his due by depicting him as a bundle of unrelated reaction tendencies. I did not write the book for any particular audience. I wrote it simply because I felt I had to define the new field of the psychology of personality as I saw it. Although there were books in the related areas of mental hygiene and abnormal psychology, I regarded my own approach as being in the tradition of academic psychology, and I felt that my emphasis should be on normality rather than on pathology. I also had a desire to avoid jargon and to try to express my thoughts in proper and felicitous English. The result was that some readers regarded the book as difficult and pretentious, others labeled it as "classic," and for twenty-five years it stood as more or less standard reading in the field. Perhaps its major importance was that it defined (for the first time) the topics which well-bred texts in the field of personality should cover.

To establish my main point (that a full-bodied psychology of the human person is possible) I had to devise and adapt a number of rather novel supporting propositions. Chief among them was the concept of *functional autonomy*. No theory of motivation, I maintained, could be adequate if based on the exclusive primacy of drives and on the reactive aspects of human nature. I hesitated to adopt McDougall's concept of purpose because it was anchored to dubious instinct theory. I felt that in the course of life, motives can, and usually do, undergo radical transformation and that the propelling force lay in the present on-moving structure of personality, not in some anachronistic conditioning of past motives. The book also emphasized the neglected topics of expressive behavior and faced up to the problem of the normative criteria for maturity. It dealt with the epistemological problem of our knowledge of other personalities and throughout reiterated the challenge that any adequate psychology of personality must deal with the essential uniqueness of every personal structure. The latter insistence, of course, scandalized readers who felt that a man's individuality was sufficiently dealt with by regarding him as a point of intersecting common dimensions. I never implied that differential psychology was irrelevant to the psychology of personality, but I did insist that our science was at fault for neglecting the problem of patterning. When at long last I undertook a complete rewriting of this text in order to update the material and simplify the exposition, I selected the title *Pattern and Growth in Personality* (1961).

While my chief intellectual love has always been personality theory, perhaps half of my research and writing has dealt with more general topics in social psychology. Even while working on *Personality* I took time off to dig as deeply as I could into the concept of "attitude," which resulted in my topical chapter, under this title, in C. C. Murchison's *Handbook of Social Psychology* (1935). A number of papers on social attitudes and newspaper psychology and a book on *The Psychology of Radio* (with Cantril, 1935) attest the same interest.

World War II placed a still heavier demand on social psychologists. Although I served with the Emergency Committee in Psychology under the APA, I avoided offers of employment in government agencies. My abilities, I felt, were not equal to the urgent and often vague demands placed upon the new agencies proliferating overnight in Washington. I felt that if I had any contribution to make, it would be best made by remaining at Harvard. Telephone lines were hot with the inquiry, "What do we know about civilian morale?" Speaking for myself, I knew nothing. But, in collaboration with Harry Murray, I decided some useful things might be discovered if we offered a seminar in "morale research." Until Murray himself was called to Washington to head an important project for the Office of Strategic Services, we directed a number of student projects, ranging in type from an analysis of Hitler's character to studies of wartime rumor and riots. A bound (but not published) volume resulted entitled *Worksheets in Morale*.

The seminar had a long-range consequence. It continued year after year, with a gradual focusing on what seemed to be the most urgent problem of national unity, namely, group conflict and prejudice. The products of this seminar over a twenty-five-year period have been numerous. I shall speak of them later.

Meanwhile there were other wartime demands. Ever since the advent of Hitler in 1933, a flood of refugee psychologists was pouring into the United States, many of them the finest type of scholar: Koffka, Stern, Köhler, Lewin, Werner, Egon and Else Brunswik, and many others. To find jobs for such stars was not difficult, but the second string of unknown refugees created a serious problem. Together with Barbara Burks, Gardner Murphy, and others, I did what I could to make contacts for them. The refugee problem had great interest for sociologists as well as for psychologists. J. S. Bruner and E. M. Jandorf collaborated with me in publishing an analysis of ninety personal documents written by Hitler fugitives under the title "Personality under Social Catastrophe" (1941).

Some of my time was given to making speeches, semipopular writing on morale, and rumor analysis, leading to a daily syndicated feature in the *Boston Traveler* entitled "Rumor

Clinic" in which we endeavored to scotch harmful wartime rumors. We classified them as of three types: "bogies," "pipe dreams," and "wedge-drivers." The third type, based on prejudice and group antagonism, was the most serious. For much of this work I leaned upon the investigations of my student Robert H. Knapp. Soon Leo Postman joined forces with me in giving a course on race relations to Boston police officers and in publishing a book *The Psychology of Rumor* (1947).

As the close of the war approached, many psychologists became concerned with the conditions required for writing a lasting and effective peace. I pointed up a statement signed by 2038 psychologists entitled "Human Nature and the Peace" and published it in the *Psychological Bulletin* (1945). In retrospect our formula for peace may seem somewhat quixotic, but it still stands as a tribute to the social ideals of our profession.

The profound public concern of most American social psychologists, not only in wartime but throughout these troubled decades, is a fact worthy of comment. In 1936 the Society for the Psychological Study of Social Issues (SPSSI) was born. Early leaders included Gardner Murphy, Goodwin Watson, George Hartmann, Kurt Lewin, Edward Tolman, and Theodore Newcomb. I served as president of the Society in 1944. My membership in this group is one that I find congenial, for at heart I am both a political liberal and a social reformer.

From my early Dartmouth days I had found close intellectual and personal companionship with my student Hadley Cantril. We both wanted to fashion a social psychology that would be accurate and applicable to significant problems. Between us we called it "L-P" (*Lebenspsychologie*). Our book about the psychology of radio (1935) was one product of our collaboration. He was director of the "Tensions Project" at UNESCO in Paris and invited me to attend a memorable conference there in 1948, resulting in the book he edited, *Tensions That Cause Wars* (1950). For it I wrote a chapter entitled "The Role of Expectancy."

As the war drew to a close, most of my colleagues and students, it seemed, were in Washington or in the armed services. For us stay-at-homes it became necessary to plan on a huge postwar influx of veterans into our universities. In particular at Harvard we faced a local situation of some urgency. Although I was continuing as chairman of the Department of Psychology it seems that some far-reaching type of change was needed. Our department, like that of sociology, was small. The interests of our own staff were clearly divided, with the "biotropes" (Boring, Stevens, Lashley, Beebe-Center) on one side and the "sociotropes" (the terms are Boring's) on the other (Murray, White, Allport). A corresponding division of interest was evident in the Department of Anthropology, with Kluckhohn, representing cultural anthropology, finding much in common with sociologists and sociotropes. Together a group consisting of Parsons, Murray, Kluckhohn, Mowrer, and myself held many meetings devising a new department. To change any basic organization within a university (especially within an older institution) is a task as cumbersome as moving a cemetery. However, plans were laid, and in January 1946 the Faculty of Arts and Sciences voted that the new department should be created.

Before leaving this era I wish to report a stroke of personal good fortune. During the last three years of my chairmanship of the Department of Psychology, Mrs. Eleanor D. Sprague served as my secretary. She continued with me in the new department, where my administrative job was chairmanship of the Committee of Higher Degrees. She was my right hand until her retirement in 1964. Thanks to her competent assistance I covered more ground than would otherwise have been possible.

1946–1966

Six P.M. was the sacred hour of adjournment for faculty meetings. At a meeting in January 1946 the faculty authorized the formation of the new department but at 5:50 P.M. had not yet christened it. The name Human Relations was suggested, but that would never do because Yale already had an institute by that name. It would be too suffocating to call it the Department of Sociology, Social Psychology, Clinical Psychology, and Social Anthropology, although that is what it was. At about 5:59 P.M. someone proposed "Social Relations," and owing to the lateness of the hour the name was adopted without debate. The new organization, involving as it did a splitting of the previous Departments of Anthropology and Psychology, was a drastic move for Harvard and startled that portion of the academic world which watches changes in Harvard's educational policies. But the war was over, the need urgent, and veterans were flocking back with a keen interest in the basic social sciences, which, they vaguely felt, must hold some solution to the troubled world's problems.

With the enthusiastic cooperation of the Provost, Paul Buck, the new department rapidly enlarged its staff with returning Harvard people (George Homans, Jerome Bruner, Brewster Smith, Donald McGranahan, and others) and with brilliant new members including Samuel Stouffer, Frederick Mosteller, and Richard Solomon. A new curriculum was offered commencing in July 1946. I myself (with George Homans) gave the introductory course for a few years. Within a year or so it became the largest elective course in college with nearly 900 Harvard and Radcliffe students registered in it. In fact soon after its beginning the department had large enrollments, a concentration of about 400 undergraduates and close to 200 candidates for the Ph.D. degree. Advanced degrees were not offered in Social Relations but rather in each of the four constituent disciplines. The problem of the department has always been to balance the needs of specialization with a measure of desired cross-disciplinary training. Our policies have followed a wavering course between specialism and integrationism, with no satisfactory proportion yet discovered.

This bold academic experiment could not have succeeded, I think, were it not for the fact that in the course of their wartime service most of our staff members had lost their strict academic identities. A man could be a good social scientist whether or not his main training had been in psychology, sociology, anthropology, statistics, or some other discipline. The war thus prepared our minds for such integration as was achieved. Intellectual leadership toward the formation of a "common language" in our field came from Talcott Parsons, joined for a time by Edward Shils and Edward Tolman. Whether the effort was premature or whether Harvard's tradition was one of individualism and dissent, it did not turn out to be possible to establish a common basic language for the department. But dyads, triads, and small clusters of colleagues did manage to work together on projects of common interest, and a general atmosphere of convergence prevailed. Much credit for such unification as was achieved goes to Parsons. For ten years he was our enthusiastic chairman and from the beginning the true leader of the enterprise.

As one of the department's founding fathers I was eager to see the experiment succeed. My specific duty was to chair the Committee on Higher Degrees (with Mrs. Sprague's able assistance) and, wherever I could, to uphold the arms of other administrative officers. (Talcott Parsons, Robert White, and David McClelland served successively as chairmen, and Samuel Stouffer and Freed Bales as laboratory directors.)

My own teaching continued much as it always had. I finally dropped the large elementary course into the able hands of Bob White and gave over formal course instruction in social psychology to younger colleagues—Jerry Bruner, Roger Brown, Gardner Lindzey, and more recently Herb Kelman, Elliot Aronson, Stanley Milgram, Kenneth Gergen, and the oncoming procession of younger talent. I gave a middle-level course in theories of personality and conducted two graduate seminars—one for second-year graduate candidates in clinical and social psychology and one a continuation of the morale seminar, which had become entirely devoted to problems of group conflict and prejudice.

It was in connection with the latter course that I directed several relevant Ph.D. theses and began a series of publications of my own, climaxed by *The Nature of Prejudice* (1954). To my mind the significance of this book, which still circulates widely in a paperback edition, lies in its table of contents. As was the case with the field of personality, I spent several years deciding what subject matter was truly central to a new, ill-defined psychological territory and what the proper order of topics should be in any comprehensive text.

While many able students collaborated in this work, one grew to the stature of a torch-bearer. I was greatly impressed by the research abilities and expository skills of Thomas F. Pettigrew, a Virginian. I invited him to accompany me to South Africa as special scholar at the Institute for Social Research at the University of Natal, where we spent six fruitful months in 1956. It was, of course, fascinating to compare the ethnic frictions of South Africa with those of the United States and thus in a way to test the cross-cultural validity of my recently published book. My conclusion was that all the personal forces making for prejudice were present in both lands, but that my own psychological bias had perhaps led me to underestimate the forces of history and of traditional social structure more strikingly evident in South Africa.

Pettigrew and I made some cross-cultural perceptual investigations in South Africa. One of them, entitled "Cultural Influences on the Perception of Movement" (1957), seemed to us to show that social factors in perception are prominent only when there is inherent ambiguity in the stimulus situation.

After a year at North Carolina, Pettigrew returned to Harvard and gradually assumed a large portion of my own teaching and administrative duties, adding them to his own heavy program of work in the field of race relations. Under his direction the long-standing seminar continues to make its contributions to the study of morale.

Returning to the field of personality theory (always central in my interests), I found myself burdened with requests for named lectures in assorted universities, sometimes single lectures, sometimes a series. Likewise there were presidential and other honorific papers to prepare, as well as chapters for symposia and handbooks. In fact most of my writing for the past twenty-five years seems to have been dictated by such obligations. Each obligation I tried to employ as an occasion to say something relevant to personality theory. Thus, to the Eastern Psychological Association I offered "The Ego in Contemporary Psychology" (1943). Sometimes this paper is cited as reintroducing the concept of self into academic psychology— a bit of an overstatement, I think. Again, the Merrick Lectures at Ohio Wesleyan and the Lowell Lectures in Boston gave me incentive to prepare *The Individual and His Religion* (1950). The assignment of the Terry Lectures at Yale resulted in *Becoming: Basic Considerations for a Psychology of Personality* (1955). A large number of additional occasional papers were gathered together in *Personality and Social Encounter* (1960). It seemed appropriate in this latter volume to list in an appendix my complete bibliography, revised in the paperback edition (1964).

To my mind there is a distinct unity in these writings, including those on prejudice. Personality, as I see it, is composed chiefly of generic attitudes, values, and sentiments. (See, for example, "Mental Health: A Generic Attitude," 1964.) Therefore the prejudice-complex, the religious sentiment, the phenomenological ego, and one's philosophy of life are important subterritories to explore in individual lives.

While giving much of my attention to these generic formations that are found in many, if not all, lives, I still place higher in my scale of scientific values the search for the pattern that binds sentiments, values, and traits within each unique individual life. I chose this theme for an address in 1961 to the *Berufsverband deutscher Psychologen* in Hamburg. The lecture was titled "Das Allgemeine und das Eigenartige in der Psychologischen Praxis" (1962). This assignment I accepted partly as an excuse for a sentimental journey. I was happy to repay the profound stimulation that German structural concepts had given me and especially to return to the scene of my studies with Stern almost forty years previously. But I felt too that German psychologists might understand my plea for morphogenic (idiographic) methods, geared to the structure of individual lives, somewhat better than did most of my American colleagues. This line of thought, of course, relates to my perennial question, "How shall a life history be written?"

For many years I had used in my teaching a remarkable series of 300 intimate letters written by a woman from the age of fifty-eight until her death twelve years later. The letters deal with a mother-son tangle and are written in a fiercely dramatic, personal style. Here surely is a unique life, calling for psychological analysis and interpretation. Having had considerable experience in teaching with the aid of these letters, I decided to present them as a challenge to others and to sketch the available modes of psychological analysis applicable to this single case; thus I produced the book *Letters from Jenny* (1965).

Among the occasional assignments that took much time and effort I should mention the chapter for Lindzey's *Handbook of Social Psychology* (1954) entitled "The Historical Background of Modern Social Psychology." I had for several years offered a course in this subject and so welcomed the opportunity to give a compendious statement of the roots of modern social psychology as I saw them to be. Although a revision of the *Handbook* is now called for, I find little to change in the chapter. Someone, however, should write a much fuller and more detailed history of the subject.

I knew, of course, that a revision of the 1937 edition of *Personality* was needed. It should be brought up to date; the account of functional autonomy required restatement, and the new movements in the fields of cognition, role studies, and existential theory should be included. *Pattern and Growth in Personality* (1961) represented this updating and likewise a simplification of exposition. Being older (and feeling personally more secure) now I can dispense with my earlier inflated vocabulary.

Meanwhile the Department of Social Relations had grown and grown. With a staff of nearly 100 instructors, further evolution and change were bound to occur. It was time to turn the controls over to younger colleagues. The department had existed for eighteen years in seven separate buildings and was largely cut off from the biotropic Department of Psychology. When the Fund for Harvard College announced as one of its goals the building of a large and inclusive Center for the Behavioral Sciences it seemed that at last a geographical union of these disparate units might be achieved. We moved into the new fifteen-story William James Hall in January 1965, just as I was entering a period of semiretirement. By arrangement with President Pusey I had agreed to teach in the fall semesters for a few years but to keep the spring terms free for writing and travel. I found it a wrench to leave Emerson Hall, which as student and teacher I had inhabited continuously for fifty years (less seven years for my work abroad and the interval at Dartmouth).

One final chapter in my formal relations with Harvard should be recorded. In March 1966 the Corporation appointed me the first Richard Clarke Cabot Professor of Social Ethics. In announcing the establishment of this new chair President Pusey took occasion to "welcome the formal reappearance of Social Ethics in a community which owes much to the dedication and example of Richard Clarke Cabot and, before him, Francis Greenwood Peabody." Pusey added that "In a time of widespread confusion about moral issues, there is also in our day a resurgence of concern for human and ethical values, especially for character and moral sensibility." Since Dr. Cabot was my first "boss" at Harvard, having much influence upon my career first and last, the appointment seemed to me to complete fittingly an intellectual cycle as well as a cycle of sentiment.

A POLEMIC-ECLECTIC

Much of my writing is critical of prevailing psychological idols. At times I have crossed swords with learning theory, dimensionalism in personality research, and with what seems to me to be an overemphasis on unconscious processes, projective tests, and simplified drive theories of motivation. I have felt that these fashionable explanatory principles are able to deal only with the peripheral or "opportunistic" layers of personality, or else that they make too much of some improbable formulations of depth psychology. (Yes, my single encounter with Freud was traumatic.)

In place of (or, more accurately, as a supplement to) these popular formulae, I have advocated what seemed to me necessary principles. These are principles dealing with "propriate" functions (anchored to the self-image), insightful capacities for learning, complex integrative generic attitudes and ways of perceiving one's world, expressive (not merely projective) behavior, the formations that mark maturity in personality, and values and orientations toward the future—in short, with the course of growth and becoming. It is within this web of concepts that one would find my personal idea.

Bergson, of course, was right in saying that no philosophic mind ever succeeds in fully realizing his idea. It is my experience also that such a mind may all the while be half-distrustful of the idea's validity. Although much of my writing is polemic in tone, I know in my bones that my opponents are partly right.

When asked to give an occasional paper at the XVII International Congress of Psychology in Washington, I titled it "The Fruits of Eclecticism: Bitter or Sweet?" (1964). In it I tried to trace eclectic trends in the psychology of the past and to argue that a systematic eclecticism is not impossible in the future. But here I insisted that no enthusiastic particularism, however fashionable, will ever be adequate. I implied that only a view of the "Open System in Personality Theory" (1960) will really serve the purpose. Any investigator, of course, has the right to restrict his variables and neglect, momentarily, irrelevant aspects of behavior, *but he has no right to forget what he has decided to neglect.*

As I have said elsewhere, some of my colleagues treat personality as a quasi-closed system. I respect their work and know that eventually their contributions will fit into the larger frame. I feel no personal animosity toward the associates with whom I have ventured to disagree. But what I dislike in our profession is the strong aura of arrogance found in presently fashionable dogmas. To my mind humility is a virtue appropriate for social and psychological scientists to cultivate. I am not fond of the label "behavioral sciences" now in vogue. From a certain point of view it is harmless enough, but to me it somehow implies that if we were all to embrace the creeds of positivism and behaviorism, all our problems would be solved. I cannot agree. Our methods would be restricted, our theories one-sided, and our students would be intimidated by a tyrannical and temporary scientism. Humility requires a more tentative position. William James was right—our knowledge is a drop, our ignorance a sea. James himself, to my mind, sets a worthy model for psychologists to follow in his open-mindedness, his respect for multiple avenues to truth, and his personal humility.

The irrelevance of much present-day psychology to human life comes from its emphasis on mechanical aspects of reactivity to the neglect of man's wider experiences, his aspirations, and his incessant endeavor to master and to mold his environment. Of course not all psychologists have this blind spot. Carl Rogers, Abraham Maslow, Gardner Murphy, Harry Murray, and many others have clearer vision.

What then is my personal idea? I suppose it has to do with the search for a theoretical system—for one that will allow for truth wherever found, one that will encompass the totality of human experience and do full justice to the nature of man. I myself have never had a strictly defined program of research, nor have I tried to establish a "school" of psychological thought. Students who have worked with me have been encouraged to tackle any significant problem, so long as it dealt with persons, with parts of persons, or with groups of persons.

Dedicated as I am to a program so broad and loose, I find it surprising that many specific honors have come my way. I shall report only one—the one that has pleased me most deeply, for it succeeds in summing up my personal idea better than I can do. In connection with the XVII International Congress of Psychology, which met in Washington in 1963, fifty-five of my former Ph.D. students presented me with two handsomely bound volumes of their own writings with the following dedicatory inscription: "From his students—in appreciation of his respect for their individuality." This is an intimate honor, and one I prize above all others.

REFERENCES

Selected Publications by Gordon W. Allport

(with F. H. Allport) "Personality traits: their classification and measurement," *J. abnorm. soc. Psychol.*, 1921, *16*, 6–40.

"An experimental study of the traits of personality: with special reference to the problem of social diagnosis." Unpublished doctoral dissertation, Harvard College Library, 1922.

"The Leipzig congress of psychology," *Amer. J. Psychol.*, 1923, *34*, 612–615.

"The standpoint of Gestalt psychology," *Psyche*, 1924, *4*, 354–361.

"Eidetic imagery," *Brit. J. Psychol.*, 1924, *15*, 99–120.

"The eidetic image and the after-image," *Amer. J. Psychol.*, 1928, *40*, 418–425.

(with F. H. Allport) "A test for ascendance-submission," *J. abnorm. soc. Psychol.*, 1928, *23*, 118–136.

"Change and decay in the visual memory image," *Brit. J. Psychol.*, 1930, *21*, 133–148.

"What is a trait of personality?" *J. abnorm. soc. Psychol.*, 1931, *25*, 368–372.

(with P. E. Vernon) *A study of values*, Boston: Houghton Mifflin, 1931; revised eds. (and G. Lindzey) 1951, 1960.

(with P. E. Vernon) *Studies in expressive movement*, New York: Macmillan, 1933.

(with H. Cantril) *The psychology of radio*, New York: Harper & Row, 1935.

"Attitudes." In C. Murchison (ed.), *A handbook of social psychology*, Worcester, Mass.: Clark Univer. Press, 1935, ch. 17.

Personality: a psychological interpretation, New York: Holt, Rinehart and Winston, 1937.

(with J. S. Bruner & E. M. Jandorf) "Personality under social catastrophe: ninety life-histories of the Nazi revolution," *Charact. & Pers.*, 1941, *10*, 1–22.

The use of personal documents in psychological science, New York: Social Science Research Council, 1942, Bull. 49.

"The ego in contemporary psychology," *Psychol. Rev.*, 1943, *50*, 451–478.

"Human nature and the peace," *Psychol. Bull.*, 1945, *42*, 376–378.

(with L. Postman) *The psychology of rumor*, New York: Holt, Rinehart and Winston, 1947.

The individual and his religion, New York: Macmillan, 1950.

"The trend in motivational theory," *Amer. J. Orthopsychiat.*, 1953, *25*, 107–119.

"The historical background of modern social psychology," in G. Lindzey (ed.), *Handbook of social psychology*, Vol. 1, Reading, Mass.: Addison-Wesley, 1954, ch. 1.

The nature of prejudice, Reading, Mass.: Addison-Wesley, 1954; abridged ed., Garden City, N.Y.: Doubleday Anchor, 1958.

Becoming: basic considerations for a psychology of personality, New Haven, Conn.: Yale, 1955.

(with T. F. Pettigrew) "Cultural influences on the perception of movement: the trapezoidal illusion among Zulus," *J. abnorm. soc. Psychol.*, 1957, *55*, 104–113.

"The open system in personality theory," *J. abnorm. soc. Psychol.*, 1960, *61*, 301–310.

Personality and social encounter: selected essays, Boston: Beacon Press, 1960; revised ed., 1964.

Pattern and growth in personality, New York: Holt, Rinehart and Winston, 1961.

"Das Allgemeine und das Eigenartige in der psychologischen Praxis," *Psychol. Beiträge*, 1962, *6*, 630–650.

"The fruits of eclecticism: bitter or sweet?" Proceedings of the XVII International Congress of Psychology, Amsterdam, 1964; also published in *Psychologia*, 1964, 7, 1–14; and in *Acta Psychol.*, 1964, *23*, 27–44.

"Mental health: a generic attitude," *J. Relig. Hlth*, 1964, *4*, 7–21.

Letters from Jenny, New York: Harcourt, Brace & World, 1965.

Christian Workers, 1960; and in Danish as *Psykologi og Religisitet* (trans. by E. E. Bugge), Copenhagen: Nyt Nordisk Forlag Arnold Busck, 1966.

The nature of personality: selected papers, Reading, Mass.: Addison-Wesley, 1950.

The nature of prejudice, Reading, Mass.: Addison-Wesley, 1954; Boston: Beacon; abridged ed., Garden City: Doubleday Anchor, 1958. Chap. I reprinted in W. O. Sutherland and R. L. Montgomery (eds.), *The reader: a study of form and content*, Boston: Little, Brown, 1960. Also published in Japanese (trans. by A. Nomura & T. Haratani), Tokyo: Baifukan, 1961; and in Spanish as *La naturaleza del prejuicio* (trans. by R. Malfe), Buenos Aires: Editorial Universitaria de Buenos Aires, 1962.

Becoming: basic considerations for a psychology of personality, New Haven: Yale University Press, 1955. Also published in Danish as *Personlighedens Udformning* (trans. by A. Madsen), Copenhagen: Nyt Nordisk Forlag Arnold Busck, 1956; in Swedish as *Personlighetens Utveckling* (trans. by A. Asker), Stockholm: Alfa Boktryckeri, 1957; in German as *Werden der Persönlichkeit* (trans. by H. von Bracken), Bern: Verlag Hans Huber, 1958; in Japanese (trans. by H. Toyosawa), Tokyo: Risoha Ltd., 1959; in Korean (trans. by Tong-He Choo), Seoul: Tong-Shin Co., 1960; in Portuguese as *Desenvolvimento da personalidade* (trans. by H. A. Simon), Sao Paulo: Editora Herder, 1962; in Italian as *Divenire: Fondamenti di una psicologia della personalita* (trans. by L. Borghi), Florence: Editrice Universitaria, 1963; and in Norwegian as *Personligheten—hvordan formes den?* (trans. by C. F. Engelstad), Oslo: Dryers Forlag, 1966.

Personality and social encounter, Boston: Beacon, 1960; paperback, 1964.

Pattern and growth in personality, New York: Holt, Rinehart and Winston, 1961; also London: Holt, Rinehart and Winston, 1963. Also published in Spanish as *La Personalidad* (trans. by I. Antich), Barcelona: Editorial Herder, 1966; and in Portuguese as *Personalidade* (trans. by M. Leite), Sao Paulo: Editora Herder, 1966.

Letters from Jenny, New York: Harcourt, Brace and World, 1965.

MONOGRAPHS

Trait-names: a psycho-lexical study (with H. S. Odbert), *Psychol. Monogr.*, 1963, 47:1–171, No. 211.
The use of personal documents in psychological science, New York: Social Science Research Council, 1942, Bull. 49.

TESTS

A-S reaction study (with F. H. Allport), Boston: Houghton Mifflin, 1928; rev. ed., Boston: Houghton Mifflin, 1949.
A study of values (with P. E. Vernon), Boston: Houghton Mifflin, 1931; rev. ed. (with G. Lindzey and P. E. Vernon), Boston: Houghton Mifflin, 1951; 3rd ed. (with G. Lindzey and P. E. Vernon), Boston: Houghton Mifflin, 1960.

ARTICLES AND REVIEWS

1921

"Personality traits: their classification and measurement" (with F. H. Allport), *J. Abnorm. Soc. Psychol.*, 1921, 16:6–40.
"Personality and character," *Psychol. Bull.*, 1921, 18:441–55.
Reviews:
  W. H. Pyle, *The psychology of learning*, *J. Abnorm. Soc. Psychol.*, 1921–22, 16:414–15.
  M. S. Pittman, *The value of school supervision;* W. S. Herzog, *State maintenance for teachers in training;* and A. G. Peaks, *Periodic variations in efficiency*, *J. Abnorm. Soc. Psychol.*, 1921–22, 16:415.

1922

Reviews:
  L. Berman, *The glands regulating personality*, *J. Abnorm. Soc. Psychol.*, 1922, 17:220–22.
  E. S. Bogardus, *Essentials of social psychology*, *J. Abnorm. Soc. Psychol.*, 1922, 17:104–06.

1923

"Germany's state of mind," *New Republic*, 1923, 34:63–65.
"The Leipzig congress of psychology," *Amer. J. Psychol.*, 1923, 34:612–15.

1924

"The study of the undivided personality," *J. Abnorm. Soc. Psychol.*, 1924, 19:132–41.

"Eidetic imagery," *Brit. J. Psychol.*, 1924, 15:99–120.

"Die theoretischen Hauptströmungen in der amerikanischen Psychologie der Gegenwart," *Zeitschrift f. Pädagog. Psychol.*, 1924, 4:129–37.

"The standpoint of Gestalt psychology," *Psyche*, 1924, 4:354–61.

Reviews:

M. P. Follett, *Creative experience, J. Abnorm. Soc. Psychol.*, 1924, 18:426–28.

W. W. Smith, *The measurement of emotion;* and H. Eng, *Experimentelle Untersuchungen über das Gefühlsleben des Kindes im Vergleich mit dem des Erwachsenen, J. Abnorm. Soc. Psychol.*, 1924, 18:414–16.

1925

Review:

W. B. Munro, *Personality in politics, J. Abnorm. Soc. Psychol.*, 1925, 20:209–11.

1926

Reviews:

K. Dunlap, *Social psychology, J. Abnorm. Soc. Psychol.*, 1926, 21:95–100.

O. Selz, *Über die Persönlichkeitstypen und die Methoden ihrer Bestimmung, Amer. J. Psychol.*, 1926, 37:618–19.

1927

"Concepts of trait and personality," *Psychol. Bull.*, 1927, 24:284–93.

Reviews:

A. A. Roback, *A bibliography of character and personality, Psychol. Bull.*, 1927, 24:309–10.

A. A. Roback, *Psychology of character, Psychol. Bull.*, 1927, 24:717–23.

W. S. Taylor (ed.), *Readings in abnormal psychology and mental hygiene, J. Abnorm. Soc. Psychol.*, 1927, 21:445–48.

1928

"The eidetic image and the after-image," *Amer. J. Psychol.*, 1928, 40:418–25.
"A test for ascendance-submission," *J. Abnorm. Soc. Psychol.*, 1928, 23:118–36.

1929

"The study of personality by the intuitive method: an experiment in teaching from *The locomotive god*," *J. Abnorm. Soc. Psychol.*, 1929, 24:14–27.
"The composition of political attitudes," *Amer. J. Sociol.*, 1929, 35:220–38.
Reviews:
E. T. Clark, *The psychology of religious awakening*, Psychol. Bull., 1929, 26:710–11.
W. McDougall, *The group mind*, J. Abnorm. Soc. Psychol., 1929, 24:123–26.
H. Meltzer and E. Bailor, *Developed lessons in psychology*, Dartmouth Alumni Bull., 1929.
T. Munro, *Scientific method in aesthetics*, Psychol. Bull., 1929, 26:711.
C. Murchison, *Social psychology*, Psychol. Bull., 1929, 26:709–10.
M. Prince, *Clinical and experimental studies in personality*, Psychol. Bull., 1929, 26:711–12.
L. T. Troland, *Fundamentals of human motivation*, J. Abnorm. Soc. Psychol., 1929, 23:510–13.

1930

"Some guiding principles in understanding personality," *The Family*, June 1930, pp. 124–28.
"The neurotic personality and traits of self-expression," *J. Soc. Psychol.*, 1930, 1:524–27.
"The field of personality" (with P. E. Vernon), *Psychol. Bull.*, 1930, 27:677–730.
"Change and decay in the visual memory image," *Brit. J. Psychol.*, 1930, 21:133–48.

Reviews:

J. E. Downey, *Creative imagination*, Psychol. Bull., 1930, 27:408–10.

K. Young, *Social psychology*, Psychol. Bull., 1930, 27:731–33.

1931

"What is a trait of personality?" *J. Abnorm. Soc. Psychol.*, 1931, 25:368–72.

"A test for personal values" (with P. E. Vernon), *J. Abnorm. Soc. Psychol.*, 1931, 26:231–48.

1932

Reviews:

W. Boven, *La science du caractère*, Amer. J. Psychol., 1932, 44:838–39.

J. C. Flugel, *The psychology of clothes*, Psychol. Bull., 1932, 29:358–59.

D. Katz and F. H. Allport, *Students' attitudes*, Psychol. Bull., 1932, 29:356–58.

F. Künkel, *Vitale Dialektik*, Psychol. Bull., 1932, 29:371–73.

A. A. Roback, *Personality*, Psychol. Bull., 1932, 29:359–60.

J. J. Smith, *Social psychology*, Psychol. Bull., 1932, 29:360.

P. M. Symonds, *Diagnosing personality and conduct*, J. Soc. Psychol., 1932, 3:391–97.

1933

"The study of personality by the experimental method," *Char. & Pers.*, 1933, 1:259–64.

"The determination of personal interests by psychological and graphological methods" (with H. Cantril and H. A. Rand), *Char. & Pers.*, 1933, 2:134–51.

"Recent applications of the *study of values*" (with H. Cantril), *J. Abnorm. Soc. Psychol.*, 1933, 28:259–73.

Reviews:

C. Bühler, *Der menschliche Lebenslauf als psychologisches Problem*, Sociologus, 1933, 9:336–38.

N. D. M. Hirsch, *Genius and creative intelligence*, Psychol. Bull., 1933, 30:365–66.

L. Klages, *The science of character* (trans. by W. H. Johnston), *Psychol. Bull.*, 1933, 30:370–71.

M. A. McLaughlin, *The genesis and constancy of ascendance and submission as personality traits*, *Amer. J. Psychol.*, 1933, 45:779–80.

1934

"Judging personality from voice" (with H. Cantril), *J. Soc. Psychol.*, 1934, 5:37–55.
Reviews:
A. Goldenweiser, *History, psychology, and culture*, *Psychol. Bull.*, 1934, 31:363–64.
A. A. Roback, *Self-consciousness and its treatment*, *Psychol. Bull.*, 1934, 31:370.

1935

"Attitudes," in C. C. Murchison (ed.), *A handbook of social psychology*, Worcester: Clark University Press, 1935, Chap. 17.
"The radio as a stimulus situation," *Acta Psychol.*, 1935, 1:1–6.
"The nature of motivation," *Understanding the child*, Jan. 1935, pp. 3–6.

1936

"Are attitudes biological or cultural in origin?" (with R. L. Schanck), *Char. & Pers.*, 1936, 4:195–205.
Review:
G. K. Zipf, *The psycho-biology of language*, *Psychol. Bull.*, 1936, 33:219–22.

1937

"The functional autonomy of motives," *Amer. J. Psychol.*, 1937, 50:141–56. Also published in C. L. Stacey and M. F. DeMartino (eds.), *Understanding human motivation*, Cleveland: Howard Allen, 1958, pp. 69–81.
"The personalistic psychology of William Stern," *Char. & Pers.*, 1937, 5:231–46. Also published (abridged) in H. Brand (ed.), *The study of personality*, New York: Wiley, 1954, pp. 149–61.

1938

"The Journal of Abnormal and Social Psychology: an editorial," *J. Abnorm. Soc. Psychol.*, 1938, 33:3–13.
"William Stern: 1871–1938," *Amer. J. Psychol.*, 1938, 51:770–74.
"Personality: a problem for science or a problem for art?" *Revista de Psihologie*, 1938, 1:1–15.
Review:
  L. B. Murphy, *Social behavior and child personality*, *J. Abnorm. Soc. Psychol.*, 1938, 33:538–43.

1939

"Dewey's individual and social psychology," in P. A. Schlipp (ed.), *The philosophy of John Dewey*, Evanston and Chicago: Northwestern University Press, 1939, Chap. 9.
"Recent applications of the A-S reaction study" (with R. Ruggles), *J. Abnorm. Soc. Psychol.*, 1939, 34:518–28.
"The education of a teacher," *The Harvard Progressive*, 1939, 4:7–9.

1940

"The psychologist's frame of reference," *Psychol. Bull.*, 1940, 37:1–28. Also published as El marco de referencia de los psicologos (trans. by A. Bernal del Riesgo), Havana. University of Havana, 1946.
"Fifty years of change in American psychology" (with J. S. Bruner), *Psychol. Bull.*, 1940, 37:757–76.
"The psychology of newspapers: five tentative laws" (with J. M. Faden), *Publ. Opin. Quart.*, 1940, 4:687–703.
"Motivation in personality: reply to Mr. Bertocci," *Psychol. Rev.*, 1940, 47:533–54. Also published in H. Brand, *The study of personality: a book of readings*, New York: Wiley, 1954, pp. 83–99; and in C. L. Stacey and M. F. DeMartino (eds.), *Understanding human motivation*, Cleveland: Howard Allen, 1958, pp. 105–20.
"Liberalism and the motives of men," *Frontiers of Democracy*, 1940, 6:136–37.
Foreword to H. Werner, *Comparative psychology of mental development* (trans. by F. B. Garside), New York: Harper, 1940; rev. ed., Chicago: Follett Pub. Co., 1948.

1941

"Liabilities and assets in civilian morale," *Ann. Amer. Acad. Pol. Soc. Sci.*, 1941, 216:88–94.

"Psychological service for civilian morale," *J. Consult. Psychol.*, 1941, 5:235–39.

"Personality under social catastrophe: ninety life-histories of the Nazi revolution" (with J. S. Bruner and E. M. Jandorf), *Char. & Pers.*, 1941, 10:1–22. Also published in C. Kluckhohn and H. A. Murray, *Personality in nature, society, and culture*, New York: Knopf, 1948, Chap. 25; and in C. Kluckhohn, H. A. Murray and D. M. Schneider, *Personality in nature, society and culture*, New York: Knopf, 1953, Chap. 27.

"Morale: American style," *Christian Science Monitor* (Weekly Magazine Section), Apr. 26, 1941, pp. 1–2, 13.

Review:

  J. M. MacKaye, *The logic of language*, *J. Abnorm. Soc. Psychol.*, 1941, 36:296–97.

1942

"The nature of democratic morale," in G. Watson (ed.), *Civilian morale*, Boston: Houghton Mifflin, 1942, Chap. 1.

"Defense seminars for morale study and morale building," *J. Soc. Psychol.*, *SPSSI Bull.*, 1942, 15:399–401.

"Report on the third front: at home," *Christian Science Monitor* (Weekly Magazine Section), Sept. 5, 1942, pp. 6, 14.

"Morale and its measurement," in *Public Policy*, Cambridge: Littauer School of Public Administration, 1942, 3:3–17.

Review:

  F. C. Bartlett, *Political propaganda*, *Sat. Rev. Lit.*, 1942, 25:18.

1943

"The productive paradoxes of William James," *Psychol. Rev.*, 1943, 50:95–120.

"Test tube for rumors," *Coronet*, 1943, 14:136–40.

"Psychological considerations in making the peace: editorial note," *J. Abnorm. Soc. Psychol.*, 1943, 38:131.

"This clinical supplement: editorial note," *J. Abnorm. Soc. Psychol.*, 38:3–5.

"Do rosy headlines sell newspapers?" (with E. C. Winship), *Publ. Opin. Quart.*, 1943, 7:205–10. Reprinted in D. Katz, D. Cartwright, S. Eldersveld and A. McG. Lee, *Public opinion and propaganda*, New York: Dryden Press, 1954:271–74.

"Social psychology and the civilian war effort" (with H. R. Veltfort), *J. Soc. Psychol., SPSSI Bull.*, 1943, 18:165–233.

"The ego in contemporary psychology," *Psychol. Rev.*, 1943, 50:451–78. Also published in C. L. Stacey and M. F. DeMartino (eds.), *Understanding human motivation*, Cleveland: Howard Allen, 1958, pp. 140–58.

"Morale research and its clearing" (with G. R. Schmeidler), *Psychol. Bull.*, 1943, 40:65–68.

"Restoring morale in occupied territory," *Publ. Opin. Quart.*, 1943, 7:606–17.

Reviews:

E. P. Aldrich (ed.), *As William James said*, *J. Abnorm. Soc. Psychol.*, 1943, 38:119–120.

M. D. Allers, *The psychology of character*, *Amer. Sociol. Rev.*, 1943, 8:735–36.

M. A. May, *A social psychology of war and peace*, *Ann. Amer. Acad. Pol. Soc. Sci.*, 1943, 229:186–87.

A. A. Roback, *William James: his marginalia, personality and contribution, New England Quarterly*, 1943, 16:143–44.

C. Schrodes, J. van Gundy and R. W. Husband (eds.), *Psychology through literature*, *J. Abnorm. Soc. Psychol.*, 1943, 38:203 (No. 2, Clin. Suppl.).

E. C. Tolman, *Drives toward war*, *J. Abnorm. Soc. Psychol.*, 1943, 38:293–96.

1944

Prefaces to *Educational opportunities in greater Boston*, Cambridge: Prospect Union Educational Exchange, 1944 and annually thereafter.

"The quest of Nellie Wise Allport," privately printed, 1944.

"The roots of religion," *Advent Paper*, No. 1, Boston: Church of the Advent, 1944. Reprinted as "La radici della religione" (trans. by Sac. Prof. G. Zunini), *Orientamenti Pedagogici*, 1958, 4:158–74

"ABC's of scapegoating" (ed. and author of Foreword), Chicago:

Central YWCA College, 1944; rev. ed., *Freedom Pamphlet Series*, New York: Anti-Defamation League of B'nai B'rith, 1948; revised, 1959. Also reprinted as *Treibjagd auf Sündenböcke* (trans. by K. C. Knudsen), Berlin: Im Christian-Verlag, 1953.

"This clinical number: editorial," *J. Abnorm. Soc. Psychol.*, 1944, 39: 147–49.

"Social psychology and the civilian war effort" (with G. R. Schmeidler), *J. Soc. Psychol.*, *SPSSI Bull.*, 1944, 20: 145–80.

"The bigot in our midst," *Commonweal*, 1944, 25: 582–86. Also published in *The Catholic Digest*, 1944, 9:93–96; and in *Common Sense* (Johannesburg, South Africa), 1945, 6: 154–56. Rev. ed., New York: Community Relations Service, 1950.

1945

"The psychology of participation," *Psychol. Rev.*, 1945, 52:117–32. Also published in *Occup. Psychol.* (London), 1946, 20:54–62; in S. D. Hoslett (ed.), *Human factors in management*, Parkville, Mo.: Park College Press, 1946; and in D. F. Sullivan (ed.), *Readings in group work*, New York: Association Press, 1952, pp. 239–58, Chap. 19.

"Human nature and the peace," *Psychol. Bull.*, 1945, 42:376–78.

"Is intergroup education possible?" *Harv. Educ. Rev.*, 1945, 15:83–86.

"Catharsis and the reduction of prejudice," *J. Soc. Issues*, 1945, 1:1–8.

"The basic psychology of rumor" (with L. Postman), *Trans N.Y. Acad. Sci.*, Section of Psychology, 1945, 8:61–81. Also published in G. E. Swanson, T. M. Newcomb and E. L. Hartley (eds.), *Readings in social psychology* (rev. ed.), New York: Holt, 1952, Part II, b, pp. 160–71; in E. E. Maccoby, T. M. Newcomb and E. L. Hartley, *Readings in social psychology* (3rd ed.), New York: Holt, 1958, pp. 54–65; in D. Katz, D. Cartwright, S. Eldersveld and A. McG. Lee, *Public opinion and propaganda*, New York: Dryden Press, 1954, 394–404; and in W. Schramm (ed.), *The process and effects of mass communication*, Urbana, Ill.: University of Illinois Press, 1954, pp. 141–55.

Review:
   G. Gallup, *A guide to public opinion, J. Abnorm. Soc. Psychol.*, 1945, 40:113–14.

1946

"Personalistic psychology as science: a reply," *Psychol. Rev.*, 1946, 53:132–35.
"Controlling group prejudice" (ed. and author of Foreword), *Ann. Amer. Acad. Pol. Soc. Sci.*, 1946, vol. 244.
"Psychology and social relations at Harvard University" (with E. G. Boring), *Amer. Psychol.*, 1946, 1:119–22.
"Some roots of prejudice" (with B. M. Kramer), published as a separate and in *J. Psychol.*, 1946, 22:9–39; rev. ed., *Roots of prejudice*, New York: American Jewish Congress, Pamphlet Series *Jewish Affairs*, 1946, 1:13.
"Geneticism *versus* ego-structure in theories of personality," *Brit. J. Educ. Psychol.*, 1946, 16:57–68.
"Effect: a secondary principle of learning," *Psychol. Rev.*, 1946, 53:335–47.
Preface to E. Simmel (ed.), *Anti-Semitism: a social disease*, New York: International Universities Press, 1946.
"The priest and the psychologist," *Bull. of General Theological Seminary*, Sept. 1946.
"An analysis of rumor" (with L. Postman), *Publ. Opin. Quart.*, 1946–47, 10.501–17. Also published in *Science Digest*, 1947, 22:58–61.
Introduction to Swami Akhilananda, *Hindu psychology*, New York: Harper, 1946.
Review:
   A. H. Leighton, *The governing of men, J. Abnorm. Soc. Psychol.*, 1946, 41:89–92.

1947

"Guide lines for research in international cooperation," *J. Soc. Issues*, 1947, 3:21–37. Also published in T. H. Pear (ed.), *Psychological factors of peace and war*, London: Hutchinson & Co., 1950, Chap. 7.
Introduction to M. I. Rasey, *Toward maturity, the psychology of*

child development, New York: Hinds, Hayden and El-dredge, 1947.
"The genius of Kurt Lewin," *J. Pers.*, 1947, 16:1–10. Also published in *J. Soc. Issues*, 1948, 4:14–21, Suppl. Series 1.
"Scientific models and human morals," *Psychol. Rev.*, 1947, 54:182–92. Also published as "Modelos cientificos y moral humana," *Rev. Psicol. Gen. Apl.* (Madrid), 1948, 3:425–47; and "Modelos cientificos y moral humana," *Actas del Primer Congreso Argentino de Psicologia*, 1 (Universidad Nacional de Tucuman, Ministerio de Educacion de la Nacion), 1955.

1948

Foreword to K. Lewin (G. W. Lewin, ed.), *Resolving social conflicts*, New York: Harper, 1948.
"Psychology," in *College reading and religion*, New Haven: Yale University Press, 1948, Chap. 3.
"The religion of the post-war college student" (with J. M. Gillespie and J. Young), published as a separate and in *J. Psychol.*, 1948, 25:3–33. Also published in J. Seidman (ed.), *The adolescent: a book of readings*, New York: Dryden Press, 1953.
Reviews:
  D. Jacobson, *The affairs of dame rumor*, Boston Sunday Post, Oct. 24, 1948.
  E. Mayo, *Some notes on the psychology of Pierre Janet*, Survey Graphic, 1948, 37:5, 267.
  A. Schweitzer, *The psychiatric study of Jesus*, Christian Register, Apr. 1948.

1949

"Psychology and the fourth R," *New Republic*, Oct. 17, 1949, pp. 23–26.
Editorial note, *J. Abnorm. Soc. Psychol.*, 1949, 44:439–42.

1950

Foreword to M. G. Ross, *Religious beliefs of youth*, New York: Association Press, 1950.
"How shall we evaluate teaching?" in B. B. Cronkhite (ed.), *A*

handbook for college teachers, Cambridge: Harvard University Press, 1950, Chap. 3.

"The role of expectancy," in H. Cantril (ed.), *Tensions that cause wars*, Urbana, Ill.: University of Illinois Press, 1950.

"A psychological approach to the study of love and hate," in P. A. Sorokin (ed.), *Explorations in altruistic love and behavior*, Boston: Beacon Press, 1950, Chap. 5.

"Prejudice: a problem in psychological and social causation" (Kurt Lewin Memorial Lecture), *J. Soc. Issues*, 1950, Suppl. Series. Also published in T. Parsons and E. A. Shils (eds.), *Toward a general theory of action*, Cambridge: Harvard University Press, 1951, Part 4, Chap. 1.

Reviews:

S. A. Stouffer *et al.*, *The American soldier* (2 vols.), *J. Abnorm. Soc. Psychol.*, 1950, 45:168–73.

"A five-volume shelf about a sickness of both individuals and society: prejudice" [M. Horkheimer and S. H. Flowerman, eds., *Studies in prejudice* (5 vols.), New York: Harper, 1950], *Sci. Amer.*, 1950, 182:56–58.

1951

"The situation we face: a psychological analysis," in A. W. Loos (ed.), *Religious faith and world culture*, New York: Prentice-Hall, 1951, pp. 35–48. Also published in *New Outlook* (Santa Monica, Calif.), 1955, 8:82–87.

"Basic principles in improving human relations," in K. W. Bigelow (ed.), *Cultural groups and human relations*, New York: Teachers College-Columbia University, 1951, Chap. 2.

Foreword to M. H. Wormser and C. Selltiz, *How to conduct a community self-survey of civil rights*, New York: Association Press, 1951.

Foreword to H. E. Kagan, *Changing the attitude of Christian toward Jew*, New York: Columbia University Press, 1951.

Foreword to E. Powers and H. Witmer, *An experiment in the prevention of delinquency*, New York: Columbia University Press, 1951.

Review:

J. La Farge, S.J., *No postponement*, *Thought*, 1951, 26:471–472, No. 102.

1952

"An evaluation of AFSC volunteer work service camps in Germany," in H. W. Riecken, *The volunteer work camp: a psychological evaluation*, Cambridge: Addison-Wesley, 1952, Appendix A, pp. 185–220.

"Resolving intergroup tensions, an appraisal of methods," in L. A. Cook (ed.), *Toward better human relations*, Detroit: Wayne University Press, 1952, Chap. 3.

"The individual and his religion," *The Andover Newton Bulletin*, 1952, 44:3–10.

"The resolution of intergroup tensions," an *Intergroup Education Pamphlet*, New York: National Conference of Christians and Jews, 1952.

"The mature personality," *Pastoral Psychol.*, 1952, 2:19–24.

"What is on the student's mind?" proceedings of the Thirtieth Annual Meeting of the *American College Health Association*, *Bulletin* No. 32, Stanford: Stanford University Press, 1952.

"Why do people join?" interview in *Adult Leadership*, 1952, 1:10–12.

"Reading the nature of prejudice," *Claremont College Reading Conference, Seventeenth Yearbook* (Claremont, Calif.), 1952, pp. 51–64.

1953

"The trend in motivational theory," *Amer. J. Orthopsychiat.*, 1953, 25:107–19. Also published as "Bemerkungen zu dem gegenwärtigen Stand der Theorie der Motivation in den USA" (trans. by H. von Bracken and Leo Canders), *Psychol. Beit.*, 1953, 1:10–28; and in C. E. Moustakas (ed.), *The self: explorations in personal growth*, New York: Harper, 1956; in E. L. and R. E. Hartley, *Outside readings in psychology*, 2nd ed., New York: Crowell, 1957, Chap. 22; and in C. L. Stacey and M. F. DeMartino (eds.), *Understanding human motivation*, Cleveland: Howard Allen, 1958, pp. 54–65.

"The teaching-learning situation," *Publ. Hlth. Rep.*, 1953, 68:875–79.

"The psychological nature of personality," *The Personalist*, 1953, 34:347–57.

1959

"Normative compatibility in the light of social science," in A. H. Maslow (ed.), *New knowledge in human values*, New York: Harper, 1959, pp. 137–50. Also published in *Relig. Educ.*, 1958, 53:62–68.

Preface to V. E. Frankl, *From death-camp to existentialism.* Boston: Beacon, 1959 (trans.).

"Religion and prejudice," *The Crane Review*, 1959, 2:1–10.

1960

"Uniqueness in students," in W. D. Weatherford, Jr. (ed.), *The goals of higher education*, Cambridge: Harvard University Press, 1960, pp. 57–75.

"Psychology and religion," in J. Clark (ed.), *The student seeks an answer*, Chap. 2. Ingraham Lectures in Philosophy and Religion, Waterville: Colby College Press, 1960, pp. 35–49.

"The open system in personality theory," *J. Abnorm. Soc. Psychol.*, 1960, 61:301–310. Also published in E. P. Hollander and R. G. Hunt (eds.), *Current perspectives in social psychology*, New York: Oxford University Press, 1963, pp. 151–162; and as "Il sistema aperto nella teoria della personalità" (trans. by P. G. Grasso), *Orientamenti Pedagogici*, 1960, 7:664–682.

"Wahrnehmung und öffentliche Gesundheitspflege" (trans. by I. Canders), of "Perception and public health" (see 1958), *Psychol. Beit.*, 1960, Heft 3–4/IV:384–404.

1961

Introduction to W. James, *Psychology: the briefer course*, New York: Harper Torchbooks, 1961.

Foreword to C. E. Lincoln, *The black Muslims in America*, Boston: Beacon Press, 1961.

Comment, in R. May (ed.), *Existential psychology*, Chap. 6, New York: Random House, 1961.

William Douglas (The man of the month), *Pastoral Psychology*, 1961, 12:6 and 66.

"Approach to mental health," reprint of portions of *The individual and his religion* (1950), *Sci. of Mind*, 1961, 34:6–11; 37–42.

"Values and our youth," *Teachers Coll. Rec.*, 1961, 63:211–219. Also published in *Image of man* (Proceed. 1961 Summer Conf.), Bellingham, Wash.: Western Washington State College *Bull.*, 1961, 3; and in R. E. Grinder (ed.), *Studies in adolescence*, New York: Macmillan, 1963, pp. 17–27.

"The psychologist's image of man," *Image of man* (Proceed. 1961 Summer Conf.), Bellingham, Wash.: Western Washington State College *Bull.*, 1961, 3.

"Prejudice in perspective" (Lucile P. Morrison Lecture), La Jolla, Calif.: Western Behavioral Sciences Institute, *Report No. 1*, 1961.

"The trend in motivational theory," reprinted (see 1953) in T. K. Menon (ed.), *Recent trends in psychology*, Calcutta: Orient Longmans Ltd., 1961; and in Martha T. and S. A. Mednick (eds.), *Research in personality*, New York: Holt, Rinehart and Winston, 1963, pp. 63–74; and in B. C. Birney and R. C. Teevan (eds.), *Measuring human motivation*, Princeton: Van Nostrand Insight Book, 1962, pp. 164–181.

1962

"Cultural influence on the perception of movement" (with T. F. Pettigrew), reprinted (see 1957) in J. A. Dyal (ed.), *Readings in psychology: understanding human behavior*, New York: McGraw-Hill, 1962, Section 27; also published in *Reprint Series in the Social Sciences*, Indianapolis: Bobbs-Merrill, P-5.

"The general and the unique in psychological science," *J. Person.*, 1962, 30:405–422. Also published in *Image of man* (Proceed. 1961 Summer Conf.), Bellingham, Wash.: Western Washington State College *Bull.*, 1961, 3. Also published as "Das allgemeine und das eigenartige in der psychologischen praxis," *Psychol. Beit.*, 1962, 6:630–50; and as "Il generale e l'unico nella scienza psicologia," *Bollettino di Psychol. Applicata*, 1963, 57–58:3–16.

"Prejudice: is it societal or personal?" *J. Soc. Issues*, 1962, 18:120–34. Also published in *Pastoral Psychology*, 1963, 14:33–45.

"Psychological models for guidance," *Harvard Educational Review*, 1962, 32:373–81. Reprinted in E. Paul Torrance and Robt. D. Strom, *Mental Health and Achievement*, New

York: John Wiley & Sons, 1965, 210–19; and in R. L. Mosher, R. F. Carle, C. D. Kehas (eds.), *Guidance: An examination*, New York: Harcourt, Brace & World, 1965, Ch. 2.
Review:
 G. C. Zahn, *German Catholics and Hitler's wars*, Unitarian-Universalist Register-Leader, 1962, 143:21.

1963

"Behavioral science, religion, and mental health," *J. Relig. & Health*, 1963, 2:187–97. Also published in *The Northeast*, Diocese of Maine, 1963, 90:13–22.
Foreword to N. L. Farberow (ed.), *Taboo topics*, New York: Atherton Press, 1963.
"The emphasis on molar problems," in M. H. Marx (ed.), *Theories in contemporary psychology*, New York: Macmillan, 1963, pp. 258–71, reprinted from "Scientific models and human morals" (see 1947).

1964

"Crises in normal personality development," *Teachers College Record*, 1964, 66:235–41.
"The fruits of eclecticism: bitter or sweet?" *Acta Psychologica*, 1964, 23:27–44.
"Imagination in psychology: Some needed steps" (York University Lecture Series) in *Imagination and the University*, Toronto: University of Toronto Press, 1964, 63–82.
"Peter Bertocci: Philosopher-Psychologist," *The Philosophical Forum* (Boston University), 1963–1964, 21:3–7.

1965

"Abraham Aaron Roback: 1890–1965," *American Journal of Psychology*, 1965, 88:689–90.
"Traits Revisited," *Psychology Today*, Journal of the Dept. of Psychology of the University of Newcastle on Tyne, 1965, 57–76. Also published in *American Psychologist*, 1966, 21:1–10.

1966

Foreword to Van Ness Bates, *Christianity and world civilization*, Boston: Christopher Press, 1966.

"Can prejudice be reduced?", *East-West Center Today*, 1966, 6:3–6.

"Prejudice and the individual," in John P. Davis (ed.), *The American Negro Reference Book*, Englewood Cliffs, N.J.: Prentice-Hall, 1966, pp. 706–13.

"The religious context of prejudice," *The Graduate Journal* (of the University of Texas), 1966, 7:115–30. Also printed in *The Journal for the Scientific Study of Religion*, 1966, 5:447–57.

"The spirit of Richard Clarke Cabot," *The Journal of Pastoral Care*, 1966, 20:102–04.

"William James and the behavioral sciences," *Journal of the Behavioral Sciences*, 1966, 2:145–47.

Reviews:

Karl Bühler, *Die Krise der Psychologie*, Journal of General Psychology, 1966, 75:201–04.

A. Koestler, *The act of creation*, Contemp. Psychol., 1966, 11:49–51.

1967

"Gordon W. Allport," in E. G. Boring & G. Lindzey (eds.), *A History of Psychology in Autobiography*, Vol. 5, New York: Appleton-Century-Crofts, 1967, 1–25.

"Personal religious orientation and prejudice" (with J. Michael Ross), *Jour. of Person. and Soc. Psych.*, 1967, 5:432–43.

"The personalistic psychology of William Stern," in B. B. Wolman (ed.), *Historical Roots of Contemporary Psychology*, New York: Harper and Row, 1967.

"The problem, the mystery: some reflections on theological education," *The Bulletin of the Episcopal Theological School*, 1967, 59:15–18.

"Six decades of social psychology," in Sven Lundstedt (ed.), *The Preparation of Social Psychologists: innovations in graduate education*, Chap. 1, Cleveland: Western Reserve Univ. Press, 1967.

INDEX OF NAMES

INDEX OF SUBJECTS